Debates in Second Language Education

Debates in Second Language Education provides an up-to-date account of the key debates and areas of controversy in the field of second language learning and teaching. Adopting a broad and comparative perspective and emphasising the importance of considering a variety of learning contexts, it encourages students and practising teachers to engage with contemporary issues and developments in learning and teaching.

Chapters are designed to stimulate thinking and understanding in relation to theory and practice, and help language educators to make informed judgements by arguing from a position based on theoretical knowledge and understanding. Bringing together leading contributors in the field, the book discusses a wide range of issues relating to second language learning and teaching including:

- the relationship between age and success in language learning
- aptitude versus motivation as predictors of successful language learning
- linguistic diversity and plurilingualism
- the teaching of grammar and vocabulary
- the value of phonics
- learning pronunciation
- the second language only versus the multilingual debate

With reflective points in every chapter, *Debates in Second Language Education* will be a valuable resource for any student or practising teacher, as well as for those engaged in initial teacher education, continuing professional development or Master's level study. It will also be of interest to second language acquisition researchers and those studying applied linguistics.

Ernesto Macaro is Emeritus Professor of Applied Linguistics at the University of Oxford. Before becoming a teacher trainer and researcher, he was a language teacher for 16 years. His current research focuses on second language learning strategies and on the interaction in second language classrooms or in classrooms where English is the Medium of Instruction.

Robert Woore is an Associate Professor in Applied Linguistics in the Department of Education at the University of Oxford. He teaches and supervises on Master's courses (including the MSc in Applied Linguistics and Second Language Acquisition), PGCE (initial teacher education) and doctoral programmes. Formerly a secondary school teacher of French and German, his research interests include the learning and teaching of second languages in instructed classroom settings, with a particular emphasis on phonology and reading. He is interested in the interface between research and classroom practice, and has undertaken various research and professional development projects in this area.

Debates in Subject Teaching
Series edited by Susan Capel, Jon Davison,
James Arthur and John Moss

Each title in the Debates in Subject Teaching series presents high-quality material, specially commissioned to stimulate teachers engaged in initial teacher education, continuing professional development and Master's level study to think more deeply about their practice, and link research and evidence to what they have observed in schools. By providing up-to-date, comprehensive coverage the books in the series support teachers in reaching their own informed judgements, enabling them to discuss and argue their point of view with deeper theoretical knowledge and understanding.

Debates in Computing and ICT Education
Edited by Sarah Younie and Pete Bradshaw

Debates in Physical Education, 2nd edition
Edited by Susan Capel and Richard Blair

Debates in English Teaching, 2nd edition
Edited by Jon Davison and Caroline Daly

Debates in Mathematics Education, 2nd edition
Edited by Gwen Ineson and Hilary Povey

Debates in Primary Education
Edited by Virginia Bower

Debates in Art and Design Education, 2nd edition
Edited by Nicholas Addison and Lesley Burgess

Debates in Second Language Education
Edited by Ernesto Macaro and Robert Woore

For more information about this series, please visit: https://www.routledge.com/
Debates-in-Subject-Teaching/book-series/DIST

Debates in Second Language Education

Edited by Ernesto Macaro
and Robert Woore

LONDON AND NEW YORK

Cover image: © Getty Images

First published 2022
by Routledge
2 Park Square, Milton Park, Abingdon, Oxon OX14 4RN

and by Routledge
605 Third Avenue, New York, NY 10158

Routledge is an imprint of the Taylor & Francis Group, an informa business

© 2022 selection and editorial matter, Ernesto Macaro and Robert Woore; individual chapters, the contributors

The right of Ernesto Macaro and Robert Woore to be identified as the authors of the editorial material, and of the authors for their individual chapters, has been asserted in accordance with sections 77 and 78 of the Copyright, Designs and Patents Act 1988.

All rights reserved. No part of this book may be reprinted or reproduced or utilised in any form or by any electronic, mechanical, or other means, now known or hereafter invented, including photocopying and recording, or in any information storage or retrieval system, without permission in writing from the publishers.

Trademark notice: Product or corporate names may be trademarks or registered trademarks, and are used only for identification and explanation without intent to infringe.

British Library Cataloguing-in-Publication Data
A catalogue record for this book is available from the British Library

Library of Congress Cataloging-in-Publication Data
Names: Macaro, Ernesto, editor. | Woore, Robert, 1973- editor.
Title: Debates in second language education / edited by Ernesto Macaro & Robert Woore.
Description: Abingdon, Oxon ; New York, NY : Routledge, 2022. | Includes bibliographical references and index. | Identifiers: LCCN 2021025659 (print) | LCCN 2021025660 (ebook) | ISBN 9780367442132 (hardback) | ISBN 9780367442163 (paperback) | ISBN 9781003008361 (ebook)
Subjects: LCSH: Second language acquisition. | Language and languages–Study and teaching. | Language and education.
Classification: LCC P118.2 .D43 2022 (print) | LCC P118.2 (ebook) | DDC 401/.93–dc23
LC record available at https://lccn.loc.gov/2021025659
LC ebook record available at https://lccn.loc.gov/2021025660

ISBN: 978-0-367-44213-2
ISBN: 978-0-367-44216-3
ISBN: 978-1-003-00836-1

DOI: 10.4324/9781003008361

Typeset in Galliard
by KnowledgeWorks Global Ltd.

To all essential workers worldwide during
the ongoing Covid pandemic

Contents

List of contributors	xi

Introduction	1
ERNESTO MACARO AND ROBERT WOORE	

PART I
Framing the debates

7

1 **Identifying key debates in second language teaching and learning** 9
ROBERT WOORE AND ERNESTO MACARO

2 **Learning English and learning languages other than English
in Asia and Europe: Current scenarios and debates** 32
BRUNA DI SABATO AND ANDY KIRKPATRICK

3 **Is there a best age for second language learning? Evidence
from across the lifespan** 52
SIMONE E. PFENNINGER AND DAVID SINGLETON

4 **Multilingual learners, linguistic pluralism and implications
for education and research** 66
HAMISH CHALMERS AND VICTORIA MURPHY

5 **Learning language by studying content** 89
DAVID LASAGABASTER

6 **Aptitude or motivation: Which is the better predictor of
successful language learning?** 106
SUZANNE GRAHAM

x *Contents*

7 Key issues in pre-service language teacher education   122
LAURA MOLWAY

8 Systemic in-service language teacher education   142
SIMON BORG

PART II
Applying the debates to second language learning contexts   163

9 Implicit versus explicit grammar learning and teaching   165
MIROSŁAW PAWLAK

10 Vocabulary learning in theory and practice: Implicit and
explicit mechanisms   183
RON MARTINEZ

11 The L2-only versus the multilingual debate   201
ERNESTO MACARO

12 Teaching phonics in a second language   222
ROBERT WOORE

13 What kind of pronunciation learning should teachers expect
of their learners?   247
SARA KENNEDY AND PAVEL TROFIMOVICH

14 Teaching the language or teaching the process   262
PETER YONGQI GU

Reflections   275
ERNESTO MACARO AND ROBERT WOORE

Index   286

Contributors

Simon Borg has been involved in language teaching for over 30 years, working as a teacher, teacher educator, lecturer, and researcher in a range of international contexts. He is recognised for his academic work on teacher cognition and teacher education and has published widely on these topics. After 15 years at the University of Leeds, he now works primarily as an educational consultant, with a particular focus on designing, implementing, and evaluating language teacher professional development projects, programmes, and policies. Details of his work (including recent publications and a blog) are available at http://simon-borg.co.uk/.

Hamish Chalmers is a Lecturer in Applied Linguistics and Second Language Acquisition in the Department of Education at the University of Oxford. His research interest centres on evaluation of pedagogical approaches to teaching children who use English as an Additional Language (EAL). In particular, his research focuses on the use of the first language as a pedagogical tool for multilingual learners in English medium classrooms. His methodological interest is in randomised trials, systematic reviews, and user engagement in science. He was a primary school teacher for the best part of two decades in both UK state schools and overseas in the International School sector. He is Vice Chair of NALDIC, the UK's subject association for EAL, and Director of IDESR.org, an organisation that curates information about systematic review in education and publishes prospective registrations for planned and ongoing systematic reviews.

Suzanne Graham is a Professor of Language and Education at the Institute of Education, University of Reading. She has led a number of large, funded research projects in the field of second language education, exploring teaching and learning in a range of different contexts, from primary through to upper secondary school education. She has published widely in the area of motivation, self-efficacy and language comprehension, with a particular focus on listening comprehension and strategic self-regulation. Formerly, a teacher of French and German in schools in England, she leads the Modern Foreign Languages Initial Teacher Education programme at the University of Reading.

xii *Contributors*

Sara Kennedy is an Associate Professor in the Department of Education at Concordia University in Montreal, Quebec, Canada. She teaches and conducts research on the teaching, learning, assessment, and use of second language speech, with a particular interest in second language pronunciation.

Andy Kirkpatrick is a Professor emeritus at Griffith University, Brisbane, Australia, and a member of the Australian Academy of the Humanities. He is editor of *The Routledge Handbook of World Englishes* (2020) and co-editor, with Anthony Liddicoat, of *The Routledge Handbook of Language Education Policy in Asia* (2019). His most recent book is *Is English an Asian Language?* (Cambridge University Press, 2020).

David Lasagabaster is a Professor of Applied Linguistics at the University of the Basque Country UPV/EHU, Spain. His research revolves around English-Medium Instruction (EMI), Content and Language Integrated Learning (CLIL), attitudes and motivation, and multilingualism. He has published widely in international journals (*Applied Linguistics, Language Teaching, International Journal of Bilingual Education and Bilingualism, The Modern Language Journal, Studies in Higher Education, Language Teaching Research, Language and Education, TESOL Quarterly*, etc.), books and edited books. Among others, he has co-edited *English-medium Instruction at Universities: Global Challenges* (Multilingual Matters, 2013), *Motivation and Foreign Language Learning: From Theory to Practice* (John Benjamins, 2014), and *Language Use in English-medium Instruction at University: International Perspectives in Teacher Practice* (Routledge, 2021).

Ernesto Macaro is an Emeritus Professor of Applied Linguistics at the University of Oxford and was founding Director of the Centre for Research and Development in English Medium Instruction in the Department of Education. He was the Director of the Department of Education from 2013 to 2016. Before becoming a teacher trainer and researcher, he was a language teacher in secondary schools in the UK for 16 years. His current research focuses on second language learning strategies and on the interaction between teachers and learners in second language classrooms or in classrooms where English is the Medium of Instruction. He has published widely on these topics.

Ron Martinez received his doctorate in Applied Linguistics from the University of Nottingham, and his master's degree in Applied Linguistics and Second Language Acquisition from the University of Oxford. He is an English Language Specialist for the US Department of State through which he advises on projects related to internationalization in higher education around the world, and currently holds the title of International Education Policy Advisor at the Universidade Federal do Paraná in Curitiba, Brazil, where is also the Director of the Academic Publishing Advisory Center (CAPA), and Coordinator of EMI faculty development programs. In addition to research and teaching, Ron is an Associate Editor of the journal *Applied Linguistics*.

Contributors xiii

Laura Molway is based at the University of Oxford, Department of Education and she specialises in second language teacher education. She became interested in teacher education during her time as a secondary school teacher of French and German, when she mentored beginning languages teachers during their school placements. Laura is currently Subject Lead for the post-graduate certificate in education (PGCE) in modern languages and she also supervises higher degrees in the fields of instructed second language learning and language teacher education. Her recent research has focussed on the use of the target language for instruction; explicit teaching of language learning strategies; students' motivation for learning languages other than English; languages teachers' professional learning needs and experiences; and formative language teacher evaluation.

Victoria Murphy is a Professor of Applied Linguistics and Deputy Director of the Department of Education, University of Oxford. She convenes the Applied Linguistics, and the Research in English as an Additional Language (R.E.A.L.) research groups. Victoria's research focuses on understanding the inter-relationships between child L2/FL learning, vocabulary, and literacy development. Her work focuses on examining cross-linguistic relationships across linguistic systems in the emergent bilingual child and how foreign language learning in primary school can influence developing first language literacy. She has published in a wide range of Applied Linguistics journals in the area of young language learners.

Mirosław Pawlak is a Professor of English at the Department of English Studies, Faculty of Pedagogy and Fine Arts in Kalisz, Adam Mickiewicz University, Kalisz, Poland, and the Faculty of Humanities and Social Sciences, State University of Applied Sciences, Konin, Poland. His main areas of interest are SLA theory and research, form-focused instruction, corrective feedback, classroom discourse, learner autonomy, learning strategies, motivation, willingness to communicate, emotions in L2 learning and teaching, study abroad, and pronunciation teaching. Mirosław Pawlak is Editor-in-Chief of the journals, *Studies in Second Language Learning and Teaching* and *Konin Language Studies*, as well as the book series, *Second Language Learning and Teaching* (Springer). He currently serves as President of the International Federation of Teacher Associations (FIPLV).

Simone E. Pfenninger is an Associate Professor of Second Language Acquisition and Psycholinguistics at the English Department of the University of Salzburg. Her principal research areas are multilingualism, psycholinguistics, and variationist SLA, especially in regard to quantitative approaches and statistical methods and techniques for language application in education. Recent books include *The Changing English Language: Psycholinguistic Perspectives* (co-edited, Cambridge University Press, 2017), and *Future Research Directions for Applied Linguistics* (co-edited, Multilingual Matters, 2017). She is co-editor of the Second Language Acquisition book series for Multilingual Matters and Vice President of the International Association of Multilingualism (IAM). In 2015, she received the Mercator Award and in 2018, the Conrad Ferdinand Meyer Prize for outstanding research.

xiv *Contributors*

Bruna Di Sabato is full Professor of Language education at the Università di Napoli Suor Orsola Benincasa. Her more recent publications in English are *Grammatical gender and translation: a cross linguistic overview* (co-author with Antonio Perri) in *The Routledge Handbook of Translation, Feminism and Gender* (L. von Flotow and H. Kamal eds, 2020) and *Multilingual Perspectives from Europe and beyond on Language Policy and Practice* (co-editor with B. Hughes, Routledge, 2021).

David Singleton is an Emeritus Fellow of Trinity College Dublin, where he was, until his retirement from that institution, Professor in Applied Linguistics. Thereafter he worked, until 2018, as Professor at the University of Pannonia, Veszprém, Hungary and at the State University of Applied Sciences, Konin, Poland. He served as President of the Irish Association for Applied Linguistics, as Secretary General of AILA and as President of EUROSLA. He is co-author of *Key Topics in Second Language Acquisition and of beyond Age Effects in Instructional L2 Learning* and co-editor of the *Multilingual Matters SLA* book series. In 2015, he received the EUROSLA Distinguished Scholar Award and in 2017 Honorary Life Membership of AILA.

Pavel Trofimovich is a Professor of Applied Linguistics in the Department of Education at Concordia University in Montreal, Quebec, Canada. His research focuses on cognitive aspects of second language processing, second language speech learning, sociolinguistic aspects of second language acquisition, and the teaching of second language pronunciation.

Robert Woore is an Associate Professor in Applied Linguistics in the Department of Education at the University of Oxford. He teaches and supervises on Master's courses (including the MSc in Applied Linguistics and Second Language Acquisition), PGCE (initial teacher education) and doctoral programmes. Formerly a secondary school teacher of French and German, his research interests include the learning and teaching of second languages in instructed classroom settings, with a particular emphasis on phonology and reading. He is interested in the interface between research and classroom practice, and has undertaken various research and professional development projects in this area.

Peter Yongqi Gu is an Associate Professor and Head of School of the School of Linguistics and Applied Language Studies, Victoria University of Wellington, New Zealand. Peter has extensive teaching and teacher education experience in New Zealand, Singapore, Hong Kong (SAR China), and mainland China. Peter was the recipient of the 2004 Thomson Heinle Distinguished Research Award from TESOL International Association. Peter's main research interests include language learning strategies, vocabulary acquisition, and language testing and assessment. Peter publishes widely on these topics. His most recent book, *Classroom-Based Formative Assessment* (Foreign Language Teaching and Research Press, 2021) focuses on the formative potential of classroom-based assessment.

Introduction

Ernesto Macaro and Robert Woore

This edited volume is entitled *Debates in Second Language Education*. We chose the title for a number of reasons. First, we were invited by Routledge to produce a follow-up to an earlier volume which had the word Debates in the title (*Debates in Modern Languages Education*, edited by Patricia Driscoll, Ernesto Macaro, and Ann Swarbrick). We were both intrigued by what constitutes a 'debate' and therefore in the book's first and what might be considered introductory chapter (by Woore and Macaro), we attempt to identify what some key debates in L2 education actually are, and what is meant by this term. Therefore, we first take a look at some edited volumes, published over four decades, which claim to identify and discuss debates or issues in the field. We then report on the findings of a survey of language practitioners (including teachers, teacher educators, and researchers) regarding what they believe are the current issues and debates in second language education. Chapter 1 thus attempts to set the scene for the first part of the book, which brings together chapters intended to 'frame the debates' in second language education. In other words, these chapters discuss issues which, whilst clearly of relevance to practitioners and students in the classroom, serve to provide a conceptual framework within which to situate some of the questions that teachers face in their day-to-day working lives.

We also decided on modifying the title to *Debates in **Second** Language Education*, because we wanted to go beyond the scope suggested by 'Modern Languages Education'. The term 'Modern Languages' was initially used to distinguish it from classical languages such as Latin and Greek. This no longer seems necessary in the second decade of the 21st century. Even the term 'foreign languages' now sounds out of place to our ears, not only because of the pejorative semantic element in the word 'foreign' but also because of the gradual evaporation of the boundaries between first and second (or third) languages in an increasingly dynamic linguistic global situation.

Clearly, there are still distinctions to be made between languages being learnt. There are divergences in the characteristics among language learning contexts and these have implications for the way that languages are valued, for the pedagogy that is employed to teach them and for how teachers are prepared for the hugely important role that they undertake. It therefore seemed to us that the term 'second language education' was the most appropriate and made the

DOI: 10.4324/9781003008361-1

2 *Ernesto Macaro and Robert Woore*

distinction sufficiently with 'first language education', which we would consider to be the formal education of young people whose 'home language' is the majority language of a country or jurisdiction.

Part I of the book therefore attempts to draw some of these broader pictures of second language education. Pfenninger and Singleton (Chapter 3) provide an overview of the evidence regarding the relationship between age and success in language learning and demonstrate that the 'received wisdom' – that the younger one starts learning a language, the better – is not supported by the research currently available. Another commonly held belief that has been around for quite some time about language learning is examined by Suzanne Graham (Chapter 6), who reflects on the construct of aptitude – the idea that people are somehow born good language learners, or that the ability to learn languages is innate and to some degree immutable. This construct is then juxtaposed by Graham with another individual difference, motivation, where it would be difficult to argue that one baby is born more motivated to learn a language than another.

A more recent debate has centred on whether it is better or more efficient to learn an L2 by studying content (that is, an academic subject not related to language learning) through the medium of that language, rather than sitting in a classroom in which the language itself is the primary focus of the teaching and learning. This more recent debate is examined by David Lasagabaster (Chapter 5) with a particular focus on English as the language in question. Lasagabaster makes a distinction between Content and Language Integrated Learning (CLIL) – where there is a requirement for teachers to develop the students' L2 – and English-Medium Instruction (EMI). In the latter, the current evidence shows, teachers are neither required in theory to develop the students' English nor do they appear to be doing so in practice.

Di Sabato and Kirkpatrick (Chapter 2) take on the highly politicized issue of the dominance worldwide of English as an L2, as opposed to the learning of other languages. They do so by comparing policy and practice in two macro-geographical areas: Asia (specifically East and South-East Asia) and Continental Europe. The linguistic diversity of the former is set in its historical and in many cases, previously colonialist context, with globalization as the driver for the dominance of English and the national policies which are dictating it. In Europe, by contrast, English has become the dominant L2 despite a policy desire – and despite several European Union initiatives – to promote linguistic diversity and plurilingualism.

The flipside of the debate about the dominance of English is taken on by Hamish Chalmers and Victoria Murphy (Chapter 4), who examine the linguistic inheritance of learners in Anglophone majority countries for whom English is an 'additional language'. They note widespread enthusiasm for 'multilingual pedagogy', in which students' home language knowledge is validated and capitalized upon in their learning of English as well as other subjects. However, they argue that whilst such an approach holds great promise as 'a practical and socially just framework for thinking about education in linguistically diverse contexts', what

Introduction 3

is now needed (and has been lacking to date) is more experimental research to demonstrate its effects on learners' outcomes.

We then come to two chapters dealing with issues in the education and professional development of language teachers. The first is by Laura Molway (Chapter 7), who presents the situation with regard to pre-service second language teacher education and notes that, as a field of research and study, it is still relatively underdeveloped when contrasted with the considerable output on *continuing* professional development. The latter is the focus of the following chapter by Simon Borg (Chapter 8). Molway lists the different forms of knowledge that language teachers need to acquire in order for effective teaching to occur – these forms collectively are often referred to as Pedagogical Content Knowledge (PCK) – and their relationship with the linguistic knowledge that prospective language teachers have when they embark on a pre-service programme. Molway observes that there is considerable debate in the languages field as to what the essential components of PCK are and, importantly, on what basis applicants to pre-service teacher programmes should be judged. Borg, on the other hand, focuses on various highly context-specific programmes which aim to promote systemic change in L2 teacher professional development, which he refers to as in-service language teacher education. These are large-scale programmes, sometimes involving tens of thousands of teachers, and unsurprisingly these are practitioners who are teaching English as an L2, mostly in the primary sector. Thus, yet again, we see a reflection of the global reach of the English language teaching industry. Borg outlines various models of in-service programmes and is keen to point to the importance of taking careful note of the local context, and not 'supplanting local educational practices' with models of teaching and teacher education imported from elsewhere.

Part II of the book shifts the focus to the classroom itself and deals with issues that language teachers face on a daily basis when preparing, teaching, and evaluating their lessons. The issues identified in Part 1, which framed these more directly classroom-based activities, are nevertheless present in the background. Teachers have to match their immediate concerns with the bigger picture.

First, Mirosław Pawlak (Chapter 9) takes on the big debate which has gone on for decades about the role that learning grammar plays in the overall learning of a second language. He presents this not as 'should we teach grammar', nor as 'should we be concerned about grammatical inaccuracy in our students' output'; rather, he asks 'should we teach grammar implicitly or explicitly'? Pawlak explores whether the distinction between implicit and explicit grammatical knowledge is theoretically and empirically justified and points to the danger of confusing L2 grammatical knowledge as a developmental process with L2 grammatical knowledge as a product.

The debate regarding the learning of a second language implicitly as opposed to explicitly is also addressed by Ron Martinez in his chapter (Chapter 9) on L2 vocabulary learning. Martinez does so by framing it historically through a theory that was prominent in the late 1970s and throughout the 1980s: that an L2 could only truly be learnt (or 'acquired') through exposure to input and

4 *Ernesto Macaro and Robert Woore*

in the same way that a child 'picks up' her/his first language: by listening and interacting with parents, older siblings, and/or caregivers. Martinez then proceeds to examine, in some detail, factors that influence vocabulary acquisition (e.g. frequency, input type) and the extent to which teaching, and direct/explicit learner engagement, can enhance acquisition.

The impact of the effectiveness of teaching is viewed from a different perspective by Peter Yongqui Gu (Chapter 14), who tackles the debate as to whether teachers should spend time teaching their students how to learn (or how to learn better), rather than simply teaching them a body of linguistic knowledge. Gu begins with a powerful example: if a language test suggests that a student has a problem learning a particular aspect of the second language, can a teacher tell whether the problem is related to an aspect of the student's second language, or rather, to the way that the student himself/herself is going about the process of learning that language? As Gu asks provocatively: 'Do learners really need to learn how to learn?' After framing the debate in a substantial historical context, he proceeds to outline research on the teaching of skills and strategies, with a particular focus on meta-analyses which have shown this teaching to have some educational value.

A typical example of 'teaching a body of linguistic knowledge' is using class time to teach students about the relationship between written letters on a page (or screen) and their sounds in alphabetic writing systems – otherwise known as the explicit teaching of phonics, which is the subject of Robert Woore's chapter (Chapter 12). In the teaching of early reading in English as a first language, the merits and demerits of phonics teaching have been the subject of long-standing and sometimes acrimonious debate. Recently, phonics has been strongly pushed by policymakers in Anglophone countries, and perhaps as a result of this, the teaching of phonics also appears to be becoming more widespread in L2 contexts as well. Woore examines some of the theoretical background and empirical evidence surrounding the teaching of L2 phonics. He argues that phonics may be a valuable component of L2 instruction in many contexts, but that its effects may differ from those in L1 settings: L2 phonics may have a positive impact on various aspects of L2 learning, including the crucial task of vocabulary acquisition.

Whilst the debate on teaching phonics can be conceived of in terms which are almost exclusively pedagogical (i.e. does it help the learner to read, to learn new words, to feel more positive about the language as a whole?), the debate pertaining to pronunciation is not only pedagogical but also sociolinguistic. Sara Kennedy and Pavel Trofimovich, in their chapter on pronunciation (Chapter 13) tackle this complex issue. Once again with particular reference to the learning of English as an L2, the debate not only centres on whether the native-like pronunciation of the L2 is possible but also whether it is desirable. In L2 learning contexts where the target language is not pervasive outside the classroom, is it *possible* to acquire the pronunciation of a native speaker of that language (the pedagogical issue)? However, a different question might be: is it *desirable* that L2 learners should strive to sound like native speakers of a language (the sociolinguistic issue)? Kennedy and Trofimovich explore both these perspectives but

Introduction 5

focus more on the 'is it possible' one by considering such aspects as the age of learning, similarities between languages, autonomy in learning, and amount of experience with the L2 (length of exposure).

In Chapter 11, Ernesto Macaro reflects on a pedagogical issue which has consistently been in the minds of both practitioners and researchers over many years: what value or place does the L1 have in second language classrooms? Macaro begins by examining the quality of the debate itself as presented by researchers and commentators in the field of second language education. He then proceeds to document: studies in a variety of contexts, which have measured how much L1/L2 is being used in classrooms; the purposes for which teachers appear to use the L1 in their L2 teaching; teacher and student attitudes to L1 use or L2 exclusivity; and the value of using the L1 in L2 vocabulary learning.

In our concluding chapter (Macaro and Woore), given the breadth of topics covered in the book, it did not seem helpful to try to offer any 'Conclusions' from the debates as a whole. Further, we were reluctant to give too much prominence to our own particular opinions, this being an edited volume rather than a co-authored one. Therefore, in our final chapter, we take a step back to offer some personal 'Reflections' on the various debates that have been covered, grouping these reflections into four main categories. First, we consider the question of 'explicit' versus 'implicit' L2 teaching, which we argue underlies various other debates in L2 education. Second, we consider the difference between debates which operate at a 'holistic' level (concerning an overall method or approach to L2 teaching) and those which are more 'atomized' (concerning the teaching and learning of a particular aspect of an L2, such as grammar or vocabulary). We argue that recent SLA research has tended to prioritize the latter, more atomized perspective, and ask what the implications of this may be for L2 teachers and policymakers seeking to use research evidence to inform their decision-making. Third, we offer some reflections on the effects of context in L2 education – that is, the extent to which and ways in which teaching and learning an L2 might differ according to the context in which they are taking place. Fourth, we look at some of the ways in which L2 education is developing, and may continue to develop, as a result of technological advancements, and ask what the implications of such developments might be for practitioners and researchers in the field.

We hope that you will enjoy reading this book and that, whether you are a second language acquisition researcher, a language teacher, or a student on a course in applied linguistics, the chapters herein will trigger in you a desire to continue engaging with these important debates.

Part I
Framing the debates

1 Identifying key debates in second language teaching and learning

Robert Woore and Ernesto Macaro

Introduction

This book attempts to bring to the reader research and commentary on some key issues and debates surrounding second language (L2) teaching and learning in the world today. But what do we actually mean by key issues and debates? This chapter begins with a theoretical and to some extent historical definition of what might be conceived of as an 'issue' or 'debate'. It then reports the results of an international survey investigating L2 practitioners' beliefs about what they consider to be key issues and debates in the field.

What are 'debates'?

In many cases, the two terms 'issue' and 'debate' are used interchangeably in the literature (and indeed in this book). However, we think it can be useful to draw a distinction between them. A useful starting point when attempting to do so might be to consult a dictionary on the meaning of these words. *The New Oxford Dictionary of English* (1998) provides the following for 'issue': "an important topic or problem for debate or discussion" (p. 969). For 'debate' it offers "formal discussion on a particular matter [...] in which opposing arguments are put forward" (p. 474). Based on these definitions, the two terms might be distinguished by the extent to which 'formal discussion' of a particular matter has taken place and 'opposing arguments' put forward. Thus, an 'issue' in L2 teaching might be some kind of problem confronting a teacher or policymaker. For example, it is last period on a Friday afternoon, and my 8th-grade class has just had a Physical Education lesson in the rain; I feel that I need to adapt my teaching to take account of these contextual factors, perhaps by reducing the linguistic demands that I might otherwise have placed on my students. However, this cannot be called a 'debate' in L2 education, since people have generally not published research into the extent to which lessons should be adapted to a 'Friday afternoon post-PE' context. It is not something that people have argued about 'formally' in the academic literature on second language acquisition (SLA). By contrast, some questions have clearly been the subject of a long-standing debate in the literature and/or the focus of systematic research investigations. Examples would be: does Content and Language Integrated Learning (CLIL) lead to better language learning outcomes than more

DOI: 10.4324/9781003008361-3

10 Robert Woore and Ernesto Macaro

traditional Foreign Language classes? Is explicit or implicit grammar instruction more effective? Which language should the teacher use to give instructions in lessons, the target language or the learners' L1? The 'debates' that this book deals with are more in the latter category, but we do not want to underplay the importance of the many 'issues' that confront language teachers on a daily basis.

Debates over time

When planning the current book, we wondered to what extent debates in L2 education had changed over preceding decades and to what extent the 'same old problems' were recurring. As we found that internet searches did not yield a particularly usable body of information about what the key debates might be, or how they might have changed over time, we tried a more traditional approach: browsing the print holdings of our departmental library. We perused the contents pages of edited volumes on the shelves, noting the date of publication and how the titles and chapters might reflect the notion of a 'debate' in our field. Table 1.1 presents, chronologically, what we found. Clearly, we are not claiming this to be a systematic or exhaustive collection of edited volumes, but we hope that it at least provides some insight into how editors have gone about presenting what they believed to be key debates in L2 education. Incidentally, we can observe that six editors opted for the term 'issues' in their titles, two used the term 'perspectives' (Johnson & Porter, 1983; Beebe, 1988), one used 'controversies' (Seidlhofer, 2003) and one used 'debates' (Driscoll et al., 2014).

Table 1.1 suggests there are two basic approaches taken by editors.

1   They decide that a particular aspect of SLA is important and then commission various chapter authors to provide research and commentary as subsections of that particular aspect. Examples are: Benati (2009), looking at aspects of L2 proficiency; Robinson (2002) on individual differences in L2 learning; Mackey (2007) on conversational interaction in SLA; and Muñoz (2006), exploring the age factor in instructed L2 learning.
2   They identify numerous aspects of SLA which need to be examined and presented as debates to their readers. They commission authors to provide research and commentary on each of these individually. Examples of this approach are: Field's (2000) *Issues in Modern Foreign Language Teaching*; Long & Doughty's (2011) *Handbook of Language Teaching*; Benati's (2013) *Issues in Second Language Teaching*; and Driscoll et al.'s (2014) *Debates in Modern Languages Education*.

We also tentatively detect from Table 1.1 a couple of trends over time, possibly reflecting the changing historical context in which SLA research and pedagogy have been operating. The first is that later edited volumes appear to have turned their attention to how SLA has been impacted by sociolinguistic factors (starting with Block & Cameron, 2002, whose use of 'globalization' in the title is picked up by Solly and Esch, 2014) or by sociocultural factors (Lantolf & Poehner, 2008; Hall et al., 2011). Second, we note that, around forty years ago,

Table 1.1 A selective, chronological overview of edited volumes in L2 education

Publication date	Editor(s)	Book title	Sections and/or chapter headings (in abbreviated or condensed form and using some of our own terminology)
1983	Johnson & Porter	*Perspectives in CLT*	CLT; curriculum design; curriculum development; CLT and teacher education; assessing communicative proficiency
1988	Beebe	*Issues in Second Language Acquisition: Multiple Perspectives*	Psycholinguistic issues; sociolinguistic approaches; neuropsychology and L2 acquisition
2000	Field	*Issues in Modern Foreign Language Teaching*	Able pupils; mixed-ability grouping; girls versus boys as learners; role of grammar; cultural awareness; use of L2/L1; assessment; role of Information technology
2002	Richards & Renandya	*Methodology in Language Teaching*	Four skills; grammar; vocabulary; pronunciation; technology; professional development
2002	Block & Cameron	*Globalization & language teaching*	The local and the global; language learning as economic commodity
2002	Robinson	*Individual Differences and Instructed Language Learning*	Motivation; anxiety; emotion; aptitude; disabilities; working memory; age
2003	Seidlhofer	*Controversies in Applied Linguistics*	(Those that apply to L2 learning) Varieties/standard language; linguistic imperialism/hegemony; psycholinguistic versus sociocultural approaches (a collection of published papers spanning some 20 years)
2003	Bourne & Reid	*Language Education*	Bilingual education; L2 support for curriculum learning; English as an additional language; policy & curriculum across countries
2005	Johnson	*Expertise in L2 Learning and Teaching*	Learner expertise in the four skills; good language learner; teacher expertise
2006	Muñoz	*Age and the Rate of FL Learning*	Role that age plays in: amount of exposure, oral fluency, vocabulary learning, morphological acquisition, writing development; strategy use
2007	Mackey	*Conversational Interaction in SLA*	Learning opportunities in interaction; feedback effect on learners
2008	Lantolf & Poehner	*Sociocultural Theory and the Teaching of L2s*	ZPD; Dynamic assessment; embodied performance; concept-based instruction; the classroom-world nexus

(Continued)

Table 1.1 A selective, chronological overview of edited volumes in L2 education *(Continued)*

Publication date	Editor(s)	Book title	Sections and/or chapter headings (in abbreviated or condensed form and using some of our own terminology)
2008	Gabryś-Barker	*Morphosyntactic Issues in Second Language Acquisition*	Language transfer; argument realization; acquisition of difficult grammatical features
2009	Benati	*Issues in L2 Proficiency*	Theories of proficiency; factors contributing to attainment in L2 proficiency
2009	Evans	*FL Learning with Digital Technology*	Potential of the internet; beliefs of trainee teachers; bilingual/cross-cultural online discourse; textbook to online materials
2009	Van den Branden et al.	*Task-based Language Teaching*	General intro to TBLT; curriculum & task design; variables affecting task-based learning; task-based language assessment
2009	Turnbull & Dailey-O'Cain	*L1 Use in Second & FL Learning*	L1 in different constituent classrooms; English and other languages; primary and secondary education; dual language programmes
2010	Moreno-Jaen et al.	*Exploring New Paths in Language Pedagogy*	Corpus-based vocabulary; corpus-based evidence in pedagogy; theory to practice
2011	Hall et al.	*L2 Interaction Competence and Development*	Interaction as social activity; development of L2 interactional competence
2011	Sanz & Leow	*Implicit and Explicit Language Learning*	Theories, practice, methodological issues involved in: morphosyntax, phonology, bilingualism
2012	Diadori	*How to Train Language Teacher Trainers*	Major issues in language teacher training; European documents on teacher assessment; multilingualism; teacher competence; teacher certification; assessment and self-assessment
2013	Benati	*Issues in Second Language Teaching*	Grammar teaching; interaction & corrective feedback; four skills;
2014	Driscoll et al.	*Debates in Modern Languages Education*	Historical overview of language teaching; cognitive processing; evidence-based practice; four skills; grammar; vocabulary; cultural awareness; motivation; strategies; progression; CLIL; primary school languages
2014	Solly & Esch	*Language Education and the Challenges of Globalization*	Globalized classrooms and equal rights; medium of instruction policy; language education of immigrant students; divisive nature of education; non-native speech acceptability

Johnson & Porter (1983) examined different 'perspectives' on communicative language teaching (CLT), yet CLT itself appears to be absent from later editorial concerns (and indeed largely absent from individual book chapters). Rather than the notion of a teaching 'approach' (let alone a method!), we have themes which are tangential to CLT. This can be seen in Mackey's (2007) volume on interaction; in Richards & Renandya's (2002) emphasis on the four language skills; and in Van den Branden et al. (2009), who turn their attention to Task-Based Language Teaching, an offshoot of CLT. It is difficult to discern why such a shift should have occurred from looking at an overall approach (CLT) to investigating more isolated components of practice. Is it because CLT has become discredited? Is it because editors are reacting to historical events or what we might call 'changing times'? Or is it that researchers have found it extremely difficult to adequately investigate and compare the efficacy of holistic approaches or methods for teaching languages?

Current debates: Stakeholders' views

Moving beyond this historical perspective, we were also keen to find out about the key current debates in L2 education – those with which language teachers, teacher educators, researchers and policymakers are grappling in the 2020s. Therefore, we created an online survey to seek the views of stakeholders in these different categories. We first asked respondents for some background information that would help us to contextualize their answers; for example, which language(s) they teach; the age, L2 proficiency and first language background of their learners; the country in which they work etc. We then posed a broad, open-ended question, asking respondents to list, in order of importance:

> … what you consider to be the THREE most important debates in second language learning and teaching. By 'debates', we mean dilemmas, controversies, questions or issues faced by second language teachers, when making decisions in their classroom, or when planning a lesson. These could also be dilemmas faced by policymakers or school leaders in relation to second language teaching.

Additionally, we asked respondents to give reasons for their choices. Once the answers to these questions had been logged, respondents then progressed to a series of closed questions. Each presented respondents with a pre-identified debate in L2 education (Table 1.2) and asked them to indicate how important they thought it was, on a four-point scale (*Very important, quite important, not very important, not important at all*). We also provided a fifth, 'no opinion' option, though in practice this was seldom used.

We emailed an invitation to complete our survey to all relevant stakeholders in our existing professional networks. We then relied on 'snowball sampling' to expand our pool of respondents: that is, we asked anyone who received our email invitation to forward it to other relevant people they knew. Below, we provide some background information on our respondents. We will then go on to summarize our findings themselves.

Table 1.2 List of debates presented in the closed questions

- The extent to which research findings should inform L2 teaching.
- The best age for starting to learn an L2 (e.g. primary school, secondary school).
- Whether it is valuable to teach students how to learn a language (e.g. learner strategy instruction), or whether it is better just to teach the language itself.
- Whether motivation to learn an L2, or 'aptitude' for learning languages, is more important in determining L2 learning outcomes.
- The extent to which it is worth teaching phonics in an alphabetic L2 (i.e. the relationships between letters and their sounds).
- The extent to which learners should aim for a native-like accent when speaking the L2.
- Whether the L2 should be used exclusively (or almost exclusively) in L2 teaching, or whether it can be valuable to use a learner's L1 to support their L2 learning.
- Whether pre-service teacher education is valuable (e.g. courses or qualifications in language teaching that you complete before starting to teach), or whether it is better simply to 'learn by doing'.
- Whether all school pupils should have the opportunity to learn an L2 (at least to some level).
- Whether it should be compulsory for all school pupils to learn an L2 (at least to some level).
- The extent to which it is important to teach pronunciation explicitly in an L2.

Who responded to our survey?

Our survey was completed in full by 100 respondents based in 21 countries around the world (Figure 1.1). However, a little over half of the respondents (58%) were based in the United Kingdom, reflecting our own geographical location. Our sample comprised 49 secondary school language teachers, 32 SLA

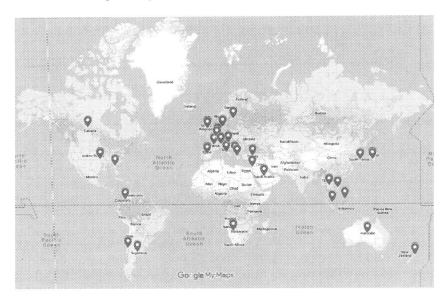

Figure 1.1 Locations of survey respondents.

researchers, 31 language teacher educators, 17 teachers of languages at the university level and 12 others, including primary school teachers, policymakers and resource creators. On average, respondents had 18 years of teaching experience, but this ranged widely, from less than 1 year to 50 years. Finally, three-quarters of our sample stated that they had completed a programme of pre-service language teacher education, whilst one-quarter said they had not.

Key debates as expressed by our respondents

As noted above, the open-ended questions in our survey invited respondents to list, in order of importance, up to three key areas of debate in L2 education. (Note that they were uninfluenced at this point by the debates which we provided in our subsequent closed questions.) Unsurprisingly, we received a wide array of responses. To make sense of the data, the first author of this chapter read through the responses and began to identify categories that seemed to 'emerge'. Each category represented a common theme or pattern. Two levels of categories were created, the first being more fine-grained (level 1 categories), whilst the second grouped these detailed categories into broader, overarching ones (level 2 categories). To illustrate, several respondents said that a key area of debate was the relative efficacy of explicit and implicit grammar teaching. These responses were labelled with the level 1 category code 'Explicit instruction', which in turn was coded as part of a broader, level 2 category relating to pedagogical approaches ('L2 Pedagogy').

Once the coding scheme was finalized, the second author independently applied it to roughly one-third of the data. This was to check that it adequately captured respondents' views and that the coding was sufficiently 'reliable'. The two authors agreed in their allocation of participants' responses to the different categories in 93% of cases, indicating very high inter-coder reliability.

Broad areas of debate

Table 1.3 summarizes participants' responses in terms of our broad 'level 2' categories. (Note that respondents were asked to give 'up to three' debates. Some provided only one or two; accordingly, the total number of responses is different for the three areas of debate in Table 1.3, with 100 responses for the 'most important' debate, but only 89 for the second most important and 61 for the third.)

We see immediately from Table 1.3 that concerns relating to 'L2 Pedagogy' – broadly speaking, how an L2 is best taught and assessed – are by far the most frequently reported in all columns. Matters relating to 'learner motivation and outcomes' are, by some margin, the second most frequent category of response overall; these also feature particularly strongly amongst the 'most important' debates. Examples in this category were questions of how best to engage L2 learners in the face of persistent demotivation or overly difficult examinations. Concerns relating to L2 education 'Policy' (for example, whether foreign language learning should be mandated for all school students in a given age group)

16   *Robert Woore and Ernesto Macaro*

Table 1.3 Numbers of responses in each of the broad 'level 2' categories

Level 2 (broad) category code	Most important debate	Second most important debate	Third most important debate	Overall tally (across all three debates)
L2 pedagogy	38	42	28	108
Learner motivation and outcomes	32	19	11	62
Policy	14	14	12	40
Teacher education and supply	5	9	8	22
Content-based instruction	6	4	2	12
Multilingual learners	5	–	–	5

were the third most frequent category overall. Finally, there were a small number of responses relating to: (a) Content-Based Instruction (such as how to teach an L2 effectively within a Content and Language Integrated Learning or 'CLIL' programme) and (b) how to cater effectively to the needs of multilingual learners (such as English language learners, or 'ELL', in the US school system).

Broad areas of debate according to the language taught

We wondered whether different groups within our overall sample of survey respondents might identify different key debates. In particular, we anticipated that different views might be held by teachers of L2 English on the one hand, and teachers of languages other than English (LOTE) on the other. For example, teaching LOTE might be expected to pose particular challenges in terms of learners' motivation in an 'English-dominant world' (Duff, 2017).

In our sample, 39 respondents stated that English was the main language they taught, while 56 gave a LOTE as their main teaching language. Note that a large majority of respondents in the LOTE group were based in secondary schools in the United Kingdom, which may have affected our results somewhat; by contrast, respondents in the L2 English group were spread across numerous different countries. Table 1.4 summarizes the key debates reported by these two groups of respondents, classified using our broad 'level 2' categories.

We ran statistical tests to see whether the English and LOTE groups of respondents differed significantly in each of their three areas of debate (their most, second most and third most important), as classified by our level 2 codes. Statistically significant differences were found between these groups of respondents in both the 'most important' and 'second most important' debates[1], though not in the third most important. Looking back at Table 1.4 shows where, specifically, the main differences occurred: namely, in the categories of 'Learner motivation and outcomes' and 'Content-based instruction'. This pattern is most clearly visible in the final column of Table 1.3, which shows the overall tally of responses in each level 2 category across all three areas of debate; Figure 1.2 presents this information in a bar chart. As can be seen, overall, when asked to

Identifying key debates 17

Table 1.4 Numbers and percentages of responses in our broad 'level 2' categories, by language being taught

Level 2 (broad) category code	Most important debate English	Most important debate LOTE	Second most important debate English	Second most important debate LOTE	Third most important debate English	Third most important debate LOTE	Overall tally (across all three debates) English	Overall tally (across all three debates) LOTE
L2 pedagogy	18 (41.9%)	20 (35.1%)	18 (41.9%)	24 (42.1%)	14 (32.6%)	14 (24.6%)	50 (45.0%)	58 (42.0%)
Learner motivation and outcomes	8 (18.6%)	24 (42.1%)	5 (11.6%)	14 (24.6%)	5 (11.6%)	6 (10.5%)	18 (16.2%)	44 (31.9%)
Policy	6 (14.0%)	8 (14.0%)	5 (11.6%)	9 (15.8%)	4 (9.3%)	8 (14.0%)	15 (13.5%)	25 (18.1%)
Teacher education and supply	1 (2.3%)	4 (7.0%)	6 (14.0%)	3 (5.3%)	5 (11.6%)	3 (5.3%)	12 (10.8%)	10 (7.2%)
Content-based instruction	6 (14.0%)	0 (0.0%)	4 (9.3%)	0 (0.0%)	2 (4.7%)	0 (0.0%)	12 (10.8%)	0 (0.0%)
Multilingual learners	4 (9.3%)	1 (1.8%)	0 (0.0%)	0 (0.0%)	0 (0.0%)	0 (0.0%)	4 (3.6%)	1 (0.7%)

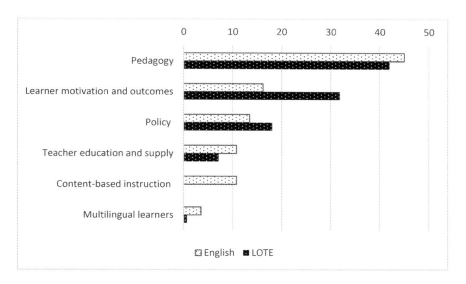

Figure 1.2 Overall percentage of responses in each of the broad 'level 2' categories, by L2 teaching group.

18 *Robert Woore and Ernesto Macaro*

identify key debates in L2 education, responses relating to learners' motivation and outcomes were much more frequent amongst the LOTE group than the English group. This is as we had expected, given the high status and instrumental value of learning English, a global lingua franca, for many learners around the world. We can also see that more English than LOTE respondents identified debates relating to Content-Based Instruction. Again, this is unsurprising, given the increasing popularity of teaching various subjects (such as Science and Maths) through the medium of English in schools and universities worldwide (Hüttner et al., 2013; Maiworm & Wächter, 2014; Lasagabaster, this volume). By contrast, teaching content through the medium of other foreign languages is much rarer in Anglophone countries.

Specific concerns

Turning to the more specific debates and issues raised by our respondents, altogether we used 43 detailed 'level 1' codes to capture these. As we do not have space to cover all 43 codes, we will focus on those which occurred ten or more times in total across all three sets of debates (i.e. across the most, second most and third most important debates). These eight codes, listed in Table 1.5 in descending order of overall frequency, account for around half of the total number of responses in each of the three sets of debates. Clearly, setting this arbitrary threshold means that we can paint only a partial picture of respondents' views, but we hope at least to give an idea of the main debates that were raised.

We will now look at some specific examples of participants' responses in each of these eight categories, following the order in which they appear in Table 1.5.

L2 curriculum

Responses in the 'L2 curriculum' category – the most frequent category overall – raised questions about what should be taught and by which methods, and about how to organize an effective L2 curriculum in broad terms. For example,

Table 1.5 Numbers of responses in the eight most frequent fine-grained ('level 1') categories

Level 1 (fine-grained) category	Most important debate	Second most important debate	Third most important debate	Overall tally (across all three debates)
L2 curriculum	5	9	9	23
Target language	6	7	5	18
Low motivation	7	5	4	16
Uptake	10	4	1	15
Exam difficulty	8	5	1	14
Washback	7	6	1	14
Explicit instruction	7	2	2	11
Low status	4	3	3	10

respondents expressed debates such as: 'what to teach and the methodology to apply'; 'what tasks to set up for foreign language learners'; and whether or not to base teaching around a textbook, since 'an entire program of study (scope and sequence and therefore learning outcomes) depends on which side of the debate you're on'. There was a sense from several respondents of a need to rethink the L2 curriculum in a way that builds and sustains learners' motivation: for example, one felt that "a lot of what they learn is really boring … It puts students off learning a language when they are learning about interesting topics in other subjects, but are stuck with boring or inappropriate material about family, school, 'my house', etc." in language lessons. Another respondent observed that "the whole basis of our teaching approach is influenced by how we were taught and yet those representations need to be challenged and updated".

There were also a number of responses in the 'L2 curriculum' category which raised questions about broad approaches to L2 teaching and the learning mechanisms underpinning these, such as the relative merits of 'games in lessons or … teacher target language as the normal means of communication' versus grammar translation and the use of 'knowledge organisers'. Two respondents referred to the importance of the 'lexical approach' to L2 teaching, based on encountering and learning chunks of language (see Racine, 2018), feeling that this approach was underdeveloped in many contexts: 'There are still very few materials, especially course books, that centre in [the] lexical approach'. Two others raised questions about the value of exposing students to 'comprehensible input' and graded language versus authentic resources, which might 'help them cope with the rather "messy"/complex patterns of discourse in spontaneous speech'. One respondent wondered about the extent to which teachers should 'introduce new vocabulary or structures and to what extend to recycle/practise previous material', an issue which might be seen in terms of the competing demands of covering a wide range of language on the one hand, and ensuring mastery of the language covered on the other. It can also be related to the broader question, raised by another respondent, of the 'role of cognitive processes underlying the four skills in determining approaches to the teaching and testing of languages'. Finally, one respondent raised the issue of informal learning and how this might be integrated with formal language teaching: "Learners (especially of English) are getting massive amounts of input from their private worlds. Classroom teaching needs to embrace this or risks being marginalised".

Target language

Zooming in from these broad-brush questions of curriculum and pedagogical approach, a number of respondents raised the more specific issue of the extent to which L1 should be used to support the learning of an L2. Indeed, this was the second most frequent category of debate mentioned overall. Six respondents made explicit reference to ongoing controversy and debate in this area; as one put it, 'It's a bone of contention with divergent and firmly held views and reasoning'. At the same time, it is an issue which must be confronted daily (and

20 *Robert Woore and Ernesto Macaro*

indeed minute-by-minute) by practitioners, at least in homogenous L1 classrooms: 'teachers need to make decisions about language use in all their lessons'; and it is one which may have a large impact on various aspects of L2 learning, including 'what vocab, grammar and skills students can acquire, the relationship they are able to build with their teacher and consequently their attitude towards language learning'. So, the stakes are high! Three responses in this category also mentioned the effects of policy on classroom practice, two of them – both secondary school teachers of EFL – from a negative perspective (talking about 'misguided policies' and 'dogma'). All this no doubt contributes to the emotional charge of this topic for teachers, for whom the issue of target language use may 'engender stress and guilt not experienced elsewhere in the curriculum'.

A few respondents seemed to see the question of L1 and L2 use as a dichotomy (e.g. 'Whether to use the students' L1 or not'; 'Whether the L2 should be used exclusively in the classroom'). Others, however, indicated that choice of language was not an either/or question: they talked instead about the 'extent' or 'amount' of each language that should be used in the classroom, or about 'balancing' the two languages for instructional purposes: 'Teachers should … understand when to use and when not to use L1'. Indeed, the majority (well over half) of responses in the 'target language' category expressed a need to recognize more nuanced positions in this debate, arguing for example that 'each classroom has its own environment', such that choice of L1 or L2 'is not so black and white'. One respondent felt that as learners' L2 proficiency increases, 'there should be a gradual decrease in the use of the mother tongue'; another noted that whilst it is important for teachers to use the L2, this must be done skilfully and in a way that is 'appropriate to the needs of students, [otherwise] students just switch off'. There were also several responses making a case for well-judged pedagogical use of the L1 as a 'learning resource' or 'mediational tool': for example, one stated that 'judicious use of learners' mother tongue is extremely useful and effective in teaching subtle points of grammar, lexis and pragmatics'. In any case, as another respondent put it, 'it is impossible to stop learners thinking in their L1', so teachers may as well embrace this rather than seek to stifle it.

Of course, many of these points of view are premised on a classroom environment in which all (or most) learners share an L1, in which the teacher is also proficient. Many L2 teaching environments around the world do not fit this description, either because there is no clear majority L1 (e.g. international language schools) or because a number of students are also learners of the dominant L1 (as in the case of English Language Learners in the United States, for example).

Low motivation

The third most frequent category of response (coming in not far behind target language use) concerned low levels of motivation and/or engagement amongst L2 learners, and how to combat this. Responses in this category referred, in various terms, to students' 'lack of enthusiasm', 'negative attitude' and 'low motivation'. (Note that we used this code only where no mention was made of other, more specific issues relating to learners' motivation. For these, we used other categories, such as 'exam difficulty', 'purposes of L2 learning', 'poor progress' and 'uptake'.) One teacher felt that low motivation was a particular problem for 'those who are less able or from less affluent families' – interestingly, the only time that social justice was raised in our survey data. In two responses, a 'lack of parental support' was also mentioned as a key factor. Four respondents (all from the United Kingdom) believed that low motivation was particularly challenging in Anglophone contexts, with students who are already 'speakers of a dominant language' and show a 'lack of interest and motivation to learn another language, because "everyone speaks English"'. Looking at the issue from a different perspective, one EFL teacher (based in Spain) felt that some of the excitement of learning English in school had been diluted by the ready access to English language resources on the internet: 'listening to a song in English class was really motivating a few years ago, but it is not so now'.

Finally, a handful of responses in this category viewed students' low motivation through the lens of the challenges of L2 learning itself. For example, one respondent felt that learning a language was more demanding than other subjects, due to the high levels of sustained commitment required. Others referred to the anxiety that language learning can provoke and the high levels of confidence needed to succeed, particularly as an adolescent in classroom settings: some 'students are fearful of speaking languages and being vulnerable'; they may be 'afraid to make mistakes or stick out in a crowd'.

Uptake

This category is closely related to the previous one; indeed, we could have included all responses in the 'uptake' category in the 'low motivation' one instead. However, we decided to separate out responses that talked predominantly about the numbers of students opting to study languages, in contexts where this is not compulsory. All of these responses included, as their main theme, some reference to 'declining', 'decreasing' or very small numbers of L2 learners in their contexts. As one respondent put it, 'fewer and fewer students are choosing to carry on studying a language once it's optional'.

Most responses in the 'uptake' category referred to the context of England, either stating this explicitly, or mentioning identifiably England-based qualifications or educational terminology. This is unsurprising, since England has seen a steady decline in the numbers of students studying languages beyond the age of 14 over roughly the last 20 years (Tinsley & Doležal, 2018; Collen, 2020). In several cases, the language used to describe this situation was highly emotive, describing the decline in L2 learning as 'disastrous' and 'a crisis', with concerns over a downward spiral from which it would be hard to recover: 'this is a vicious circle: not enough young people are studying languages, leading to a shortage of teachers'. With few students learning a language to age 18, it was feared that universities would 'be forced to close [foreign language] departments' and that there would be 'a lack of employees with language skills' in the wider workforce.

22 Robert Woore and Ernesto Macaro

Various reasons were suggested for the decline in uptake of language study in schools. These included: a general lack of motivation for L2 learning ('student apathy'; 'lack of interest'); the greater difficulty of languages compared to other subjects; poor understanding by students of the benefits of L2 learning; competition from other school subjects, like Science and Maths, seen to have higher instrumental value; lack of support from senior staff in schools; and, in England, the impact of 'Brexit', with 'insular attitudes' and a fear that 'we are breeding a narrow minded, inward-facing society'.

Exam difficulty

This category is again closely linked to the two previous ones but was used for responses where the main theme was the difficulty of public examinations in foreign languages compared to other subjects. Responses in this category were fairly homogenous, all expressing the view that, in languages, 'examinations are unfairly difficult', making it 'more difficult to get a high grade'; the marking is 'severe', 'overly-strict' and 'harsh'. This, in turn, was felt to be 'demoralizing for students' and stressful for staff, who were under pressure to achieve good results for their students 'within our current target-driven system'. Numerous respondents commented that the problem of 'over difficult and inaccessible exams' was a major cause of the decline in post-compulsory language study in schools: 'pupil numbers suffer due to the idea that they will achieve a lower grade'.

Interestingly, almost all responses in the 'exam difficulty' category referred explicitly to the English GCSE (General Certificate of Secondary Education) and/or A-Level (Advanced Level), national examinations taken at ages 16 and 18, respectively.

Washback

'Washback' refers to the influence exerted by tests and examinations (usually high-stakes ones) on curriculum design and pedagogy. Three respondents used the term 'washback' itself, whilst several others talked about 'teaching to the test' or 'teaching to the examination'. Comments in this category were again fairly homogeneous, raising the question of 'how to address the tension between teaching students to speak a language and teaching students to pass exams'; how to balance '"true" language learning versus "completing the exam" learning'. One respondent, a secondary school teacher, eloquently captured their dilemma:

> We are so much focused on passing the exam (...) Everything we do in the classroom is with the exam in mind, teaching them strategies on how to approach this or that question in the exam, rather than teaching them how to use the language in the country whose language they are learning.

Two respondents also highlighted that this focus on exam preparation stifled pedagogical creativity, reducing teachers' ability to experiment with 'innovative and active learning techniques' and to 'do interesting things in and around the classroom'.

Explicit instruction

Responses in this category concerned the relative merits of explicit and implicit teaching methods. As with the target language debate, many responses (around half) appear to frame this question in binary terms – i.e. *either* explicit *or* implicit instruction; one actually used the term 'dichotomy'. Further, although it is possible to see this question as one which 'frames decisions around how to present/practise most aspects of language teaching', all but two respondents related it specifically to teaching grammar. One respondent questioned the 'tendency to assume that EFL learners can acquire the grammatical foundations of English by using it in "communicative" classroom activities, and/or in task-based curricula'; another, however, warned against explicit grammar teaching, since 'it will make students get bored very easily'. One respondent neatly summed up the debate by asking:

> Do we just expect correct grammar to sink in, or do we do explicit grammar exercises, and if so, how do we get our learners to transfer a perfect grammar exercise into good productive language?

Low status

Responses in this category noted the low status of languages relative to other subjects in the curriculum. In turn, 'schools where languages are not valued often do not have adequate teaching time, support from Senior Management, funding, or resources', thus making it difficult 'for students to make progress or develop a love of the subject'. There is a sense of languages being 'crowded out by the demands of "more important" subjects, e.g. maths, English and science', and of teachers having to 'fight' for the place of languages in the curriculum. One respondent notes that children are often taken out of language lessons for catch-up work in other subjects, creating a mismatch between their school's rhetoric around valuing languages and what happens in practice: 'In theory, my school values languages. In practice they have other priorities and a crowded curriculum'. From another respondent came what sounded like a heartfelt comment:

> Teachers feel alone in their daily job, without any support from the Administration [and] very little quality training.

Specific issues according to the language taught

Once again, we wished to examine the extent to which the specific issues raised by our respondents might differ between those teaching L2 English and those teaching LOTE. To this end, Figure 1.3 shows the percentages of all responses made by our English respondents and our LOTE respondents in each of the eight fine-grained categories outlined above. In this figure, we have again amalgamated responses across all three areas of debate (i.e. the most, second most

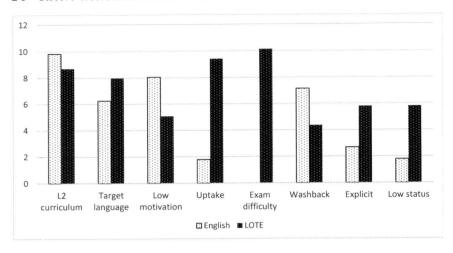

Figure 1.3 Overall percentages of responses in each of the most frequent 'level 1' categories, by language group.

and third most important), in order to increase the numbers in each category and allow more meaningful comparisons to be drawn. Statistical testing found statistically significant differences between the two language groups in terms of the distribution of their responses across these eight categories.[2]

In line with our comments above, this chart shows that the overwhelming majority of responses in the 'uptake' and 'exam difficulty' categories were made by LOTE respondents – most of whom were UK-based. Contrary to predictions, there is actually a slightly higher percentage of English than LOTE respondents in the 'low motivation' category. However, this is because many comments about poor student motivation were included separately in the 'uptake' and 'exam difficulty' categories, which were entirely or almost entirely represented by LOTE respondents. Comments on the explicit/implicit debate and on the low status of languages were also slightly more prevalent in the LOTE group, whereas the negative effects of exam washback were mentioned slightly more often by the English group. Broad questions of pedagogical approach and curriculum design (the 'L2 curriculum' category), and questions about the balance of L1 and L2 in the classroom ('Target language'), were both raised in roughly equal proportion by both groups.

It is also worth noting that, taken together, the eight categories in this chart cover a greater percentage of the total number of responses for the LOTE group (57.2% of all their responses) than for the English group (37.5%). This is because the responses of the English group were more widely distributed across a larger number of categories overall, perhaps reflecting the wider range of different countries and educational contexts in which these respondents worked. Our LOTE group, by contrast, was more homogeneous, based overwhelmingly in the UK Modern Foreign Languages sector.

Identifying key debates 25

There were also some categories of response which occurred less frequently overall (and so were not included in the eight categories above), but which were represented entirely, or almost entirely, by respondents in the L2 English group. The most frequent of these categories were:

1 'Language politics', concerning the relative status of certain languages compared to others. This category accounted for 7.1% of responses in the English group but only 0.7% of responses in the LOTE group. This imbalance presumably reflects concerns over what respondents called the 'dominant status' and 'hegemonic position' of English, seen by some as 'a threat to multilingualism'.

2 Questions of 'CBI (Content-Based Instruction) pedagogy' (7.1% of responses in the English group but not mentioned at all by the LOTE group). As noted above, this reflects the widespread use of English-Medium Instruction (or English CLIL) for subjects such as Science and Maths, whereas teaching through the medium of other L2s is much rarer.

3 Concerns over institutional 'Native speaker bias' (4.5% of responses in the English group; not mentioned by LOTE respondents). Again, native-speakerism and native-speaker teacher bias are widely recognized issues in L2-English contexts (e.g. see Holliday, 2006).

4 Questions of 'Technology' and how to use this effectively to support L2 learning (4.5% of responses in the English group; not mentioned in the LOTE group). Tentatively, we wonder whether this could reflect a greater prevalence of online material in English, thus making this concern more salient for teachers of English.

Closed questions: Respondents' views on 11 'debates'

As described earlier, our survey also included a series of closed questions. Here, we identified eleven potential areas of debate in L2 education, and invited respondents to state how important they felt each one was, using a four-point scale (very important, quite important, not very important, not important at all). There was also a fifth 'no opinion' option, but this was rarely used (2.6% of responses overall). Table 1.6 summarizes the responses. For each debate, we show both the number of respondents who chose each response option, and the average level of importance reported by the sample as a whole. To calculate the latter, we allocated zero points for each response of 'not important at all', one point for 'not very important', two points for 'quite important' and three for 'very important'. We then took the mean score for each item (disregarding, for this purpose, the very small number of 'no opinion' responses). Thus, a mean score of 3 would indicate that all respondents considered a given debate to be 'very important', while a score of 0 would indicate that all respondents considered it to be 'not important at all'. A mean score above the mid-point (1.5) can be taken to indicate that, on average, a given debate was felt to have some importance by the sample as a whole; conversely, a mean score below 1.5 indicates that the debate was, on

Table 1.6 Perceived importance of eleven debates in L2 education across the sample as a whole

	Debate	Not important at all	Not very important	Quite important	Very important	No opinion	Mean agreement score (standard deviation)
1	Whether all school pupils should have the opportunity to learn an L2 (at least to some level).	1	2	27	68	1	2.6 (0.7)
2	The extent to which research findings should inform L2 teaching.	0	9	26	61	3	2.5 (0.7)
3	Whether pre-service teacher education is valuable, or whether it is better simply to 'learn by doing'.	0	11	35	49	4	2.4 (0.6)
4	Whether it is valuable to teach students how to learn a language (e.g. learner strategy instruction), or whether it is better just to teach the language itself.	0	7	45	46	1	2.4 (0.8)
5	Whether it should be compulsory for all school pupils to learn an L2 (at least to some level).	3	7	34	53	2	2.4 (0.8)
6	The best age for starting to learn an L2 (e.g. primary school, secondary school).	3	16	41	38	1	2.3 (0.8)
7	The extent to which it is important to teach pronunciation explicitly in an L2.	1	14	48	32	4	2.1 (0.9)
8	Whether the L2 should be used exclusively (or almost exclusively) in L2 teaching, or whether it can be valuable to use a learner's L1 to support their L2 learning.	4	17	36	40	2	2.1 (0.7)
9	The extent to which it is worth teaching phonics in an alphabetic L2 (i.e. the relationships between letters and their sounds).	1	20	40	32	6	2.1 (0.6)
10	Whether motivation to learn an L2, or 'aptitude' for learning languages, is more important in determining L2 learning outcomes.	3	24	43	26	3	2.0 (0.8)
11	The extent to which learners should aim for a native-like accent when speaking the L2.	13	30	46	9	1	1.5 (0.7)

average, not considered important. The debates in Table 1.6 appear in decreasing order of mean agreement score; thus, the first debate in the list is the one to which respondents overall attributed the highest level of importance.

Table 1.5 shows that respondents broadly agreed that almost all of these debates were important. Only for item 11, the last debate in the list (the extent to which learners should aim for a native-like accent when speaking the L2) is the mean agreement score not positive overall, being 1.5 (or neutral). It is true that from item 6 (the best age for starting to learn an L2) onwards, we start to see considerable numbers of respondents (15% or more) rating the debates as either 'not very' or 'not at all' important. Nonetheless, for all debates in our list (even item 11), there are still more respondents who rate them as either quite/ very important than not very/not at all important.

Of course, caution is needed in interpreting these findings, since there may be a tendency for respondents to agree that a given debate is important, once they are asked to consider it. In other words, respondents may have been unlikely to say that any of the debates were *not* very important, once they saw them in a list and were asked to think about them. (It is for this reason that we began our survey with the open-ended questions, judging that these might provide a more unbiased insight into respondents' views.)

Once again, we broke down our findings from the closed questions according to language group, comparing the views of (a) respondents involved in teaching L2 English and (b) those involved in teaching LOTE. However, statistical tests found only one significant difference between these groups. This was in respect of item 7 in Table 1.6 ('the extent to which it is important to teach pronunciation explicitly in an L2').[3] For this item, the mean agreement score for the English group was 1.8, while for the LOTE group it was 2.4. Overall, therefore, this debate was considered more important by our LOTE group than our English group. Table 1.7 shows the percentages of respondents in each language group who chose each of the five response options for this item. We can see that almost a third of L2 English respondents, but very few LOTE respondents, considered this debate unimportant. By contrast, almost all LOTE respondents (93%) felt that this was an important area of debate.

Table 1.7 Percentages of English and LOTE respondents choosing each response option on item 7 ('the extent to which it is important to teach pronunciation explicitly in an L2')

	Not important at all	Not very important	Quite important	Very important	No opinion	Mean agreement score (and standard deviation)
Teachers of English	2.4	28.6	47.6	16.7	4.8	1.8 (0.7)
Teachers of LOTE	0.0	3.5	49.1	43.9	3.5	2.4 (0.6)

Conclusions

Stepping back to reflect on what we have explored in this chapter, two key points seem to emerge. The first is the fact that L2 teaching is, inescapably, a highly contested sphere of activity. Responses to our survey highlight the sheer range and complexity of challenges faced by L2 educators. Further, responses in the broad 'L2 pedagogy' category make clear just how many key decisions L2 teachers must take in the course of their daily practice, many against a backdrop of controversy and uncertainty. There is a lack of consensus even on some of the most fundamental bases of L2 education and 'design principles' of an effective L2 curriculum. To make matters worse, pedagogical debates in these areas often appear to take the form of binary choices between opposing (and sometimes deeply entrenched) poles of opinion: for example, grammar translation versus CLT; explicit versus implicit grammar instruction; L1 versus L2 as the routine language of classroom communication. All L2 teachers must inevitably take a position in many of these debates, even if only implicitly, through their classroom practice: for example, which language (L1 or L2) should they talk to their students in at time X in lesson Y for purpose Z?

Our rough analysis of some of the edited volumes published in the field over the last forty years also shows how the contested nature of L2 education has persisted over time. There have been some shifts in the topics of debate – reflecting changes in social, political and educational contexts, as well as advances in SLA research; but there are also some key controversies which have stubbornly endured (e.g. L1 versus L2; explicit versus implicit instruction). We would further observe that some debates in L2 education have been (or have been perceived to be) between different groups of stakeholders, such as classroom practitioners on the one hand and researchers or policymakers on the other; an example might be the target language debate (see Macaro, this volume). In other cases, topics have been hotly contested within a given group of stakeholders, as exemplified by various recent exchanges between language teachers on social media, or by academic debates on topics like the effectiveness of written corrective feedback (e.g. Truscott, 1999 versus Lyster et al., 1999). Thus, it is not the case that practitioners can simply turn to research for 'the answers': as Ellis (2005: 210) puts it, 'research and theory do not afford a uniform account of how instruction can best facilitate language learning'. Overall, it appears that the question of how to teach an L2 effectively is far from settled!

But why should this be, given the vast amount of intensive research activity that has been conducted within the realm of SLA? Why do we still seem to have so much debate and so few answers? One reason may simply be the enormous complexity of the object of study itself (i.e. the learning of an additional language), all the more so when literacy is involved as well as oral proficiency. Another reason may be that SLA is (relatively speaking) "still a very young field of study" (Ellis, 2005: 209), for example, when compared to Physics or Medicine. Finally, L2 learning and teaching take place within a huge range of diverse settings.

Identifying key debates 29

This leads us on to the second key point, which, for us, emerges from the current chapter: the importance of context. On the one hand, there may be some universals in SLA (and indeed this is an assumption of much research and theorizing in the field: e.g. Hall & Cook, 2012), for example, in terms of the cognitive processes of learning or the principles underpinning instruction. Yet, on the other hand, our survey data makes clear the powerful effects of context on some of the key issues and debates that confront teachers and learners. Drawing on examples from our survey responses, these contextual effects may operate at various levels. First, they may reflect broad societal or geopolitical realities (e.g. the dominant status of English as a global lingua franca; the impact of Brexit). Second, they may flow from national policies (e.g. whether language learning is compulsory for students of a given age in a given country). Third, they may reflect decisions taken at an institutional level (e.g. how much time is available for language study within the curriculum of a given school; whether learners are withdrawn from languages in order to catch up in other subjects). Fourth, they may reflect the needs and developmental trajectories of learners themselves (e.g. adolescent secondary school students feeling reluctant to speak a foreign language in front of classmates). Finally, we could add to these points the kinds of 'micro'-contextual issues that we discussed at the start of this chapter (e.g. it is Friday afternoon after a rainy PE lesson; student X has just fallen out with student Y). All of these kinds of contextual features are ones to which a teacher must respond, and which may, out of practical necessity, end up taking priority over more general pedagogical principles derived from SLA research and theory. In other words, L2 teaching and learning (indeed, all teaching and learning) is inevitably a contextualized process. Long (2009: 374) sums this up nicely:

> On the classroom floor, rather abstract strategic prescriptions and proscriptions take a back seat to the 101 tactical decisions teachers must make as even the slowest-paced lesson unfolds.

This, however, is not to deny the value of research-informed theories and principles as the underpinnings of classroom practice. Though SLA research could never hope to tell teachers precisely what to do at any given point in time (e.g. in which language to address their students at time X in lesson Y for purpose Z), it can offer guiding lights, points on the horizon towards which effective practice can be steered.

Relating the issues raised in this chapter to your own context:

1 Do you believe that there are some universal principles about language teaching? If so, which are they and what aspects of pedagogy do you believe are very much context-dependent?
2 To what extent do you believe that Second Language Education research has provided a theoretical framework for teaching languages in your educational context?

Notes

1 $p =.004$, two-tailed Fisher's exact test and $p =.040$, two-tailed Fisher's exact test, respectively.
2 Two-tailed Fisher's exact test, $p =.016$.
3 Two-tailed Fisher's exact test, $p < .001$. A Bonferroni correction was applied for multiple comparisons, giving an alpha level of .005.

References

Beebe, L. M. (Ed.) (1988). *Issues in Second Language Acquisition: Multiple Perspectives*. New York: Newbury House.

Benati, A. (Ed.) (2009). *Issues in Second Language Proficiency*. London: Bloomsbury.

Benati, A. (Ed.) (2013). *Issues in Second Language Teaching*. Sheffield: Equinox Publishing.

Block, D. & Cameron, D. (Eds.) (2002). *Globalization & Language Teaching*. London: Routledge.

Bourne, J. & Reid, E. (Eds.) (2003). *Language Education*. London: Kogan Page.

Collen, I. (2020). Language trends 2020. *Language Teaching in Primary and Secondary Schools in England. Survey Report*. London: British Council.

Diadori, P. (Ed.) (2012). *How to Train Language Teacher Trainers*. Newcastle Upon Tyne: Cambridge Scholars Publishing.

Driscoll, P., Macaro, E. & Swarbrick, A. (Eds.) (2014). *Debates in Modern Languages Education*. London: Routledge.

Duff, P. A. (2017). Commentary: Motivation for learning languages other than English in an English-dominant world. *The Modern Language Journal*, 101(3), pp. 597–607.

Ellis, R. (2005). Principles of instructed language learning. *System* 33(2005), pp. 209–224.

Evans, M. (Ed.) (2009). *Foreign Language Learning with Digital Technology*. London: Continuum.

Field, K. (Ed.) (2000). *Issues in Modern Foreign Language Teaching*. London: Routledge.

Gabryś-Barker, D. (Ed.) (2008). *Morphosyntactic Issues in Second Language Acquisition*. Clevedon: Multilingual Matters.

Hall, G. & Cook, G. (2012). Own-language use in language teaching and learning. *Language Teaching*, 45(3), pp. 271–308.

Hall, J. K., Hellerman, J. & Doehler, S. P. (Eds.) (2011). *L2 Interaction Competence and Development*. Clevedon: Multilingual Matters.

Holliday, A. (2006). Native-speakerism. *ELT Journal*, 60(4), pp. 385–387.

Hüttner, J., Dalton-Puffer, C. & Smit, U. (2013) The power of beliefs: Lay theories and their influence on the implementation of CLIL programmes. *International Journal of Bilingual Education and Bilingualism*, 16(3), pp. 267–284.

Johnson, K. (Ed.) (2005). *Expertise in L2 Learning and Teaching*. London: Palgrave Macmillan.

Johnson, K. & Porter, D. (Eds.) (1983). *Perspectives in Communicative Language Teaching*. London: Academic Press.

Lantolf, J. P. & Poehner, (Eds.) (2008). *Sociocultural Theory and the Teaching of Second Languages*. Sheffield, UK: Equinox Publishing.

Long, M. (2009) Methodological principles for language teaching, in M. H. Long and J. Doughty (eds.) *The Handbook of Language Teaching*. Oxford: Blackwell. pp. 373–394.

Lyster, R., Lightbown, P. and Spada, N. (1999). A response to Truscott's 'What's wrong with oral grammar correction'. *Canadian Modern Language Review*, 55(4), pp. 457–467.

Identifying key debates 31

Mackey, A. (Ed.) (2007). *Conversational Interaction in SLA*. Oxford: Oxford University Press.

Maiworm, F. & Wächter, B. (Eds.) (2014). *English-Taught Programmes in European Higher Education: The State of Play in 2014*. ACA papers on international cooperation in education. Bonn: Lemmens.

Moreno-Jaen, M., Serrano-Valverde, F. & Calzada-Perez, M. (Eds.) (2010). *Exploring New Paths in Language Pedagogy: Lexis and Corpus-Based Language*. Sheffield, UK: Equinox Publishing.

Muñoz, C. (Ed.) (2006). *Age and the Rate of FL Learning*. Clevedon: Multilingual Matters.

Racine, J. P. (2018). Lexical approach. *The TESOL Encyclopedia of English Language Teaching*, 2, pp. 1–7.

Richards, J. & Renandya, W. A. (Eds.) (2002). *Methodology in Language Teaching; An Anthology of Current Practice*. Cambridge: Cambridge University Press.

Robinson, P. (Ed.) (2002). *Individual Differences and Instructed Language Learning*. Amsterdam: John Benjamins.

Sanz, C. & Leow, R. P. (Eds.) (2011). *Implicit and Explicit Language Learning: Conditions, Processes, and Knowledge in SLA and Bilingualism*. Washington DC: Georgetown University Press.

Seidlhofer, B. (Ed.) (2003). *Controversies in Applied Linguistics*. Oxford: Oxford University Press.

Solly, M. & Esch, E. (Eds.) (2014). *Language Education and the Challenges of Globalization*. Newcastle Upon Tyne: Cambridge Scholars Publishing.

Tinsley, T. & Doležal, N. (2018). Language trends 2018. *Language Teaching in Primary and Secondary Schools in England. Survey Report*. London: British Council.

Truscott, J. (1999). What's wrong with oral grammar correction. *Canadian Modern Language Review*, 55(4), pp. 437–456.

Turnbull, M. l. & Dailey-O'Cain, J. (Eds.) (2009). *First Language Use in Second and Foreign Language Learning*. Clevedon: Multilingual Matters.

Van den Branden, K., Bygate, M. & Norris, J. M. (2009). *Task-Based Language Teaching: A Reader*. Amsterdam: John Benjamins.

2 Learning English and learning languages other than English in Asia and Europe

Current scenarios and debates

Bruna Di Sabato and Andy Kirkpatrick

Introduction

In this chapter, we look at issues surrounding the learning and teaching of English and other languages in the school systems of two widely different contexts, namely Asia (East and Southeast) and Continental Europe (primarily countries within the European Union), identifying major trends. We shall show that, while there are significant differences with regard to language education policy within these two broad contexts, there are also some interesting similarities. The following sections will outline the salient features of these two areas referring to official data and statistics where available, and trying to identify the sociocultural and political mainsprings. Convergences and discrepancies between the two contexts will be critically appraised, highlighting debatable issues for the development of future policies. Apart from meeting economic and financial needs, ideally, these should also bring about equitable and peaceful societies where people can communicate easily, overcoming both language and ideological barriers, and granting the same access to knowledge and progress to all.

East and Southeast Asia

We first consider East and Southeast Asia. In this chapter, East Asia is considered to comprise China, Korea and Japan and Southeast Asia the ten countries which make up the Association of Southeast Asian Nations (ASEAN). These ten countries are, in alphabetical order, Brunei, Cambodia, Indonesia, Laos, Malaysia, Myanmar, The Philippines, Thailand, Singapore and Vietnam. When compared with Europe, East and Southeast Asia is linguistically extremely diverse. Indeed, Asia itself is the most linguistically diverse region in the world, being home to some 34% or 2301 of the world's 7102 living languages. Europe is less linguistically diverse, being home to only 286, or 4% of the world's living languages. With regard to specific countries of East and Southeast Asia, Indonesia is the most linguistically diverse with 707 living languages. Other countries within the region with more than 100 living languages are China (300), the Philippines (193), Malaysia (146) and Myanmar (117)[1]. As we will show, despite – or perhaps

DOI: 10.4324/9781003008361-4

Learning languages other than English in Asia and Europe 33

because of – this diversity, few of these languages are being learned in schools across East and Southeast Asia.

English, by contrast, is playing increasingly important roles in each of these countries and in order to explain the presence of English some historical background is necessary. Many of the countries of Southeast Asia were colonies of English-speaking empires. These include Brunei, Myanmar, Malaysia and Singapore, which were part of the British empire, and the Philippines, which was an American colony from 1898 until 1946. Being part of English-speaking empires, English established institutional roles in these countries and regional varieties of English developed. These include, for example, the Filipino, Malaysian and Singaporean varieties of English. Braj Kachru, the leading figure in the field of World Englishes, proposed the so-called 'circles' classification of countries, based on the role of English within them (e.g. Kachru 1982, 1985). Countries where English was spoken as a first language by the majority of the population he called 'Inner Circle' countries. These included the United States, Australia and Great Britain itself. Countries which had English imported to them in their position as part of empire, he classified as 'Outer Circle' countries. These included countries such as Singapore, the Philippines and Malaysia, but also countries such as India. Over time, Outer Circle countries reshaped the English that had been imported by developing their own norms of English, resulting in the varieties of English noted above (Schneider 2007). In countries where English played a minimal role and was only taught as a school subject, Kachru was classified as Expanding Circle countries. Such countries were norm-dependent, relying upon inner-circle varieties of English to provide the models of English for the classroom. These included countries such as China and Japan. Following Kachru's circles classification, the countries of Continental Europe would be classed, therefore, as countries of the Expanding Circle.

Even though the countries of the Outer Circle mentioned above have all achieved independence, the roles of English have been maintained and in many Expanding Circle countries, the roles of English have increased dramatically. As Bolton and Bacon-Shone note:

> Since the era of European decolonisation in Asia, which largely took place from the late 1940s to the 1960s, there has been a massive expansion in the spread of English throughout the whole of the region, in both Outer Circle and Expanding Circle societies.
>
> (Bolton & Bacon-Shone 2020, 49)

Why are so many people learning English? To take China as an example, where English is now a compulsory subject from the third year of primary school and given equal weighting with maths and Chinese itself in the infamous *gao kao*, the national university entrance exam, a major reason is that English is seen as a conduit which allows people to connect to the world. As Bolton, Botha and

34 *Bruna Di Sabato and Andy Kirkpatrick*

Zhang (2020) point out, English connects Chinese people to the world "either directly, through travel or education abroad, or even symbolically, by connecting young people to life outside mainland China, at a range of levels, from popular culture to current affairs or to various forms of academic knowledge". The feeling that English connects people to the world is shared across much of East and Southeast Asia and helps explain its popularity. In addition, the Association of Southeast Asian Nations has officially made English the only working language of the group (Kirkpatrick 2010). Article 34 of the ASEAN Charter, which was signed by all member states in 2009, simply states the "the sole working language shall be English". By making English the only working language of the group, the language policy of ASEAN makes a startling contrast with that of the European Union, where all member states were given the opportunity to choose which languages they wanted to be recognized as official languages of the Union. One similarity that can be seen in both the Asian and European contexts is the call for a spirit of 'unity in diversity'. Article 2 of the ASEAN Charter lists a number of principles that ASEAN member states are expected to follow and these include "respect for the different cultures, languages and religions of the peoples of ASEAN while emphasising their common values in the spirit of unity in diversity" (Kirkpatrick 2010, 7). This echoes the official European slogan of 'United in Diversity' which we discuss further below. Its realization in Indonesian, *Bhinneka tunggal ika*, is, incidentally, also the official slogan of Indonesia. Yet despite this call for unity in diversity and respect for local cultures and languages, the importance of English is continually stressed, as this 2013 quote from the then Secretary General of ASEAN, Le Luong Minh, makes clear:

> With the diversity in ASEAN reflected in our diverse histories, races, cultures and belief systems, English is an important and indispensable tool to bring our Community closer together. [...] Used as the working language of ASEAN, English enables us to interact with other ASEAN colleagues in our formal meetings as well as day-to-day communications. [...] In order to prepare our students and professionals in response to all these ASEAN integration efforts, among other measures, it is imperative that we provide them with opportunities to improve their mastery of the English language, the language of our competitive global job market, the lingua franca of ASEAN.
>
> (ASEAN 2013)

Thus, in addition to the usual reasons given for the apparent need for English – which include countries wanting to participate in globalization and to keep up with developments in science and technology – there is a popular demand for English which means that, in many cases, governments and people agree that English is somehow important for the development of both country and individuals. Evidence for this can be seen in the language education policies adopted by the countries of East and Southeast Asia. In a recent study of language education

Learning languages other than English in Asia and Europe 35

policy across Asia, Kirkpatrick and Liddicoat (2019,12) identified five major trends, namely:

1. the promotion of the respective national language as a symbol of national identity and unity;
2. the promotion of English as the second language of education;
3. as a result of point 2 an increasing division between the 'have' and 'have nots', as government schools often face shortages of qualified English teachers and lack access to suitable materials;
4. limited support for indigenous languages in education, and often these languages are present in policy documents but not in reality;
5. as a result of points 2 and 4, many children have to learn in languages they do not understand.

What these trends indicate is that, in most of the countries of East and Southeast Asia, language education policy dictates that the two major languages of education are the respective national language and English. Other languages, whether these be indigenous local languages or foreign languages, are neglected. There are exceptions to this, and perhaps the most noteworthy is the language education policy recently adopted by the Philippines. For many decades, language education policy in the Philippines was represented by the Bilingual Education Policy (BEP). Through this policy, from the first year of primary school, maths and science subjects, as well as English itself, were taught through the medium of English, and other subjects through the national language, Filipino. But, as noted above, the Philippines is home to 193 languages. It should also be noted that the national language, Filipino, is based on Tagalog, the language spoken in and around the capital, Manila. While today, most Filipinos are able to use Filipino, at the time of the introduction of the BEP in 1974, few people outside Manila itself would have been able to speak it. At the same time, few, apart from the affluent middle and upper classes, knew English. This meant that many Filipino children in the multilingual Philippines were forced to learn in two languages that they did not understand. This led the Filipino linguist Andrew Gonzales to despair that:

> The formula for success in Philippine education is to be a Tagalog living in Metro Manila, which is highly urbanized, and studying in a private school considered excellent. And of course, the formula for failure is the opposite: being non-Tagalog, studying outside of Metro Manila, in a rural setting, in a public or government school considered sub-standard.
>
> (Gonzalez 1996, 333)

As a result of decades of lobbying, the Philippines Government eventually abandoned the BEP and, in 2009, introduced the policy of mother tongue-based multilingual education (MTBMLE) (Martin 2020). MTBMLE nominates 19 languages that are to be used as media of instruction for the first three years of primary school, after which Filipino and English assume the roles of media of instruction and the other languages are taught as subjects. While the policy of MTBMLE represents a radical shift in language education policy away from the BEP, proponents of MTBMLE remain critical of the government, being uncertain why only 19 languages have been gazetted as languages of instruction and also arguing that MTBMLE should entail the use of these languages as media of instruction throughout the course of primary school, not just for the first three years (Young & Igcalinos 2019).

In Indonesia, the most linguistically diverse country under review here, the national language, *Bahasa Indonesia* is the sole language of education. Local governments have some autonomy and some of the larger languages such as Sundanese and Javanese are taught in secondary schools. Local languages with fewer speakers such as Buginese are taught in some areas where Buginese is the native language, but not in all of them (Koehler 2019). Generally speaking, however, only a handful of the seven hundred or so languages of Indonesia are taught in schools.

As with Indonesia, the language education policy of China prioritizes the teaching of the national language. The Chinese Language Law, implemented in 2000, is clear. *Putonghua*, the variety of Mandarin spoken around the capital Beijing and its written form, Modern Standard Chinese, is prescribed as the sole language of education (Kirkpatrick & Xu 2001). In making one language of a multilingual nation the national language, China is reflecting what many other nations in the region have done. Believing that a national language is vital for establishing a national identity, governments across the region have striven to promote one language as the national language. In the case of China, other Chinese languages such as Cantonese and Shanghainese are thus not allowed to be used as languages of education. Hong Kong and Macau remain the only two polities where Cantonese is used as a language of education. And, as noted above, English is the second major language of education in China. The Language Law does, however, allow the use of the languages spoken by the national minorities in China as languages of education. Thus languages such as Zhuang, Tibetan, Mongolian and Yi are used as languages of education but with limited success, in part because parents see that Putonghua is a more important language for their children to learn in school than their home language (Feng & Adamson 2019). In the vast majority of cases, the two languages being learned in Chinese schools are the national language and English.

There is no doubt that English is now China's second language. But how many learners and speakers of English are there in China? It is difficult to obtain precise figures, but perhaps the most reliable recently compiled figures for English learners and users can be found in Bolton & Bacon-Shone (2020). Using data from government censuses and language surveys, they compiled sets of figures for English language speakers across Asia. As shown in Table 2.1, the figure for the number of English speakers in China is 276 million. Table 2.1 also shows their estimate of English speakers across Asia's Expanding Circle countries as a whole, illustrating how important English has become even in these contexts. The data indicate the percentages and the total number of the population that speaks English.

Learning languages other than English in Asia and Europe   37

Table 2.1 Knowledge of English in Expanding Circle Asian societies

Society	Current estimates	Approximate total of English speakers
Nepal	30%	8.5 million
Macau	28%	0.2 million
China	20%	276.0 million
Myanmar (Burma)	10%	5.2 million
Japan	10%	12.5 million
South Korea	10%	5.1 million
Taiwan	10%	2.4 million
Thailand	10%	6.5 million
Vietnam	10%	4.6 million
Cambodia	5%	0.8 million
Indonesia	5%	13.0 million
Laos	5%	0.3 million
Total		**335.1 million**

Source: Adapted from Bolton & Bacon-Shone (2020).

Table 2.2 shows their estimates for the percentages and the current number of English speakers in the Outer Circle countries of Asia.

If we add the totals of these two tables together, we see that the overall number of English speakers in Asia is around 800 million, a total which shows that there are almost twice as many English speakers in Asia alone than there are native speakers of English. But these figures need to be treated with caution, as does the very notion of a 'speaker of English'. How much English does a 'speaker of English' actually know? How often does a 'speaker of English' actually use English? How successfully are Asians learning English? These are questions that are extremely difficult to answer. The most recent EF English Proficiency Index (EPI) calculated the English proficiency of 100 countries based on the test results of 2.3 million adults who took their test in 2018 (EF 2019). Singapore

Table 2.2 Knowledge of English in Outer Circle Asian societies

Society	Current estimates	Approximate total of English speakers
Singapore	80%	3.1 million
Philippines	65%	66.7 million
Brunei	60%	0.2 million
Hong Kong	53%	3.9 million
Malaysia	50%	15.5 million
Pakistan	25%	50.9 million
Sri Lanka	25%	5.3 million
Bangladesh	20%	32.6 million
India	20%	260.0 million
Total		**438.2 million**

Source: Adapted from Bolton & Bacon-Shone (2020).

38   Bruna Di Sabato and Andy Kirkpatrick

was the only Asian country of the 14 which was rated in the top 'Very High' band. Malaysia and the Philippines were rated in the 'High' band. China and India were both rated in the 'Moderate' band, Indonesia, Japan and Vietnam in the 'Low' band and Myanmar and Thailand in the lowest 'Very Low' band. But these results are based on adults who voluntarily took their tests. Similar caution must be exercised when considering results obtained by the IELTS and TOEFL international tests of English, as they are based on the results of people who actually took these tests and who thus merely represent a small fraction of the total number of people learning English.

These figures take no note of the millions of children across East and Southeast Asia who are learning English in primary school but failing to complete their primary schooling, dropping out for a variety of reasons, one of which, according to UNESCO, is that education is not provided in the children's mother tongue. As Kirkpatrick and Liddicoat noted in the fifth language education policy trend above, the current almost universal prioritizing of the national language and English as languages of education in the language education policies of these countries means that many children are having to learn in languages they do not understand. The UNESCO report, *Education for All by 2015* (2007), stressed the importance of providing multilingual education and education in a child's home language to improve primary school retention rates across Asia.

A further point to stress is that for speakers of the languages of East and Southeast Asia, English is linguistically a truly foreign language, in that it belongs to a different language family (Kirkpatrick 2010). In contrast, European children learning European languages at school are learning languages which are, with exceptions such as Hungarian, from the same language family. There are, to varying degrees, levels of connection between the languages. Many European languages share cognates. They share the same script, with only minor variations. Literacy in one language can help with literacy in another. For Asian children learning English, if there are cognates (as in '*polis*' in Malay), they come from borrowings from English into the local languages. Asian learners of English may have to learn a new script. All this makes English harder for children who speak Asian languages to learn, but the typological difference between English and Asian languages – greater than between the Romance and Germanic languages of Europe – and the significance of this for learning the language are not taken into account by language education policymakers.

In this first section of this chapter, we have noted that, generally speaking, in the Asian countries under review, language learning is restricted to learning the respective national language of the country and English. This is also true of both Japan and South Korea. Other local and foreign languages are neglected. Chinese (*Putonghua*) is, after English, the most popular foreign language taught throughout the region, but this is often in private schools. But all government schools teach English, often from the third year of primary school. Despite the widespread teaching of English in East and Southeast Asian school systems, no official recognition of the particular difficulties associated with learning a language that is typologically distinct from the children's first languages is given. Neither is

Learning languages other than English in Asia and Europe 39

there official recognition of local varieties of English or the role of English as a lingua franca, and this makes the learning and teaching of English even more problematic, as only a tiny minority of English language teachers in the region possesses a native speaker variety of English (Kirkpatrick 2010, 2018). There are indications, however, that scholars and educational professionals in countries such as Indonesia and Vietnam are beginning to promote the teaching of English as a lingua franca rather than a native speaker variety of English in these countries (e.g. Zein 2018; Van Canh et al. 2019). These educational professionals argue that the major use of English in Asia is as a lingua franca (ELF) and that ELF does not require users to acquire native speaker varieties of the language.

We have not said much about the teaching of European languages other than English in this first section of the chapter for the reason that these are only taught as electives, most commonly in tertiary education. French, Spanish and German are the most common, with *Putonghua* Chinese being the most widely taught Asian language. The teaching of these languages is often supported by agencies such as the Confucius and Goethe Institutes. In Asia, foreign language education has thus become synonymous with the teaching and learning of English; other foreign languages have at best a minimal role in education, especially in schools (Kirkpatrick & Liddicoat 2019).

To summarize the first part of this chapter, the teaching of languages in East and Southeast Asian countries is dominated by the teaching of the respective national language and English. It is as if, in the struggle for unity in diversity, local governments have promoted the national language as the symbol of unity and identity at the expense of the diversity represented by literally hundreds of local languages. At the same time, the governments' and their people's perception of the importance of English for both national and individual development has made English the second most important language of education in each of these countries. It is dangerous to put precise figures on the numbers of Asian speakers of English, but perhaps the most reliable figure would be around 800 million, representing almost twice the number of native speakers of it. It is even more difficult to define what is meant by a speaker of English in these contexts, but there is clearly a cline of proficiency both within and between the countries reviewed here. Local languages other than the national language do not feature in any systematic way as languages of education and, where they are taught, are often the responsibility of NGOs rather than governments (Kosonen 2019). An exception is the Philippines and, in some cases, the languages of the national minorities of China. Foreign languages other than English are not predominant in the school system, with Putonghua being the foreign language most learned. In the second part of the chapter, we turn to examine the situation in continental Europe.

Europe

In this part of the chapter, we will concentrate on the trends in second and foreign language learning in Continental Europe, especially within the European Union (EU).[2] By focusing on policies and their outcomes, the following pages will attempt to offer an organic view of the learning of English and languages other than English in Europe. It will soon become clear that member states are expected to adopt similar policies in line with recommendations agreed upon and shared by the countries' representatives in such institutions. A common thread emerges across Europe, then, though differences exist because of the sociocultural and historical features typical of a multifaceted and therefore culturally rich continent.

The concept of 'unity in diversity' was mentioned in the previous section when referring to the promotion of national languages by local Asian governments as a symbol of unity and identity. In the European context, the official motto 'United in diversity' encapsulates Europe's will "to work for peace and prosperity, while recognizing and respecting the continent's many different cultures, traditions and languages" (European Union 2019). Much as in the Asian context, the status of English as the most used and studied first foreign language is also a feature of the European continent. Languages are felt to be a source of enrichment for EU citizens and language diversity is promoted and protected, despite a level of diversity which might appear scarcely relevant when compared to the wealth of languages spoken in Asia.

This respect for linguistic diversity is considered a fundamental value of the Union, as stated in the consolidated version of the founding Treaty of the European Community: art. 149 (1997) emphasizes that its action shall be aimed at "developing the European dimension in education, particularly through the teaching and dissemination of the languages of the Member States" (European Union 1997), while fully respecting cultural and linguistic diversity within the states' education systems. This position is in line with the wider perspective represented by UNESCO: the international organization, which counts 193 member states and 11 associate members, has also promoted several initiatives to foster cultural and linguistic diversity. The UNESCO Universal Declaration on Cultural Diversity (2001, Annex 2) specifically highlights the importance of linguistic diversity at all levels of education, as does their report, *Education for All by 2015*, mentioned above. In April 2019, 'Foreign language teaching and linguistic diversity' were included as items for discussion, and the Executive Board invited member states to support the implementation of quality education in at least two foreign languages at as early an age as possible, and to invest more in the training of language teachers "so that the proficient multilingualism thus imparted can foster mobility and employability" (UNESCO 2019, 2).

The language patrimony of the EU consists of 24 official languages; these are, in alphabetical order: Bulgarian, Croatian, Czech, Danish, Dutch, English, Estonian, Finnish, French, German, Greek, Hungarian, Irish, Italian, Latvian, Lithuanian, Maltese, Polish, Portuguese, Romanian, Slovak, Slovenian, Spanish and Swedish. However, the EU is also home to more than 60 regional languages (also named as 'non-dominant' if compared to a 'dominant' language, namely the State language or the language of instruction) used by more than 40 million citizens (European Commission 2019a). Over the years, the migratory trends endemic to the EU have also led to the presence of extra-European languages such as Arabic, Turkish, Urdu, Hindi and Chinese.

Learning languages other than English in Asia and Europe   41

Besides the drive towards linguistic diversity, language policy throughout the EU is also based on the ambitious objective of reaching widespread plurilingualism[3], with all citizens able to communicate in at least two languages other than their mother tongue (Mezzadri 2016). The 2002 Barcelona European Council Recommendation that at least two foreign languages should be imparted to all pupils from a very early age (art. 44) has been implemented in a range of measures across Europe (European Council 2002). It is variously applied within the field of compulsory secondary education, where the teaching and learning of a second language are either mandatory or are offered to students as one of the curricular options.

A present-day snapshot of language learning and language education throughout the European continent (based on the latest data for 2018 published by the European Commission – Eurostat 2012 onwards) illustrates that, as in Asia, in most of the EU member states a majority of pupils study English at primary school. In Austria, Cyprus, Liechtenstein, Malta, Spain, North Macedonia and Norway, 99% to 100% of pupils do so, followed by a slightly lower number in Croatia, France, Greece, Italy, Latvia and Poland. A different situation is to be found in the countries from the eastern and northern block, which became European Member States in 2004 or 2007, and where learning Russian was a compulsory aspect of the educational system. Statistics now show that in 2017, more than 50% of primary school pupils were studying English in most of these countries. A third aspect is represented by a number of multilingual countries, where more than one language has some sort of official recognition, such as Belgium, Luxembourg and the non-EU Switzerland. Here, the language needs are different, because the co-existence of citizens speaking different first languages grants priority to such languages. For instance, in Luxembourg, where Luxembourgeois, French and German are used by the administration and by the judiciary, primary education grants space to the three, while English is introduced only later at secondary school (Ministère de l'Éducation Nationale de l'Enfance et de la Jeunesse 2017). After Luxembourg, in 2017, Belgium, Greece, Romania and Spain were recorded as the countries with the most primary school children learning French as a foreign language. German was the main foreign language taught at primary school in Luxembourg, while just over one-fifth of primary school pupils were taught German in Croatia and Hungary.

As for language learning in upper secondary general education, in 2017, a massive 94.7% of students across the EU were studying English as a foreign language; slightly more than one-fifth (22.3%) were studying Spanish, while less than a fifth were studying French (18.1%) or German (17.4%). Data show that from 2012 to 2017, the number of secondary school students studying Spanish rose while those studying French fell; and a considerable increase in the number of pupils studying English was recorded in Greece, Hungary and Portugal (European Commission – Eurostat 2012, last update 2019). The study of a second foreign language is, however, not strongly endorsed by all member states (Eurydice 2017). When the study of an additional language is offered, the most common choices are French, German, Spanish and Italian. In 2017, the only

EU Member State where every pupil in upper secondary general education was consistently learning two or more languages was Luxembourg; although figures close to 100% were also recorded in France, Romania, Czechia, Slovakia and Finland, where more foreign languages than just the four mentioned above were studied. The lowest numbers of upper secondary school students studying two or more foreign languages were recorded in Greece (1.0%), and Portugal (6.0%). Among the non-EU "foreign" languages, Russian, Chinese and Arabic hold prime position, and Latin and Classical Greek still figure among the options.

Interestingly, the 2018 Council Recommendation points to the fact that a curious vicious circle is emerging: although a second foreign language may be part of the lower secondary school syllabus, students usually cease to study it over the years. The disappearance of the second foreign language is a controversial issue. Although plurilingualism is recognized as one of the pillars of lingua-cultural heritage and educational policy, member states opt for different measures not only for economic reasons but also for cultural ones. A second foreign language is occasionally seen as usurping the place of another subject. In Italy, for instance, the strongly Catholic heritage resists the replacement of Latin by a foreign language. The ensuing outcome is a decrease in the demand for foreign languages in tertiary education and consequently a dearth of qualified language teachers. It is also relevant that although language learning now starts at a younger age (usually before the age of eight), the amount of time devoted to language lessons is still inadequate (Eurydice 2017). It is therefore not surprising that the Eurobarometer 2012 survey (European Commission 2012a), albeit not particularly recent, reports that over 40% of respondents claim to be unable to hold a conversation in a language other than their mother tongue (see also European Commission 2012b).

As for English, the already mentioned EF EPI index data for 2019 confirm an unequal level of English competence across Europe: while the Netherlands holds the top position in the 'Very High' band, followed by the other Northern European countries (Sweden, non-EU Norway, Denmark and Finland with slightly lower results) other countries such as France, Spain and Italy are in the 'Moderate' band. However, no EU countries are listed in the 'Very Low' band, the lowest positions being filled by the non-EU Turkey and Azerbaijan. This suggests that EU language policies are exerting their influence across member states, although some differences have been registered in the different regions.

Most of the European educational systems also refer to the teaching of regional or minority languages, which may be compulsory for students from a minority background or those living in specific geographical areas. Official documents mention over 60 regional or minority languages, though the landscape varies on the basis of favourable or unfavourable political commitments and the specific linguistic make-up of each country. In Croatia, Lithuania, North Macedonia, Slovakia, Spain and Sweden, official documents report a number of regional or minority languages ranging from five to ten; in France, Hungary, Italy, Poland, Romania and Serbia, the figure is higher than ten, with Poland and Serbia reaching fifteen. In many European educational systems, amongst which are France and Sweden, the teaching of regional or minority languages in schools is supported by a legal framework and sometimes by specific Ministerial guidelines and funding: the learning and visibility of regional or minority languages across Europe are also promoted thanks to funding programmes like Erasmus+ and Creative Europe (Eurydice 2019). In addition to schools offering regional or minority languages besides the main language of instruction, a number of educational systems now have schools in which all or most subjects are taught in such languages. This happens, for instance, in Slovenia, where some schools provide education in Italian and other bilingual schools provide education in Slovenian and Hungarian.

The general framework described so far illustrates that, besides several EU actions to promote plurilingual education, plurilingualism also seems to stem from sociocultural features inherent to the different regions of Europe. This is indirectly confirmed by recent initiatives designed to promote further actions on behalf of member states. Following the Commission's aim to establish a European Education Area by the year 2025 in which, "in addition to one's mother tongue, speaking two other languages has become the norm" (European Commission 2017, 11), the Council Recommendation of 22 May 2019 on a comprehensive approach to the teaching and learning of languages (2019/C 189/03) advocates that member states promote a series of actions to help learners gain a 'competence level' in another European language, besides the language of schooling, and also acquire a 'degree of fluency' in a third language. The terms chosen to define language ability appear to be deliberately vague and unspecific, as they employ neither the generic 'elementary/advanced' spectrum nor the current CEFR levels. This may be an attempt to avoid controversy by allowing each country to subjectively comply with the Commission's aim, while guaranteeing the success of the 2025 objective. The language of schooling itself takes on a multiple dimension, becoming plural(istic). In this context, the languages of schooling are all those present in the educational environment and are all equally significant for the learner's language competence. The very idea of the '*Language as a subject*', i.e. the majority language in the geographical area where the school is located (Italian in Italy, French in France, etc.) has been revised by policymakers. As many schools are now multilingual and the range of learners' first languages is increasingly wide, the teaching of the majority language has to extend beyond first language teaching and embrace tenets of second language teaching. At the same time, a perspective of '*Language(s) in other subjects*' (which includes the CLIL – Content and Language Integrated Learning – environment) is promoted, i.e. the view of language as a tool through which students learn content matter in subjects such as geography, history or mathematics (see Lasagabaster, this volume). Literacy in content subjects empowers learners to acquire and exchange knowledge. In order to attain such objectives, a whole-school language policy must be developed in which all teachers – those of majority languages, second languages, regional, minority and migration languages, foreign languages (modern and classical) and other subjects – join forces and cooperate.

44   *Bruna Di Sabato and Andy Kirkpatrick*

To further such aims, a number of guidelines have been put forward by the Council to encourage:

- continuity in language education across the curriculum;
- learners' competencies in the languages of schooling with a special regard for those from refugee, migrant or any form of disadvantaged background;
- commitment on behalf of non-language teachers to raising awareness of specific registers and vocabulary in the languages of schooling;
- linguistic diversity and forms of informal language resources across the learning path, contemplating the assessment and validation of extra-curricular competences (see also Council of the European Union 2012 on the validation of non-formal and informal learning);
- learners' mobility by, whenever possible, exploiting EU funding incentives;
- adherence to the CEFR as a reference framework;
- the autonomy of scholastic institutions in terms of language teaching strategies within the boundaries of national legislations (Council of the European Union 2019).

Indeed, the upsurge in interest in the use of minority languages and dialects is a further sign of the times in terms of educational policy. Both the European Commission and the Council of Europe recognize "the value of learning and maintaining any language which is part of a person's individual interests and circumstances" (European Commission 2019a, 6). This plurilingual dimension within school environments now includes migrants' linguacultural heritage and, on a par, the teaching of a national language to migrants as an initial form of integration.

These two aspects have been the object of debate for the last twenty years or so, i.e. since the European continent became aware that migration flows would play a significant role in the years to come. The impact of such a phenomenon on school education, and in particular on language education, is self-evident. In recent years, European countries, institutions, researchers and policymakers have faced the need to integrate the people settling in Europe from two different standpoints: an approach which favours learning the host country language as a form of integration; the other which encourages migrant pupils to keep their mother tongue (Volpe & Crosier 2019). The former, which Eurydice terms "The monolingual paradigm", is dominant in most publicly funded schools across Europe and is due to historical reasons, whereby the use of one common language within a nation state was part of the nation-building process, a phenomenon also seen more recently across Asia. Monolingual instruction was seen as crucial to ensure the existence of one common language (the 'state language') within national borders. The language diversity pervading European societies (due to migration but also globalization, increasing travel opportunities, technologies etc.) is leading away from the 'monolingual paradigm'. Plurilingualism is currently actively promoted by academic research and the European institutions. By quoting Cummins (2001), "to reject the child's language in the

Learning languages other than English in Asia and Europe 45

school is to reject the child" (19), Eurydice supports this policy in the recent Report on *Integrating Students from Migrant Backgrounds into Schools in Europe* (2019). Many earlier studies in bilingual education in the United States (Genesee 1987, Thomas & Collier 1997) are mentioned in the Report to highlight well-grounded research on the advantages of bilingual programmes which enable students "to acquire the language of instruction more rapidly even though it means less instruction time for it, as part of the language curriculum time is used for teaching home languages" (Eurydice 2019, 137). The Report provides data on the different educational policies across member states illustrating the prevalent attitude to adopt some form of home language teaching. However, such measures are often adopted with the main aim to help migrant children to achieve proficiency in the language of instruction, not in the home country's language.

Multilingualism is also mentioned by the European Commission as one of the eight key competencies for lifelong learning. Multilingualism comprises:

> the ability to use different languages appropriately and effectively for communication. It broadly shares the main skill dimensions of literacy: it is based on the ability to understand, express and interpret concepts, thoughts, feelings, facts and opinions in both oral and written form (listening, speaking, reading and writing) in an appropriate range of societal and cultural contexts according to one's wants or needs. Language competences integrate a historical dimension and intercultural competences. It relies on the ability to mediate between different languages and media, as applied in the Common European Framework of Reference. As appropriate, it can include maintaining and further developing mother tongue competences, as well as a country's official language(s).
>
> (European Commission 2019b, 7)

This holistic view of language learning promoted at a European level embraces the much-stressed attention to learners' needs, common to current instructional philosophy. Intercultural understanding and competence are of crucial importance today, as they allow us to address the root causes of some of the worst plagues in today's societies: discrimination, racism, hate speech and so on. This view of plurilingualism within the wider perspective of intercultural competence is not new to European institutions; in fact, it was present as early as 2001 in what the Common European Framework defined as "plurilingual and pluricultural competence":

> the ability to use languages for the purposes of communication and to take part in intercultural interaction, where a person, viewed as a social agent has proficiency, of varying degrees, in several languages and experience of several cultures. This is not seen as the superposition or juxtaposition of distinct competences, but rather as the existence of a complex or even composite competence on which the user may draw.
>
> (Council of Europe 2001, 168)

Languages stand as the expression both of different cultures and of differences within the same culture. Plurilingual and intercultural education in school contexts should be viewed as a form of global language education, stretching across all languages and all disciplinary domains. Through their content and scope, all disciplines contribute to this language education (Council of Europe 2009), and new pedagogical practices are now acknowledged throughout the EU. Among these, translanguaging practices stem from the awareness that learners can transfer skills, mindsets and strategies from one language to the other(s), establishing (what is now considered by this line of thought 'effective') communication while at the same time maximizing their social, emotional and cognitive development. The attention to translanguaging in educational contexts stems from the response to current social practices in multilingual settings, and entails the removal of a hierarchy among the languages which constitute the linguistic repertoire of the individual speaker. Languages are no longer viewed as distinct codes and the focus shifts to the individual's ability to resort to a variety of resources to create and interpret signs (Blackledge et al. 2018). Translanguaging has crucial effects in instructional contexts because it implies the development of a different idea of language education and language competence focused on the learner rather than on the language(s). It goes beyond code-switching by focusing on the learners' fluid use of their linguistic repertoire and their ability to create and employ original and complex trans-linguistic discursive practices. Consequently, assessment practices also need to be re-considered and the *Guide for the Development and Implementation of Curricula for Plurilingual and Intercultural Education* (Beacco et al. 2016) encourages the pursuance of reference frameworks which take into account the skills linked to a plurilingual mode of operation and to cross-cultural competences.

Finally, the role of digital tools needs to be highlighted. As a great many learners today are digital natives, the use of such instruments (virtual online environments, web-based learning, language applications, etc.), rather than more traditional methods, can foster interest and motivation both inside and out of the classroom. This awareness is taken for granted in pedagogical environments. But in the case of language learning, this inbuilt propensity towards the digital world favours English above and beyond other foreign languages. Proficiency cannot be attributed to, or restricted to, formal learning alone. Non-formal and informal exposure (media, tourism, computer-mediated communication, etc.) can make significant contributions. The English language holds pole position as the most taught foreign language in European countries, a "kind of basic unavoidable skill" in much the same way as new technologies: among the many reasons for this "privileged position", the study on plurilingual and intercultural education commissioned by the Council of Europe in 2009 (Cavalli et al. 2009) argues that there might also be an economic justification which leads the educational system to opt for "a common 'lingua franca' which facilitates the least costly response to the problems of the organisation of the teaching of foreign languages" (12).

This section on the main trends in language education in Europe has illustrated the general tendency of national institutions to promote language learning competencies in line with European indications. While such indications are nominally shared by all EU member states, limited space is still devoted to foreign languages in the school curricula, and teachers still lack adequate training. At the same time, a new perspective on current communication needs within multilingual social and vocational settings is generating a revision of the very concept of language competence, which in turn leads to different language teaching practices. All in all, it seems that Europe is experiencing a fruitful and constructive trend with the emergence of a binary paradigm where 'English' and 'languages other than English' (LOTE) stand at the two extremities. Stakeholders must be aware that, although English is now an intrinsic part of the language curriculum, it alone cannot meet a society's language needs and can only marginally promote the developmental purposes of plurilingual and intercultural education (Cavalli et al. 2009).

Conclusion

What comparisons can be drawn from these summaries of foreign language learning and teaching across the school systems of East and Southeast Asia and Europe? Firstly, it is clear that, in both contexts, English is by far the most important foreign language of education. In the primary and secondary schools of Asia, the learning and teaching of English have displaced the learning and teaching of Asian languages, other than the respective national languages. In Europe, English is overwhelmingly the most popular foreign language taught at both primary and secondary. Secondly, in both Asia and Europe, the official policy calls for the respect for the diverse languages and cultures of the region, with both geographical regions adopting some version of the slogan 'unity in diversity'. However, the extent to which this is realized differs across Asia and Europe. While, generally speaking, Europe has been comparatively successful in implementing a policy whereby school students learn – or are at least introduced to – two languages in addition to their first languages, the same cannot be said for East and Southeast Asia. There, with the rare exception of countries such as the Philippines, school students learn only their respective national language and English. The national language is seen as integral to nation building and English as essential for participating in the global economy. Asian languages, other than the respective national language, are seldom part of national curricula. *Putonghua* Chinese is the most common 'foreign' Asian language taught, as is the case in Europe.

In the final analysis, a strong contrast emerges between East and Southeast Asia and Europe. In East and Southeast Asia, national educational policies promote unity and intercultural communication through the teaching of the national language and English. In Europe, the current trend is diametrically opposite, with the implementation of language education policies aimed at the promotion and safeguarding of minority languages as part of the European heritage. Europe is also promoting the use of migrants' home country languages in

48 *Bruna Di Sabato and Andy Kirkpatrick*

school contexts. There is some irony here. Europe, the least linguistically diverse region in the world, is developing and promoting educational policies to favour the study and use of non-dominant languages. Such policies stem from sociocultural (the need to foster inclusion and cohesion) and educational (the cognitive advantages of multilingualism) grounds, which take the wider perspective of a multilingual landscape into account. In stark contrast, Asia, the most linguistically rich region in the world, is doing little to promote and safeguard its linguistic diversity, despite official rhetoric urging nations to respect the linguistic and cultural variety of the region. Such heterogeneity calls for views and approaches to language teaching which recognize and seek to maintain this diversity. The challenge will be to develop language education policies which successfully promote the teaching and learning of local and regional languages while making English an additional language in any speaker's repertoire.

Relating the issues raised in this chapter to your own context:

1 How many languages are spoken in your country? How many and which ones are taught in the school system?
2 In your own educational context, are there policies and/or projects aimed at widening the learners' multilingual competence(s)?

Notes

1 These figures are taken from Ethnologue (ethnologue.com).
2 At the time of writing, the United Kingdom was in the process of leaving the European Union. Therefore, the United Kingdom is mentioned only when statistical data were still available.
3 While the two terms multilingualism and plurilingualism are frequently used interchangeably, a distinction is provided by Beacco et al. (2016, 20): "Plurilingualism is the ability to use more than one language – and accordingly sees languages from the standpoint of speakers and learners. Multilingualism, on the other hand, refers to the presence of several languages in a given geographical area, regardless of those who speak them."

References

ASEAN. (2013, June). *Educating the next generation of workforce: ASEAN perspectives on innovation, integration and English.* Keynote address presented at the British Council Conference, Bangkok.

Beacco, J.C., Byram, M., Cavalli, M., Coste, D., Egli Cuenat, M., Goullier, F., Panthier, J., 2016. *Guide for the Development and Implementation of Curricula for Plurilingual and Intercultural Education*, Council of Europe, Language Policy Division. Available at: https://www.coe.int/en/web/language-policy/guide-for-the-development-and-implementation-of-curricula-for-plurilingual-and-intercultural-education [Accessed 10 Feb. 2020].

Blackledge, A., Creese, A., Baynham, M., Cooke, M., Goodson, L., Hua, Z., Wei, L., 2018. "Language and Superdiversity. An Interdisciplinary Perspective". In A. Creese, A. Blackledge, eds., *The Routledge Handbook of Language and Superdiversity*. Abingdon and New York: Routledge, 1–29.

Learning languages other than English in Asia and Europe 49

Bolton, K., Bacon-Shone, J., 2020. "The Statistics of English across Asia". In K. Bolton, W. Botha, A. Kirkpatrick, eds., *The Handbook of Asian Englishes*. Hoboken, NJ: Wiley-Blackwell, 49–80.

Bolton, K, Botha, W., Zhang, W., 2020. "English in Contemporary China". In K. Bolton, W. Botha, A. Kirkpatrick, eds., *The Handbook of Asian Englishes*. Hoboken, NJ: Wiley-Blackwell, 503–528.

Cavalli, M., Coste, D., Crişan, A., van de Ven, P., 2009. *Plurilingual and Intercultural Education as a Project*, Council of Europe Language Policy Division. Available at: https://rm.coe.int/plurilingual-and-intercultural-education-as-a-project-this-text-has-be/16805a219f [Accessed 10 Feb. 2020].

Council of Europe, 2001. *Common European Framework of Reference for Languages: Learning, Teaching, Assessment*. Cambridge: Cambridge University Press.

Council of the European Union, 2012. "Recommendation of 20 December 2012 on the Validation of Non-formal and Informal Learning". *Official Journal of the European Union*, C 398/01. Available at: https://eur-lex.europa.eu/legal-content/EN/TXT/?uri=celex%3A32012H1222%2801%29 [Accessed 10 Feb. 2020].

Council of the European Union, 2019. "Recommendation of 22 May 2019 on a Comprehensive Approach to the Teaching and Learning of Languages". *Official Journal of the European Union*, C189/15. Available at: https://op.europa.eu/en/publication-detail/-/publication/7216390d-876b-11e9-9f05-01aa75ed71a1/language-en/format-HTML/source-106024285 [Accessed 10 Feb. 2020].

Cummins, J., 2001. *Bilingual Children's Mother Tongue: Why Is It Important for Education?* Available at: http://www.lavplu.eu/central/bibliografie/cummins_eng.pdf [Accessed 10 May 2020].

EF, 2019. *English Proficiency Index* EPI. Available at: https://www.ef.com/__/~/media/centralefcom/epi/downloads/full-reports/v9/ef-epi-2019-english.pdf [Accessed 10 Feb. 2020].

European Commission, 2012a. *Europeans and Their Languages*. Special Eurobarometer Report 386. Available at: https://ec.europa.eu/commfrontoffice/publicopinion/archives/ebs/ebs_386_en.pdf [Accessed 10 Feb. 2020].

European Commission, 2012b. *First European Survey on Languages Competences*. Final Report. Available at: http://ec.europa.eu/languages/eslc/docs/en/final-report-escl_en.pdf [Accessed 10 Feb. 2020].

European Commission, 2017. *Communication from the Commission to the European Parliament, the Council, the European Economic and Social Committee of the Regions Strengthening European Identity through Education and Culture. The European Commission's Contribution to the Leaders' Meeting in Gothenburg, 17 November 2017*. Available at: https://eur-lex.europa.eu/LexUriServ/LexUriServ.do?uri=COM:2017:0673:FIN:EN:PDF [Accessed 10 Feb. 2020].

European Commission, 2019a. *The Teaching of Regional or Minority Languages in Schools in Europe*. EACEA/Eurydice Report. Luxembourg: Publications Office of the European Union. Available at: https://eacea.ec.europa.eu/national-policies/eurydice/sites/eurydice/files/minority_languages_en.pdf [Accessed 10 Feb. 2020].

European Commission, 2019b. *Key Competences for Lifelong Learning*. Publication Office of the European Union. Available at: https://op.europa.eu/en/publication-detail/-/publication/297a33c8-a1f3-11e9-9d01-01aa75ed71a1/language-en [Accessed 10 Feb. 2020].

50 Bruna Di Sabato and Andy Kirkpatrick

European Commission – Eurostat, 2012 (last update 31–01–2020). "Pupils by Education Level and Number of Modern Foreign Languages Studied – Absolute Numbers and % of Pupils by Number of Languages Studied". In *Foreign Language Learning Statistics*. Available at: https://appsso.eurostat.ec.europa.eu/nui/show.do?dataset=educ_uoe_lang02 [Accessed 10 Feb. 2020].

European Council, 2002. *Barcelona European Council 15 and 16 March 2002. Presidency Conclusion*. Available at: http://aei.pitt.edu/43345/1/Barcelona_2002_1.pdf [Accessed 10 Feb. 2020].

European Council, 2019. *Recommendation of 22 May 2019 on a Comprehensive Approach to the Teaching and Learning of Languages*. Available at: https://eur-lex.europa.eu/legal-content/EN/TXT/?uri=CELEX%3A32019H0605%2802%29 [Accessed 27 May 2020].

European Union, 1997. *Treaty Establishing the European Community* (Consolidated Version). Rome Treaty, 25 March 1957. Available at: https://www.refworld.org/docid/3ae6b39c0.html [Accessed 29 May 2020].

European Union, 2019. *The EU Motto*. In About the EU section. Available at: https://europa.eu/european-union/about-eu/symbols/motto_en. Last published 13/02/2019. [Accessed 10 Feb. 2020].

Eurydice, 2017. *Key data on Teaching Languages at school in Europe*. EACEA, Eurydice Brief. Available at: https://eacea.ec.europa.eu/national-policies/eurydice/content/key-data-teaching-languages-school-europe-%E2%80%93-2017-edition_en. [Accessed 29 May 2020].

Eurydice, 2019. *Integrating Students from Migrant Backgrounds into Schools in Europe: National Policies and Measures*. EACEA, Eurydice Report. Luxembourg: Publications Office of the European Union. Available at: https://op.europa.eu/en/publication-detail/-/publication/39c05fd6-2446-11e9-8d04-01aa75ed71a1/language-en/format-PDF. [Accessed 29 May 2020].

Feng, A., Adamson, R.A., 2019. "Language Policies in Education in the People's Republic of China". In A. Kirkpatrick, A. Liddicoat, eds., *The Routledge International Handbook of Language Education Policy in Asia*. London and New York: Routledge, 45–59.

Genesee, F., 1987. *Learning through Two Languages: Studies of Immersion and Bilingual Education*. Cambridge, MA: Newbury House.

Gonzalez, A., 1996. "Evaluating Bilingual Education in the Philippines: Towards a Multidimensional Model of Education in Language Planning". In M.L.S. Bautista, ed., *Readings in Philippine Sociolinguistics*. Manila: De la Salle University Press, 327–340.

Kachru, B., 1982. *The Other Tongue: English Across Cultures*. Urbana, IL: University of Illinois Press.

Kachru, B., 1985. "Standards, Codification and Sociolinguistic Realism: The English Language in the Outer Circle". In R. Quirk, H. Widdowson, eds., *English in the World*. Cambridge: Cambridge University Press, 11–30.

Kirkpatrick, A., 2010. *English as a Lingua Franca in ASEAN: A Multilingual Model*. Hong Kong: Hong Kong University Press.

Kirkpatrick, A., 2018. "Conclusion". In N. Sifakis, N. Tsantilla, eds., *ELF for EFL Contexts*. Clevedon: Multilingual Matters, 229–241.

Kirkpatrick, A., Liddicoat, A., 2019. "Introduction". In A. Kirkpatrick, A. Liddicoat, eds., *The Routledge International Handbook of Language Education Policy in Asia*. London and New York: Routledge, 3–13.

Kirkpatrick, A., Xu, Z., 2001. The New Language Law of the People's Republic of China. *Australian Language Matters*, 9(2): 14–18.

Learning languages other than English in Asia and Europe 51

Koehler, M., 2019. "Language Education Policy in Indonesia: A Struggle for Unity in Diversity". In A. Kirkpatrick, A. Liddicoat, eds., *The Routledge International Handbook of Language Education Policy in Asia*. London and New York: Routledge, 286–297.

Kosonen, K., 2019. "Language Education Policy in Cambodia". In A. Kirkpatrick, A. Liddicoat, eds., *The Routledge International Handbook of Language Education Policy in Asia*. London and New York: Routledge, 216–228.

Martin, I., 2020. "Philippine English". In K. Bolton, W. Botha, A. Kirkpatrick, eds., *The Handbook of Asian Englishes*. Hoboken, New Jersey: Wiley-Blackwell, 479–500.

Mezzadri, M., 2016. "Le politiche linguistiche europee: tra continuità e cambiamento". In C. Melero (a cura di), *Le lingue in Italia, le lingue in Europa: dove siamo, dove andiamo*. Venezia: Edizioni Ca' Foscari, 11–19.

Ministère de l'Éducation nationale de l'Enfance et de la Jeunesse, 2017. *Langues à l'école luxembourgeoise*. Available at: http://www.men.public.lu/fr/themes-transversaux/langues-ecole-luxembourgeoise/index.html [Accessed 10 Feb. 2020].

Schneider, E., 2007. *Postcolonial English. Varieties around the World*. Cambridge: Cambridge University Press.

Thomas, W.P., Collier V.P., 1997. *School Effectiveness for Language Minority Students*. Washington, DC: National Clearinghouse for Bilingual Education.

UNESCO, 2001. *Universal Declaration on Cultural Diversity*. Available at: http://portal.unesco.org/en/ev.php-URL_ID=13179&URL_DO=DO_TOPIC&URL_SECTION=201.html [Accessed 10 Feb. 2020].

UNESCO, 2007. *Education for All by 2015. Will We Make It?* Oxford: Oxford University Press. Available at: http://unescdoc.unesco.org/images/0015/001547/15473e.pdf [Accessed 10 Feb. 2020].

UNESCO, 2019. *Foreign-Language Teaching and Linguistic Diversity*. 206 EX/37, Executive Board. Available at: https://unesdoc.unesco.org/query?q=Conference:%20%22UNESCO.%20Executive%20Board,%20206th,%202019%22&sf=sf:* [Accessed 10 Feb. 2020].

Van Canh, Le, Nguyen, H.T.M., Nguyen, T.T.M., Barnard, R., eds., 2019. *Teacher Capacity Building for Standards-based ELT: Insights from Vietnam*. London and New York: Routledge.

Volpe, A.M., Crosier, D., 2019. "Should Immigrants Be Taught in Their Mother Tongue at Schools?" *EPALE – Electronic Platform for Adult Learning in Europe*. Available at: https://epale.ec.europa.eu/en [Accessed 10 May 2020].

Young, C., Igcalinos, T., 2019. "Language-in-Education Policy Development in the Philippines". In A. Kirkpatrick, A. Liddicoat, eds., *The Routledge International Handbook of Language Education Policy in Asia*. London and New York: Routledge, 165–184.

Zein, M.S., ed. 2018. *Teacher Education for English as a Lingua Franca: Perspectives from Indonesia*. London: Routledge.

3 Is there a best age for second language learning? Evidence from across the lifespan

Simone E. Pfenninger and David Singleton

Introduction

Most people would undoubtedly answer the question posed in the title in the affirmative and would elaborate their response with some version of the cliché "the younger the better". This would not by any means seem an unreasonable reaction. Since first language (L1) development happens in infancy, the general inference that children are better equipped for language acquisition than adolescents or adults looks reasonable. Indeed, our observation of life around us may be interpretable as suggesting that starting to learn *anything* early in life – the violin, chess, tennis – may be rewarded with rich advantages. We shall see, however, that this commonsensical wisdom has its limits, and in certain circumstances may be just plain wrong.

In Second Language Acquisition (SLA) research, studies on the age factor may have reached a crossroads. In all of the phases up until the present time, the focus of quantitative and qualitative work has been on identifying and exploring the weight of age of onset (AO) compared to other individual differences (e.g. motivation, L1 literacy skills, and so on) in their relationship to second language (L2) attainment at a given point (e.g. the end of mandatory schooling). Furthermore, despite the heightened attention to age in both scientific discourse and policy design – whether treating age as a central variable (i.e. the main focus of interest) or as a socio-demographic control, included in statistical models to assist the study of something else – there has been a marked failure to attend to the understanding of the social process of aging. Research has tended to rely rather on the popular portrayal of ageing as decay and forgetfulness or on 'common-sense' assumptions about age (e.g. "the earlier the better"). In so doing, researchers as well as laypeople crystallize the concept of age into a discourse of 'age as internal causal factor', useful as a rhetorical tool in scientific argumentation and policy recommendations, in a manner which largely disregards current conceptualizations of age in social theory (see e.g. Rughiniş & Humă, 2015).

However, after more than 50 years of research in both SLA and education, scholars are finally beginning to (a) direct their attention to individuals' actual developmental process, by tracking change with dense measurements and plotting their behaviour and interactions; (b) examine the way different individuals

DOI: 10.4324/9781003008361-5

Is there a best age for second language learning? 53

are differentially affected by AO; and (c) seek holistic accounts of maturational effects and general age effects[1]. For instance, it has become abundantly clear from recently emerged complexity theories that the findings obtained in traditional research designs (group data at one moment in time, or measurements at two data points, or on cross-sections comparing groups of learners at different levels) may not be representative for a longer period of time and cannot predict much about any individual's behaviour at any given point in time. Our goal in this chapter is to take a critical look at L2 learning across the lifespan and to show that maturation effects are less important in this regard than other (contextual, socio-affective) factors, positive and negative, which may be the concomitants of ageing. A comprehensive synthesis of relevant research is beyond the scope of this chapter. The goal is rather to expose the essential nature of the age factor by the use of selected examples.

Age as a complex, socio-cultural variable

The current view of age as a complex, socio-cultural variable arises from the recognition that age is associated with a myriad of factors, "crucially indicating that starting age cannot be seen as the cause of non-native-likeness in the deterministic way advocated by the maturational constraints position" (Muñoz, 2019, p. 432). In an early paper, R. Ellis (1994) went as far as to suggest excluding age from the inventory of individual differences (IDs). He advocated the view that age transcends these categories and potentially impacts on all of them, thus *contributing* to, rather than representing, IDs in L2 learning. In part, age owes its special status to its role as a 'macro-variable': like other ID variables, age has a way of interacting with external variables, thus creating a joint impact on the outcome variable. AO may, for example, condition learner variables such as the extent to which an individual is motivated to acquire an L2 to high levels of proficiency, to engage in the L2 culture, and to identify with L2 speakers (e.g. Dörnyei & Skehan, 2003; Moyer, 2014).

A focus on the role of *experience* in interaction with the age factor in language acquisition and processing provides a crucial source of evidence that bears strongly upon core issues in theories of L2 acquisition. This has become evident in studies that have investigated 'critical period' effects versus experiential sources of variability. The Critical Period Hypothesis (CPH) is associated with two key predictions: across-the-board 'non-nativelikeness' and 'discontinuity' (Birdsong & Vanhove, 2016). In other words, first, L2 attainment to nativelike levels amongst adults is impossible because they have passed a critical period for successful learning. Second, the relationship between AO and ultimate L2 attainment is not considered to be linear, as there is an age-determined threshold "after which the decline of success rate in one or more areas of language is much less pronounced and/or clearly due to different reasons" (DeKeyser, 2012, p. 445).

However, defining what constitutes sufficient evidence for nativelikeness is difficult if not impossible on epistemological grounds: the absence of evidence for non-nativelikeness in late starters, for instance, does not equal evidence for

54 Simone Pfenninger and David Singleton

nativelikeness (Birdsong & Vanhove, 2016). For one thing, both native speakers and L2 learners exhibit grammatical idiosyncrasies and other types of variability in representations of linguistic structure (Dabrowska, 2012). Also, according to Birdsong's (2018) review of critical period effects vs. bilingualism effects, one would need evidence of across-the-board monolingual-likeness in the L2, which is of course impossible. Considering, for instance, Cook's (1997) notion of multicompetence, neither the L1 nor the L2 of bilinguals can be expected to resemble, under scrutiny, that of monolinguals in either language. Multi-competence thus presents a view of L2 acquisition based on the L2 user as a whole person rather than on the norms of the monolingual native speaker.

As for the search for a biologically regulated threshold, so far there has been no convincing evidence for a CPH-compatible discontinuity in the relationship between AO and ultimate attainment. Different statistical methods applied to the same data may result in different shapes of the AO–attainment function (Birdsong, 2018; Vanhove, 2013), thus introducing an additional dimension of inter-individual variability. With increasing AO, the learners' L2 results become more dispersed, goals for L2 learning become more diverse, and there is an increase in inter-individual effects of progressive cognitive decline, progressive L1 entrenchment and education on L2 attainment (Birdsong, 2018). In studies of ageing, individual differences in cognition that increase with age have been attributed to differences in lifestyle, education and overall health, amongst others (Carlson et al., 2012; Christensen, 2001; Pliatsikas et al., 2019). What is more, even within the individual, cognitive performance is far from stable and can manifest significant day-to-day or even within-day fluctuations based on the current state of health, cognition or social interactions (Neupert & Allaire, 2012). Unsurprisingly, day-to-day fluctuations in L2 motivation, too, have been found to occasion intra-individual differences in L2 performance (Dörnyei, Henry, & MacIntyre, 2014), which again calls for an individualized and dynamic conceptualization of L2 development.

Analyzing the high degree of variability in the performance of the late-arriving learners in Johnson and Newport's (1989) L2 grammaticality judgement data, Vanhove (2013) attributes the essentially random dispersal of late learners' scores to factors such as age-conditioned inter-individual differences in literacy, education, opportunities for L2 use, and motivation – that is, to factors unrelated to critical period constraints. Similarly, Werker and Hensch's (2015) work, describing the cascading sequence of multiple, overlapping periods of plasticity that enable the development of phonetic perception in the native language, suggests that at the level of the individual child, the duration of critical periods in speech perception development can be varied through bilingual experience.

Hence, Birdsong (2018) describes AO as a "proxy for the L2 acquisition initial state" (p. 2), i.e. the sum of an individual's cognitive, neurological, and linguistic development, along with motivational, identificational, attitudinal and experiential characteristics at the point at which L2 learning begins. In this sense, AO is understood not as the determinant of the "age factor" but rather as a "meta-variable" (Flege, 1999).

Optimal age of onset across different L2 settings: Life rather than age

It is thus not surprising that age as a predictor of L2 learning outcomes is not the silver bullet it was formerly deemed to be. In naturalistic settings, it has been well-documented that linguistic variables (e.g. intra- and inter-learner variation), neurobiological variables (e.g. plasticity), and socio-affective variables (e.g. motivation, investment) are all, directly or indirectly, modulated by the age when L2 learning begins (Birdsong, 2018). That said, it seems more and more likely that the reason why, in the long run, younger L2 starters in a naturalistic environment tend to end up more proficient than older starters is attributable to a range of socio-affective factors, to how they *experience* the L2, rather than to the maturational dimension as such.

To take as an example the case of younger and older arrivals in a host country, there are significant differences in the experience of younger and older immigrants in terms of various aspects of their life in the new country, which can plausibly be seen as impinging on both proficiency attainment in the host country language and on the role this language has for immigrants arriving at different ages. These relate *inter alia* to the different stages of development of linguistic-cultural identity, which in turn impact on openness to friendships amongst different groups. Thus, in a much-cited study of child and adolescent immigrants, Jia & Aaronson (2003) found that the children enjoyed more L2 contexts of use than the adolescents, having a large number of L2-speaking friends, while the adolescents chose more L1-speaking peers as their friends.

In children who grow up bilingual (whether sequential bilinguals or child L2 learners), younger age of acquisition is not necessarily predictive of better language outcomes in all circumstances in immersive contexts at home (see e.g. Blom & Paradis' special 2016 issue on age effects in child language acquisition). To the contrary, older age can mean more rather than fewer cognitive resources for learning the language. In these learning contexts, age is thus described as being multi-faceted and indexical not only of maturational effects and plasticity but also of changing availabilities of cognitive and environmental resources, and growing connectivity as a function of environmental stimuli (Blom & Paradis, 2016; Paradis, Tulpar & Arppe, 2016).

Nor should it be thought that adults are incapable of reaching very high levels of proficiency. In this latter connection, one can cite Kinsella and Singleton's (2014) study involving 20 native English speakers whose average age of significant exposure to French was 28.6 years. All resided in France, and all occasionally reportedly passed for native speakers of French. These participants (and a control group of native French speakers) were asked to identify the accents of some French regions and to complete a lexical and grammatical test. Three of the twenty participants scored within native-speaker ranges on these tasks (outperforming many of the French native speakers on the accent recognition task); all three had married French spouses.

56 Simone Pfenninger and David Singleton

With regard to the adult population, the general assumption is that ageing brings a serious decline in the capacity to master L2s. In this realm too, however, a growing body of evidence from research in education, psycholinguistics, cognitive science and neurolinguistics challenges the conventional view that the age factor is the non-plus-ultra predictor of L2 learning outcome. For instance, the neurocognitive ageing literature, on the whole, suggests that the brain preserves large parts of its plasticity even at an advanced age and remains receptive towards new languages (e.g. Park & Reuter-Lorenz, 2009; Peltzer-Karpf, 2003; Raz & Lindenberger, 2013; Schlegel, Rudelson & Tse 2012). Furthermore, findings to date indicate a wide variance in L2 acquisition attainment in older adults based on inter-individual differences such as cognitive functioning and auditory acuity (e.g. Giroud et al., 2018). For instance, attention and cognitive control capacities have been shown to distinguish individuals on the basis of previous L2 experience or social class (Bialystok & Poarch, 2014; Cullum et al., 2000). Finally, a steadily accumulating body of evidence in the domain of linguistic cognition – notably by Blanco et al. (2016), Ramscar et al. (2010, 2013a, 2013b, 2014. 2017) – indicates that there is no neurobiological evidence for any declines in the processing capacities of healthy older adults, except in the case of neurological diseases where there is evidence of pathology (see e.g. Strauss, Sherman, & Spreen, 2006). Along those lines, Ramscar et al. (2014, 2017) were able to show in computational simulations that the patterns of response change in lexical decision tasks – in which subjects make a speeded judgement as to whether a letter string is a word or not, which are typically taken as evidence for (and measures of) cognitive decline – arise out of basic principles of learning and emerge naturally in learning models as they acquire more knowledge: experience inevitably increases the overall range of knowledge and skills any individual possesses, increasing the amount of information in (and complexity of) his or her cognitive systems. Thus, processing all this extra information in combination with the increased vocabulary search must inevitably have a cost.

With regard to classroom settings, similarly, the current scientific view offered on the age factor in foreign language (FL) classrooms is that "success" in additional languages is a function of the quantity and quality of language experience rather than simply a matter of maturational or general age effects – and that this applies to both the childhood/adolescence end of the spectrum (e.g. Pfenninger & Singleton, 2017, 2019a) and to third age language learning (e.g. Pfenninger & Singleton, 2019b; Singleton & Zaborska, 2020). The introduction of early FL learning and teaching into the elementary school curriculum in Europe is the result of a top-down approach including various factors, including European policies such as multilingualism requirements (see e.g. the Barcelona objectives 2002, European Commission, 2011), parental encouragement, the steady growth of English as a lingua franca on an international level, and the misguided transplantation of research findings obtained in naturalistic settings to classrooms: "findings from second language learning in naturalistic contexts have been generalized to FL learning in instructed contexts" (Muñoz, 2006, p. 6).

The implementation of early FL programmes has been described as hasty (Piske, 2013), with a lack of teacher preparation and training for elementary and secondary teachers (Edelenbos, Johnstone, & Kubanek, 2006), and neglecting the available research in the field of L2 acquisition (Schmelter, 2010). In popular wisdom, children's language learning at an early age in pre- or elementary school is often described as 'spongelike', 'fun' or 'playful', 'fast' and 'more efficient', but these statements have to be considered carefully within the particular educational context and with learners' individual differences in mind (Piske, 2013). As early as the 1970s, studies were being conducted (e.g. Burstall, 1975; Carroll, 1975) which failed to demonstrate the capacity of early instruction to deliver higher proficiency attainment levels than later instruction, and this has been the consistent finding since (see Muñoz & Singleton, 2011). In Canada and the United States, it has also been found that older immersion learners are as successful as younger learners (e.g. Swain & Lapkin, 1989; Turnbull et al., 1998).

Huang (2016) refers to 42 empirical studies that were published in the past 50 years and was unable to find unequivocal evidence for a younger learner advantage. As part of the five-year longitudinal Beyond Age Effects (BAE) study conducted in Switzerland, Pfenninger and Singleton (2017, 2019a) explored what underlies age effects in L2 learning and investigated how learning contexts shape processes of L2 development. In this study, the English language skills of 636 secondary school students were assessed, who had all learned Standard German and French at primary school, but only half of whom had learned English from age 8, the remainder having started English five years later. The results suggested that age-related attainment effects were overshadowed by other effects (L2 learning motivation, L1 literacy skills, family circumstances, classroom effects, to name but a few), yielding diverse outcomes according to individual differences and contextual effects mediating FL outcomes. An earlier age of learning proved beneficial only for children raised as biliterate simultaneous bilinguals receiving substantial parental support, as opposed to monolinguals and non-biliterate (simultaneous or sequential) bilinguals.

In a recent attempt to "provide a point of comparison for results from Switzerland" (i.e. for the results reported in the BAE study by Pfenninger and Singleton, 2017, 2019a), Baumert et al. (2020) examined the long-term effects of early English instruction on receptive language proficiency (reading and listening comprehension) at the end of full-time compulsory schooling in Germany. Drawing on data from the BISTA ("Überprüfung des Erreichens von Bildungsstandards") assessment of national educational standards, they aimed to establish whether or not secondary-level instruction takes account of and builds on the knowledge of early-start students, while meeting the basic condition for counterfactual analysis, namely ignorability of assignment criteria. In other words, the samples of early and late starters were equivalent, and assignment to the two groups (early versus late) was random. This decreases the likelihood that systematic differences can arise between the experimental and the control group (i.e. early and late starters).

58 Simone Pfenninger and David Singleton

On the basis of results from this large, non-selective sample (19,653 students), the authors conclude the following, inter alia:

> In sum, this study found no evidence for the expected positive effects of early-start English. After 5 years of English at secondary level, the exposure advantage of students who had English at elementary level was eroded. This result is consistent with the findings of Pfenninger and Singleton (2017), who— without controlling for relevant covariates ... – found that early starters' (A0: 8 years) exposure advantage (440 hours) was no longer detectable after 6 years of English at Swiss Gymnasium schools [academically oriented high schools].
>
> (p. 1122)

As Baumert et al. (2020) rightly point out, such findings do not necessarily refute the effectiveness of an early start in a formal, instructional setting per se. Rather, the authors of the BISTA study attribute the results to some of the same phenomena as were considered in the BAE study: (1) secondary school teachers responding "maladaptively by not acknowledging and building on what students actually know and can do"; and (2) a lack of "enough qualified teachers to ensure high-quality instruction at elementary level" (for a discussion of this see also Chambers, 2014; Courtney et al., 2015; Graham et al., 2016; Jaekel et al., 2017; Muñoz, Tragant, & Camuñas, 2015; Nikolov & Mihaljevic Djigunovic, 2011). Besides these critical issues in relation to the transition in FL instruction from primary to secondary school, Pfenninger and Lendl (2017) point out that L2 proficiency outcomes from primary schools vary greatly; thus, since secondary schools receive students from several primary schools, teachers are required to be particularly thorough in assessing the initial skills of incoming students.

To sum up, cumulative empirical evidence indicates that age plays a significant role in the process of developing proficiency in another language in some ideal learning conditions. However, much of the effect of starting age is the consequence of its co-varying relationship with non-biological factors (Muñoz & Singleton, 2011). This may also answer the question as to what accounts for the differential attainment amongst late learners in naturalistic settings. The answers lie again in the individual difference (ID) variables – aptitude, motivation, personality, socio-economic status, gender, learning history, and the like. That said, these variables do not supplant age effects; rather, the ID variables interact with age-related maturational constraints and exert a differential impact on learners of early and later AOs. What is more, conclusions are limited by our view of age as an independent, separate entity and by measuring its effects at one point in time, rather than longitudinally. This is not by any means a novel argument; in practice, however, few studies pay attention to the variable nature of age effects over longer periods of time. Another lesson that we can learn from the above-described studies is that in order to faithfully capture the construct, age is properly operationalized and analyzed as a continuous subject factor. As with any other continuous variable, participant assignment to

Is there a best age for second language learning? 59

age categories may mask intra-group variability and result in loss of statistical power (e.g. Altman, 1998). This leads us to our next topic, that is, the variability of age effects.

The age factor as a potentially dynamic entity

Some researchers have long questioned treating learner IDs as modular (i.e. discrete, separate, isolated), stable, and context-independent traits (see Serafini, 2017). Instead, they have argued for the need to consider the multiple ways IDs and their sub-components dynamically interact with one another and with the external environment (e.g. Dörnyei, 2010). This view aligns with a broader, more holistic approach adopted by a growing number of L2 researchers that entails seeing language learning and language learners themselves as dynamic, complex, adaptive systems within which all factors interact and affect one another (Douglas Fir Group, 2016). In L2 development, many internal states (cognitive ability, motivation, attitude, emotions, and so on) and external states or events (the general context in which a language is learned, a particular teacher, an illness, a particular usage event, and so on) at any given moment may have an effect on the developmental path. All these interrelated factors may cause any part of the learner's language system to fluctuate from one moment to the next. Such a conceptual shift is informed by principles within Complex Dynamic Systems Theory (CDST), which has inspired a continuously growing wave of L2 research (De Bot, Lowie, & Verspoor, 2007; Larsen-Freeman, 1997, 2019; Ortega & Zhao-Hong, 2017). In relation to learner IDs, a dynamic systems perspective necessitates a change in conceptualization "from stable and monolithic traits to dynamic and multicomponential resources" (Serafini, 2017, p. 370). Cross-sectional research, comparing different individuals or groups under distinct conditions or proficiency levels at a given point in time, may point to inter-individual differences and their causes, but it is only through the close and repeated tracking of language within individuals or groups that the essence of development will be made observable (Norris & Manchón, 2012).

A recent study known as the Age and Immersion (AIM) study has been the first longitudinal study to explore the best time for regular versus bilingual language exposure in (pre)primary programmes, using multiple measures over time so as to focus on fluctuations, trends and interactions in individual data as well as intra-individual variation over time (Pfenninger, 2020, 2021). The study investigated the L2 English development of 146 children who received 50/50 bilingual instruction in German and English (so-called 'partial content and language integrated learning [CLIL]' programmes) as well as 105 children in 'minimal CLIL' programmes with almost uniquely monolingual German instruction (90% German, 10% English). Of the 251 participants in total, 231 were from German-speaking homes (new to English), while 20 were from English-speaking homes (new to German). They varied in their age of first CLIL instruction (5, 7, 9 or 11). In the cross-sectional part of the study

60 *Simone Pfenninger and David Singleton*

at the end of primary education (age 12), their German and English oral and writing skills were assessed. For 91 of them, data collection occurred four times annually over eight school years (ages 5–12) via oral and written L2 production tasks, motivation questionnaires, interviews, and parental and teacher questionnaires. Following CDST-inspired studies (e.g. Chan et al., 2015), the L2 data was coded for various aspects of accuracy, complexity, fluency and lexical richness, systematically integrating quantitative analyses and qualitative content analyses. The main goals were: (1) to find out if there are advantages associated with the early provision of CLIL instruction with respect to rate and outcome of FL learning, as compared to a later CLIL introduction; and (2) to investigate the dynamic multicausality of the emerging language system, the meaningfulness of intra-learner variability over time, and the potential socio-affective and contextual reasons for individual developmental jumps.

Results showed that, like other ID variables, the age factor behaves like a dynamic entity that changes over time and affects L2 development differentially at different times. For instance, while the L2 development rate was fastest towards the end of primary school for all participants, irrespective of their AO, AO had less of an influence on L2 proficiency in the later primary grades. Furthermore, none of the 91 participants in the longitudinal design showed the mean pattern of the group. Thus, the findings of a snapshot analysis of age effects may not be representative for a longer period of time and cannot predict much about any individual's behaviour at any given point in time; this reminds us of the need to treat cross-sectional studies with caution.

Conclusion

Part of the answer to our original question – concerning the notion of the best age for additional language learning – is that answering it very much needs to take account of the circumstances of learning. Just starting young in a normal classroom with two hours a week of L2 classes will not work the oracle. Starting young in an immersion situation with plenty of reading and writing plus parental support just may – but so may immersive circumstances in adulthood, especially when one is living in a loving situation with a speaker of the target language.

The recent stalemate in our understanding of the effects of age on second language learning basically stems from a narrowness of view. Instead of looking across the human lifespan at both younger and older learners in all their variety of learning contexts, the field's focus has typically been on narrowly identifying age effects, often with characterizations of adult learners being sparse and inaccurate. We believe that an adequate understanding of the age factor must necessarily include a close and a nuanced look not only at younger learners but also at older learners in all the rich variety of learning contexts in which they find themselves. Treating either group as monolithic is likely to constrain our view, limit our understanding and lead to mistaken inferences.

Is there a best age for second language learning? 61

Relating the issues raised in this chapter to your own context:

1 In your own second language education context, is there a trend to offer English (or any other L2) through early childhood education and care (i.e. formal childcare and pre-school services for children under five years of age)?
2 To what extent is there a consensus amongst practitioners, in your own context, about sufficient resources and training for early FL teaching?

Note

1 According to Birdsong (2018), maturational effects are often thought of as taking place within, but not beyond, the 'critical period'. For this reason, a distinction is sometimes drawn between maturational effects and general age effects over the lifespan and a similar distinction may be drawn between maturational effects and AO effects.

References

Altman, D. G. (1998). Categorizing continuous variables. In P. Armitage & T. Colton (Eds.), *Encyclopedia of Biostatistics* (pp. 563–567). New York, NY: Wiley.

Baumert, J., Fleckenstein, J., Leucht, M., Köller, O., & Möller, J. (2020). The long-term proficiency of early, middle, and late starters learning English as a foreign language at school: A narrative review and empirical study. *Language Learning, 70*(4), 1091–1135.

Bialystok, E., & Poarch, G. J. (2014). Language experience changes language and cognitive ability. *Zeitschrift Für Erziehungswissenschaft, 17*(3), 433–446.

Birdsong, D. (2018). Plasticity, variability and age in second language acquisition and bilingualism. *Frontiers in Psychology, 9*. Retrieved from https://doi.org/10.3389/fpsyg. 2018.00081 (26/2/2020).

Birdsong, D., & Vanhove, J. (2016). Age of second-language acquisition: Critical periods and social concerns. In E. Nicoladis & S. Montanari (Eds.), *Bilingualism across the Lifespan: Factors Moderating Language Proficiency* (pp. 163–182). Berlin/Washington, DC: De Gruyter Mouton/American Psychological Association.

Blanco, N. J., Love, B. C., Ramscar, M., Otto, A. R., Smayda, K., & Maddox, W. T. (2016). Exploratory decision-making as a function of lifelong experience, not cognitive decline. *Journal of Experimental Psychology: General, 145*, 284–297.

Blom, E., & Paradis, J. (2016). Introduction: Special issue on age effects in child language acquisition. *Journal of Child Language, 43*(3), 473–478.

Burstall, C. (1975). Factors affecting foreign-language learning: A consideration of some relevant research findings. *Language Teaching and Linguistic Abstracts, 8*, 105–125.

Carlson, M. C., Parisi, J. M., Xia, J., Xue, Q.-L., Rebok, G. W., Bandeen-Roche, K., & Fried, L. P. (2012). Lifestyle activities and memory: Variety may be the spice of life. The women's health and aging study II. *Journal of the International Neuropsychological Society, 18*(2), 286–294.

Carroll, J. B. (1975). *The Teaching of French as a Foreign Language in Eight Countries: International Studies in Evaluation*. Stockholm: Almqvist & Wikse.

Chambers, G. N. (2014). Transition in modern languages from primary to secondary school: The challenge of change. *Language Learning Journal, 42*(3), 242–260.

62 Simone Pfenninger and David Singleton

Chan, H., Verspoor, M., & Vahtrick, L. (2015). Dynamic development in speaking versus writing in identical twins. *Language Learning, 65*(2), 298–325.

Christensen, H. (2001). What cognitive changes can be expected with normal ageing? *Australian & New Zealand Journal of Psychiatry, 35*(6), 768–775.

Cook. V. J. (1997) Monolingual bias in second language acquisition research. *Revista Canaria de Estudios Ingleses, 34,* 35–49.

Courtney, L., Graham, S., Tonkyn, A., & Marinis, T. (2015). Individual differences in early language learning: A study of English learners of French. *Applied Linguistics, 38*(6), doi:10.1093/applin/amv071

Cullum, S., Huppert, F. A., McGee, M., Dening, T., Ahmed, A., Paykel, E. S., & Brayne, C. (2000). Decline across different domains of cognitive function in normal ageing: Results of a longitudinal population-based study using CAMCOG. *International Journal of Geriatric Psychiatry, 15*(9), 853–862.

Dabrowska, E. (2012). Different speakers, different grammars: Individual differences in native language attainment. *Linguistic Approaches to Bilingualism, 2,* 219–253.

De Bot, K., Lowie, W., & Verspoor, M. (2007). A dynamic systems theory approach to second language acquisition. *Bilingualism: Language and Cognition, 10*(1), 7–21.

DeKeyser, R. (2012). Age effects in second language learning. In S. M. Gass & A. Mackey (Eds.), *The Routledge Handbook of Second Language Acquisition* (pp. 442–460). London: Routledge.

Dörnyei, Z. (2010). The relationship between language aptitude and language learning motivation: Individual differences from a dynamic systems perspective. In E. Macaro (Ed.), *Continuum Companion to Second Language Acquisition* (pp. 247–267). London: Continuum.

Dörnyei Z., & Skehan, P. (2003). Individual differences in second language learning. In C. J. Doughty & M. Long (Eds.), *The Handbook of Second Language Acquisition* (pp. 275–298). Oxford: Blackwell.

Dörnyei, Z., Henry, A., & MacIntyre, P. D. (Eds.) (2014). *Motivational Dynamics in Language Learning* (Vol. 81). Clevedon: Multilingual Matters.

Douglas Fir Group. (2016). A transdisciplinary framework for SLA in a multilingual world. *Modern Language Journal, 100*(Supplement 2016), 19–47.

Edelenbos, P., Johnstone, R., & Kubanek, A. (2007). *The Main Pedagogical Principles Underlying the Teaching of Languages to Very Young Learners. Languages for the Children of Europe. Published Research, Good Practice & Main Principles.* Retrieved from http://ec.europa.eu/languages/policy/language-policy/documents/young_en.pdf

Ellis, R. (1994). *The Study of Second Language Acquisition.* Oxford: Oxford University Press.

European Commission (2011). *Europeans and Their Languages.* Special Eurobarometer 243. Brussels, Belgium: Commission of the European Communities.

Flege, J. E. (1999). Age of learning and second language speech. In D. Birdsong (Ed.), *Second Language Acquisition and the Critical Period Hypothesis* (pp. 101–131). Mahwah, NJ: Lawrence Erlbaum Associates.

Giroud, N., Hirsiger, S., Muri, R., Kegel, A., Dillier, N., & Meyer, M. (2018). Neuroanatomical and resting state EEG power correlates of central hearing loss in older adults. *Brain Structure & Function, 223*(1), 145–163. doi:10.1007/s00429-017-1477-0

Graham, S., Courtney, L., Tonkyn, A., & Marinis, T. (2016). Motivational trajectories for early language learning across the primary-secondary school transition. *British Educational Research Journal, 42*(4), 682–702.

Huang, B. H. (2016). A synthesis of empirical research on the linguistic outcomes of early foreign language instruction. *International Journal of Multilingualism*, *13*, 257–273. doi: 10.1080/14790718.2015.1066792.

Jaekel, N., Schurig, M., Florian, M., & Ritter, M. (2017). From early starters to late finishers? A longitudinal study of early foreign language learning in school. *Language Learning*, *67(3)*, 631–664.

Jia, G., & Aaronson, D. (2003). A longitudinal study of Chinese children and adolescents learning English in the United States. *Applied Psycholinguistics*, *24*, 131–161.

Johnson, J. S. and Newport, E. L. (1989) Critical period effects in second language learning: The influence of maturational state on the acquisition of English as a second language. *Cognitive Psychology*, *21*, 60–99.

Kinsella, C., & Singleton (2014). Much more than age. *Applied Linguistics*, *35*(4), 441–446.

Larsen-Freeman, D. (1997). Chaos/complexity science and second language acquisition. *Applied Linguistics*, *18*(2), 141–165.

Larsen-Freeman, D. (2019). On language learner agency: A complex dynamic systems theory perspective. *Modern Language Journal*, *103*(Supplement 2016), 61–79.

Moyer, A. (2014). What's age got to do with it? Accounting for individual factors in second language accent. *Studies in Second Language Learning and Teaching*, *4*(3), 443–464.

Muñoz, C. (Ed.) (2006). *Age and the Rate of Foreign Language Learning*. Clevedon: Multilingual Matters.

Muñoz, C. (2019). A new look at age: Young and old L2 learners. In J. W. Schwieter & A. Benati (Eds.), *The Cambridge Handbook of Language Learning* (pp. 430–450). Cambridge: Cambridge University Press.

Muñoz, C., & Singleton. D. (2011). A critical review of age-related research on L2 ultimate attainment. *Language Teaching*, *44*(1), 1–35.

Muñoz, C., Tragant, E., & Camuñas, M. (2015). Transition: Continuity or a fresh start? *APAC Quarterly*, *89*, 11–16.

Neupert, S. D., & Allaire, J. C. (2012). I think I can, I think I can: Examining the within-person coupling of control beliefs and cognition in older adults. *Psychology and Aging*, *27*(3), 742–749.

Nikolov, M., & Mihaljevic Djigunovic, J. (2011). All shades of every color: An overview of early teaching and learning of foreign languages. *Annual Review of Applied Linguistics*, *31*, 95–119.

Norris, J. M., & Manchón, R. (2012). Investigating L2 writing development from multiple perspectives: Issues in theory and research. In R. Manchón (Ed.), *L2 Writing Development: Multiple Perspectives* (pp. 221–244). Berlin: de Gruyter.

Ortega, L., & Zhao-Hong, H. (Eds.) (2017). *Complexity Theory and Language Development*. Amsterdam: John Benjamins.

Paradis, J., Tulpar, Y., & Arppe, A. (2016). Chinese L1 children's English L2 verb morphology over time: Individual variation in long-term outcomes. *Journal of Child Language*, *43*, 553–580.

Park, D. C., & Reuter-Lorenz, P. (2009). The adaptive brain: Aging and neurocognitive scaffolding. *Annual Review of Psychology*, *60*, 173–196.

Peltzer-Karpf, A. (2003). The role of neural plasticity in foreign language learning. In R. Ahrens (Ed.), *Europäische Sprachenpolitik – European Language Policy* (pp. 369–393). Heidelberg: Universitätsverlag Winter.

Pfenninger, S. E. (2020). The dynamic multicausality of age of first bilingual language exposure: Evidence from a longitudinal CLIL study with dense time serial measurement. *Modern Language Journal*, *104*(3), 662–686.

64 Simone Pfenninger and David Singleton

Pfenninger, S. E. (2021). Emergent bilinguals in a digital world: A dynamic analysis of long-term L2 development in (pre)primary school children. (Special issue on "CDST & Transdisciplinary Research Methods", eds. P. Hiver and A. Al-Hoorie.) *International Review of Applied Linguistics IRAL* (special issue on "CDST & Transdisciplinary Research Methods", eds. P. Hiver and A. Al-Hoorie). https://doi.org/10.1515/iral-2021-0025.

Pfenninger, S. E., & Lendl, J. (2017). Transitional woes: On the impact of L2 input continuity from primary to secondary school. (Special issue, "L2 Grammar Acquisition", eds. T. Angelovska.) *Studies in Second Language Learning and Teaching, 7*(3), 443–470.

Pfenninger, S. E., & Singleton, D. (2017). *Beyond Age Effects in Instructional L2 Learning: Revisiting the Age Factor.* Bristol: Multilingual Matters.

Pfenninger, S. E., & Singleton, D. (2019a). Starting age overshadowed: The primacy of differential environmental and family support effects on L2 attainment in an instructional context. *Language Learning, 69*(S1), 207–234.

Pfenninger, S. E., & Singleton, D. (2019b). A critical review of research relating to the learning of additional languages in the third age. *Language Teaching, 52*(4). doi:10.1017/S0261444819000235

Piske, T. (2013). Frühbeginn allein ist nicht genug.: Welchen Einfluss haben Faktoren wie Alter, sprachlicher Input, Geschlecht und Motivation auf die Aussprechentwicklung und die grammatischen Kenntnisse von Zweitsprachenlernern? In C. Bürgel & D. Siepmann (Eds.), *Thema Sprache–Wissenschaft fur den Unterricht: Vol. 6. Sprachwissenschaft–Fremdsprachendidaktik. Neue Impulse* (pp. 117–144). Baltmannsweiler, Germany: Schneider Verlag Hohengehren.

Pliatsikas, C., Veríssimo, J., Babcock, L., Pullman, M. Y., Glei, D. A., Weinstein, M., Golcman, N., & Ullman, M. T. (2019). Working memory in older adults declines with age, but is modulated by sex and education. *Quarterly Journal of Experimental Psychology, 72*(6), 1308–1327.

Ramscar, M., Dye, M., & Klein, J. (2013). Children value informativity over logic in word learning. *Psychological Science, 24*(6), 1017–1023.

Ramscar, M., Dye, M., & McCauley, S. M. (2013). Error and expectation in language learning: The curious absence of mouses in adult speech. *Language, 89*, 760–793.

Ramscar, M., Hendrix, P., Shaoul, C., Milin, P., & Baayen, H. (2014). The myth of cognitive decline: Non-linear dynamics of lifelong learning. *Topics in Cognitive Science, 6*, 5–42.

Ramscar, M., Sun, C. C., Hendrix, P., & Baayen, H. (2017). The mismeasurement of mind: Life-span changes in paired-associate-learning scores reflect the "cost" of learning, not cognitive decline. *Psychological Science, 28*(8), 1171–1179.

Ramscar, M., Yarlett, D., Dye, M., Denny, K., & Thorpe, K. (2010). The effects of feature-label-order and their implications for symbolic learning. *Cognitive Science, 34*, 909–957.

Raz, N., & Lindenberger, U. (2013). Life-span plasticity of the brain and cognition: From questions to evidence and back. *Neuroscience & Biobehavioral Reviews, 37*(9), 2195–2200.

Rughiniș, C., & Humă, B. (2015). Who theorizes age? The "socio-demographic variables" device and age–period–cohort analysis in the rhetoric of survey research. *Journal of Aging Studies, 35*, 144–159.

Serafini, E. J. (2017). Exploring the dynamic long-term interaction between cognitive and psychosocial resources in adult second language development at varying proficiency. *The Modern Language Journal, 101*(2), 369–390.

Schlegel, A. A., Rudelson, J. J., & Tse, P. U. (2012). White matter structure changes as adults learn a second language. *Journal of Cognitive Neuroscience, 24*(8), 1664–1670.

Schmelter, L. (2010). (K)eine Frage des Alters–Fremdsprachenunterricht auf der Primarstufe. *Zeitschrift für Interkulturellen Fremdsprachenunterricht, 15*, 26–41.

Singleton, D., & Zaborska, D. (2020). Adults learning additional languages in their later years: The pain, the profit and the pleasure, *Journal of Multilingual Theories and Practices, 1*(1), 112–124.

Strauss, E., Sherman, E. M. S., & Spreen, O. (2006). *A Compendium of Neuropsychological Tests: Administration, Norms, and Commentary*. Oxford: Oxford University Press.

Swain, M., & Lapkin, S. (1989). Aspects of the sociolinguistic performance of early and late French immersion students. In R. Scarcella, E. Anderson & S. Krashen (Eds.), *On the Development of Communicative Competence in a Second Language* (pp. 41–54). Cambridge, MA: Newbury House.

Turnbull, M., Lapkin, S., Hart, D., & Swain, M. (1998). Time on task and immersion graduates' French proficiency. In S. Lapkin (Ed.), *French Second Language Education in Canada: Empirical Studies* (pp. 31–55). Toronto: University of Toronto Press.

Vanhove, J. (2013). The critical period hypothesis in second language acquisition: A statistical critique and a reanalysis. *PLoS One, 8*(7): e69172. doi:10.1371/journal.pone.0069172.

Werker, J. F., & Hensch, T. K. (2015). Critical periods in speech perception: New directions. *Annual Review of Psychology, 66*(1), 173–196.

4 Multilingual learners, linguistic pluralism and implications for education and research

Hamish Chalmers and Victoria Murphy

Introduction

In this chapter, we address issues concerning multilingual pupils in linguistically diverse classrooms. Taking Britain as an example, we begin with a very brief history lesson which demonstrates that this country has long been, and continues to be, a multilingual society. We share concerns over the terminology used to denote multilingual pupils in the UK (and beyond) and then turn our attention to whether and to what extent a multilingual pedagogy does/could have benefits to pupils. In particular, we argue that while there has been some compelling descriptive and qualitative research that argues for an approach which directly capitalizes on the home language knowledge of multilingual pupils, we need more controlled, experimental work to establish any causal links between drawing on the home language on the one hand, and enhanced second language (L2) and academic outcomes on the other. We discuss the theoretical background which justifies the need for this research, and we present relevant past research that has attempted to examine the impact of multilingual approaches. We conclude by arguing that while what has been done is of significant value in our efforts to understand and articulate best practice for multilingual pupils, we still need more and more experimental, research to establish causal links between practice and outcomes in linguistically diverse classrooms.

Britain: A well-established multilingual society

The UK has a long history of educating multilingual learners. While acknowledging the presence of multilingual learners in the UK since time immemorial, Costley (2014) notes that the 1950s provided somewhat of a watershed moment. It was here, in response to the 1948 British Nationality Act (11 & 12 Geo. 6 c. 56), that the UK saw the beginning of significant and sustained inward migration (British Nationality Act, 1948). This started with the 'Windrush Generation' (British citizens from former British colonies, named for one of the ships that brought the first wave of migrants from the Caribbean in 1948) and has continued consistently ever since. This period saw the arrival of people from all over the British Commonwealth and with them languages such as Bangla, Urdu, Punjabi, Hindi, Patwa, and Swahili. Contrary to the common assumption

DOI: 10.4324/9781003008361-6

at the time – that migrants were merely temporary sojourners, here for a short while until the time came for them to return 'home' (Stubbs, 1985; Levine, 1996) – large numbers of the Windrush generation, and every generation of migrants since, have settled, made the UK their home and become an important part of the fabric of British society. So too have their languages.

An Act of Parliament (Immigration Act, 1971) marked the end of the Windrush period, stopping free movement to the UK of British overseas passport holders, and replacing it with the need for Commonwealth citizens to have both a work permit and a parent or grandparent born in the UK before being considered for settlement (BBC, 2020). However, two years later, in 1973, the UK joined the European Economic Community and thus signed up to the principle of free movement of labour within that coalition of nations, a principle that was reaffirmed in 1992 with the signing of the Treaty of Maastricht and the creation of the European Union (EU) (1992). As one might expect, the free movement of people within the EU brought many more migrants to the UK and, as with the Windrush generation, many more languages. Figures from the Centre of Migration, Policy and Society (Vargas-Silva & Walsh, 2020) show that the number of British residents born in the EU rose from an estimated 1.6 million in 2004 to approximately 3.7 million in 2019. Over the same period, numbers of UK residents born outside the UK but not in the EU rose from an estimated 3.8 million to nearly 6 million. This inward migration is associated with an increase in the numbers of multilingual learners in UK schools, as the Department for Education notes that a significant proportion is accounted for by mothers born outside the UK giving birth to children in the UK (Department for Education, 2019).

The UK's decision to leave the EU, taken in 2016 and finally consecrated on the first of January 2021, might be thought to apply limiting pressure on the rate of increase in migration. While the total number of EU-born residents living in the UK dipped only slightly following the 2016 referendum that precipitated the UK's decision to leave the EU, movement of people from the EU to the UK dropped off sharply. Between 2015 and 2019, new arrivals from the EU fell by 34%. However, over the same period, inward migration from non-EU countries started to rise (Vargas-Silva & Walsh, 2020). Regardless of the UK's decision to leave the EU, it will continue to need migrant labour for its own economic prosperity (HM Government, 2018) and will continue to be bound by international law to accept applications for asylum from people fleeing trauma. There is every reason to suspect, therefore, that inward migration will continue to bring multilingual families into the British school system and that the British-born children of settled migrants will continue to contribute positively to the linguistic profile of this nation, its society and schools. Britain is, and will remain, a multilingual society.

How is linguistic diversity represented in UK schools?

Recent figures from the UK's Department for Education – which help to contextualize the relationship between immigration to the UK and the impact on the country's school population – put the number of learners classified as hailing

68   Hamish Chalmers and Victoria Murphy

from multilingual home environments at around 19% of the pupil population (Department for Education, 2019), a figure that had risen steadily from about 11% in 2006 when these data began to be regularly reported.

In England, among the 19% of the school population who can be thought of as multilingual, more than 300 different non-English languages are represented (Bailey & Marsden, 2017). In Scotland, the proportion of multilingual children in government-funded schools is about 10%. Among these, 153 different home languages in addition to English are represented, including Scots (Scottish Government, 2020). In Wales, the proportion is approximately 8% (StatsWales, 2020). However, while the Welsh figures incorporate pupils speaking one of the more than 155 languages represented among Welsh school pupils, the relevant statistical release collapses first language Welsh and first language English speakers into one figure, thus underestimating the number of multilingual pupils in the system as a whole. In Northern Ireland, the equivalent figure is approximately 5%, with about 90 different home languages represented (Meredith, 2018). As in Wales, this figure does not take into account pupils who speak Irish, which is collapsed into one figure with English.

Our national education system is thus unquestionably multilingual. The term provided by the British education system to describe this significant minority within the school population is pupils who have English as an Additional Language, or simply EAL. The implications of this term are discussed in the next section.

English as an additional language: What's in a name?

> A pupil is recorded to have English as an additional language if she/he is exposed to a language at home that is known or believed to be other than English. This measure is not a measure of English language proficiency or a good proxy for recent immigration.
>
> (Department for Education, 2019:9)

Arguably, this somewhat paltry explanation of what it means to be an EAL learner invokes more questions about that classification than it clarifies. If 'exposure' to a language other than English is the defining characteristic, then what does it mean to be exposed to another language? Is it enough for pupils to hear their grandmother or uncle using a non-English language when on a phone call to relatives in another country? Does the presence of foreign-language newspapers in the family home count as exposure? If a child hears music in their heritage language, or is present when other members of the family are watching non-English movies or TV programmes, is that sufficient? The strict interpretation of the term would suggest that, yes, all of these and any other one might think of would place a pupil into the category of EAL.

Of course, 'exposure' could also mean that the pupil uses non-English languages with a proficiency equal to or superior to that of their English language.

Linguistic pluralism and implications 69

So, we find ourselves subsuming under the banner of EAL everything from ostensibly monolingual English pupils, whose ambient home environment features non-English languages which they may not use or understand, through pupils who use only a non-English language at home and who are in the process of learning or acquiring English at school, to pupils who are fully conversant with English and one or more non-English language. Note also that it is sufficient for any of these contexts to be 'believed' to characterize the linguistic environment of the pupil, though believed by whom is undeclared. This all-encompassing characterization of EAL has led some to brand it 'reckless' (TES, 2018, no page). EAL as a defining characteristic tells us nothing of the nature or extent of the exposure to either English or the non-English language. Crucially, therefore, it tells us nothing of the type of education that would be best suited to any individual classified as EAL.

In Northern Ireland, official classification is more informative. A decision was taken by the Northern Irish Department of Education in 2010 to dispense with the term EAL "due to difficulties in the interpretation of the above definitions [of EAL] encountered by schools when completing their census returns" (Department of Education, 2010:3). The term chosen to replace it was 'Newcomer', defined as "a child or young person who has enrolled in a school but who does not have the satisfactory language skills to participate fully in the school curriculum and does not have a language in common with the teacher" (Department of Education, 2010:3). This definition matches more closely definitions used in other parts of the world, notably the United States, where children who require additional support to access the curriculum because of their English language skills are referred to as Limited English Proficiency (LEP). Importantly, and unlike the EAL designation used in England, this categorization makes explicit reference to the child's developing linguistic proficiency in the medium of instruction.

EAL may have its limitations as a diagnostic indicator for linguistic and other educationally relevant characteristics of multilingual pupils, but it does something that other terms do not. It explicitly places English as an *addition* to the existing linguistic repertoires of pupils. It does so without implying a hierarchy of languages, as, for example, the more globally familiar ESL (English as a Second Language) does. Neither does it draw attention to what nascent multilingual children cannot do, as Limited English Proficient does. Instead, it invites the view that multilingualism is an asset. Whether or not the orientation towards 'additive bilingualism' (Lambert, 1981) is intentional, and more specifically *well intentioned* – Cunningham (2019), for example, argues that 'EAL' cannot escape negative ideological associations and language attitudes and is thus inevitably problematic – we believe that users of the term should seize the opportunity it presents to frame 'EAL' as descriptive of the kind of linguistic competence we aspire to for all of our children. That is, EAL can be seen as reflective of a society where languages are things to be added to our shared repertoire, where multilingualism is seen as an unremarkable aspect of everyday life, and linguistic pluralism is something to aspire to.

Does a multilingual society benefit from a multilingual pedagogy?

We have established that we live in a multilingual society. Children at various stages of multilingualism, from those just beginning to acquire an additional language to those with an impressive command of a number of them, make up a fifth of the pupil population in the UK. Similar patterns of societal multilingualism exist the world over. A turning point in the way that applied linguists have begun to think about the implications of a society in which different languages coexist was codified in the publication of two books both using the term 'The Multilingual Turn' in their titles (Conteh & Meier, 2014; May, 2014). In both volumes, the authors explore what it means to live in a global society where multilingualism is the norm rather than the exception, and explore the implications of this for personal identities, social cohesion, language learning, and language pedagogies and curricula.

Conteh and Meier (2014) consists of a number of different contributions which explore issues around language ideologies and identity in linguistically diverse societies, language education in schools and communities and pedagogies and classroom practice. The volume challenges the notion of a monolingual mainstream and promotes the reality (and advantages) of multilingualism throughout all aspects of society, but education in particular. The majority of the contributions were based in complementary schools, those educational settings that fall outside of formal education and in which many multilingual families send their children to develop more advanced heritage language skills. Research on linguistically diverse classrooms is often carried out in such contexts, as teachers in 'mainstream' formal education do not tend (at present) to engage in multilingual pedagogical approaches.

May's (2014) volume is also a compilation of contributions from authors around the world, each of whom in their own way address important issues within the context of linguistically diverse classrooms and multilingual learners. Works such as these, which focus on the needs, issues, challenges and education of multilingual learners, are increasingly pertinent as our society slowly recognizes the reality of the multilingual world in which we live. For the purposes of this chapter, we will focus on the implications of the multilingual turn as it relates to pedagogical approaches for multilingual learners.

At its heart, work advocating the multilingual turn argues for acceptance of, and support for, multilingualism. Within educational settings, this means that instead of viewing linguistically diverse classrooms as problems to be overcome, they should rather be viewed as resources from which one can support language development (in the round) in all students, regardless of their linguistic profile. A much-discussed notion relating to this, particularly from a pedagogical perspective, is 'Translanguaging'. Wei (2018), for example, has noted that the term translanguaging can be conceived as a practical theory of language, where the notion of using more than one code within and across utterances is a language practice engaged in by multilinguals around the world. It can be directly

Linguistic pluralism and implications 71

relevant to classrooms as well, as highlighted by García (2009) and Creese and Blackledge (2015) among others (see also Conteh, 2018). From a pedagogical point of view, the notion is that multilingual children should be able to draw on all of their languages (i.e. their full linguistic repertoire) to enhance their learning across the curriculum.

An example of how using the home language can support learning in classrooms can be found in Early and Cummins (2011) and Cummins et al. (2015). Cummins et al. (2015) discuss the notion of identity negotiation and how students' identities within specific social groups influence academic achievement. Multilingual learners often under-achieve academically (though note that they often excel too) (Murphy, in press). Academic achievement is influenced by numerous variables, including linguistic proficiency, literacy skill and home language environment. Social status and the *perceived* social status of students and their respective languages are also argued to be a significant factor in achievement. Indeed, Cummins (2000) powerfully articulates the social justice issues associated with educating multilingual learners, arguing that many of the problems they tend to experience from an educational perspective can be attributed to the implicit and explicit prejudices levied against ethnic minority pupils and their families.

Cummins et al. (2015) discuss the notion of 'identity texts', which is where teachers encourage multilingual pupils to use their multilingualism as a cognitive tool to broaden the range of modalities they can use to create literature and art. In turn, this can serve to enhance their literacy skills and help them develop a stronger, and more positive, self-identity. In their work, Cummins et al. (2015) present a model where such a process (in which multilingual pupils use their full linguistic repertoire) can support literacy engagement, and ultimately literacy attainment. Importantly (and taking a translanguaging perspective), this approach allows students to create dual-language texts, even in educational settings where the teacher does not know the home language of the pupils. Cummins et al. (2015) report the pride felt by the pupils in terms of the work they created, and argue that literacy-based practices that affirm multilingual pupils' identity and use of their home languages can have direct, positive impacts, particularly with respect to their academic achievement. Indeed, they go so far as to suggest a causal relationship between an approach like that used in identity texts on the one hand and enhanced literacy skill on the other. This is because, they argue, approaches such as these increase pupils' engagement with literacy, and engagement has been demonstrated to be associated with higher literacy achievement.

All of these ideas are intuitively appealing to those of us who are predisposed to view multilingualism, wherever it is found, as more interesting and positive than the monolingual norm. There are powerful reasons to assume that adopting pedagogical approaches which allow multilingual pupils to draw from their home language knowledge and experience will lead to enhanced proficiency in the majority language (their L2) and improved academic outcomes. We submit, however, that at this point in the development of work in this area, we still lack the critical mass of research – and of a particular kind of research – that will unambiguously demonstrate the power of the multilingual turn in

72 Hamish Chalmers and Victoria Murphy

educational settings. In short, we would argue that while there is a sound body of work arguing for the benefits of translanguaging approaches in mainstream classrooms, until and unless we have rigorous experimental methods applied to this question, we will not be able to demonstrate unequivocally the benefits for majority language development or academic achievement. Importantly we need Randomized Controlled Trials (RCTs), in which a multilingual pedagogy is directly compared with the monolingual norm, and where clear outcomes (language and/or academic) are compared across both types of learning conditions. Very little work of this type has yet been conducted, and without it, what we have are compelling descriptions of what individual teachers, classrooms and/or schools have done that *might* be effective. What we don't have is convincing causal evidence, evidence that could be incorporated into teacher education programmes to support future teachers, and which can also be brought to government departments to argue for promoting multilingualism throughout the curriculum. We are hopeful that such research, once conducted, will bear fruit and demonstrate advantages in defined outcomes. The reason for our optimism stems from a body of theorizing and research to which we now turn.

Leveraging language to leverage learning

To start to explore the possibilities, it is worth revisiting our theoretical understanding of the way that multiple languages coexist in the minds of language learners and the potential that this cohabitation in cognitive space might have on overall linguistic development. In 1979, Cummins published his Linguistic Interdependence Hypothesis, followed shortly thereafter (in 1980) by his theory of a Common Underlying Proficiency (Cummins, 1979a, 1980). These continue to be extremely influential in shaping the way we think about the cognitive development of multilingual learners and its implications for their linguistic and academic development (Cummins, 2008; Thomas & Mady, 2014; Forbes, 2019). Both theories will be familiar to many readers, but to recap: they do not see languages as separate entities that exist in splendid isolation from one another in the mind of a multilingual individual (and therefore entities that compete in a zero-sum game for cognitive resources, as earlier conceptualizations of bilingualism would have it: e.g. Darcy, 1953). Instead, the theory sees the cognitive skills that inform linguistic proficiency in either language as being housed in the same central engine. As such, cognitive-linguistic skills developed initially through one language inform the use of both (or all) languages. Cummins characterized this interrelatedness most famously with a diagram of a dual-peaked iceberg. The peaks of the iceberg emerging from the waterline represent the surface features of each of two languages: pronunciation, lexis and grammar. These are the features of language that we see and hear when an individual uses one or other of their languages. Beneath the waterline, abstract and invisible, is where the cognitive resources that inform the use of the surface features are represented. According to Cummins, this collection of skills is unitary, informing both languages. Working from this assumption, Cummins posits that

Linguistic pluralism and implications 73

teaching to develop the cognitive-linguistic skills that reside in the submerged central engine – using either of the languages known to the learner – will inform development in both. A child who has learned to tell the time in one language, for example, does not need to re-learn the semantics of words like 'past', 'to' and 'o'clock', they just need learn the labels for these concepts in the other language (Cummins, 2001). The languages are interdependent; thus the skills informing meaning-making in one of them can be brought to bear on meaning-making in the other.

Evidence for Cummins' central engine

Cummins based his theories in large part on findings from the then relatively nascent field of bilingual education research in the 1970s (e.g. Lambert & Tucker, 1972; Cohen, 1974; Swain, 1975) and from studies assessing the correlation between academic language proficiency in learners' first language (L1) and in their L2 (e.g. Cummins, 1977; Lapkin & Swain, 1977; Genesee, 1979). We will explore some of this work below.

Research on bilingual education programmes

At the time that Cummins and others were first exploring the notion of linguistic interdependence, research was more concerned with assessing whether bilingual education was *detrimental* to cognitive development rather than exploring the possibility that it might be advantageous. The findings of studies like Lambert and Tucker (1972) and Cohen (1974) tended to demonstrate that the fears which some held about bilingualism were unfounded. Bilingual education did not damage the development of the L1, nor did it appear to have any detrimental effect on cognitive development, and it resulted in superior learning of the target language (French in the case of Lambert and Tucker, Spanish in the case of Cohen). Another influential study informing the Common Underlying Proficiency theory was Swain (1975), which looked in some detail at the development of specific writing characteristics in the L1 of her participants (English), who were Grade 3 learners in a bilingual French immersion programme in Canada. Outcomes measures were text length, proportion of complex and simple sentences, lexical variety, lexical misuse, morphological errors, spelling and creativity. Swain found that, compared to English children studying French as a stand-alone subject in an English-medium programme, the writing of English L1 children in the bilingual programme was longer, more complex, equally lexically diverse, contained fewer lexical and morphological errors and was "at least as creative" (Swain, 1975:20). It did contain slightly more punctuation and spelling errors, but Swain points out that the French immersion pupils' writing was longer and more complex, so the opportunity to make these kinds of errors was greater.

The success of bilingual programmes in Canada helped to usher in what might arguably be called the heyday of bilingual education in the USA, following the 1974 amendment to the Bilingual Education Act, when States were encouraged

74   *Hamish Chalmers and Victoria Murphy*

to provide bilingual programmes as a matter of routine. The prevailing conditions provided an opportunity to assess the effects of these programmes, and a number of studies were conducted in the 70s and 80s that did so. Several systematic reviews and meta-analyses of research conducted during this period demonstrate that these bilingual programmes were associated with improved educational outcomes for minority language students (Willig, 1985; Greene, 1998; McField, 2002; Rolstad, Mahoney & Glass, 2005; Slavin & Cheung, 2005). Across this body of research, children from minority language backgrounds who attended bilingual programmes either matched or outperformed their peers (who attended monolingual English schools) on measures such as reading, writing, vocabulary, oral language, mathematics, problem-solving, science, social studies and measures of general intelligence.

More recently, and adding important international evidence to a body of literature that had principally been focused on North America, research on the effects of bilingual programmes in Europe was synthesized in a systematic review by Reljić, Ferring and Martin (2015). In their review, they performed an exceptionally thorough search for studies that evaluated European bilingual programmes in comparison to programmes conducted only in the target language (normally the language of the European state in which the schools were located). They found seven reports that add support to the general findings of the North American research. The studies assessed bilingual programmes that used six different L1s (Urdu, Asturian, Basque, Catalan, Gaelic and Turkish) and four target languages (English, Spanish, Norwegian and Dutch). The studies reported on outcomes such as literacy, mathematics, civics, linguistic creativity and written expression, both in the L1 and in the target languages. As with previous studies, Reljić, Ferring and Martin's synthesis found a small but statistically significant positive effect on academic and linguistic attainment for students in bilingual schools compared to students in target-language-only schools. They conclude that their review "supports bilingual education in Europe, which specifically includes the home language of language minority children" (Reljić, Ferring & Martin, 2015:29).

In the bilingualism literature, we have evidence, therefore, that when multilingual children are educated in both of their languages, there are detectable and meaningful advantages, especially for children who belong to language minority communities, as is often the case for EAL leaners in the UK. While in this literature there are clear implications for multilingual approaches to teaching multilingual learners, it is not clear how important context is to these overall findings. For example, it is important to remember that mainstream schools in the UK are quite a different to bilingual programmes in Los Angeles or Montréal, in more ways than just the languages that are used for instruction.

Correlational studies

The correlational studies that informed Cummins' (1979a, 1980) reasoning about the interdependence of languages in the minds of bilingual (or aspiring bilingual)

Linguistic pluralism and implications 75

learners focused on assessing the relationships between academic attainment and proficiency in what he called Cognitive/Academic Language Proficiency or CALP (Cummins, 1979b). Earlier explorations of the relationships between language proficiency and academic attainment, notably by Oller, focused on the influence of what he called a "language factor" (Oller, 1978:412). This was a global measure of linguistic proficiency that was examined as a correlate of academic attainment. The language factor, according to Oller, explains about 79 percent of the variance in academic attainment across a variety of measures.

Cummins, however, took issue with the language factor as a measure of the type of linguistic proficiency that would lead to success in school. The basis of his criticism was that, rather than there being a single language factor, there are instead two dimensions to language proficiency. The first dimension he called Basic Interpersonal Communicative Skills or BICS (Cummins, 1980), with the second being CALP. The distinction is important. Proficiency in BICS – social, concretely contextualized, everyday, and chiefly oral language – is, with very rare exceptions, acquired by everyone in their L1, regardless of IQ or academic aptitude. It is also relatively rapidly acquired in an L2, assuming adequate exposure and opportunities to use it. As such, BICS introduces a ceiling effect into the measurement of language proficiency. If everyone by the time they reach school age, or soon after, has attained high levels of BICS, it ceases to be a useful correlate, as everyone is at (or close to) ceiling. Much better for assessing the relationship between language proficiency and academic success, says Cummins (1980), is CALP. CALP is the dimension of language that is harder to acquire without explicit teaching. It requires conscious knowledge of the language, such that it can be manipulated, synthesized and used in decontextualized cognitive/academic operations.

By disaggregating CALP from BICS and assessing the relationship between the former and learners' academic attainment, a better understanding of how language development contributes to overall academic development can be determined. More importantly, for the purposes of this discussion, assessing the extent of CALP knowledge in either or both of the languages known to an individual, and comparing the extent to which these correlate with academic attainment, can provide insight into whether cultivating CALP in one language has implications for the development of the same set of skills in the other. Cummins asserted that CALP can be distinguished empirically from BICS by the type of assessment used. For example, oral fluency tests say very little about CALP when compared with oral cloze tests – the latter requiring the manipulation of linguistic knowledge to be successfully completed (Cummins, 1979b).

To illustrate the importance of the CALP/BICS distinction, Cummins drew on a number of studies that assessed the relationships between CALP skills in L1, CALP skills in L2, aptitude, IQ and scores on achievement tests (Swain, Lapkin & Barik, 1976; Cummins, 1977; Lapkin & Swain, 1977; Carey & Cummins, 1979; Genesee, 1979; Genesee & Hamayan, 1980; Taft & Bodi, 1980). This body of literature demonstrated moderate to strong positive

76   *Hamish Chalmers and Victoria Murphy*

correlations between all of these measures. That is, L1 CALP was positively correlated with L2 CALP; and both were positively correlated with IQ, aptitude and achievement. Cummins took this as evidence for the veracity of his Common Underlying Proficiency theory. That is: "both L1 and L2 CALP are manifestations of the one underlying dimension" (Cummins, 1979b:199). Moreover, Cummins' analysis of these data also revealed an association with the age at which the L2 was introduced. Specifically, the older that learners were when they first started learning the L2, the more likely they were to demonstrate an advantage in their mastery of L2 syntax and morphology as well as the cognitive/academic skills manifested through the L2. The implication from this latter finding is that CALP skills already manifested in the L1 are quickly absorbed into the L2, assuming adequate exposure and some direct teaching. Using the L1 to support EAL learners might, therefore, have a facilitative effect, if it works from the basis established in the stronger language to build competence in the weaker one.

More recent correlational studies, conducted since the body of work that first influenced Cummins, have largely confirmed his initial position. Preevo et al. (2016), for example, conducted a meta-analysis of studies exploring relationships between oral language proficiency in L1 and L2 and academic proficiency among bilingual children with an immigration background. Results from 86 studies published between 1976 and 2013, covering bilingual learners from pre-school to age 18 with a variety of L1 backgrounds, were synthesized. The synthesis revealed that oral language proficiency in the L1 was moderately positively correlated with early L2 literacy (phonological awareness, letter knowledge and initial awareness of literacy concepts) ($r = .22$) and more weakly correlated with L2 reading proficiency ($r = .12$). Both correlations were statistically significant. Adding support for the position that instruction in the L1 may facilitate development in the L2, the correlations found in the constituent studies in this meta-analysis tended to vary in strength according to school type: the strongest correlations were associated with bilingual programmes, and weaker correlations were found among children who attended schools in which the language of instruction was exclusively the L2.

Another meta-analysis (Melby-Lervåg & Lervåg, 2011) explored the relationships between L1 and L2 oral language proficiency, L1 and L2 phonology (operationalized by the authors as decoding and phonological awareness), and L1 and L2 reading comprehension. They searched for reports published between 1976 and 2009 that assessed the relationships between at least two of these variables in school-age learners. They located 47 eligible studies, across a variety of contexts, including a variety of L1s and L2s. The findings of these studies were statistically synthesized in five meta-analyses. These revealed a small positive meta-correlation ($r = .16$) for L1 and L2 oral language proficiency; a large positive meta-correlation ($r = .54$) between L1 and L2 decoding; a large meta-correlation ($r = .60$) between L1 and L2 phonological awareness; and a moderate meta-correlation ($r = .24$) between L1 decoding and L2 reading comprehension. The only meta-correlation calculated in this study that did not show clear evidence of an association was that of L1 oral language proficiency and L2 reading comprehension, perhaps reflecting the BICS/CALP distinction in the cognitive-linguistic skills required for each task.

In addition, some work has added to our understanding about whether the linguistic interdependence associated with CALP is confined to structurally similar languages or whether the relationship holds for structurally dissimilar languages. Chuang, Joshi & Dixon (2011) explored relationships between competence in Mandarin Chinese literacy and English literacy among secondary school learners in Taiwan. The orthographic systems of these languages are very dissimilar. Mandarin Chinese uses a logographic script, in which symbols represent entire words or morphemes. English uses an alphabetic script, in which letters represent the individual phonemes that make up words and morphemes. The dissimilarity of these orthographic systems led Chuang, Joshi & Dixon (2011) to question whether we would see the transfer of literacy competence in Mandarin Chinese to literacy competence in English, or whether the influence of proficiency in Mandarin literacy would be an impediment to developing similar skills in English. Mandarin and English test results from a random sample of 30,000 Taiwanese ninth-grade students, over a six-year period were compared. Using linear regression modelling, they determined that 62% of the variation in English literacy proficiency could be accounted for by the participants' level of Mandarin literacy. The inclusion of other predictors in the model (gender; rural or urban school districts; length of time learning English) had negligible effects on the bottom-line finding. This study, and other similar ones (Bialystok, Luk & Kwan, 2005; Bialystok, McBride-Chang & Luk, 2005; Wang, Perfetti & Liu, 2005; Wang, Cheng & Chen, 2006; Keung & Ho, 2009), lend important support to the notion that, even when languages are structurally quite different, "students' L1 reading ability plays a significant role during the process of L2 reading comprehension acquisition" (Chuang, Joshi & Dixon, 2011:114).

Findings like these tantalize educators who wish to capitalize on the linguistic diversity represented by multilingual learners in their classrooms. Operationalizing this understanding in terms of pedagogy is eagerly hypothesized about by researchers and practitioners alike (NALDIC, 2019). Chuang, Joshi & Dixon (2011), for example, urge the Taiwanese Ministry of Education to adapt their national curriculum to "tailor L2 [English] reading instruction to capitalize on reading knowledge and strategies already familiar to students through the L1 learning process" (114).

What are the implications of this body of work for multilingual pedagogies?

We have devoted quite some space to characterizing and updating research that was first conducted more than four decades ago, to explain the basis for the claim that a multilingual approach to the education of EAL learners might be a fruitful avenue to pursue. The consistency in findings across this forty-year period is remarkable. What is perhaps even more remarkable is that more recent research in this area does not appear to have moved us much further forward in our understanding of the pedagogical implications of this theory than we were in the 1980s. In the four decades since Cummins first told us to adopt multilingual pedagogical approaches, conceptual replications of the work that informed this instruction have very little to add to, or clarify, Cummins' essential argument. One might well ask how many correlational studies of linguistic interdependence we need before we are satisfied that Cummins' theory is sound. How many evaluations of bilingual programmes need to be conducted in order to conclude that children who want to participate in them should be able to? Or, perhaps, what could researchers be doing with their time and energy instead of re-litigating old arguments?

One area that we believe should be receiving much more attention from researchers who are interested in the potential of multilingual pedagogies is the exploration of the substantive effects of adopting these approaches on meaningful educational outcomes for multilingual learners.

A new research focus

The challenge for teachers of EAL learners relates to the operationalization of the lessons learned from the research summarized above in the linguistically diverse contexts that characterize their classrooms.

A body of literature aimed squarely at teachers has grown out of the multilingual turn, and especially under the banner of translanguaging (García & Wei 2014). These have produced volumes of advice on how to incorporate other languages into the educational diet of multilingual learners. We have already mentioned the work of Cummins et al. (2015). As a further example, Gibbons (2009: 92) suggests that teachers should "use the students' first language to explain the key points of the text [...] prior to having them read it in English". The Department for Education for England suggests to teachers that students' "[h]ome language can be used to develop higher-order literacy and cognitive skills" (Bourne, 2002:76) by, for example, discussing the rhetorical devices used in literary texts or exploring cause and effect in science lessons. Celic and Seltzer (2012) and Chumak-Horbatsch (2012) have produced compendia of multilingual approaches to teaching, including activities such as: dual language note-taking; reading in one language, discussing the text in the other; using translation software such as Google Translate; and so on.

However, the efficacy of these interventions outside the context of bilingual education lacks a secure evidential basis. Most of the research on multilingual approaches to teaching EAL learners has been observational in nature and has a tendency to use proxy measures for actual linguistic and academic outcomes. There is, however, a small body of literature that evaluates the substantive educational effects of multilingual approaches to teaching, using methodological approaches that can help reduce uncertainty about these effects. We will describe both these bodies of literature next.

Observational research on the effects of multilingual pedagogies

We are informed about the potential pedagogic role of multilingual approaches to teaching by research that examines the purposes to which it is put by multilingual learners when they engage in educational activities. When given the opportunity to use their L1, multilingual learners use it in ways that seem likely to support their learning. For example, research using think-aloud protocols that observes and classifies the purposes of L1 use by students working together or responding to L2 tasks finds that L1 is used for planning and reviewing work, meta-linguistic exploration, and for staying on task (Swain & Lapkin, 2000; Scott & de la Fuente, 2008; Duarte, 2016).

In addition, research has examined the relationship between L1 use and student wellbeing (in the UK and elsewhere). This has shown that students feel valued when their linguistic background, and by extension, their cultural heritage, is acknowledged and actively promoted by their teachers (Parke et al., 2002; Kenner et al., 2008). Similarly, aspects of social justice are the main drivers of the translanguaging movement. Some proponents of translanguaging make the strong argument that by failing to promote explicitly the dynamic use of the full linguistic repertoires of multilingual learners, the education system is marginalizing and oppressing these students (Flores & García, 2017; Kleyn & García, 2019; García, 2019). It is legitimate to look at how multilingual learners and their advocates view linguistic plurality, and the multilingual turn in language teaching and learning reinforces this burgeoning rejection of what some call the monolingual (and especially monolingual *English*) hegemony (Major, 2018).

There is an expectation that teachers' practice should be based on the best available evidence about what is likely to work most effectively in their contexts. To that end, we take the position that it is important to determine whether multilingual approaches can help multilingual learners (such as EAL students in the UK) to understand better what they are being taught and to express better what they have learned, in the majority language (e.g. English in the UK). This should not diminish the argument that multilingual learners are entitled to be valued for who they are.

Observational research like that described in this chapter helps us to speculate about the potential advantage to EAL learners that multilingual approaches may have, and it makes a strong social justice case. However, these alone do not inform us about the substantive academic and linguistic outcomes of these approaches. In order to demonstrate that the educational outcomes for multilingual learners will be improved by multilingual pedagogies, experiments that compare these pedagogical approaches to alternatives must be conducted. It is a basic principle of educational research, aiming to tease out causal relationships between teaching and learning, that a promising teaching approach should be carefully compared with a realistic alternative in a fair test (Campbell & Stanley, 1963). Too much of the existing literature on multilingual pedagogies does not do that. Far more often, we see causal claims made on the basis of research designs that cannot be said reliably to support them. Often the designs adopted do not provide valid comparisons and do little to address the potential biases which may have influenced findings. As such, our capacity to judge the merits of a given multilingual approach relative to an alternative is compromised. When researchers make the effort to reduce the potential that biases have to influence our understanding – by, for example, using random allocation to create comparison groups – we are in a far stronger position to assess reliably the relative effects of these approaches. Studies in which that effort has been made in the area of multilingual pedagogy are notable by their scarcity.

Experimental research on the effects of multilingual pedagogies

Empirical support for the above arguments is derived from a recent systematic review of research addressing this question (Chalmers, 2019). The review sought to locate studies using experimental and quasi-experimental designs that evaluated teaching strategies making use of participants' home languages, and where linguistic and/or academic outcomes in the target language were measured. A comprehensive search for research that met these criteria revealed only eleven eligible studies.

The eleven studies addressed a variety of learning strategies and outcomes. Three studies explored the effects of using learners' L1 on outcomes related to reading (Walters & Gunderson, 1985; Sánchez, 2004; Huennekens, 2013). These used read-alouds in the L1, translations of school texts into L1, and dialogic reading in the L1 as vehicles for incorporating L1 into L2 classrooms. They assessed the effects of these strategies on L2 reading comprehension and L2 phonic knowledge. Taken together, their findings are equivocal. Huennekens (2013) found in favour of using the L1, Sanchez (2004) found in favour of not using the L1, and Walters and Gunderson (1985) found that it appeared to make little difference, as participants in all groups did equally well.

In another study included in Chalmers' (2019) review, Yiakoumetti (2006) compared two groups of Cypriot Greek speakers, whose language of instruction at school was Standard Modern Greek (SMG). One group was taught using a technique in which features of SMG were explicitly and systematically compared and contrasted with similar features in Cypriot Greek. The other group continued with their usual SMG literacy curriculum. The group who had used the language comparison technique made significantly fewer errors in their production of SMG (both written and oral) compared to the other group.

One study in the review (Chalmers, 2014) assessed the effects of asking the parents of EAL learners to discuss the events of a short story using either English or their L1. The completeness and quality of subsequent written recounts of those stories were then compared. Both the English-only and the L1 group did equally well on these outcomes. Notable for educational contexts such as the UK (see section "Britain: A well-established multilingual society"), this was the only study located for the review which was conducted in a linguistically diverse setting; that is, a setting in which more than one L1 was represented among participants.

Linguistic pluralism and implications 81

A more promising avenue for exploration emerges from six studies included in the review that addressed the use of the L1 to support vocabulary teaching in the L2. All but one of these used some variation on identifying keywords in a shared text and discussing these words using the L1s of the participants. Lugo-Neris et al. (2010) used a randomized crossover design with kindergarten-aged Spanish-L1 children in Florida to assess whether stopping to talk in Spanish about keywords in an English language story improved the subsequent understanding of those keywords relative to talking about them in English only. They found that participants were better able to define the keywords in both English and Spanish following the L1-mediated intervention. A similar approach was taken by Lee and Macaro (2013). The authors took advantage of pre-existing Korean primary school classes in which English was taught either by monolingual English teachers or by bilingual Korean/English teachers. Comparison classes were selected on the basis of the teachers' professional experience, class sizes, pupils' ages, socio-economic backgrounds and English proficiency of the students (that is, participants were not randomly allocated to class type, but instead existing classes were 'matched' on these characteristics). In their reading lessons, when they encountered preselected target words, the bilingual teachers translated them and discussed their meaning in Korean. The monolingual teachers used English to explain the words' meanings. In tests of recall and recognition of the target words, the authors found that those who had been given Korean language input on meanings performed statistically significantly better than those who had been given English language explanations.

Two other studies follow a very similar structure (Sieh, 2008; Codina Camó & Pladevall Ballester, 2015). Sieh's study contained two experiments, which took place in Taiwan with 4th Grade Mandarin learners of English. In both experiments, the teacher read a story to the children in English. When she reached preselected target words, she either showed the children a flashcard with an illustration of the word and its written English form or she showed the flashcard and orally translated the word into Mandarin Chinese. In one of the two experiments, there was a statistically significant difference in the receptive knowledge of the target words, with those in the L1 condition faring better. In the other experiment, no difference in outcomes was detected.

Codina Camó and Pladevall Ballester (2015) followed a very similar procedure. They used an animated adaptation of The Tales of Peter Rabbit as a stimulus with 5th Grade Catalan learners of English. When preselected words appeared in the video, the teacher paused it and either showed the participants a flashcard containing the English word and an illustration of it or showed the flashcard and orally translated its meaning into Catalan. The group who were taught using Catalan performed statistically significantly better on tests of receptive knowledge of the target words, both one week and one month after the intervention, compared to the group using only English.

The final study addressing vocabulary knowledge included in Chalmers' (2019) synthesis, Tonzar, Lotto and Job (2009), was somewhat different, and arguably less representative of typical classroom practice. Using a projector, 123 Italian L1 4th Grade students were shown a series of 40 English or German words (there were two target languages in this study). After each word, either a picture to illustrate its meaning or an Italian translation of the word was shown. On tests of recall of the target words, those words that had been followed by an illustration were statistically significantly better recalled than those for which an Italian translation had been provided.

In assessing the methodological rigour of all the studies that met the review's eligibility criteria, Chalmers (2019) found that very few had adopted the most trustworthy designs for causal inference (randomized trials, for example), and that there were significant shortcomings in terms of scale in most of them. With regards to the debate we are entertaining in this chapter, we might tentatively say that there appears to be promise in the use of multilingual approaches when teaching L2 vocabulary to multilingual learners (e.g. English vocabulary to EAL pupils). However, we are hard pressed to say much more than that. The literature exposes an embarrassing lack of quality evidence that would inform us either way about a pedagogical approach that has become something of a *cause célèbre* in the field.

Keeping 'the multilingual turn' turning

The enthusiasm that has been steadily building for multilingual approaches to educating not just our multilingual learners but also their monolingual peers demonstrates a seriousness about valuing the linguistically plural societies that characterize our world. In the UK, the EAL community is generally excited by the pedagogical possibilities implied by 'the multilingual turn'. As Macaro (2018:204) notes, "For the past 20 years or so, the presence of the L1 in the classroom has ceased to become a controversial issue in the SLA [Second Language Acquisition] community". Nonetheless, echoes of earlier academic concerns around the appropriateness of anything other than 'all L2, all the time' that characterized academic discourse can still be heard among decision-makers not immediately invested in the field of EAL. Macaro continues: "the argument is no longer among researchers and commentators but among the teachers they are researching." Teachers are torn between a growing call to adopt multilingual pedagogies on the one hand and years of policy, practice, beliefs and experience that implicitly or explicitly reject this on the other.

The switch to a different way of teaching does not come without a cost. This may be in terms of money: buying multilingual textbooks or employing multilingual teachers and assistants, for example. It may be in terms of effort and time: training teachers and adapting curricula, for example. Or it may be simply in terms of opportunity: resources are finite and educational decisions in this respect are zero sum. Resources invested in one area cannot also be invested in another. Teachers should be confident that any investment in switching to multilingual pedagogies is worthwhile. As we have noted, on the grounds of

Linguistic pluralism and implications 83

its substantive educational effects, far too little existing research can give them this confidence. In the light of the paucity of trustworthy evidence from experiments on multilingual approaches to teaching EAL learners, is it reasonable to expect practitioners to make that investment? We would not blame them if they demurred.

We recognize the vital contribution that works in the translanguaging sphere, and on multilingualism more generally, is making towards social justice. We have articulated the importance of correlational and observational studies in helping us to understand the theoretical foundations upon which multilingual pedagogies are constructed. If we are to keep 'the multilingual turn' turning, however, it is incumbent on us as researchers to invest more effort in robustly assessing the effects of multilingual pedagogies on outcomes that are important to teachers and EAL learners. We should ensure that this is done in ways that allow us to make confident interpretations about the substantive effects of these approaches as they compare to realistic alternatives. This means more experiments, conducted in contexts that more accurately reflect reality for teachers and EAL learners in mainstream education.

While we, as authors, celebrate multilingualism in our society, we nonetheless take the position that proficiency in the majority language of education is a *sine qua non* in terms of educational success for multilingual learners in any given context (e.g. proficiency in English for EAL pupils in the UK). It is this language through which multilingual learners are expected to demonstrate their knowledge and understanding of the things that they are taught in school. For better or for worse, English proficiency will continue to play an important part in the lives of EAL learners when they leave school. We believe a good starting point to address the uncertainty, if not outright scepticism, about multilingual pedagogies held by some decision-makers, therefore, is to build on the few experimental studies we have reported above and put well-defined multilingual strategies to the test. There is no shortage of well-reasoned and creative approaches to incorporating multilingual learners' linguistic repertoires into their mainstream education with which this could be done (Celic & Seltzer, 2012; Chumak-Horbatsch, 2012; Hesson, Seltzer & Woodley, 2014; Espinosa, Ascenzi-Moreno & Vogel, 2016). All of these publications come with the promise of improved educational outcomes for EAL learners, but few have been robustly empirically evaluated. If it can be established that adopting multilingual pedagogies improves proficiency in the majority linguistic currency of our educational system, this would add important leverage in the hands of those advocating for this substantial minority group of learners.

In conclusion, the multilingual turn – and the enthusiasm with which it has been seized by advocates for multilingual learners – offers a practical and socially just framework for thinking about education in linguistically diverse contexts. If we are to build on the promise that was ignited in the 1970s, but which in important respects has failed to move much further forward in the years since, we must take seriously the need to complete the thought experiments, of which we have plenty, with real experiments, of which we have few.

84 Hamish Chalmers and Victoria Murphy

Relating the issues raised in this chapter to your own context:

1 What do you see as your role as it relates to the multilingualism in the communities you serve? Do you see it as your responsibility to foster multilingualism among your language learners or to concentrate exclusively on the target language?
2 What kinds of research would be most relevant to you in helping to inform your thinking around the wider pedagogical implications of adopting multilingual teaching approaches?

References

Bailey, E., & Marsden, E. (2017). Hundreds of languages are spoken in the UK, but this isn't always reflected in the classroom. *The Conversation*. Available at: https://theconversation.com/hundreds-of-languages-are-spoken-in-the-uk-but-this-isnt-always-reflected-in-the-classroom-82289 [Accessed 1 November 2020].

BBC (2020). *Windrush generation: Who are they and why are they facing problems?* Available at: https://www.bbc.co.uk/news/uk-43782241 [Accessed 13 October 2021].

Bialystok, E., Luk, G., & Kwan, E. (2005). Bilingualism, biliteracy, and learning to read: Interactions among languages and writing systems. *Scientific Studies of Reading*, 9, 43–61.

Bialystok, E., McBride-Chang, C., & Luk, G. (2005). Bilingualism, language proficiency, and learning to read in two writing systems. *Journal of Educational Psychology*, 97, 580–590.

Bourne, J. (2002). *Home languages in the literacy hour in the national literacy strategy: Supporting pupils learning English as an additional language.* London: DfES.

British Nationality Act (1948). Available at: https://www.legislation.gov.uk/ukpga/Geo6/11-12/56/enacted [Accessed 28 July 2020].

Campbell, D., & Stanley, J. (1963). *Experimental and quasi experimental designs for research.* Boston: Houghton Mifflin Co.

Carey, S. T., & Cummins, J. (1979). *English and French achievement of grade 5 children from English and mixed French-English home backgrounds attending the Edmonton separate school system English-French immersion program.* Report submitted to the Edmonton separate school system.

Celic, C., & Seltzer, K. (2012). *Translanguaging: A CUNY-NYSIEB guide for educators.* New York: CUNY-NYSIEB.

Chalmers, H. (2014). *Harnessing linguistic diversity in polylingual British curriculum schools. Do L1 mediated home learning tasks improve learning outcomes for bilingual children? A randomised trial.* Masters Dissertation. Oxford Brookes University. Available at: https://www.teachingenglish.org.uk/sites/teacheng/files/harnessing_linguistic_diversity_for_bc_v2.pdf [Accessed 3 February 2021].

Chalmers, H. (2019). *Leveraging the L1: The role of EAL learners' first language in their acquisition of English vocabulary.* Unpublished PhD Thesis. Oxford Brookes University. Available at: https://doi.org/10.24384/fhr0-jr57 [Accessed 4 February 2021].

Chuang, H.-K., Joshi, R. M., & Dixon, L. Q. (2011). Cross-language transfer of reading ability. *Journal of Literacy Research*, 44(1), 97–119.

Chumak-Horbatsch, R. (2012). *Linguistically appropriate practice.* Toronto: University of Toronto Press.

Codina Camó, A., & Pladevall Ballester, E. (2015). The effects of using L1 translation on young learners' foreign language vocabulary learning. *Elia*, 15, 109–134.

Cohen, A. D. (1974). The Culver City Spanish immersion program: The first two years. *The Modern Language Journal*, 58, 95–103.

Conteh, J., & Meier, G. (2014). *The multilingual turn in languages education: Opportunities and challenges.* Bristol: Multilingual Matters.

Conteh, J. (2018). Translanguaging. *ELT Journal*, 72(4), 445–447.

Costley, T. (2014). English as an additional language, policy and the teaching and learning of English in England. *Language and Education*, 28(3), 276–292.

Creese, A., & Blackledge, A. (2015). Translanguaging and identity in educational settings. *Annual Review of Applied Linguistics*, 35, 20–35.

Cummins, J. (1977). A comparison of reading achievement in Irish and English medium schools. In V. Greaney (ed.), *Studies in reading.* Dublin: Educational Co. of Ireland.

Cummins, J. (1979a). Linguistic interdependence and the educational development of bilingual children. *Review of Educational Research*, 49(2), 222–251.

Cummins, J. (1979b). Cognitive/academic language proficiency, linguistic interdependence, the optimum age question and some other matters. *Working Papers on Bilingualism*, 19, 198–205

Cummins, J. (1980). The construct of language proficiency in bilingual education. In J. E. Alatis (ed.), *Georgetown University Round Table on languages and linguistics 1980.* Washington, DC: Georgetown University Press, 81–103.

Cummins, J. (2000). *Language, power and pedagogy: Bilingual children in the crossfire.* Clevedon: Multilingual Matters.

Cummins, J. (2001). Bilingual children's mother tongue: Why is it important for education? *Sprogforum*, 7(19), 15–20.

Cummins, J. (2008). Teaching for transfer: Challenging the two solitudes assumption in bilingual education. In: N. H. Hornberger (ed.), *Encyclopedia of language and education.* Boston, MA: Springer. https://doi.org/10.1007/978-0-387-30424-3_116.

Cummins, J., Hu, S., Markus, P., & Montero, M. K. (2015). Identity texts and academic achievement: Connecting the dots in multilingual school contexts. *TESOL Quarterly*, 49(3), 555–581.

Cunningham, C. (2019). Terminological tussles: Taking issue with "EAL" and "languages other than English". *Power and Education*, 11(1), 121–128.

Darcy, N. T. (1953). A review of the literature on the effects of bilingualism upon the measurement of intelligence. *The Journal of Genetic Psychology*, 82, 21–57.

Department for Education (2019). *Schools, pupils and their characteristics.* Available at: https://assets.publishing.service.gov.uk/government/uploads/system/uploads/attachment_data/file/812539/Schools_Pupils_and_their_Characteristics_2019_Main_Text.pdf [Accessed 1 April 2020].

Department of Education (2010). *Newcomers.* Available at: https://www.education-ni.gov.uk/sites/default/files/publications/de/newcomer-guidelines-for-schools.pdf [Accessed 7 November 2020].

Duarte, J. (2016). Translanguaging in mainstream education: a sociocultural approach. *International Journal of Bilingual Education and Bilingualism*, 22(2), 150–164.

Early, M., & Cummins, J. (eds.). (2011). *Identity texts: The collaborative creation of power in multilingual schools.* Stoke-on-Trent: Trentham books.

Espinosa, C., Ascenzi-Moreno, L., & Vogel, S. (2016). *A translanguaging pedagogy for writing: A CUNY-NYSIEB guide for educators.* New York: CUNY-NYSIEB.

European Union (1992). Treaty on European Union (Consolidated Version), Treaty of Maastricht, 7 February 1992. *Official Journal of the European Communities*, C 325/5; 24 December 2002. Available at: https://www.refworld.org/docid/3ae6b39218.html [Accessed 29 October 2020].

Flores, N., & García, O. (2017). A critical review of bilingual education in the United States: From basements and pride to boutiques and profit. *Annual Review of Applied Linguistics*, 37, 14–29.

Forbes, K. (2019). Teaching for transfer between first and foreign language classroom contexts: Developing a framework for a strategy-based, cross-curricular approach to writing pedagogy. *Writing & Pedagogy*, 11, 101–126.

García, O. (2009). *Bilingual education in the 21st century: A global perspective.* Oxford: Wiley-Blackwell.

García, O. (2019). Decolonizing foreign, second, heritage and first languages: Implications for education. In: D. Macedo (ed.), *Decolonizing foreign language education.* New York: Routledge, 152–168.

García, O., & Wei, L. (2014). *Translanguaging: Language, bilingualism and education.* Basingstoke: Palgrave Macmillan.

Genesee, F. (1979). Acquisition of reading skills in immersion programs. *Foreign Language Annals*, 2(1), 71–77.

Genesee, F., & Hamayan, E. (1980). Individual differences in young second language learners. *Applied Psycholinguistics*, 1(1), 95–110.

Gibbons, P. (2009). *Multilingual learners' literacy and thinking.* Portsmouth, NH: Heinemann.

Greene, J. (1998). *A meta-analysis of the effectiveness of bilingual education.* Claremont, CA: Thomas Rivera Policy Institute.

Hesson, S., Seltzer, K., & Woodley, H. H. (2014). *Translanguaging in curriculum and instruction: A CUNY-NYSIEB guide for educators.* New York: CUNY-NYSIEB.

HM Government (2018). The UK's future skills-based immigration system. Available at: https://assets.publishing.service.gov.uk/government/uploads/system/uploads/attachment_data/file/766465/The-UKs-future-skills-based-immigration-system-print-ready.pdf [Accessed 31 October 2020].

Huennekens, M. E. (2013). *The cross-linguistic effects of dialogic reading on young English language learners.* Unpublished PhD Thesis. Virginia Commonwealth University, Virginia, USA.

Immigration Act (1971) c.77. Available at: https://www.legislation.gov.uk/ukpga/1971/77/enacted [Accessed 13 October 2021].

Kenner, C., Al-Azami, S., Gregory, E., & Ruby, M. (2008). Bilingual poetry: Expanding the cognitive and cultural dimensions of children's learning. *Literacy*, 42(2), 92–100.

Keung, Y.-C., & Ho, C. S.-H. (2009). Transfer of reading-related cognitive skills in learning to read Chinese (L1) and English (L2) among Chinese elementary school children. *Contemporary Educational Psychology*, 34, 103–112.

Kleyn, T., & García, O. (2019). Translanguaging as an act of transformation: Restructuring teaching and learning for emergent bilingual students. In: L. de Oliveira (ed.), *Handbook of TESOL in K-12.* Malden: Wiley, 69–82.

Lambert, W. E. (1981). Bilingualism: Its nature and significance. In: W. E. Lambert, C. E. Snow, B. A. Goldfield, A. U. Chamot, & S. R. Cahir (eds.), *Bilingual educational series 10: Faces and facets of bilingualism.* Washington DC: Centre for Applied Linguistics, 1–6.

Lambert, W. E., & Tucker, G. R. (1972). *Bilingual education of children: The St. Lambert experiment.* Rowley: Newbury House.

Lapkin, S., & Swain, M. (1977). The use of English and French cloze tests in a bilingual education program evaluation: Validity and error analysis. *Language Learning*, 27, 279–310.

Lee, J. H., & Macaro, E. (2013). Investigating age in the use of L1 or English-only instruction: Vocabulary acquisition by Korean EFL learners. *The Modern Language Journal*, 97(4), 887–901.

Levine, J. (1996). Voices of the newcomers. In: M. Meek (ed.), *Developing pedagogies in the multilingual classroom: The writing of Josie Levine*. Staffordshire: Trentham Books, 11–24.

Lugo-Neris, M. J., Jackson, C. W., & Goldstein, H. (2010). Facilitating vocabulary acquisition of young English language learners. *Language, Speech, and Hearing Services in Schools*, 41, 314–317.

Macaro, E. (2018). *English medium instruction*. Oxford: OUP.

Major, J. (2018). Bilingual identities in monolingual classrooms: Challenging the hegemony of English. *New Zealand Journal of Educational Studies*, 53, 193–208.

May, S. (2014). *The multilingual turn: Implications for SLA, TESOL and bilingual education*. New York: Routledge.

McField, G. (2002). *Does program quality matter? A meta-analysis of select bilingual education studies*. Unpublished PhD Thesis, University of Southern California. Available at: http://digitallibrary.usc.edu/cdm/ref/collection/p15799coll16/id/255011 [Accessed 4 February 2021].

Melby-Lervåg, M., & Lervåg, A. (2011). Cross-linguistic transfer of oral language, decoding, phonological awareness and reading comprehension: A meta-analysis of the correlational evidence. *Journal of Research in Reading*, 34(1), 114–135.

Meredith, R. (2018). Ninety first languages spoken in NI schools. *BBC News*. Available at: https://www.bbc.co.uk/news/uk-northern-ireland-43211979 [Accessed 1 November 2020].

Murphy, V. A. (in press). Myths and misconceptions in bilingual language development. In: H. Chalmers (ed.), *The researchED guide to English as an additional language: An evidence-informed guide for teachers*. Woodbridge: John Catt Educational.

NALDIC (2019). Translanguaging. *EAL Journal*, 8, Spring 2019.

Oller, J. (1978). The language factor in the evaluation of bilingual education. In: J. Alatis (ed.), *Georgetown University Round Table on languages and learning 1978 international dimensions of bilingual education*. Washington, DC: Georgetown University Press.

Parke, T., Drury, R., Kenner, C., & Robertson, L. H. (2002). Revealing invisible worlds: Connecting the mainstream with bilingual children's home and community learning. *Journal of Early Childhood Literacy*, 2(2), 195–220.

Preevo, M., Malda, M., Mesman, J., & van IJzendoorn, M. (2016). Within- and cross-language relations between oral language proficiency and school outcomes in bilingual children with an immigrant background: A meta-analytical study. *Review of Educational Research*, 86(1), 237–276.

Reljić, G., Ferring, D., & Martin, R. (2015). A meta-analysis on the effectiveness of bilingual programs in Europe. *Review of Educational Research*, 85(1), 92–128.

Rolstad, K., Mahoney, K., & Glass, G. V. (2005). The big picture: A meta-analysis of program effectiveness research on English language learners. *Educational Policy*, 19(4), 572–594.

Sánchez, L. Z. (2004). *Effects of parent participation using first language curriculum materials on the English reading achievement and second-language acquisition of Hispanic students*. Unpublished PhD Thesis. Lehigh University, Pennsylvania, USA.

Scott, V. M., & de la Fuente, M. J. (2008). What's the problem? Use of the L1 consciousness-raising, L2 learners. *The Modern Language Journal*, 92(1), 100–113.

88 Hamish Chalmers and Victoria Murphy

Scottish Government (2020). *Pupil census: Supplementary statistics*. Available at: https://www.gov.scot/publications/pupil-census-supplementary-statistics/ [Accessed 31 October 2020].

Sieh, Y.-C. (2008). A possible role for the first language in young learners' processing and storage of foreign language vocabulary. *Annual Review of Education, Communication, and Language Sciences*, 5, 136–160.

Slavin, R. E., & Cheung, A. (2005). A synthesis of research on language of reading instruction for English language learners. *Review of Educational Research*, 75(2), 247–284.

StatsWales (2020). *Pupils in nursery, primary, middle and secondary schools acquiring English as an additional language by local authority and stage of development*. Available at: https://statswales.gov.wales/Catalogue/Education-and-Skills/Schools-and-Teachers/Schools-Census/Pupil-Level-Annual-School-Census/Ethnicity-National-Identity-and-Language/pupilsacquiringenglishasadditionallanguage-by-localauthorityregion-stagedevelopment [Accessed 31 October 2020].

Stubbs, M. (1985). *The other languages of England. Linguistic minorities project*. London: Routledge & Kegan Paul.

Swain, M. (1975). Writing skills of grade three French immersion pupils. *Working Papers on Bilingualism*, 7, 1–41.

Swain, M., & Lapkin, S. (2000). Task-based second language learning: The uses of the first language. *Language Teaching Research*, 4(3), 251–274.

Swain, M., Lapkin, S., & Barik, H. C. (1976). The cloze test as a measure of second language proficiency for young children. *Working Papers on Bilingualism*, 11, 32–42.

Taft, R., & Bodi, M. (1980). A study of language competence and first language maintenance in bilingual children. *International Review of Applied Psychology*, 29(1–2), 173–182.

TES (2018). Why using the term EAL can be reckless. *Times Educational Supplement*, 16 May 2018. Available at: https://www.tes.com/news/why-using-term-eal-can-be-reckless [Accessed 1 November 2020].

Thomas, R., & Mady, C. (2014). Teaching for transfer: insights from theory and practices in primary-level French-second-language classrooms. *McGill Journal of Education*, 49(2), 399–416.

Tonzar, C., Lotto, L., & Job, R. (2009). L2 vocabulary acquisition in children: Effects of learning method and cognate status. *Language Learning*, 59(3), 623–646.

Vargas-Silva, C., & Walsh, P. W. (2020). *EU Migration to and from the UK*. Migration Observatory briefing, COMPAS, University of Oxford. Available at: https://migrationobservatory.ox.ac.uk/wp-content/uploads/2020/10/Briefing-EU-Migration-to-and-from-the-UK.pdf [Accessed 29 October 2020].

Walters, K., & Gunderson, L. (1985). Effects of parent volunteers reading first language (L1) books to ESL students. *The Reading Teacher*, 39(1), 66–69.

Wang, M., Cheng, C., & Chen, S.-W. (2006). Contribution of morphological awareness to Chinese–English biliteracy acquisition. *Journal of Educational Psychology*, 98, 542–553.

Wang, M., Perfetti, C. A., & Liu, Y. (2005). Chinese–English biliteracy acquisition: Cross-language and writing system transfer. *Cognition*, 97, 67–88.

Wei, L. (2018). Translanguaging as a practical theory of language. *Applied Linguistics*, 39(1), 9–30.

Willig, A. C. (1985). A meta-analysis of selected studies on the effectiveness of bilingual education. *Review of Educational Research*, 55(3), 269–317.

Yiakoumetti, A. (2006). A bidialectal programme for the learning of standard modern Greek in Cyprus. *Applied Linguistics*, 27(2), 295–317.

5 Learning language by studying content

David Lasagabaster

Introduction

The burgeoning number of content and language integrated learning (CLIL) and English-medium instruction (EMI) courses and programmes epitomizes the crave for English learning throughout the world. The spread of such programmes is based on the belief that, by teaching content in English in school or university settings where English is not the L1 of most students, their foreign language proficiency will improve significantly.

Since the vast majority of EMI programmes do not contemplate language learning objectives and many EMI university teachers staunchly believe that language learning falls outside their remit, in this chapter, I will distinguish between CLIL (the most frequent label at pre-university level) and EMI (typically used at tertiary level). Although it is widely believed that both CLIL and EMI have a positive impact on students' English development, many questions still remain unanswered. In this chapter, I will try to tackle some of the most recurrent questions in the field, including the following: Has English as a foreign language (EFL) failed or does it just complement CLIL/EMI? Is the teaching of content through English the best way forward? Does students' English proficiency really improve as a result of teaching content in English? If so, do all language skills benefit to the same extent? Who should be responsible for teaching language through content?

Although the results analyzed in the review of the literature carried out in this chapter are *grosso modo* applicable to any other foreign language, I will focus on English for two main reasons. Firstly, because globally it is the most widely learned foreign language (Crystal, 2019; see also Di Sabato and Fitzpatrick, this volume) and, secondly, because a large proportion of content-based courses taught in a foreign language are in English (Doiz, Lasagabaster and Sierra, 2012; Hu, Li and Lei, 2014; Murata, 2019). Interestingly the first few content and language integrated learning (CLIL) programmes in Germany in the 1960s were in French. This remained the main target language for 20 years before English took over in the early 1990s, becoming the most popular CLIL language by far (Rumlich, 2016). This development parallels what has happened in many other countries. However, my review of the CLIL literature will mainly

DOI: 10.4324/9781003008361-7

90 *David Lasagabaster*

revolve around the European context, not only due to the fact that the acronym CLIL was coined by a group of European experts and it was rapidly adopted in the European context but also due to space constraints.

Defining CLIL

In this chapter, I distinguish between CLIL and EMI on the grounds that, whereas integration of content and language teaching is one of the main features of CLIL programmes at pre-university level, EMI is the label habitually used at university level, as EMI programmes do not usually include any language objectives and actual integration is rare in university classes (Costa, 2012; Lasagabaster, 2018). Whereas one of the main teaching principles of CLIL is that language and content have to be taught in an integrated manner, this tenet is alien to university EMI in the vast majority of contexts and pedagogical practices tend not to aim at such integration. In addition, at university level, English proficiency is regarded as a prerequisite rather than an expected learning outcome (Dafouz, Camacho and Urquia, 2014), which is why English language teaching plays second fiddle or is simply ignored in most EMI courses. Conversely, at pre-university level, English proficiency is far from taken for granted. It has nevertheless to be acknowledged that the term CLIL is vague and realized in different forms (in terms of age of onset, school subjects involved, explicit objectives and intensity, to name but a few), and this is so not only across diverse countries but even within the same local context.

A side-effect of the overwhelming role of English as the current main *lingua franca* is reflected in the burgeoning number of CLIL and EMI courses and programmes all over the world. With this global trend in mind, Macaro (2018: 290), among many others, wonders why countries decide to switch from mother-tongue instruction to foreign language instruction. The main reason may lie in the fact that the desire to improve English proficiency has led the boards of many educational institutions to embrace CLIL/EMI in the belief that it is the best solution to overcome a linguistic deficit in the foreign language, while content learning and – also importantly – L1 development are not negatively affected. Since EFL (English as a foreign language) classes seem not to ensure high proficiency due to the limited exposure to English (in many education systems, exposure amounts to just three or four hours per week), CLIL and EMI programmes allow more time to be devoted to English without taking up additional time in an already overcrowded curriculum.

But has EFL failed? And should EFL complement CLIL/EMI?

One of the most prevailing courses of action in order to improve learners' foreign language proficiency has consisted in starting its teaching ever earlier, to the extent that many schools start teaching it as early as grade 1. This early teaching is based on the common assumption that *the younger the better*. However,

Muñoz and Singleton (2011: 2; see also Pfenninger and Singleton, this volume) claim that "insufficient attention has been paid to a range of other potentially important factors, such as amount and quality of input, learners' orientations and attitudes, and the specific conditions under which the L2 is encountered."

In Canada, Netten and Germain (2004) analyzed traditional French as a foreign language teaching (core French) and concluded that the limited hours of instruction per week in a non-intensive time distribution proved ineffective. In fact, these authors point out that studies carried out in their context found that only 23% of the time in core French classes was spent on teaching communication, as most of the time was devoted to formal language study, while teachers were prone to closely following teaching materials. The authors considered that the main factor responsible for the low French proficiency reached by the end of compulsory education was the lack of sufficient time, as students usually spent overall only 1000 hours from grade 4 to grade 12 in short periods of about 40 minutes in length. Netten and Germain claimed that learning to communicate requires large amounts of authentic language use and this is hard to achieve in a few short sessions per week.

In Spain, many schools teach English from the age of six onwards and some even in infant education, when learners are as young as 3–5 years old. Nevertheless, studies reveal that this early introduction does not produce better results because the "opportunities for implicit learning and practice are minimal" due to limited exposure (Muñoz, 2006: 33). Older learners are usually quicker when it comes to acquiring declarative knowledge or explicit learning and tend to outstrip younger learners when both groups are compared after the same hours of instruction. When it comes to ultimate attainment (understood here as the English proficiency level obtained at the end of the L2 acquisition process at school), "the proficiency levels attained are known to fall very short of native-like proficiency" (Muñoz, 2008: 580). Even if some readers may not feel comfortable with the use of native-like proficiency as a benchmark, ultimate attainment remains unsatisfactory after so many years of formal instruction of the foreign language. The main reason for these discouraging results lies in the fact that the optimal learning conditions are not met because in the vast majority of foreign language learning contexts, the input is neither quantitatively nor qualitatively rich enough, and the learning experience is less intensive than in naturalistic language settings.

What is more, when early starters have had greater exposure, they have not shown a significant advantage over later starters (Muñoz, 2008). In contrast, late immersion students have significantly outperformed early immersion students, which has been attributed to the massive amount of exposure to which the former are exposed in an intensive manner. In a similar vein, CLIL/EMI should provide a teaching situation in which the greater presence of the foreign language in the curriculum will allow and foster the development of communicative skills (mainly receptive skills), an approach that stems from the positive results obtained in immersion programmes in different parts of the world (Tedick and Cammarata, 2012).

92   *David Lasagabaster*

Although some authors (Bruton, 2019; Dallinger et al., 2016) propose that an increase in the number of EFL classes might be as effective as CLIL implementation with regards to foreign language learning, the fact is that in most curricula, the possibility of including more EFL classes is simply not viable. Even if this possibility were ever envisaged, it would entail reducing the time given to the rest of the curriculum – highly controversial, as it is unlikely that other subject teachers would embrace the idea of having their class hours cut. Cenoz (2013: 392) asserts that "there is no reason to believe that learning content matter through the foreign language produces better results than having the same amount of instruction in foreign language classes." Although she may be right, it is simply unrealistic to think of a context in which foreign language classes can be increased at the expense of the other school subjects.

It, therefore, seems that the only reasonable and feasible way to increase the presence of the foreign language is by spreading CLIL/EMI in the curriculum, which led Graddol (2006) to forecast that CLIL/EMI may end up replacing EFL. According to Graddol, English teachers will eventually lose their subject and will carry out other tasks such as a support or remedial role. However, as Hüttner and Smit (2014: 162) cogently point out, "In compulsory education, where CLIL in Europe mostly takes place, there would be an uproar if students in state schools were supposed to learn content through a foreign language without any specific provision in that language." Therefore, in European educational systems, CLIL plus foreign language lessons (mostly English) is the main option by default and, in fact, to my knowledge, there is no European country where the introduction of CLIL in primary or secondary education has brought about the elimination of the foreign language class. Similarly, at university level, ESP (English for specific purposes) and EAP (English for academic purposes) courses are deemed to play a paramount role when it comes to supporting students "with the English language needs for disciplinary study" (Basturkmen, 2019: 319). Therefore, EFL and ESP/EAP are regarded as a basic complement to underpin CLIL and EMI across the board.

Is CLIL effective when it comes to language learning?

Advocates of CLIL tend to present a plethora of reasons to underpin their belief that this approach provides an enriching learning context that will eventually produce more competent English language speakers. The following are some of the arguments habitually highlighted in CLIL literature:

- Input is enhanced because the amount is substantially increased in CLIL settings. Moreover, the input is more meaningful (they are encouraged to use the foreign language due to the predominant focus on meaning), authentic (established by the content subject's curriculum), and richer (it triggers a deeper level and cognitively more demanding processing of semantic meaning).
- It helps to boost the affective parameter, as students will feel more motivated by using this innovative approach.

Learning language by studying content 93

- Students will learn not only general English but also the specific language of different disciplines, which will be very useful in their future academic and professional careers.
- It will foster intercultural communication and students will become better at communication across different cultures and social groups.
- It is an approach in which product and process orientations are foregrounded through task- and project-based teaching.
- It promotes implicit learning since classes are focused on meaning and communication rather than on discrete grammatical items for their own sake.
- It strengthens not only the teacher-student interaction but also the student-student interaction and communication in the foreign language.
- It will foster internationalization, a buzzword in education which entails the need to be fluent at least in one foreign language.
- And last but not least, and as a result of the combination of all the previous benefits, CLIL will help to improve foreign language competence, especially students' speaking ability, one of the language skills most often neglected in many diverse education systems.

Despite all the virtues extolled above, the answer to the question put forward in the title of this section is anything but straightforward once the empirical evidence available so far is taken into account. In fact, two opposing visions are found in the literature: one which corroborates CLIL's linguistic benefits, and another which warns that the data available is far from conclusive.

On the one hand, some authors consider that CLIL/EMI students do benefit in the case of some particular language skills, but not all. In their review articles, Dalton-Puffer (2011) and Pérez-Cañado (2012) underscore that CLIL students are better in some language areas, while others seem not to benefit from the CLIL approach. Pérez-Cañado (2012: 329–330) summarizes these results as follows:

> The positive effect is felt on global communicative competence, on receptive skills, speaking (greater fluency is displayed), morphology (with increased automatization and appropriacy of use being found), vocabulary (particularly technical and semi-technical terms), writing (fluency and lexical and syntactic complexity), creativity, risk-taking, and emotive/affective outcomes (learner motivation) [...] However, pronunciation, syntax, writing (accuracy and discourse skills), informal and nontechnical language, and pragmatics remain largely unaffected, perhaps owing to an insufficient focus on form in CLIL classrooms.

On the other hand, some authors are critical about the idyllic picture portrayed in the CLIL literature. In this vein, Macaro (2018: 293) states that "the research evidence to date is remarkably flimsy"; Rumlich (2016: 243) concludes that "The only thing we know empirically about the effects of CLIL is that we do not know a lot"; and Dallinger et al. (2016: 30) go even further and affirm that "the question arises why one should introduce CLIL at all, given its null-effect on

94 David Lasagabaster

the content subject and the limited positive outcomes in English." These authors also claim that whenever CLIL students outscore their non-CLIL counterparts, causation is not evident, that is, that CLIL *per se* may not be the reason for the former's better linguistic performance.

The reasons that lie behind the critical perspectives of the second group of authors are varied but could mainly be due to the following factors. Firstly, it has to be noted that CLIL is usually implemented alongside EFL classes, which brings about a greater exposure to English than that of their EFL counterparts. Secondly, some authors have also warned that CLIL groups are sometimes made up of students who are more motivated, as pioneering groups often included highly motivated students and teachers (Admiraal, Westhoff and de Bot, 2006). Besides, the label *elitism* is often associated with the approach (Pérez-Cañado, 2019). Thirdly, some other researchers have claimed that CLIL students were already more proficient in English before joining CLIL groups, an initial significant difference that has not been adequately controlled in some studies. Fourthly, too many studies have been based on the participants' perceptions rather than on actual measurements, and the former should always be analyzed with caution. All these factors (to a greater or lesser degree) would be held responsible for higher achievement in the foreign language on the part of CLIL students, but at the same time, they cast doubt about the real impact of CLIL.

Since some of the studies included in the aforementioned two review articles (Dalton-Puffer, 2011 and Pérez-Cañado, 2012) have come in for criticism on methodological grounds, due to the lack of control at baseline or *a priori* between-groups differences, my review will focus on only a few studies that have controlled for such differences and which include large samples within a longitudinal research design.

Particular attention will be paid to Rumlich's (2016) study due to its methodological thoroughness and the large sample involved. Following a multivariate approach that incorporated cognitive, affective-motivational, and additional individual variables, Rumlich scrutinized the performance of almost a thousand students over a two-year period to examine, among other things, the impact of CLIL on English proficiency. In his study, CLIL and regular students progressed quite similarly and the results revealed that time had a significant effect but on both groups. In fact, English proficiency improved over the two-year period but no statistically significant interaction was found between the variables time and group. However, Rumlich's study relied on a written text and, therefore, other skills such as speaking and listening that may benefit from CLIL were not considered. This could partially explain why, despite the fact that the CLIL students participating in Rumlich's study represented a selected group with a higher self-concept that had moreover received one additional school year of EFL teaching, their results did not reveal any benefit on English proficiency.

In a very recent study, Pérez Cañado (2019) tried to test whether some of the main qualms about CLIL could be confirmed or refuted by means of data gathered in Spain. The participants were 2042 primary education and secondary education students from 12 different Spanish provinces. The author controlled the three variables which are usually held responsible for CLIL groups' better results and associated with CLIL's purported elitism, namely English language grades, motivation, and verbal intelligence. She also controlled the impact of three other variables: socioeconomic status (SES), rural versus urban school setting, and type of school (public, private, or charter). On these variables, CLIL and non-CLIL groups were found to be comparable in the vast majority of cases. One of the reasons for this is that in Spain many schools do not carry out any selective process and implement the CLIL approach to all the students in the school (some schools do not have non-CLIL parallel groups). The results showed the following: (1) CLIL students obtained better English results irrespective of the type of school; (2) SES affected primary education and secondary educations students' results, but both in the case of CLIL and non-CLIL groups; (3) the usual rural/urban divide was mitigated by CLIL, as this contextual variable had a more substantial effect in non-bilingual schools; and (4) CLIL succeeded in a school located in a disadvantaged context, although a caveat must be acknowledged because the study was limited to this single non-elite school. With these results in mind, the author claims that the use of the label 'elitism' to refer to CLIL experiences needs to be questioned.

Apart from the opposite results obtained in these two large-scale studies that controlled for some key variables, other studies have also produced contradictory results. In the group of studies that indicate that CLIL does not always yield positive linguistic effects, Roquet and Pérez-Vidal (2017) compared a group following an EFL approach with a CLIL group in secondary education with regards to their writing skills and found no significant difference (in accordance with Rumlich, 2016). Students' compositions were assessed twice over on academic year for complexity, accuracy, and fluency (quantitatively) and for task fulfilment, organization, grammar, and vocabulary (qualitatively). Both groups improved by the end of the study, but the only significant results were found in accuracy. Nor did Pladevall-Ballester and Vallbona (2016) find significant differences in reading skills among primary education students in what the authors label as a minimal input context (an additional CLIL hour per week). The participants took a language test at four different times during two academic years, while exposure to English was kept the same in both groups. Unexpectedly, the non-CLIL group outscored the CLIL group in listening skills, which led the authors to conclude that more intensive exposure may be needed for CLIL benefits to bloom in the long run.

After controlling for a range of student, classroom, and teacher features, Dallinger et al. (2016) found that CLIL significantly increased listening comprehension among more than 1800 German secondary school students. The authors conducted their longitudinal study with two measurement stages at the beginning and at the end of bilingual History instruction in grade 8. General English skills were measured via a C-test following a holistic approach which consisted of 159 gaps/items distributed over seven subtexts. The differences also increased regarding the general English skills between time 1 and time 2, but "once differences in prior achievement at the beginning of Grade 8 were

96 *David Lasagabaster*

considered (Model 2), the CLIL-advantage was substantially reduced and became statistically insignificant" (Dallinger et al., 2016: 28). The other language skills (reading, writing, and speaking) were not measured in this large-scale study. However, as the authors themselves acknowledge, it is important to investigate the other language skills, for the C-test may fall short when it comes to gauging the whole linguistic repertoire of CLIL students. This is a limitation of the three aforementioned studies (Dallinger et al., 2016; Pladevall-Ballester and Vallbona, 2016; Roquet and Pérez-Vidal, 2017), as they all measured a single language skill.

On another note, results such as those obtained by Rumlich (2016) bring to the fore the question of CLIL programmes' intensity. In a study carried out in Spain with 157 students, Somers and Llinares (2021) observed that low-intensity students were less motivated both intrinsically and instrumentally, not only due to the fewer CLIL subjects (6 hours per week versus 13 hours per week for the high-intensity groups) but also because the subjects were "less academically inclined" (p. 11): Arts, Physical education, Musical education for low-intensity groups versus Biology and Geology, History and Geography or Technology for the high-intensity participants. This greater motivation may also help to explain the results obtained by Merino and Lasagabaster (2018). These authors conducted a longitudinal study spanning one year in which almost 400 secondary education students enrolled in three different programmes: A non-CLIL group (exposed to English in 11.3% of the curriculum), a CLIL group with 3.4 CLIL sessions per week (22.5% exposure), and a CLIL group with an average of 8.4 CLIL sessions per week (41% exposure). The results indicated that there were no significant differences between the non-CLIL group and the low-intensity CLIL group (the improvement of both groups was similar once the initial differences were considered), which leads the authors to conclude that CLIL seems to exert a significant impact on foreign language proficiency only when it is part of a high-intensity programme, as these students outperformed the other two groups.

Last but not least, it is also worth mentioning that few studies have compared CLIL and non-CLIL groups with the same amount of exposure to the foreign language by equating the number of hours of exposure to English (CLIL learners being therefore younger than the non-CLIL counterparts). One was carried out by Gené-Gil, Juan-Garau and Salazar-Noguera (2015), who focused only on writing skills. They observed that non-CLIL students progressed significantly more in lexical complexity, but CLIL students obtained higher scores overall. However, Olsson (2015) analyzed four written assignments over three years, finding that CLIL and non-CLIL groups did not show any significant difference. The author put this down to the lack of attention to general academic vocabulary (the author distinguishes between domain-specific vocabulary used in different disciplines and general academic vocabulary). Since both studies controlled for between-group comparability, these results only make interpreting the available research more complex.

The conclusion is that we cannot yet draw clear-cut conclusions regarding CLIL's effectiveness with regard to foreign language learning. This is due to a lack of information regarding some of CLIL's important features and the diversity of contexts where research has been undertaken and analyzed. We may be able to glean more from the teaching strategies and practices used in different contexts. However, we will leave that for the discussion section. Let us focus now on tertiary education.

Is EMI effective when it comes to language learning?

It is worth noting that much of the research hitherto undertaken at the tertiary level is based on students' and teachers' beliefs and perceptions (Doiz, Lasagabaster and Sierra, 2011, 2014; Jensen and Thøgersen, 2011: Kirkgöz, 2009), but beliefs do not always match reality. In fact, research reveals that students' own assessment of their language proficiency is not always reliable, as they tend to have a "higher perception of their English skills than objective assessment shows" (Hernández-Nanclares and Jiménez-Munoz, 2017).

If the number of cogently designed studies aimed at measuring the development of English proficiency at pre-university level is limited, research at university level is even scarcer, which is why, in this section, the review will not be limited to the European context. Nonetheless, some studies found in our review have been discarded because they were based on holistic impressions and did not consider whether the differences between groups were statistically significant (Bosisio, 2015), or because they were exploratory in nature and relied on small samples (Tai, 2015). Although these discarded studies present pertinent experiences and bring to light interesting analyses (Rubio-Alcalá et al., 2019), their research designs and/or lack of statistical analyses prevent us from including them in this review.

The studies completed in higher education can be divided into two main groups: those that focus on specific language skills and those that measure general English proficiency.

In the first group, Aguilar and Muñoz (2014) focused on grammar and listening through within-group comparisons in the Spanish context. The participants were 63 engineering students enrolled in seven different courses for one semester (60 hours). The authors underscore that there was no CLIL methodological adaptation. After a semester, only the pre- and post-listening test differences were statistically significant (with a small effect size). After distributing students into three proficiency groups, the researchers observed that only the students with the lowest level of proficiency (elementary level or Oxford Placement Test Band 3) improved significantly in both tests, whereas the higher proficiency students (OPT Band 6) showed no gain and even obtained worse results in the grammar post-test.

Chostelidou and Griva (2014) focused on the development of 270 Greek accountancy students' reading skills in L2 English. An experimental syllabus and specially designed materials were developed for the EMI group, while the non-EMI group only received EFL classes. No between-groups baseline differences were observed at the pre-test stage. After one academic semester,

98 David Lasagabaster

and although both groups made significant progress in terms of reading skills, the post-intervention measurement revealed a statistically significant greater improvement on the part of the EMI group, whose exposure to English had been greater due to the implementation of the experimental syllabus.

In a study conducted in Taiwan with 638 undergraduates, Chou (2018) compared full EMI and partial EMI students' speaking development over a semester. The potential bias of self-selection was minimized because all participants were required to take EMI courses at the four universities under scrutiny, and the author ensured that their command of English was similar before starting EMI. The speaking scores by the end of the semester showed significant differences (medium effect size; eta squared = .06) in favour of the full EMI students since they had more opportunities to communicate in English, while they also reported less speech anxiety, greater confidence in speaking, and more positive feelings towards EMI courses. It would have been interesting if the study had also compared non-EMI students.

As for the second group of studies, Rogier (2012) conducted a study in the United Arab Emirates with a view to measuring longitudinally whether general English proficiency tested by the IELTS exam improved after a four-year EMI undergraduate programme. The primary (i.e. main) participants were 59 female Emirati students, but the author also compared the results of 327 students from different degree courses (secondary participants). Rogier observed a significant score gain in the four language skills of the primary participants, but this was especially so in speaking, followed by reading, writing, and then listening. However, students were expected to graduate with a 6.0 IELTS score but they only improved half a band on average (5.5 IELTS). Therefore, there was an improvement but it was "minimal" (p. 84) after four years. In the case of the secondary participants, the percentage of students who did not reach 6.0 IELTS was as follows: reading (65%), writing (51%), listening (48%), and speaking (14%). Therefore, in the case of the larger sample, speaking was also the skill that benefitted most from EMI. Since the IELTS exam plays a key role in this study (and in all the analyses made in this institution) and the faculty of the programme wondered whether the test is adequate to measure the language used in the classroom. in the discussion section the impact of exams on language proficiency measurement will be considered. Because of these poor results, the institution has decided to put into action a pilot programme to provide students with extra support from specially trained language teachers.

In the Chinese context, Lei and Hu (2014) compared EMI and non-EMI students. The participants were 136 Business Administration undergraduates enrolled in EMI and Chinese-medium programmes. Both groups took college English classes and initial English tests showed no differences between EMI and non-EMI students. English proficiency was measured via the national standardized College English Test Band 6, a test designed for students who major in any specialization other than English. By the time EMI students took the English test, they had received one-year EMI courses (2–3 EMI courses per semester). The test consists of four sections: listening, reading, error correction, writing/translation. The results revealed no differences between the EMI and non-EMI groups, but nor did EMI students hold more positive attitudes towards English or feel less anxious when speaking English. Based on interviews with the participants, Lei and Hu (2014: 119) warn that the EMI programme was "inefficient in important ways" and highlight the faculty members' inadequate command of English and the "poor pedagogical strategies adopted to cope with language difficulties," among others.

In Taiwan, Yang (2015) measured EMI students' language development in the four skills by means of a national general English proficiency test. The sample consisted of only 29 EMI students enrolled in an international tourism programme at a national polytechnic university. The programme was entirely taught in English except for Chinese language and general education courses. The pre- and post-General English tests, which included the four language skills, were completed after two years on the programme. Interestingly, high achievers in the pre-test still outperformed their classmates in the post-test, unlike in Aguilar and Muñoz's study (2014). As was also the case in the previous study by Rogier (2012), Yang had no comparison group to rely on within the same institution. However, the author compared the results obtained by the EMI participants in his study with those of non-EMI universities in national level measurements and found that the former outscored the latter in the receptive skills but not in the productive ones (p. 369). The reasons adduced are that the EMI courses (CLIL is the label used by the author, but no integration is mentioned) are lecture-based and that students have no opportunity to practice their productive skills.

In Spain, Hernández-Nanclares and Jiménez-Munoz (2017) reported a study conducted in BA in Business Administration during two semesters (one EMI subject per semester). In this EMI programme, a Spanish content teacher collaborated with a native language expert and a linguist and teacher trainer with extensive CLIL experience. The 172 EMI students self-assessed their English competence in the four language skills, which was then compared with objective assessment. Whereas subjective results showed a clear improvement in all skills, objective results offered a less optimistic view and gave EMI students half a CEFR (Common European Framework of Reference) level less than their perceptions. However, the objective measures at the beginning and at the end of the year did show a significant improvement in reading (from B2.1 to C2.1), writing, listening, and speaking (from B1.1 to B2.1 in the latter three). Therefore, collaboration between content and language experts seems to exert a very positive influence on students' English proficiency, in accordance with studies undertaken at pre-university level (San Isidro and Lasagabaster, 2019).

Discussion

It is widely believed that the sooner students start learning English, the better their proficiency will eventually become. However, this will only take place if they have massive exposure to the target language, something unattainable in foreign language classes because they are typically limited to a few small doses

100 David Lasagabaster

per week (Muñoz, 2008; Muñoz and Singleton, 2011). That is why CLIL advocates claim that this approach will enhance students' motivation and foreign language learning since exposure to the target language will be substantially increased and more meaningful. However, some other authors are not so optimistic and even criticize the "overabundance of reasons brought forth mainly in contrast to the language learning setting in regular EFL classes" (Rumlich, 2016: 162). The latter usually take for granted that CLIL students are selected and this is the main reason for the positive results obtained in some contexts and for an overestimation of CLIL-related linguistic benefits. However, recent studies (Pérez-Cañado, 2019) have also shown that this selection process does not always take place and that CLIL really can boost foreign language learning. It can thus be concluded that CLIL results are contradictory, which has sparked much debate in the last few years among researchers in the field, the main reason being that longitudinal research on CLIL is limited and – making interpretation more complex – conflicting and inconsistent.

The review of the literature in this chapter has brought to light that more methodologically sound research on the impact of CLIL/EMI programmes on English proficiency is sorely needed. One of the major shortcomings of the studies undertaken so far has to do with the lack of longitudinal studies that control for potential initial hidden differences between the CLIL and the non-CLIL groups. But we need to go a step further and delve into the teaching and pedagogical practices implemented in CLIL and EMI programmes, as this may be one of the main reasons underlying the conflicting results found in the literature.

The aforementioned surprising results obtained by Rumlich (2016) are worth considering. Since his CLIL participants had not only a higher self-concept but had also received one additional school year of EFL teaching but still did not outperform their non-CLIL counterparts, it seems that methodology and the integration of content and language are a key question to which more attention should have been paid. One possible explanation for the unexpected results obtained by Rumlich could be found in the lack of actual integration on the part of content teachers. Unfortunately, rarely do studies provide a description of how pedagogy was actually being integrated. The mere implementation of CLIL seems not to yield the expected results and pedagogical considerations should come to the fore. It is striking that pre-selected students who have been exposed to a larger amount of input in English do not outperform their non-CLIL counterparts. This is an issue that undoubtedly deserves further attention so that the causes for these counterintuitive results can be unearthed.

The evidence garnered in higher education EMI is also anything but definitive. In fact, in the seven studies detected in the literature where actual measurement of English was carried out, the results could not be more diverse. Lei and Hu (2014) found no differences, in Rogier (2012) EMI students improved in speaking, while in Yang (2015) they were better at receptive skills but not at the productive ones; in Chostelidou and Griva's (2014) study, EMI students scored higher in reading comprehension, in Aguilar and Muñoz's (2014) in listening and grammar but only in the case of those students with the lowest proficiency

Learning language by studying content 101

level, whereas in Hernández-Nanclares and Jiménez-Muñoz's (2017) EMI students obtained better results in all four language skills. In Chou's (2018) study, full EMI students outperformed partial EMI students in speaking. At first sight, these results seem to make it impossible to draw any cogent conclusion from the available empirical evidence, since not only is the number of studies limited but also the skills under consideration vary considerably from one study to another, which impedes any attempt to draw generalizable implications. However, a closer look at the studies indicates that three factors are to be considered: first, the intensity of the EMI experience; second, the pedagogical practices implemented in each context; and third, the tools used to measure language proficiency.

As for intensity, this review suggests that the benefits of EMI will only be reaped if longer periods of EMI implementation and higher intensity are considered. Immersion education results should be borne in mind, because, as we have seen, intensity is a key question. A single-subject taught in English during a semester cannot be expected to have such a significant impact. This would explain why only low-proficiency students benefitted from EMI in Aguilar and Muñoz's (2014) study. The impact of intensity can also be observed in Chou's (2018) results, as students receiving partial EMI exhibited higher speech anxiety, a greater lack of confidence, and more negative feelings towards EMI than their full EMI counterparts, whose speaking scores were significantly better. This also applies to CLIL studies on low-intensity programmes (e.g. Pladevall-Ballester and Vallbona, 2016). However, the higher intensity does not automatically produce significant improvement (Rogier, 2012), which leads us on to pedagogical practices.

As for pedagogical practices, some of the studies emphasize that teaching strategies were inefficient and poor (Lei and Hu, 2014). If this is the case, small wonder EMI does not yield positive results in some contexts. The collaboration between language and content teachers could help to bridge the content/language gap (Lasagabaster, 2018), as the results obtained by Hernández-Nanclares and Jiménez-Munoz (2017) seem to confirm. Although it is often taken for granted that just by teaching content in English, students' foreign language proficiency will improve, the studies reviewed above indicate that this is not always the case and that methodological adjustments have to be put into action if this objective is to be achieved.

University content teachers repeatedly claim that the teaching of language aspects does not fall within their remit, as they are not experts in the field (Lasagabaster, 2021). In fact, the EMI syllabus does not usually include any language goals and makes no reference to language skills (Airey 2012). Several authors (Lasagabaster, 2018; Lo, 2015) have highlighted a need to foster collaboration between language and content teachers, so that a counterbalanced approach can be bolstered (Llinares, Morton and Whittaker, 2012; Lyster, 2007), in which learners explicitly focus on features of the target language. Implementing a proactive approach could be a key factor, wherein explicit heed is paid to the development of language skills, in opposition to a reactive approach characterized by spontaneous and unplanned feedback on language issues (Lyster, 2007: 97).

102 *David Lasagabaster*

Nowadays, researchers concur that it is of paramount importance to integrate form-focused instruction into EMI/CLIL to enable students to notice non-salient language features.

At university level, EMI content teachers are willing to foster collaboration with their language expert colleagues, and so are EMI students (Lasagabaster, 2021). This collaboration would allow language-related objectives to be established (EMI programmes are currently characterized by their absence) and would have an impact on the quality of teaching. The responsibility to teach language should therefore be shared to a certain degree by content and language teachers, although the latter should pave the way for this symbiosis and take on the leading role.

Last but not least, a third question to bear in mind is that English tests are currently not tailored. If we are to measure CLIL/EMI's impact, we need to develop tests that measure the language skills that are fostered through this approach (Lei and Hu, 2014; Rogier, 2012; Swain, 2000). Subject-specific skills should therefore be considered, as most standardized language tests are usually too focused on linguistic knowledge and disregard more communicative abilities (such as giving a presentation on the propagation of a virus) that may benefit most from CLIL/EMI courses. Tedick and Cammarata (2012) also discuss this question and claim that some tasks are not appropriate for middle or high school learners and do not elicit the academic language that better distinguishes CLIL from non-CLIL groups.

Conclusion

The upward pressure due to the popularity of CLIL in secondary education requires the design of international studies in which EMI programmes in diverse settings are compared. In the next few years, an increasing number of CLIL students will be reaching university and they will more than likely demand courses delivered in English. Empirical evidence is therefore necessary in order to make decisions about how such courses can be best implemented.

CLIL/EMI-related foreign language learning advantages need to be confirmed, because otherwise the adequacy of its implementation will be put into doubt. After the promising results of early experiences (Dalton-Puffer, 2011; Pérez-Cañado, 2012), it is time for English medium instruction at pre-university level to be solidly underpinned by cogent empirical studies that help to dispel the doubts raised during the last decade. Obviously, this also applies to higher education.

Future research should include a more detailed description of CLIL/EMI programmes, so that comparisons can later be made, but also closer examination of the teaching and pedagogy displayed in each context. Although instruction in English potentially provides students with more opportunities to benefit from greater contact with the foreign language, it is the actual teaching practice that guarantees meaningful exposure and opportunities for students' relevant and substantial language practice.

Relating the issues raised in this chapter to your own context:

1 Do EMI content teachers pay attention to language issues in your context? If not, what initiatives could be taken to promote their attention to language issues in their EMI classes?
2 How could the collaboration between content and language teachers be boosted in your context?

Acknowledgements

This chapter falls within the work carried out in the following research projects: FFI2016-79377-P (Spanish Ministry of Economy and Competitiveness; AEI/FEDER, EU) and IT904-16 (Department of Education, University and Research of the Basque Government).

References

Admiraal, W., Westhoff, G. and de Bot, K. (2006). Evaluation of bilingual secondary education in the Netherlands: Students' language proficiency in English. *Educational Research and Evaluation* 12, 75–93.

Aguilar, M. and Muñoz, C. (2014). The effect of proficiency on CLIL benefits in engineering students in Spain. *International Journal of Applied Linguistics* 24, 1–18.

Airey, J. (2012). 'I don't teach language.' The linguistic attitudes of physics lecturers in Sweden. *AILA Review* 25, 64–79.

Basturkmen, H. (2019). ESP teacher education needs. *Language Teaching* 52, 318–330.

Bosisio, N. (2015). CLIL in the Italian university. A long but promising way to go. *Elle* 4, 133–154.

Bruton, A. (2019). Questions about CLIL which are unfortunately still not outdated: A reply to Pérez-Cañado. *Applied Linguistics Review* 10, 591–602.

Cenoz, J. (2013). Discussion: Towards an educational perspective in CLIL language policy and pedagogical practice. *International Journal of Bilingual Education and Bilingualism* 16, 389–394.

Chostelidou, D. and Griva, E. (2014). Measuring the effect of implementing CLIL in higher education: An experimental research project. *Procedia – Social and Behavioral Sciences* 116, 2169–2174.

Chou, M.-H. (2018). Speaking anxiety and strategy use for learning English as a foreign language in full and partial English-medium instruction contexts. *TESOL Quarterly* 52, 611–633.

Costa, F. (2012). Evidence on form in ICLHE lectures in Italy. Evidence from English-medium science lectures by native speakers of Italian. *AILA Review* 25, 30–47.

Crystal, D. (2019). *The Cambridge encyclopedia of the English language*. Third edition. Cambridge: Cambridge University Press.

Dafouz, E., Camacho, M. M. and Urquia, E. (2014). 'Surely they can't do as well': A comparison of business students' academic performance in English-medium and Spanish-as-first-language-medium programmes. *Language and Education* 28, 223–236.

Dallinger, S., Jonkmann, K., Hollm, J. and Fiege, C. (2016). The effect of content and language integrated learning on students' English and history competences – killing two birds with one stone? *Language and Instruction* 41, 23–31.

104   David Lasagabaster

Dalton-Puffer, C. (2011). Content-and-language integrated learning: From practice to principles? *Annual Review of Applied Linguistics* 31, 182–204.

Doiz, A., Lasagabaster, D. and Sierra, J. M. (2011). Internationalisation, multilingualism and English-medium instruction. *World Englishes* 30, 345–359.

Doiz, A., Lasagabaster, D. and Sierra, J. M. (eds.) (2012). *English-medium instruction at universities: Global challenges*. Bristol: Multilingual matters.

Doiz, A., Lasagabaster, D. and Sierra, J. M. (2014). Language friction and multilingual policies at higher education: The stakeholders' view. *Journal of Multilingual and Multicultural Development* 35, 345–360.

Gené-Gil, M., Juan-Garau, M. and Salazar-Noguera, J. (2015). Development of EFL writing over three years in secondary education: CLIL and non-CLIL settings. *The Language Learning Journal* 43, 286–303.

Graddol, D. (2006). *English next: Why global English may mean the end of 'English as a foreign language.'* London: British Council.

Hernández-Nanclares, N. and Jiménez-Muñoz, A. (2017). English as a medium of instruction: Evidence for language and content targets in bilingual education in economics. *International Journal of Bilingual Education and Bilingualism* 20, 883–896.

Hu, G., Li, L., and Lei, J. (2014). English-medium instruction at a Chinese university: Rhetoric and reality. *Language Policy* 13, 21–40.

Hüttner, J. and Smit, U. (2014). CLIL (content and language integrated learning): The bigger picture. A response to: A. Bruton. 2013. CLIL: Some of the reasons why ... and why not. *System* 44, 160–167.

Jensen, C., and Thøgersen, J. (2011). Danish university lecturers' attitudes towards English as the medium of instruction. *Ibérica* 22, 13–34.

Kirkgöz, Y. (2009). Students' and lecturers' perceptions of the effectiveness of foreign language instruction in an English-medium university in Turkey. *Teaching in Higher Education* 14, 81–93.

Lasagabaster, D. (2018). Fostering team teaching: Mapping out a research agenda for English-medium instruction at university level. *Language Teaching* 51, 400–416.

Lasagabaster, D. (2021). Team teaching: A way to boost the quality of EMI programmes? In D. Coyle and F. Rubio-Alcalá (eds.), *Developing and evaluating quality bilingual practices in higher education* (pp. 163–180). Clevedon: Multilingual Matters.

Lei, J. and Hu, G. (2014). Is English-medium instruction effective in improving Chinese undergraduate students' English competence? *International Review of Applied Linguistics in Language Teaching* 52, 99–126.

Llinares, A., Morton, T. and Whittaker, R. (2012). *The roles of language in CLIL*. Cambridge: Cambridge University Press.

Lo, Y. Y. (2015). A glimpse into the effectiveness of L2-content crosscurricular collaboration in content-based instruction programmes. *International Journal of Bilingual Education and Bilingualism* 18(4), 443–462.

Lyster, R. (2007). *Languages learning and teaching through content: A counterbalanced approach*. Amsterdam/Philadelphia: John Benjamins.

Macaro, E. (2018). *English medium instruction*. Oxford: Oxford University Press.

Merino, J. A. and Lasagabaster, D. (2018). The effect of content and language integrated learning programmes' intensity on English proficiency: A longitudinal study. *International Journal of Applied Linguistics* 28, 18–30.

Muñoz, C. (ed.) (2006). *Age and the rate of foreign language learning*. Clevedon: Multilingual Matters.

Learning language by studying content 105

Muñoz, C. (2008). Symmetries and asymmetries of age effects in naturalistic and instructed L2 learning. *Applied Linguistics* 29, 578–596.

Muñoz, C. and Singleton, D. (2011) A critical review of age-related research on L2 ultimate attainment. *Language Teaching* 44, 1–35.

Murata, K. (ed.) (2019). *English-medium instruction from an English as a lingua franca perspective: Exploring the higher education context.* London and New York: Routledge.

Netten, J. and Germain, C. (2004). Theoretical and research foundations of intensive French. *Canadian Modern Language Review* 60(3), 275–294.

Olsson, E. (2015). Progress in English academic vocabulary use in writing among CLIL and non-CLIL students in Sweden. *Moderna Sprak* 109, 51–74.

Pérez-Cañado, M. L. (2012). CLIL research in Europe: Past, present and future. *International Journal of Bilingual Education and Bilingualism* 15, 315–341.

Pérez Cañado, M. L. (2019). CLIL and elitism: Myth or reality? *The Language Learning Journal* 48, 4–17.

Pladevall-Ballester, E. and Vallbona, A. (2016). CLIL in minimal input contexts: A longitudinal study of primary school learners' receptive skills. *System* 58, 37–48.

Rogier, D. (2012). *The effects of English-medium instruction on language proficiency of students enrolled in higher education in the UAE* (PhD dissertation). University of Exeter, UK. Retrieved from: https://ore.exeter.ac.uk/repository/bitstream/handle/10036/4482/RogierD.pdf?sequence=2

Roquet, H. and Pérez-Vidal, C. (2017). Do productive skills improve in content and language integrated learning (CLIL) contexts? The case of writing. *Applied Linguistics* 38, 489–511.

Rubio-Alcalá, F. D., Arco-Tirado, J. L., Fernández-Martín, F. D., López-Lechuga, R., Barrios, E. and Pavón-Vázquez, V. (2019) A systematic review on evidences supporting quality indicators of bilingual, plurilingual and multilingual programs in higher education. *Educational Research Review* 27, 191–204.

Rumlich, D. (2016). *Evaluating bilingual education in Germany: CLIL students' general English proficiency, EFL self-concept and interest.* Frankfurt am Main: Peter Lang.

San Isidro, X. and Lasagabaster, D. (2019). The impact of CLIL on pluriliteracy development and content learning in a rural multilingual setting: A longitudinal study. *Language Teaching Research* 23, 584–602.

Somers, T. and Llinares, A. (2021). Students' motivation for content and language integrated learning and the role of programme intensity. *International Journal of Bilingual Education and Bilingualism* 6, 839–854.

Swain, M. (2000). French immersion research in Canada: Recent contributions to SLA and applied linguistics. *Annual Review of Applied Linguistics* 20, 199–212.

Tai, H.-Y. (2015). Writing development in syntactic complexity, accuracy and fluency in a content and language integrated learning class. *International Journal of Language and Linguistics* 2, 149–156.

Tedick, D. J. and Cammarata, L. (2012) Content and language integration in K-12 contexts: student outcomes, teacher practices, and stakeholder perspectives. *Foreign Language Annals* 45, 28–53.

Yang, W. (2015). Content and language integrated learning next in Asia: Evidence of learners' achievement in CLIL education from a Taiwan tertiary degree programme. *International Journal of Bilingual Education and Bilingualism* 18, 361–382.

6 Aptitude or motivation
Which is the better predictor of successful language learning?

Suzanne Graham

Introduction

Variation across learners in terms of how successful they are at learning a second or foreign language is a familiar phenomenon for most teachers. That variation can be associated with what we call individual differences – for example, learners' age or their gender (Dörnyei, 2005). Two key areas in which individuals can vary are language aptitude and motivation for language learning. They have long been considered to be the strongest predictors of success (Skehan, 1991). However, the relative importance of each remains a subject of debate. This chapter considers how language learning aptitude and motivation have been defined and investigated over the last few decades; more importantly, it reviews the research evidence regarding their respective contributions to language learning outcomes and what implications that might have for the classroom.

How teachers teach, whatever their subject area, is in many ways influenced by beliefs they bring to the classroom (Meijer, Verloop, & Beijaard, 1999). In an early session in the language teacher education course I run, I usually ask trainee teachers, preparing to teach high school learners of French, German or Spanish in England, to reflect on some of the beliefs they have about learning. I do that as a way of prompting them to consider whether those beliefs could be challenged and questioned. One resource I often draw on is the questionnaire from Spada and Lightbown's (2006) *How languages are learned,* that presents popular beliefs about language learning. Two items in that questionnaire, in particular, have always provoked a lot of discussions:

> *Highly intelligent people are good language learners*
> *The best predictor of success in second language acquisition is motivation*

The first of these statements implies that learners are either good at languages or they aren't – that they have some kind of inborn talent, one that we tend to call 'aptitude'. Of course, aptitude is not really the same as 'intelligence', although for some people, the two may amount to much the same thing, and high levels of intelligence, as measured by such instruments as Intelligence Quotient (IQ) tests, can and often do go hand in hand with language aptitude (Li, 2016).

DOI: 10.4324/9781003008361-8

Language aptitude is something that for lay people is an evident reality, in the same way that being good at music and sport, or maths, is often seen as some sort of innate ability, rather than something that can be developed. As Horwitz (1988) argues, in regard to language learning, there is a "widespread belief [...] that acquiring another language is a special 'gift' that some people have and that most people do not have" (Simon, 1980, in Horwitz, 1988, p. 283). Such views are also reflected in Ortega's (2010) keynote talk on language acquisition research for language teachers, who, she suggests (although without citing evidence to back up her claim), have "intuitive notions" about aptitude. These include the view that "Language aptitude is genetic (we're born with it)", that it "has to do with intelligence, good memory, or a musical ear", and that it is "fixed [...] 'either or': Either one has it, or one doesn't. So... there is little teachers can do about it...!"

Key questions

The terminology often used for high ability in areas such as music, maths, sport, and languages also strongly implies that it is innate or inborn. For example, in England, learners who are very good at 'academic' subjects like maths or languages are described as 'gifted', those who are very good at sport or performing arts, 'talented'. Both terms suggest ability handed down at birth, that is immutable, with the added implication that such ability is a prerequisite for success. While the definition of language aptitude given by two prominent researchers in the field does not specifically mention 'innateness', the use of the term talent implies it: "there is a specific talent for learning foreign languages which exhibits considerable variation between individual learners" (Dörnyei & Skehan, 2003: 590).

Language learning motivation, by contrast, is something that is potentially more amenable to development, to nurturing, more readily created from scratch rather than inborn, but also therefore less stable and unpredictable. Does that make it more or less important than language aptitude? Is successful language learning possible with *either* motivation *or* aptitude, or are both necessary? The answer to those questions depends in part on answers to some other key questions. The first is: what do we mean by 'successful' language learning? Do we mean the highest level of attainment, as measured by some sort of proficiency test or examination? And does that mean attainment at a specific point in time, or ultimate attainment – that is, the end-point of learners' language study? And what kind of proficiency are we talking about – is attainment perceived as doing well on tests of, say, grammatical knowledge, written accuracy, or communicative language use? Or does 'successful' mean something else, less easily measured – for example, enjoyable, rewarding, leading to changed attitudes about other cultures, and so on. Success might also mean achieving one's personal goals for language learning, perhaps helped by a teacher who is able to nurture learners so that they achieve a level of attainment that is meaningful for them. How we define 'success' is therefore likely to influence how important aptitude and motivation might be as predictors.

108 *Suzanne Graham*

Another question relates to the kind of learners we are talking about, and the context in which they are learning. An adult learner studying English as a required part of their undergraduate degree, in a country where English proficiency is vital for gaining a good job, may well be influenced by different factors than a 12-year-old learner of German in England, where language learning is only compulsory until the age of 14 and is seen as less vital for future prospects.

These are some of the issues this chapter will seek to explore, taking each of aptitude and motivation in turn.

Aptitude

What is language aptitude? One of the most influential scholars in the field, Carroll (1981), identified it as the "initial state of readiness" (p. 86) for learning a foreign language. Importantly, Carroll argued that aptitude influences how *easily* and *quickly* people learn another language, rather than the level of proficiency they reach at the end of their learning. In other words, aptitude is not the same thing as language achievement. Carroll did, however, develop a battery of tests designed to predict how successful people would be in language learning in the areas of pronunciation, grammar, and vocabulary. Those tests formed the Modern Language Aptitude Test (MLAT), which was first published in 1959 by Carroll and Sapon and which remains the most widely used tool for measuring language aptitude. Over the years, other tests such as the LLAMA (Meara, 2005) have emerged, although often focusing on the same areas of testing as the MLAT. As Li (2019) reports, while Carroll saw aptitude as having four main components (grammatical sensitivity, inductive learning ability, phonemic coding ability, and associative memory or rote-learning ability), he also believed it to be 'unitary'. That is, aptitude depends on all of these four components together; individuals are either high or low in aptitude, rather than having a mixture of different strengths. Not all aptitude researchers agree with that view, however. Skehan (2002), for example, views aptitude as made up of different components that come into play in different stages of L2 learning, namely noticing different linguistic forms, identifying rules and patterns in language, and applying that knowledge in actual language use (Skehan, 2002, 2012).

Within the MLAT, grammatical sensitivity and inductive learning reflect the ability "to recognize the grammatical functions of words (or other linguistic entities) in sentence structures" (Carroll, 1981: 105) and the ability "to infer or induce the rules governing a set of language materials' (p. 105) respectively. Phonemic coding ability is defined as "the ability to identify distinct sounds, to form association between those sounds and symbols representing them, and to retain these associations" (p. 105). Finally, associative memory or rote-learning ability reflects "the ability to learn associations between sounds and meanings rapidly and efficiently, and to retain these associations" (p. 105).

It is worth pointing out, as Li (2015, 2019) does, that the areas of learning the MLAT was designed to predict are ones that underpinned language teaching as it was in the 1950s, namely the audiolingual, behaviourist and grammar-translation

Aptitude or motivation 109

approaches, rather than the communicative approach that developed in the 1970s and 1980s. The areas are also noticeably concerned primarily with language comprehension rather than language production, and seem to have little to do with the ability to use language communicatively (Li, 2019). That suggests that aptitude is especially important in classroom contexts, where the focus is more on explicit, conscious learning of grammar and linguistic features than would be the case for learning a language in a naturalistic setting. Indeed, Ranta (2002) found that language aptitude was not strongly related to success in communicative settings. By contrast, Wen and Skehan (2011) argue that the MLAT also predicts learning in such settings, and Harley and Hart (1997) found that aptitude predicted success in L2 learning through immersive, content-based teaching. It is fair to say, however, that many of the aptitude studies to date have been conducted in America, in audiolingual rather than communicative classrooms, so we know relatively little about how important it is for high school, mixed-attainment communicative classrooms in other countries.

That may be in part because research into language aptitude fell out of favour in the last decades of the 20th century, also reflecting a view that it may be unhelpful, even elitist, to seek to identify those who might be likely to be more or less successful at language learning (Dörnyei, 2005). More recently, however, aptitude has attracted greater interest. Important insights come from Li (2015, 2016, 2017, 2019), who undertook three meta-analyses of research into aptitude. In a meta-analysis, the author takes the findings of a number of related studies and pools them to come up with an overall conclusion. Li's work continues to show that aptitude is an important predictor of successful language learning but that its impact varies.

One area where aptitude seems to be especially important is the development of grammatical knowledge. Li (2015) found that across 53 studies, aptitude emerged as moderately related to grammar acquisition, especially for high-school learners, when grammar teaching was explicit. Language analytic ability was particularly important for that kind of learning, as might be expected. Li comments, however, that the relationship his analysis established between aptitude and learning success is weaker than some researchers have claimed, concluding that aptitude "is predictive of initial L2 grammatical competence and less so of later stages of learning, and that it is a conscious construct that affects learning outcome in explicit conditions" (p. 407).

In a second meta-analysis, Li (2016) looked at whether language aptitude predicted other aspects of language proficiency than grammar, and whether different aspects of aptitude are more important for some language skills than for others. Overall aptitude was a strong predictor for L2 learning in general. By contrast, it was related only fairly moderately to the skills of reading, listening, and speaking. Its relationship with writing was not statistically significant, and there was only a weak, if statistically significant relationship with vocabulary learning. Phonetic coding ability appeared to be the strongest predictor when the individual aspects of aptitude were examined (except for listening, interestingly, where it was the weakest predictor).

110   *Suzanne Graham*

Language aptitude, then, appears to most strongly predict the ability to learn from explicit grammar teaching. That might also suggest that aptitude is closely related to general academic ability, or even intelligence, given that grammar knowledge is often an important focus in traditional academic contexts. While intelligence is a broad capacity, influencing "how well a student will understand directions and explanations, or will make inferences about them from the content of any given learning experience" (Gardner & MacIntyre, 1992: 216), language aptitude is much more specific. But they are strongly related on a statistical level (Li, 2016), and we might say they are very similar, if not identical.

How useful is the notion of aptitude for the languages classroom?

It could be argued that by saying language aptitude 'predicts' successful L2 learning, we are implying that it is 'useful' for that learning. But is that really true? Does knowing that a student has high or low language aptitude help or hinder a teacher's work?

One use to which such information might be put could be to place learners in teaching groups according to their aptitude levels. There is a lot of debate about the merits or otherwise of such an approach, which space does not permit me to consider here. Perhaps of greater relevance is a small body of research that suggests that good use can be made of language aptitude information by matching teaching methods and materials to learners' different aptitude profiles. For example, Wesche (1981) grouped learners by their memory or analytic abilities: one group had high analytic ability, one high memory ability, and one had high ability for both areas. Different types of instruction, to match those profiles, was then given to an intervention group. A comparison group received unmatched instruction (that is, all learners were taught in the same way). Greater learning gains were made by learners in the 'matched' condition.

More recent studies have looked at how aptitude interacts with different types of instruction, as reviewed by Li (2017) in a further meta-analysis investigating three main areas. First, corrective feedback. Li found that there was a stronger link between high aptitude and benefiting from explicit corrective feedback than was the case for implicit feedback. Second, explicit or implicit grammar instruction, where again the link between benefits and high aptitude was stronger for the explicit form. Third, deductive or inductive instruction. In the former, learners are explicitly given a grammar rule and then practise it; in the latter, they work with language materials (e.g. written or spoken texts) and have to draw out the grammatical rules themselves (but there is still an explicit focus on such rules). The evidence reviewed by Li (2017) points to higher aptitude learners benefiting more from inductive instruction (presumably because their aptitude enables them to identify rules and patterns easily themselves) and lower aptitude learners doing better with deductive approaches. Li concludes that teachers might make use of all of these research findings either by taking a varied approach (using, for example, both explicit and implicit types of feedback during

Aptitude or motivation   111

the course of a lesson) or by providing extra support for lower aptitude learners in areas such as grammar learning. They might, for example, provide an explicit statement of a grammatical rule on a handout during more inductive activities, he argues.

By contrast, less helpful consequences can occur from paying attention to the notion of aptitude, especially if teachers adhere to the commonly held view (supported by some, but not all, research – see, for example, Sáfár and Kormos, 2008) that language aptitude is a fixed trait, not influenced by instruction. Viewing aptitude in that way implies, on the one hand, that there is in fact no need to offer different types of instruction to learners of differing levels of aptitude, as aptitude is deterministic. On the other hand, it implies that some students can achieve in a second language and others cannot. Clearly, such a view may have a negative impact on both learners and teachers.

Impact on learners

If learners have strong beliefs about the link between language aptitude and success in L2 learning, even if these are at a fairly unconscious level, then potentially they may see little point in continuing with language study if they feel their own level of aptitude is low. Such an issue is particularly problematic in Anglophone contexts such as England and Australia, where language study is not compulsory across all years of schooling and where there are decreasing numbers of secondary school pupils choosing to study a foreign language beyond the optional stage. Research suggests that learners in England see foreign languages as very difficult to achieve in, especially when compared with other areas of the curriculum (Graham, 2004; QCA, 2006). But there has been surprisingly little research conducted into pupils' conceptions of language learning ability or aptitude, what it is and how amenable it is to development. This is surprising because there is evidence from other curriculum areas (e.g. mathematics, Blackwell et al., 2007) to suggest that pupils' conceptions of ability, their so-called 'implicit theories of ability' (Dweck & Leggett, 1988), are relevant to their levels of engagement, performance, and achievement. In such a framework, 'ability' appears as similar to 'aptitude', something which learners with a 'fixed' view of it perceive as immutable and inborn. We know very little about the extent to which such different implicit theories of ability regarding foreign language study are held by secondary school learners, although there is evidence (Graham, 2004; Williams, Burden, & Lanvers, 2002) that those in England tend to attribute any lack of success they experience to ability factors, and that perceived proficiency declines over time (Williams et al., 2004). Whether ability is perceived by such learners as fixed or mutable is not, however, clear and is worthy of further investigation, as it may shed further light on the issue of low motivation for language learning, a question considered in more depth later in this chapter.

Furthermore, we know very little about teachers' implicit theories of language learning ability or language aptitude. Research does suggest that teachers' beliefs about the nature of ability influence the goals they set for students (Lynott &

112   *Suzanne Graham*

Woolfolk, 1994), and may also contribute to pupils' experiences in the languages classroom. Evidence of this appears in a study by Mitchell and Lee (2003), where they explored language teaching in classrooms in the UK and Korea. Teacher 'E' in England in particular talked about some learners reaching their "linguistic ceiling" or being "very willing but not terribly able", while others were referred to as "linguists" (p. 51). The authors conclude that such views led Teacher E to lower her expectations, to be "inwardly pessimistic about the ultimate progress of at least some of her students" and to adjust her teaching accordingly (p. 58). Research also suggests similar attitudes among school leaders, who can, furthermore, associate lower socio-economic status (SES) with lower aptitude or suitability for language study. Across geographically diverse contexts such as Mexico (Sayer, 2018) and Australia (Black, Wright, & Cruickshank, 2018), foreign language education for lower SES students tends to take a non-communicative, "back to basics" (Sayer, 2018: 66) approach which, according to the teacher in Sayer's study, is supposedly made necessary by "their general lack of academic knowledge and skills through which to learn an additional language" (p. 66). In other words, views about the importance of aptitude and its influence on success in language learning can have negative implications for who gets to study a language at school and the form that instruction takes.

Motivation

We have therefore seen that, one way or another, language aptitude is an important predictor of how far students succeed in language learning, but not always in straightforward ways, in so far as beliefs about language aptitude may be as important as the thing itself. That is particularly the case if such beliefs lead students to give up language study, taking us to the role of motivation in language learning success.

Just as for language aptitude, several studies have explored statistically how far motivation predicts language learning outcomes, generally by taking scores on a questionnaire assessing such motivation and looking at their relationship with scores on language tests. In other words, does having 'more' motivation lead to higher levels of language attainment? While the majority of studies show that motivation is a very important predictor of learning outcomes, the relationship is almost always weaker than is the case for language aptitude. For example, Ehrman and Oxford (1995) administered aptitude tests (MLAT) together with questionnaires and other tests that elicited scores for motivation, anxiety, language learning strategies, learning styles, self-esteem, and personality traits. They found that aptitude measures most strongly correlated with proficiency, more strongly than was the case for motivation. The same was true of a study by Kiss and Nikolov (2005), investigating 12-year-old learners of English in 10 schools in Hungary, and one by Sparks et al. (2009) studying young secondary school learners in the USA.

As Li (2016) points out, however, most studies exploring the relative importance of motivation and aptitude have assessed the former with a questionnaire

Aptitude or motivation 113

that does not necessarily reflect current thinking about what motivation is and how it should be measured. That is, most have used the Attitude/Motivation Test Battery (AMTB) by Robert Gardner (1985). Gardner's model of motivation tended to present motivation as a largely stable characteristic, largely made up of attitudes towards the L2 and its speakers, as well as attitudes towards the L2 learning situation. If we consider motivation to be why people select a particular activity, how long they are willing to persist in it and what effort they invest in it (Dörnyei, 2001), then the AMTB, focusing as it does on attitudes, is arguably more a measure of factors that influence choices about the *initiation* of language learning, rather than a measure of degrees of persistence or effort. AMTB scores thus represent something relatively fixed, which may explain why researchers have then tried to explore direct relationships between such scores and attainment (Dörnyei, 2001). We return to this issue later.

Are aptitude and motivation related to each other at all? Li (2016), looking at a number of studies, found that aptitude and motivation were only weakly related on a statistical level. Yet, another well-known measure of language aptitude, the Pimsleur battery, suggests that they may be. The Pimsleur Language Aptitude Battery (PLAB; Pimsleur et al., 2004) includes assessments of attitudes and motivation as part of aptitude (Snow, 1991). Or language aptitude and motivation might be indirectly related, in so far as motivation might *result* from language learning success, itself arising from aptitude, rather than motivation being the *cause* of language learning success. Such a view is, in part, shared by Sparks and Ganschow (1991), who argue that low motivation could stem from learners having "underlying native language problems" (p. 6), including difficulties relating to L1 reading which in turn one might relate to language aptitude.

So, the evidence suggests, fairly convincingly, that aptitude predicts language proficiency more strongly than motivation does, generally speaking, when the two variables are compared across statistical tests that compare their ability to foretell language attainment levels. Nevertheless, as Dörnyei (2005: 43) points out with reference to Carroll himself, language aptitude "does not predict whether an individual can learn a foreign language or not", but instead suggests how quickly a learner is likely to make progress "under optimal conditions of motivation, opportunity to learn, and quality of instruction" (Carroll, 1973, p. 6). This suggests that aptitude alone cannot bring about 'successful' language learning; to be successful in an L2, ultimately you have to study an L2. Again, this argument is very relevant in many contexts, where learning another language is not compulsory for more than a relatively short period of time. As Larson-Hall and Dewey (2012) also argue, an adult in the USA is not compelled to learn German; if they decide not to, then no amount of aptitude will result in any learning at all. Learners' ultimate level of attainment also depends to a large degree on how long they continue learning a language for. No matter how much aptitude they have, if they stop learning a language after, say, a year, then they are unlikely to get much beyond the beginner stage. Therefore, in contexts where learners have a choice about whether they persist with language study or not, motivation is likely to be as important as aptitude, if not more so.

114 *Suzanne Graham*

The impact of motivation on learning outcomes is therefore what we might call an indirect one. As argued by Dörnyei and Csizér (2005), "motivation is only indirectly related to learning outcomes/achievement because it is, by definition, *an antecedent of behavior rather than of achievement.* In other words, motivation is a concept that explains why people behave as they do rather than how successful their behavior will be" [emphasis added] (p. 20). Previous research makes the mistake, in their view, of implying a "false linear relationship between motivation and learning outcomes" (p. 20). Thus, they suggest that rather than looking at the relationship between language achievement measures and motivation itself, as measured by surveys of factors such as attitudes towards the target language community, it would be more sensible to look at what they call "the mediating link, motivated behaviour" (p. 20). There is also an argument that, as motivated behaviour and persistence are likely to fluctuate over the course of language learning, longitudinal rather than cross-sectional studies are needed if we are to understand fully the relationship between motivation and learning outcomes. How valid is it to measure motivation at one point in time and then to examine whether it predicts attainment? Papi and Hiver (2020), in a study using interviews to trace six learners' motivation 'stories', show convincingly how motivation can fluctuate over time and depending on the learning context, such as the phase of education (middle or secondary school, university). It therefore seems rather futile to try to establish a linear relationship between motivation and outcomes.

What factors, then, affect motivated behaviour? One of the most influential theories of L2 learning in recent years, The Ideal L2 Self (Dörnyei, 2005), suggests that a key driving force is learners' future self-image of themselves as a competent speaker of the L2. Studying secondary school and university learners of English in Chile, Kormos, Kiddle, and Csizér (2011) found a strong link between motivated behaviour and the Ideal L2 self. Likewise, in a large-sample study of Iranian adult learners of English, Papi and Teimouri (2014) found that motivated behaviour was most strongly influenced by the Ideal L2 self and instrumentality (learning a language for specific rewards, such as getting a good job). By contrast, in Lamb (2012), a study of younger learners of English in junior high school in Indonesia, classroom experiences emerged as a stronger predictor of motivated behaviour than the Ideal L2 self (which was also not a significant predictor of language learning outcomes). Learning contexts (school or university, for example) and age of learners may therefore influence the relevance of the Ideal L2 self, as well as other factors such as the status of the language being learnt.

The Ideal L2 self suggests that learners exert motivated behaviour to try to reduce any discrepancy between their current position as a language learner and that 'ideal' future self, influencing in turn how much effort and time they spend on language learning. The link between motivated behaviour and outcomes is illustrated in an interesting study by Larson-Hall and Dewey (2012). Based on a sample of English-speaking missionaries learning L2 Japanese, they investigated the relationship between a measure of speaking and grammatical

Aptitude or motivation 115

development (through an elicited imitation or 'EI' task) and sections of the LLAMA aptitude test, as well as measures of motivation via a questionnaire that aimed to tap into features of the ideal L2 self (Dörnyei, 2005). They also included the amount of time learners had spent in the country where the target language was spoken, namely Japan. They found that aptitude and motivation had similar levels of importance for predicting how well the missionaries did in the EI task; but what was much more important was the amount of input they had had, in terms of how long they had spent in studying the language. Arguably, the quantity of input is related to how motivated one is to learn the language.

That idea is also suggested in a study by Saito et al. (2018). Like Dörnyei (2005) and colleagues, they argue that L2 learning behaviour (such as practising using the language) is influenced by learners' visions of themselves as an L2 user, which in turn influences how highly they achieve. The amount and quality of practice learners have with the language is important for how well they acquire it, as is the extent to which they engage deeply with the language itself. This is arguably especially true for speaking skills (Saito et al., 2018), who looked at the relationship between measures of motivation and speaking outcomes over a period of time. They found that for 108 Japanese English as a foreign language (EFL) students, greater enjoyment in L2 learning and a stronger sense of Ideal L2 self-predicted how much they practised speaking and how much their speaking skills developed over three months.

There are, however, other perspectives that have been taken on what influences motivated behaviour or persistence for language learning. A growing body of work argues that learners' expectations of success, the degree of confidence they have in their ability to succeed at specific tasks – their self-efficacy (Bandura, 1997) – is a very important factor that forms a sub-component of language learning motivation and influences motivated behaviour (Dörnyei, 1994; Yun, Hiver, & Al-Hoorie, 2018). Self-efficacy is then in turn related to the kinds of explanations learners give for their success or failure on different tasks, known as 'attributions'. Learners who attribute failure to factors that are uncontrollable – such as low ability or innate aptitude – are more likely to give up when tasks are challenging. In a study of learners of French in England, Graham (2004) found that learners who made ability-related attributions were less likely to continue with language study when it was no longer compulsory and hence were less likely to go on to achieve higher levels of attainment. In a number of studies, furthermore, self-efficacy has been found to be an important predictor of learning outcomes – in subjects such as mathematics (Pajares & Schunk, 2001), but increasingly for language study. Reviewing studies that have specifically explored the role of self-efficacy in language learning, Raoofi, Tan, and Chan (2012) identified 12 studies that established a strong relationship between self-efficacy and learning outcomes, either in general terms or for specific skills. A notable study is by Hsieh and Schallert (2008). They investigated how far self-efficacy predicted attainment for 500 undergraduates in Spanish, German, and French, along with the explanations students gave for how well they did in those languages

116 *Suzanne Graham*

(their attributions). They found that self-efficacy and attributions together were strong predictors of course grades, explaining around 45% of the variation in learners' course grades.

Self-efficacy, or how competent learners feel they are in respect of a given area of learning, is hence a strong predictor of learning outcomes. But it is important not to view it in isolation. It forms only one-half of the expectancy-value equation (Eccles, 1983), which is one of the dominant theories of achievement motivation. The expectancy-value equation considers that individuals' level of motivation is influenced by (a) their expectations of success in a given area and (b) the value they place on such success. Value includes interest, enjoyment, and sense of importance of the activity. Both halves of the equation are believed to be essential for motivation and indeed are related to one another, as several large-scale studies across different curriculum areas have found. For example, in a study across 57 countries of motivated behaviour for science (i.e. wanting to continue studying it), Nagengast et al. (2011) point out emphatically: "The essence of the noncompensatory, multiplicative relation between expectancy and value is that both have to be high. It is not sufficient to either enhance academic self-concept or to enhance value; teachers must be sufficiently skilled to simultaneously enhance both constructs. If teachers focus on one to the exclusion of the other, then the influence of each is undermined" (p. 1064). Such research also indicates that while expectancy beliefs (self-efficacy) have a strong influence on achievement, value beliefs have a stronger influence on choice, effort, and persistence.

Both self-efficacy and value are, arguably, things that a teacher can do something about. By contrast, it is relatively difficult – if not, in the view of some, impossible – to influence a learner's level of aptitude. That arguably makes motivation a more important classroom variable than aptitude, especially if we consider 'successful' language learning to be more than mere attainment in the form of course grades. As Dörnyei and Muir (2019: 720) argue, "boring but systematic teaching can be effective in producing, for example, good test results, but rarely does it inspire a lifelong commitment to the subject matter".

What factors might influence the development of that lifelong commitment? For school-age learners, the classroom experience is very important, and is something over which the teacher has some control. For example, Guilloteaux and Dörnyei (2008) explored teachers' use of motivational teaching strategies with 1,300 learners of English in South Korea, who were between 12 and 15 years of age. The strategies included setting tangible tasks not linked to language outcomes, bringing in an element of creativity and fantasy linked with students' interests, giving opportunities for personal and emotional expression, and giving feedback free from personal criticism. Their use was strongly related to student motivated behaviour and explained a large proportion of the variation in it (Guilloteaux & Dörnyei, 2008).

Dörnyei and Muir (2019) provide further insights into many teaching strategies that might promote motivation, including how to ensure healthy and productive group dynamics and student-teacher relationships. They additionally

Aptitude or motivation 117

highlight three motivation phases that teachers would do well to consider: "(a) generating initial motivation, (b) maintaining and protecting motivation, and (c) encouraging positive retrospective self-evaluation" (p. 729). The first of these can be enhanced by addressing the two aspects of the expectancy-value equation we discussed earlier. Teachers can raise learners' awareness of different forms of value in language learning. That can include making the teaching materials relevant for the learners, not only linked to the world outside the classroom but also to what learners themselves see as the purpose of language learning. Such purpose may relate to achieving linguistic competence to get a job or similar (instrumental value), or to a desire to learn about other cultures in the broadest sense, for the enjoyment and interest that it generates (integrative and intrinsic value). In Papi and Hiver (2020), the authors argue convincingly that motivation is influenced by a complex interaction of factors, relating not only to a sense of competence but also to what they call 'truth', in which is included the desire to learn about the target language and its related culture. The role of cultural contact has also been explored extensively in a number of publications by Csizér and Kormos (2008), which highlight that for 13/14-year-old learners of English and German in Hungary, motivated behaviour was determined not only by language-related attitudes but also by the views that the students held about the perceived importance of contact with those from other cultures (Csizér & Kormos, 2008). The latter, in turn, was influenced by exposure to L2 cultural artefacts, such as films, videos, books, magazines, and music, not only for English but also for German. Such contact is arguably something that teachers can influence.

Returning to the first half of the expectancy-value equation, maintaining motivation is linked to improving learners' expectation of success, achievable firstly by helping learners set realistic goals based on a shared understanding of what is possible to achieve in a given amount of time (Dörnyei & Muir, 2019). Second, the expectation of success can come through the encouragement of 'Positive Retrospective Self-Evaluation' – whereby the teacher encourages positive attributions and sense of control, through feedback that is informative and shows learners how to improve through strategies over which they have some control, rather than through rewards and merits (Dörnyei & Muir, 2019). This aligns with an approach that emphasizes the link between enhanced motivation and giving learners concrete strategies by which they can become more successful. As Macaro (2003, p. 115) claims: "Demotivated learners have to be given the tools with which to find the subject [language learning] easier and make more rapid progress".

Some studies that have investigated how to improve language learning motivation have had considerable success by giving learners such 'tools'. For example, working with Year 7 and 8 learners of French, Macaro and Erler (2008) not only helped improve learners' ability to read in French by teaching them how to apply learner strategies to solve reading 'challenges' (through a structured programme of reading strategy instruction over 14 months) but also they saw an improvement in the learners' level of motivation for reading and for French overall.

118 *Suzanne Graham*

An important role was played by feedback on the extent to which learners had used the strategies they had been taught, and how this had led the learners to solve the particular language challenges that they faced.

Conclusion

What can we conclude from the above discussions about the relative importance of aptitude and motivation for successful language learning? As for many things in education, the answer has to be 'it depends': not only on how we are defining 'successful' but also on how we are defining 'importance', along with a whole host of other issues such as the kind of learner, learning, and context we are talking about. While it is fairly clear that, on a statistical level, measures of language aptitude predict higher learning outcomes more strongly than measures of motivation do – especially for learning of a fairly explicit, grammar-focused kind – it is also clear that without motivation, language learning is likely to come to a halt or perhaps not even start in the first place. Perhaps more essentially, if we consider 'importance' to mean how much weight teachers should attach to each factor, then for me, motivation wins hands-down, as something that is amenable to change, and hence something worth paying particular attention to.

Relating the issues raised in this chapter to your own context:

1 In your own second language education context, are there national or institutional policies or recommendations for grouping learners by language aptitude?
2 To what extent are you aware of practitioners, in your own context, believing language aptitude to be an inborn quality that is fixed and not amenable to change?

References

Bandura, A. (1997). *Self-efficacy: The exercise of control.* New York: Freeman.

Black, S., Wright, J., & Cruickshank, K. (2018). The struggle for legitimacy: Language provision in two "residual" comprehensive high schools in Australia. *Critical Studies in Education, 59*(3), 348–363. doi:10.1080/17508487.2016.1197139

Blackwell. L. S., Trzesniewski, K. H., & Dweck, C. S. (2007). Implicit theories of intelligence predict achievement across an adolescent transition: A longitudinal study and an intervention. *Child Development, 78*(1), 246–263.

Carroll, J. B. (1973). Implications of aptitude test research and psycholinguistic theory for foreign language teaching. *International Journal of Psycholinguistics, 2*, 5–14.

Carroll, J. B. (1981). Twenty-five years of research on foreign language aptitude. In K. C. Diller (Ed.), *Individual differences and universals in language learning aptitude* (pp. 83–118). Rowley, MA: Newbury House.

Csizér, K., & Kormos, J. (2008). The relationship of intercultural contact and language learning motivation among Hungarian students of English and German. *Journal of Multilingual and Multicultural Development, 29*(1), 30–48, doi:10.2167/jmmd557.0

Dörnyei, Z. (1994). Motivation and motivating in the foreign language classroom. *The Modern Language Journal, 94*, 273–284.

Dörnyei, Z. (2001). New themes and approaches in L2 motivation research. *Annual Review of Applied Linguistics, 21*, 43–59.

Dörnyei, Z. (2005). *The psychology of the language learner: Individual differences in second language acquisition.* Mahwah, NJ: Lawrence Erlbaum.

Dörnyei, Z., & Csizér, K. (2005). The internal structure of language learning motivation and its relationship with language choice and learning effort. *The Modern Language Journal, 89*, 19–36.

Dörnyei, Z., & Muir, C. (2019). Creating a motivating classroom environment. In X. A. Gao (Ed.), *Second handbook of English language teaching.* New York: Springer.

Dörnyei, Z., & Skehan, P. (2003). Individual differences in second language learning. In C. J. Doughty & M. H. Long (Eds.), *The handbook of second language acquisition* (pp. 589–630). Oxford: Blackwell.

Dweck, C. S., & Leggett, E. (1988). A social-cognitive approach to motivation and personality. *Psychological Review*, 95, 256–273.

Eccles, J. (1983). Expectancies, values and academic behaviors. In J. T. Spence (Ed.), *Achievement and achievement motives: Psychological and sociological approaches* (pp. 75–146). San Francisco, CA: Freeman.

Ehrman, M., & Oxford, R. (1995). Cognition plus: Correlates of language learning success. *The Modern Language Journal, 79*, 67–89.

Gardner, R. C. (1985). *The attitude/motivation test battery.* Technical report. Retrieved from: https://publish.uwo.ca/~gardner/docs/AMTBmanual.pdf

Gardner, R. C., & MacIntyre, P. D. (1992). A student's contributions to second-language learning. Part I: Cognitive variables. *Language Teaching, 25*, 211–220. doi:10.1017/S026144480000700X

Graham, S. (2004). Giving up on modern foreign languages? Students' perceptions of learning French. *The Modern Language Journal, 88*, 171–191.

Guilloteaux, M. J., & Dörnyei, Z. (2008). Motivating language learners: A classroom-oriented investigation of the effects of motivational strategies on student motivation. *TESOL Quarterly, 42*, 55–77.

Harley, B., & Hart, D. (1997). Language aptitude and second language proficiency in classroom learners of different starting ages. *Studies in Second Language Acquisition, 19*, 379–400.

Horwitz, E. K. (1988). The beliefs about language learning of beginning university foreign language students. *The Modern Language Journal, 72*(3), 283–294.

Hsieh, P. H. P., & Schallert, D. L. (2008). Implications from self-efficacy and attribution theories for an understanding of undergraduates' motivation in a foreign language course. *Contemporary Educational Psychology, 33*, 513–532. doi:10.1016/j.cedpsych.2008.01.003

Kiss, C., & Nikolov, M. (2005). Developing, piloting and validating an instrument to measure young learners' aptitude. *Language Learning, 55*, 99–150.

Kormos, J., Kiddle, T., & Csizér, K. (2011). Systems of goals, attitudes, and self-related beliefs in second-language-learning motivation. *Applied Linguistics, 32*, 495–516. doi:10.1093/applin/amr019

Lamb, M. (2012). A self system perspective on young adolescents' motivation to learn English in urban and rural settings. *Language Learning, 62*(4), 997–1023. doi:10.1111/j.1467-9922.2012.00719.x

Larson-Hall, J., & Dewey, D. 2012. An examination of the effects of input, aptitude, and motivation on the language proficiency of missionaries learning Japanese as a second language. In L. Hansen (Ed.), *Second language acquisition abroad: The LDS missionary experience* (pp. 45–51). Amsterdam: John Benjamins.

120 *Suzanne Graham*

Li, S. (2015). The associations between language aptitude and second language grammar acquisition: A meta-analytic review of five decades of research. *Applied Linguistics, 36*, 385–408 doi:10.1093/applin/amu054

Li, S. (2016). The construct validity of language aptitude. *Studies in Second Language Acquisition, 38*, 801–842.

Li, S. (2017). The effects of cognitive aptitudes on the process and product of L2 interaction: A synthetic review. In L. Gurzynski-Weiss (Ed.), *Expanding individual difference research in the interaction approach: Investigating learners, instructors, and other interlocutors* (pp. 41–70). Amsterdam: John Benjamins Publishing Company.

Li, S. (2019). Six decades of language aptitude research: A comprehensive and critical review. In Z. Wen, P. Skehan, A Biedron, S. Li, & R. Sparks (Eds.), *Language aptitude: Advancing theory, testing, research and practice.* New York: Routledge.

Lynott, D.-J., & Woolfolk, A. E. (1994). Teachers' implicit theories of intelligence and their educational goals. *The Journal of Research and Development in Education, 27*(4), 253–264.

Macaro, E. (2003). *Teaching and learning a second language: A review of recent research.* London: Continuum.

Macaro, E., & Erler, L. (2008). Raising the achievement of young-beginner readers of French through strategy instruction. *Applied Linguistics, 29*, 90–119.

Meara, P. (2005). *LLAMA language aptitude tests: The manual.* Swansea: Lognostics.

Meijer, P. C., Verloop, N., & Beijaard, D. (1999). Exploring language teachers' practical knowledge about teaching reading comprehension. *Teaching and Teacher Education, 15*, 59–84.

Mitchell, R., & Lee, J. H.-W. (2003). Sameness and difference in classroom learning cultures: Interpretations of communicative pedagogy in the UK and Korea. *Language Teaching Research, 7*, 35–63. doi:10.1191/1362168803lr114oa

Nagengast, B., Marsh, H. W., Scalas, L. F., Xu, M. K., Hau, K. T., & Trautwein, U. (2011). Who took the "x" out of expectancy value theory? A psychological mystery, a substantive-methodological synergy, and a cross-national generalization. *Psychological Science, 22*, 1058–1066, doi:10.1177/0956797611415540

Ortega, L. (2010). *Language acquisition research for language teaching: Apply, even if with caution!* Keynote address delivered at the Österreichische Gesellschaft für Sprachendidaktik Conference, Innsbruck, 23–25 September 2010.

Pajares, F., & Schunk, D. H. (2001). Self-beliefs and school success: Self-efficacy, self-concept, and school achievement. In R. J. Riding & S. G. Rayner (Eds.), *International perspectives on individual differences, Vol. 2. Self perception* (pp. 239–265). London: Ablex Publishing.

Papi, M., & Hiver, P. (2020, in press). Language learning motivation as a complex dynamic system: A global perspective of truth, control, and value. *The Modern Language Journal.* doi:10.1111/modl.12624

Papi, M., & Teimouri, Y. (2014). Language learner motivational types: A cluster analysis study. *Language Learning, 64*, 493–525.

QCA (2006). *Pupils' views on language learning.* Available at: http://www.school-portal. co.uk/GroupDownloadFile.asp?GroupId=338117&ResourceID=2339971.

Pimsleur, P., Reed, D. J., & Stansfield, C. W. (2004). *Pimsleur language aptitude battery: Manual 2004 edition.* Rockville, MD: Language Learning and Testing Foundation.

Ranta, L. (2002). Learners' language analytic ability in the communicative classroom. In P. Robinson (Ed.), *Individual differences and instructed language learning* (pp. 159–180). Amsterdam: John Benjamins Publishing Company.

Aptitude or motivation 121

Raoofi, S., Tan, B. H., & Chan, S. H. (2012). Self-efficacy in second/foreign language learning contexts. *English Language Teaching*, 5, 60–73. doi:10.5539/elt.v5n11p60

Sáfár, A., & Kormos, J. (2008). Revisiting problems with foreign language aptitude. *International Review of Applied Linguistics in Language Teaching*, 46, 113–136.

Saito, K., Dewaele, J.-M., Abe, M., & In'nami, Y. (2018). Motivation, emotion, learning experience and second language comprehensibility development in classroom settings: A cross-sectional and longitudinal study. *Language Learning*, 68, 709–743.

Sayer, P. (2018). Does English really open doors? Social class and English teaching in public primary schools in Mexico. *System*, 73, 58–70. doi:10.1016/j.system.2017.11.006

Skehan, P. (1991). Individual differences in second language learning. Studies in Second Language Acquisition, 13, 275–298. doi:10.1017/S0272263100009979

Skehan, P. (2002). Theorizing and updating aptitude. In P. Robinson (Ed.), *Individual differences and instructed language learning* (pp. 69–94). Amsterdam, John Benjamins Publishing Company.

Skehan, P. (2012). Language aptitude. In S. Gass & A. Mackey (Eds.), *Handbook of second language acquisition* (pp. 381–395). New York: Routledge.

Snow, R. E. (1991). Aptitude-treatment interaction as a framework for research on individual differences in psychotherapy. *Journal of Consulting and Clinical Psychology*, 59, 205–216.

Spada, N., & Lightbown, P. (2006). *How languages are learned*. Oxford: Oxford University Press.

Sparks, R., & Ganschow, L. (1991). Foreign language learning difficulties. Affective or native language aptitude differences. *Modern Language Journal*, 75, 3–16.

Sparks, R., Patton, J., Ganschow, L., & Humbach, N. (2009). Long-term relationships among early first language skills, second language aptitude, second language affect, and later second language proficiency. *Applied Psycholinguistics*, 30, 725–755.

Wen, Z., & Skehan, P. (2011) A new perspective on foreign language aptitude research: Building and supporting a case for "working memory as language aptitude". *Ilha do Desterro*, 60(60). doi:10.5007/2175-8026.2011n60p015.

Wesche, M. B. (1981). Language aptitude measures in streaming, matching students with methods, and diagnosis of learning problems. In K. C. Diller (Ed.) *Individual differences and universals in language learning aptitude*. Rowley, MA: Newbury House.

Williams, M., Burden, R., & Lanvers, U. (2002). "French is the language of love and stuff": Student perceptions of issues related to motivation in learning a foreign language. *British Educational Research Journal*, 28, 503–549.

Williams, M, Burden, R, Poulet, G., & Maun, I. (2004). Learners' perceptions of their successes and failures in foreign language learning. *Language Learning Journal*, 30, 19–29.

Yun, S., Hiver, P., & Al-Hoorie, A. J. (2018). Academic buoyancy: Exploring learners' everyday resilience in the language classroom. *Studies in Second Language Acquisition*, 40, 805–830. doi:10.1017/S0272263118000037

7 Key issues in pre-service language teacher education

Laura Molway

Introduction

Second Language Teacher Education (SLTE) as a field of study within teacher education is still relatively small. The field is often subdivided into the teaching of English as a Second or Foreign Language (ESL/EFL) and the teaching of other Modern Foreign Languages (MFL), but this chapter takes a generalist approach of relevance to the preparation of teachers for any type of instructed second, foreign or additional language learning classroom.

The purpose of language teaching

Why learn an additional language? The answer to this question has profound implications for the preparation of languages teachers, since underpinning conceptions about the aims and nature of language learning influence the role and status that different aspects of second language (L2) teaching may have within an SLTE programme. For example, SLTE course designers strike a balance between a range of different aims, such as the development of listening, reading, writing, speaking and translation skills; grammatical awareness; intercultural understanding; and depth and breadth of vocabulary knowledge. The aims of a language learning course (and by extension the aims of an associated SLTE course) are also reflected in the vocabulary that is included in the curriculum – for example, a course designed to prepare learners to use an L2 in the business world might focus on transactional language relevant to that context, whilst a course designed to develop more general communicative competence might focus on high-frequency vocabulary in everyday use.

Since the early 1980s, the dominant international model of L2 teaching and learning has been known as 'Communicative Language Teaching'. This approach prioritizes competent *use* of the L2, as opposed to a grammar-translation approach emphasizing knowledge *about* the linguistic system of the L2. However, there is an ongoing debate surrounding the ideal balance between the development of communicative competence and the development of knowledge about the workings of the language.

DOI: 10.4324/9781003008361-9

In the last decade, increased globalization has contributed to a growing recognition of the need for intercultural understanding to be foregrounded as an additional key aim of language education programmes (Moeller & Nugent, 2014), as reflected in a Council of Europe report (Byram et al., 2002, p. 5):

> [L2 teaching should] give learners intercultural competence as well as linguistic competence; to prepare them for interaction with people of other cultures; to enable them to understand and accept people from other cultures as individuals with other distinctive perspectives, values and behaviours; and to help them to see that such interaction is an enriching experience.

The knowledge base of language teaching

Schulman (1986) identifies seven main categories of teacher knowledge (detailed in Table 7.1). Whilst most of the categories of knowledge outlined in Table 7.1 are self-explanatory, the category of *pedagogical content knowledge* (PCK) or, in the European tradition, *didactic transposition* (Chevallard, 1986) may be less immediately apparent. PCK involves knowledge of '*the ways of representing and formulating the subject that make it comprehensible to others*' (Shulman, 1986, p. 9). Amongst other things, when focussing on students' knowledge *about* the language, L2 teachers must have an assortment of effective examples and explanations at hand to elucidate their subject and to tackle pupils' misconceptions about the nature and workings of the language. They also require an understanding of how knowledge progression occurs in languages and what pupils are likely to find difficult.

Alongside teachers' need for well-integrated content knowledge, pedagogic knowledge and curricular knowledge, Schulman highlights the moral, normative dimension to teaching, requiring decision-making based around a set of core professional values and ideals about the purposes of education. Finally, he underlines the need for these decisions to be carefully calibrated according to local socio-cultural conditions and the nature of the learners.

Returning for a moment to Schulman's first category of knowledge needed for teaching, descriptions of L2 teachers' *content knowledge* often distinguish

Table 7.1 Forms of knowledge needed for teaching according to Shulman (1986)

1	Content knowledge
2	General pedagogical knowledge
3	Curricular knowledge
4	Pedagogical content knowledge
5	Knowledge of educational ends, purposes and values
6	Knowledge of learners and their characteristics
7	Knowledge of contexts

124   *Laura Molway*

between the interrelated domains of teachers' declarative knowledge *about* language (knowledge of grammar, vocabulary, pronunciation and syntax) and their automatized, procedural knowledge *of* the language (underpinning communicative proficiency). Of course, in practice, the boundaries between these two knowledge domains are blurred. For example, the process of rendering target language (TL) input comprehensible to learners requires teachers to draw simultaneously on their knowledge of and about language and their PCK. Andrews (2003) explores the multiple and simultaneous pedagogic purposes of teachers' TL, explaining that learners listen to their teachers' TL in order to (a) comprehend instructions regarding the details of their learning tasks; (b) understand teachers' representations and explanations of language as an object of study and (c) engage with the input, developing their second language listening skills and noticing new vocabulary. In this way, in L2 classrooms, '*teaching and what is taught are inseparable*' (Freeman & Johnson, 1998, p. 413).

The PCK and content knowledge that teachers of languages require have been the subject of some debate (Freeman, 2002), leading Agudo (2014, p. 1) to claim that '*there is no consensus in the field of SLTE as to what the essential knowledge base of SLTE is, either in terms of disciplinary knowledge or pedagogical content knowledge*'. Issues of grammar teaching or of first language (L1) and TL use within the L2 classroom are examples of key aspects of L2 teaching about which there is not yet a '*consensual body of knowledge*' (McIntyre, 1995, p. 371) to inform teacher education. These issues must be confronted by curriculum designers for SLTE, who must make decisions about which evidence to present to beginning teachers concerning how to incorporate grammar explanations and TL within their own classroom practice. (Chapters in Part 2 of this book explore these issues in more detail.) In part as a response to the ongoing debates in Second Language Acquisition (SLA) research and also in acknowledgement of the need for teachers to make choices about which implications from SLA literature are most relevant to learners in their own classroom contexts, Ellis (2010, p. 192) notes that those delivering SLTE have moved away from traditional roles as transmitters of knowledge about SLA towards more of an emphasis on an awareness-raising role, '*encouraging teachers to examine their own teaching practice as in a reflective model of education*'.

Current debates in SLTE

Beyond these underpinning debates about the aims and knowledge base of L2 teaching, SLTE course designers must engage with a range of perennial and contemporary issues in language teacher preparation, including the following:

- How should applicants to SLTE be selected? What knowledge, skills and personal attributes are desirable in a prospective L2 teacher?
- How does knowledge progression occur in the beginning L2 teachers? How can SLTE develop teachers' knowledge, beliefs, attitudes and practices?
- What content should SLTE courses include?

- How long should the SLTE course be and how should the content be sequenced?
- How should field experiences be related to theoretical understandings developed in the SLTE classroom? What is the role of SLA research?
- How should beginning teachers' progress within SLTE courses be evaluated?

The sections that follow outline some of the key lines of argument put forwards in relation to these questions and are intended to stimulate further discussion and reflection.

Selection of applicants for SLTE courses

In many programmes across the globe, the selection and rejection of applicants for SLTE is based in large part on candidates' prior academic attainment in the subject(s) they wish to teach (McGraw & Fish, 2018). One key question is therefore what level of subject knowledge is adequate. Related to this, should adequate subject knowledge be assumed at the point of selection, or should SLTE courses include opportunities for beginning teachers to develop their subject knowledge? Bale (2016, p. 394) points out that student teachers do not just require general proficiency in the TL, *'but also knowledge of, and experience with, the specialized language needed to deploy pedagogical moves'* such as providing TL explanations and repairs when negotiating meaning with learners. The extent to which an SLTE course is able to enhance student teachers' general and pedagogical TL proficiency depends on a range of factors such as: the course length and therefore the time available for language knowledge enhancement activities; how easy it is to recruit prospective teachers with adequate subject knowledge; and the proficiency levels of the students that the course is preparing teachers to work with. It is common across Europe to require a C1 or C2 proficiency level in the Common European Framework for languages (CEFR, 2013) for entry to SLTE. This is roughly equivalent to a Bachelor's degree in the language or an Advanced High level in the proficiency guidelines of the American Council on the Teaching of Foreign Languages (ACTFL, 2012). Where the SLTE programme is focussed on developing teachers of EFL, there is widespread evidence of bias towards native speakers of English both in the selection of candidates and in future employability (Clark & Paran, 2007; Moussu, 2006). This is of great concern, especially since it has been argued that bilingual teachers who share a language with their learners may, in some respects, be better positioned to help their learners make efficient progress in their learning (Llurda, 2005).

Whilst it is clearly vital to have an in-depth understanding of your subject in order to teach it, it is also true that first-rate subject knowledge on its own cannot prepare a teacher to engage a student who sees no point in learning an L2 or to assist a student who is struggling to grasp something that, to the teacher, appears to be self-evident! A narrow focus on measures of academic competence in the selection process is short-sighted since this fails to capture anything about

126 *Laura Molway*

a candidate's understanding of the processes of learning a language; their motivation to teach; their ability to form meaningful relationships with learners; their capacity for reflective thinking; or their relevant life experiences. In selecting candidates for such a person-centred profession, programme designers need to ask themselves what personal and emotional characteristics might be desirable in a teacher as well as what intellectual characteristics are necessary to take on the role.

Regarding L2 teachers' knowledge, another debate of interest is the question of whether successful completion of an SLTE course can equip teachers with all the knowledge and skills that they might need in the course of a life-long career – a notion dismissed as absurd by Freeman (2002). In light of the ever-growing body of research in education in general and in SLA in particular, Lange (1983) highlights the importance of maintaining up-to-date language and pedagogical skills and suggests that lifetime certification for language teachers be scrapped in favour of periodic relicensing. Such radical structural changes are unlikely to be pursued in most contexts. However, SLTE courses could usefully consider how they might prepare beginning teachers to maintain an academic curiosity about their profession and to seek continued opportunities to learn and develop throughout their careers.

Models of SLTE

SLTE commonly takes the following forms: short, intensive courses completed either online or face-to-face (e.g. courses preparing native speakers to teach their own languages such as TEFL[1] or FLE[2] certification); university undergraduate degree programmes that combine a subject specialism focus with preparation for teaching; national postgraduate certification courses; or predominantly school-based models such as *School Direct* in England or *Teach for America* (Maier, 2012).

In addition to these different organizational models of SLTE, there are different underpinning conceptualizations of the process of learning to teach. Three dominant conceptualizations have been described by Winch et al. (2013) as: (1) a craft or apprenticeship model (involving an emphasis on on-the-job training); (2) a technician or 'theory into practice' model (involving initial input of academic content that is later implemented into classroom practice); and (3) a professional or integrated model (involving both practical and theoretical learning opportunities). In this third model, a beginning teacher is supported to make critical judgements about their classroom practice, drawing on three complementary and indispensable strands of knowledge: situated understanding, technical knowledge, and theoretical knowledge. The idea (associated with this third model) that '*student teachers should question, and test against diverse criteria, whatever ideas for practice are presented to them as well as those which they bring with them*' (McIntyre, 1995, p. 371) is known variously as a process of '*practical theorising*' or '*clinical reasoning*' (a term borrowed from the medical profession – see Kriewaldt & Turnidge, 2013).

Integrated models of teacher education, in which theoretical input is interwoven with practical experiences, offer a potential means to increase the professionalism and status of teachers, preparing them to be both consumers and creators of new knowledge about teaching and to develop adaptive expertise and problem-solving skills that enable career-long professional learning (BERA and RSA, 2014). This approach is in line with recent calls for teachers to become *'competent and confident professionals [...] able to engage in enquiry rich practice [...] to analyse and interrogate evidence and arguments, drawing critically and self-critically from a wide range of evidence to make informed decisions in the course of their practice'* (UCET, 2020, p. 1). However, it is important to note that the merits of introducing beginning teachers to the complexities of practical theorising (i.e. the process of critical reflection described above) at an early stage of learning to teach have been questioned on the grounds that this might undermine their confidence and sense of self-efficacy (Burn & Mutton, 2018). An alternative approach might involve an initial apprenticeship phase of teacher education where student teachers are asked to follow clear frameworks with a view to developing automaticity in some basic, practical teaching skills, before subsequently being asked to adopt an inquiry stance (Cochran-Smith & Lytle, 2009) and synthesize evidence from multiple sources to design their own research-informed and contextualized teaching methodologies.

Building research literacy in integrated models

Integrated models can help beginning L2 teachers to identify productive tensions between what is observed in classroom field experiences and what is suggested by educational research. Course designers might seek to explicitly acknowledge these tensions and place emphasis on beginning teachers (a) reflecting on research-informed principles that seem likely to foster good language learning, and (b) developing *'situated methodologies'* (Ur, 2013), which are effective in their individual school and classroom contexts. In order to facilitate L2 teachers' engagement with SLA research, attempts have been made to synthesize findings and construct some guiding pedagogical principles that L2 teachers can use to inform their teaching (Ellis, 2005; Lightbown, 2003; Macaro et al., 2016; Nation & Macalister, 2010; Smith & Conti, 2016). SLTE course designers might draw on these resources as a starting point for engaging beginning teachers with some of the underpinning SLA research.

One issue with the use of SLA research to inform SLTE programmes is that much of this research is based in contexts where English is the L2 being learned (ESL/EFL). It is likely that the process of learning a language differs depending on the L1(s) spoken by the learners and the nature and status of the L2 that is targeted for learning. For example, student teachers learning to teach French in high schools in the USA will encounter learners with very different motivational profiles and prior exposure to the L2 than, say, student teachers learning to teach

128 *Laura Molway*

English in bilingual schools in India. SLTE courses need to be sensitive to these differences and consider how best to help student teachers to select the most appropriate research evidence to inform their teaching. This might entail a programme designed to build the research literacy of beginning teachers, enabling them to identify and critically reflect on the relevance, validity and reliability of SLA research findings. There is a key accessibility issue to be resolved in that much SLA research that is still published in pay-to-access academic journals. SLTE courses could therefore ensure that student teachers are introduced to open-access sources of reading (and perhaps journals linked to national subject associations) that are likely to remain accessible to teachers once they have completed their studies.

Relative weighting of practical experience

Across the world, over the last two decades, there has been a 'practicum turn' in teacher education, with increasing importance being placed on beginning teachers gaining substantial amounts of practical 'field' experience of teaching in real classrooms. In some contexts, a move to privilege teaching experience has been made in direct opposition to the idea that teachers should engage with theory and reflection (Ellis & Orchard, 2014). However, extended opportunities for beginning teachers to learn from experience have also been integrated into courses where research-informed theoretical knowledge is drawn on alongside knowledge generated by observation, reflection and action within the field of practice. This is either done via blocked practicum (five days a week in the field for a number of weeks) or distributed practicum (usually between two to four days a week in the field over an extended period of time, interleaved with study in the university). The integration of extensive field experience with research-informed theoretical input has implications for overall course length: most SLTE courses last for a period from a few months to no longer than two years. Longer courses self-evidently offer student teachers more opportunities to synthesize their learning from multiple sources within an integrated model, and to master the complex process of developing practical theories of teaching for their individual classroom contexts.

An increase in the proportion of time that beginning teachers spend gaining field experience brings with it an expansion of the role and influence of field-based professional mentors. Much of experienced teachers' classroom behaviour is known to be automatized, unconsciously guided by a range of social, cognitive, affective and motivational drivers (Korthagen, 2016). Field-based mentors have sometimes been found to struggle to articulate their expert pedagogical knowledge (because this has become routinized over time, and thus subconscious) or to explain the reasoning behind their classroom actions for the benefit of student teachers under their guidance. SLTE course designers therefore need to think carefully about how they might best support colleagues in the field who take on this role.

Demand for new forms of SLTE

Around the world, one driving force of change in L2 education is the adoption of bilingual education programmes (such as CLIL in mainland Europe), where learners study one or more curriculum subjects in their L2 alongside their usual L2 lessons. Modelled on French/English immersion programmes in Canada, this approach offers learners sustained exposure to the L2 and is fast becoming a mainstream model of education in countries such as Spain and Germany. (See chapter 4 in this volume for an in-depth discussion of CLIL). For SLTE, there is therefore increasing demand for programmes that can equip teachers to teach both a language and a non-language subject. There is also growing demand for SLTE programmes that are designed to support content subject specialists to take on an additional language teaching role.

As many countries recognize the importance of L2 learning, there also is an ongoing shift towards beginning the teaching of an L2 earlier in learners' educational journey. Almost all European countries have a long-established expectation that children begin learning an L2 at elementary school, and majority English-speaking countries such as New Zealand and the UK have made recent moves to introduce L2 learning earlier, reflecting a desire to improve the proficiency level reached by the end of formalized education. In countries where L2 teaching expertise is underdeveloped at elementary level, such policy changes present significant challenges for SLTE, as generalist elementary school teachers may need to upskill to meet demand (a need identified, for example, by 48% of primary schools surveyed in England by Tinsley & Board in 2017).

Knowledge progression when learning to teach an L2

Student teachers do not arrive at SLTE courses as blank slates: they bring with them a wealth of previous learning and teaching experiences. Time spent in classrooms as a learner shapes an individual's conception of teaching and acts as a powerful *'apprenticeship of observation'* (Lortie, 1975) or indeed, an *'anti-apprenticeship of observation'* (Moodie, 2016), which prospective L2 teachers (perhaps unconsciously) draw on for default models of what (not) to do in the classroom. Since those who wish to teach an L2 are likely to have, themselves, experienced success in their previous language studies, they may rely relatively uncritically on models of L2 teaching and learning that have worked well for them personally, unless prompted to reflect deeply on these models' effectiveness for a wide range of other learners. Research into the processes of teacher learning has therefore emphasized the importance of engaging with student teachers' initial conceptions and creating safe spaces within which pre-existing ideas about effective teaching can be subjected to rigorous challenge over an extended period (Wright, 2010).

Alongside the cognitive challenges of learning to teach, there is also an emotional and existential process of change that unfolds as student teachers take on a new professional identity and develop a range of interpersonal relationships.

130 *Laura Molway*

Teacher education programmes often struggle to find ways to support student teachers through this process of evolving a new definition of oneself as a teacher and more research is needed in this area (Malderez et al., 2007). We do know that the journey towards becoming an effective teacher is often marked by progression from a preoccupation with one's own teaching performance (what am *I* doing in the classroom and am *I* doing it right?) towards an increasing focus on the learning processes and outcomes of one's students (what are *my students* doing and what are *they* learning?). This shift in focus can be traced through all stages of the teaching process: pre-action (planning), inter-action (teaching) and post-action (reflection and evaluation) (Mutton et al., 2011). In SLTE courses, student teachers' desire to teach through the medium of the L2 may amplify their preoccupations with their own language and teaching performance. It is therefore likely to be helpful if SLTE programme leaders acknowledge these performativity concerns whilst also gently supporting student teachers to worry less about their own performance and more about the quality of the learning opportunities created for their learners.

It is well documented that changes in a beginning teacher's knowledge following exposure to new ideas do not necessarily lead to changes in their deeply held beliefs. Acting on newly received ideas, a beginning teacher may try out new practices in their classroom, but if these practices do not align with their existing beliefs and attitudes, then they are unlikely to be adopted into their practice in the longer term (Opfer & Pedder, 2011). Clarke and Hollingsworth (2002) propose a multidirectional model of teacher growth (see Figure 7.1),

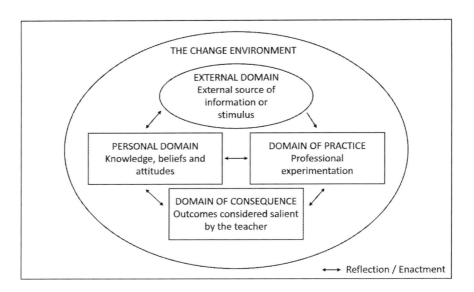

Figure 7.1 Model of teacher growth.

Source: Based on Clarke & Hollingsworth, 2002.

Key issues in pre-service language teacher education 131

which theorizes teacher change as a process mediated by both reflection and enactment. (Enactment describes teachers' actions driven variously by: external stimuli; personal knowledge and beliefs; and/or evidence of impacts). This model suggests that teachers' professional growth can be initiated, potentially simultaneously, in any of four dimensions and it acknowledges that the nature of teacher learning is also affected by the context in which it occurs (represented within the model as the 'change environment').

Given what is known about the non-linear, complex nature of teacher learning, there are clear issues with the way in which many SLTE courses are structured around a linear syllabus (typically involving a series of 'input' sessions, each with a specific theme such as 'developing listening skills', 'behaviour management', 'grammar teaching' and 'assessment for learning'). Linear syllabi may limit the opportunities for student teachers to reflect on and enact changes across the four domains (see Figure 7.1), even when the theoretical and practical elements of an SLTE course are well-integrated. For example, a student teacher who is focussed on resolving pressing behaviour management issues in their practicum at the time when a session on 'assessment for learning' is delivered may find that the content of this input session is a distant memory by the time they come to wrestle with conflicting approaches to marking and feedback in their own practice. When resolving issues that arise in their practice, unless they have had recent opportunities to reflect on relevant educational theory and research, student teachers are likely to rely heavily on practices that they have observed within the field and that align with their own prior knowledge and beliefs. In order to provide opportunities for student teachers to be repeatedly exposed to ideas relating to a range of issues within languages teaching, SLTE course designers could look to create a spiral syllabus, consisting of sessions that integrate several skills, each of which is revisited several times. This would entail an integrated structure, interweaving field experiences with input sessions. Such a design might increase the likelihood that student teachers would find themselves in a position to reflect on relevant field experiences in light of external ideas from research and to rigorously interrogate each source of knowledge with reference to the other. There are many practical issues to designing a spiral syllabus, such as the one envisaged here. However, the use of educational technology may offer some possible solutions (as explored by Khine & Lourdusamy, 2003). Restrictions on face-to-face teaching during the current pandemic have raised teacher educators' awareness of the potential advantages of both synchronous and asynchronous online learning. For example, the development of a repository of pre-recorded inputs about various aspects of SLA could enable student teachers to access ideas from theory and research as and when these are most relevant to their own developing classroom practice.

Tools and activities

SLTE courses use a plethora of tools and activities to help student teachers to develop expertise in planning, teaching and evaluation. These include: lectures and seminars; guided reflection tasks; investigative research tasks and written

132   *Laura Molway*

assignments to engage student teachers with and in research; collaborative planning tasks; micro-teaching episodes; lesson modelling (placing student teachers in the shoes of L2 learners); observation templates; lesson planning templates; feedback from observers of student teachers' lessons; and video footage of student teachers' lessons and/or other teachers' practices for analysis. Much has been written about the pros and cons of various learning tools and activities in the education of teachers, but in this section, I focus on just a few of the ongoing debates.

Lesson planning templates

One ubiquitous tool is the lesson planning template: a standardized format produced by the SLTE course in order to guide student teachers to consider a range of aspects of lesson design that are considered important and to write down a detailed account of the steps of their lesson, usually mapped against the desired learning outcomes. Whilst the structure of such a template can be helpful in the beginning stages of learning to teach, John (2006) warns that student teachers must not become slaves to a rigid outline, as this can stifle the development of problem-solving skills and creativity. A linear, objective-driven approach to planning has also been criticized as leading student teachers to see their lesson plan as a script that should not be deviated from, which may shut off opportunities for learning something valuable that is not pre-determined in the lesson plan (Allwright, 2005; Elliott, 2001). Given the widespread availability of textbooks and online resources to support language teaching and learning, it is also important that SLTE courses support student teachers to create lesson plans that draw on and adapt existing plans created by others. Mutton et al. (2011, p. 410) suggest that '*too often perhaps we work from the assumption that planning is always something that individual student teachers must do for themselves*'. To assist student teachers in the process of learning to plan creatively and flexibly, SLTE courses could encourage collaborative planning. This can create opportunities for student teachers to access the thought processes of more experienced colleagues and to understand the ways in which experienced teachers visualize the possible unfolding of a plan in the context of a specific classroom. The process of collaborative planning also offers field-based colleagues some insight into the student teacher's current thinking and understanding.

Written assignments

Written assignments are important tools in the education of teachers with the aim of them developing a strong professional rationale for actions taken within the classroom. To maximize the potential of written assignments to support student teachers' development of personal theories of practice, students should be encouraged to write about an issue of direct relevance to their own teaching and the structure of the assignment should enable the genuine testing out of ideas for language teaching and learning, integrating knowledge from theory

Key issues in pre-service language teacher education 133

and practice. Mutton et al. (in press) found that L2 student teachers in their SLTE programme experienced tensions between the dual use of assignments as (1) tools to assess their academic competence and (2) tools to support their practical theorising. Course designers should be aware of these tensions and the fact that assignment structures that promote the processes of practical theorising may not necessarily fit the traditional, linear structure of the Social Sciences research tradition.

Modelling

Hockly (2000) suggests that modelling is a strategy currently underused in most teacher education programmes. He suggests that course tutors could model a range of teaching strategies with a focus on different skills (listening, writing, etc.) so that student teachers can experience these strategies first-hand and analyse their effectiveness. This may be particularly effective if done in a language that is not spoken by any of the student teacher cohort since, perhaps for the first time in a while, this offers them a chance to experience the joys and frustrations of language lessons as an individual learner within a class of other beginners. This type of experiential learning provides a stimulus for student teachers to articulate their own beliefs about the process of language learning and a safe space within which these beliefs can be subjected to critical examination.

Medium of instruction

Many SLTE methods courses cater to candidates who are aspiring teachers of multiple languages, which means that the dominant L1 (i.e. in England, English) is the default medium of instruction (Tedick, 2009) and the readings that are drawn on tend to be in that L1. Bale's (2016) small-scale study introduced TL activities and readings into an SLTE methods course and found that the student teachers reported gaining both proficiency in the L2 they were training to teach and also an insight into the experiences of being an L2 learner. For example, some reported that being asked to speak the TL in front of peers was anxiety-inducing. It seems that in contexts where SLTE courses seek to develop student teachers' subject knowledge alongside their pedagogical expertise, it may be fruitful to consider the inclusion of reading materials in the TL that student teachers are training to teach and the use of the TL as the language of instruction for some aspects of the programme.

Video-based observation

Over the last decade, the potential of video recordings of classroom teaching for the purposes of teacher education and evaluation has been the subject of much discussion (Hockly, 2018). There is a range of inexpensive tools that enable teachers to film their own classroom teaching and to easily edit and annotate the resulting footage, which can subsequently be used for analysis and reflection.

134 *Laura Molway*

When designing development opportunities using video as part of an SLTE programme, Baecher and Connor (2016, p. 1) suggest that the focus should be on the potential of self-videoed footage for *'empowerment and growth and for insights made by the viewer, rather than as a means for external evaluation'*. The student teacher should maintain control over the choice of which elements of the footage they are happy to share and discuss with others in order to avoid the developmental potential of the tool becoming distorted by the pressures of performance assessment.

Assessing student teachers' performance within SLTE programmes

There has been a global movement towards competency-based approaches to teacher qualification or licensure and these are often written in such a way that they can be applied across all subject areas. The European portfolio offers an exception in that it identifies 193 descriptors of competences related specifically to language teaching (Newby et al., 2007). Performance indicators such as these offer a transparent and often evidence-informed description of what is considered to be high-quality work in teaching, but a competency-based approach has also been criticized for turning the complex and reciprocally interacting skills of teaching into a tick list of separate skills to be acquired. Performance indicators also tend to focus only on the most visible aspects of teachers' work, sometimes omitting dimensions of teachers' roles that may be less easy to assess. Indeed, an unintended consequence of an overreliance on a competency-based approach may be that it leads student teachers to *focus on target achievement to the detriment or neglect of other less measurable tasks and responsibilities* (Evetts, 2011, p. 415). For example, within SLTE, student teachers' development of their learners' intercultural competence is often left neglected and their performance in this area is often unassessed in SLTE courses.

As student teachers go through their SLTE courses, most receive substantial formative feedback about their classroom teaching performance from course tutors and/or experienced teachers who observe them in the field. However, it is much less common in practice for student teachers to receive meaningful formative feedback specifically in relation to their planning and this is an aspect of learning to teach that may benefit from more careful consideration (Mutton et al., 2011).

The end-of-course assessment of beginning teachers' performance for licensure often consists of a combination of evaluation of a portfolio of evidence compiled by the student teacher (lesson plans, resources, evaluations and feedback) and practical assessments in the form of observations of the student teacher's lessons. Integrated teacher education models often also include assessment in the form of written academic assignments, sometimes at the Master's level. There is an ongoing debate about the subjective nature of assessments in the form of observations of student teachers' lessons. The large-scale Measures of Effective Teaching (MET) project found that even when observers are carefully trained

Key issues in pre-service language teacher education   135

in the use of a research-informed observation protocol, the ratings provided by a single observer are often highly volatile and unreliable (Bill & Melinda Gates Foundation, 2012). For this reason, it may be preferable to avoid an over-reliance on high-stakes observations in the assessment process. The portfolio approach helps to ensure that no one source of evidence is given undue weight and the performance of the student teacher over an extended period of time is considered.

Evaluating the effectiveness of SLTE programmes

The ultimate goal of any SLTE programme is to educate competent and effective L2 teachers who can enhance their students' learning. However, it is extremely difficult to find fair, reliable and valid ways to determine the success of individual SLTE programmes in accomplishing this goal.

The performance of initial teacher education programmes is often evaluated and compared based on a combination of one or more of the following: evaluation of student teachers' performance during their SLTE course; student teachers' own judgements about how well-prepared they feel to teach following their course; and/or the achievement scores of students taught by course graduates in the early years of their career following completion of the SLTE course (Cochran-Smith & Power, 2010). It has been established that high-quality teaching is the most important school-based factor associated with student achievement scores (Schleicher, 2016) and so on the surface, it might seem reasonable to include the test scores of future students (those whom graduates go on to teach once in post) when measuring the success of an SLTE programme. However, as Mayer (2017, p. 10) explains, *what is not so easily agreed upon are the most appropriate ways for determining the impact of teacher education, and indeed the teacher, on student learning.* The validity of student test scores as a measure of the impact of teacher education is undermined by the plethora of other situational variables that can affect students' performance and the performance of a teacher once she has graduated from a teacher education programme. This type of evaluation cannot account for the impact of students' prior learning experiences with their previous teachers and it also usually fails to take account of harder-to-measure outcomes such as students' enjoyment and wellbeing.

Whilst systems of evaluation at the national level may be beyond the influence of individual SLTE course designers, there is nonetheless important work to be done at individual course level to evaluate the impact of SLTE on student teachers' knowledge, belief and practices. Mayer (2017, p. 11) argues that teacher education courses should engage in *regular and systematic evidence-informed analysis,* drawing on research as well as data generated within the provider's own system. Each course should then make appropriate changes to the programme in response to this analysis and subsequently investigate the effect of those changes to determine whether or not they result in improvements.

Given programme designers' vested interest in examining the impact of their work, readers may be surprised to hear that there is, as yet, little conclusive research evidence to show that SLTE programmes have a significant impact on

136 *Laura Molway*

teachers' beliefs and subsequent classroom practices. Whilst there is some evidence of impact (Brouwer & Korthagen, 2005; Yook & Lee, 2016), there are also studies that suggest that such impact is limited (Macaro, 2001; Molway et al., 2020; Peacock, 2001). Studies have also looked at the extent to which graduates of SLTE courses develop adaptive expertise and practical theories to inform their classroom practices. Issues with the flow of relevant SLA research findings to practitioner-focussed publications are known to limit the extent to which graduates of SLTE programmes are able to continue to develop their knowledge of relevant research (Marsden & Kasprowicz, 2017). The available evidence suggests that many L2 teachers do not engage with SLA research in any form following the completion of their training year (Borg, 2010) and one study conducted in England found that very few L2 teachers referred to theory or methodological principles when prompted to explain their teaching practices (Borg & Burns, 2008). Rather than dismissing SLTE as ineffective, it seems likely that the available research has failed to adequately capture the processes of teacher change associated with participation in SLTE programmes and more needs to be done to explore this issue. Inconsistency in study results may be explained by factors such as: methodological issues in study designs; differences in the various SLTE course aims and models; student teachers' own diverse prior learning experiences (Borg, 2003); and the influence of the particular contexts within which they go on to teach.

Concluding comments

I have argued in this chapter for a conception of language teaching as a highly-skilled profession, which is both academic and practical. L2 teachers need to develop an adaptive skillset that prepares them for the challenges of myriad unknown future classrooms and equips them with the confidence to access, generate and respond to new knowledge about the processes of learning and teaching a second language. This conception of the language teaching profession offers a challenge to designers of SLTE programmes: in order for student teachers to engage critically both with practices observed in the field and with the ideas they encounter in the literature, using each to interrogate the other, SLTE courses need to be structured in such a way that field experiences are interleaved with opportunities to reflect on research-informed ideas and theories about effective L2 teaching. I question whether the majority of SLTE courses at present are designed to enable the richly connected learning over an extended period of time that is needed to develop this level of professional expertise.

In a world that is rapidly changing and becoming ever more interconnected, the landscape for SLTE is also shifting rapidly and there are seemingly limitless drivers and possibilities for innovation, drawing on the affordances of new technologies and advances in SLA research, educational psychology and related fields. SLTE courses should engage with these possibilities and be willing to evaluate the aims, curriculum and impact of their current practices in light of new evidence.

Key issues in pre-service language teacher education   137

It is, of course, also important to remember that SLTE sits within international and national policy contexts which shape course aims, content and delivery. At a global level, the education of teachers is affected by movement towards a focus on international measurement and comparison of educational outcomes in order to drive improvements in education systems (Ellis & McNicholl, 2015). This has led to an increasing focus on demonstrating the impact of both student teachers and teacher education programmes in terms of desired student outcomes. It is crucial to scrutinize the impact of SLTE since, through the classroom practices of the teachers it educates, SLTE affects the experiences of innumerable learners. However, there is a continuing need to problematize high-stakes assessment processes both within and of SLTE programmes, since there are concerns about: (a) the validity and reliability of both observations and student outcomes as a proxy for teacher performance; and (b) the potential unintended effects of accountability systems, as they may serve to inflate the perceived importance of measurable aspects of teaching whilst undervaluing less measurable, but nonetheless highly important, elements of a teacher's role. In order to gather more meaningful data about the impact of SLTE, there is an urgent need for longitudinal studies that follow pre-service L2 teachers into later employment. Such studies could combine pupil perception surveys, observations and teachers' self-report data to establish the extent to which ideas and methodologies engaged with during SLTE are reflected in teachers' theories about teaching and their classroom practices.

Relating the issues raised in this chapter to your own context

1   What are the dominant models of SLTE in your own context and to what extent do they enable beginning teachers to synthesize their learning both from practical field experiences and from academic scholarship?
2   Is there a national framework of standards for the accreditation of second language teachers in your own context? What evidence is used when assessing beginning teachers and how robust and reliable do you think this evidence is?

Notes

1   Teaching English as a Foreign Language.
2   Français Langue Étrangère.

References

ACTFL. (2012). *Assigning CEFR Ratings to ACTFL Assessments.* 4. https://www.actfl. org/sites/default/files/reports/Assigning_CEFR_Ratings_To_ACTFL_Assessments.pdf
Agudo, J. de D. M. (Ed.). (2014). *English as a Foreign Language Teacher Education: Current Perspectives and Challenges.* Rodopi. https://ebookcentral.proquest.com/lib/oxford/detail.action?docID=1686926
Allwright, D. (2005). From Teaching Points to Learning Opportunities and beyond. *TESOL Quarterly, 39*(1), 9–31.

138 *Laura Molway*

Andrews, S. (2003). Teacher Language Awareness and the Professional Knowledge Base of the L2 Teacher. *Language Awareness, 12*(2), 81–95. https://doi.org/10.1080/09658410308667068

Baecher, L., & Connor, D. (2016). Video as a Tool in Teacher Learning. *New Educator, 12*(1), 1–4. https://doi.org/10.1080/1547688X.2015.1066912

Bale, J. (2016). Language Proficiency in an Era of Accountability: Using the Target Language to Learn How to Teach. *Journal of Teacher Education, 67*(5), 392–407. https://doi.org/10.1177/0022487116667196

BERA & RSA. (2014). *Research and the Teaching Profession: Building the Capacity for a Self-Improving Education System.* http://www.bera.ac.uk/project/research-and-teacher-education

Bill & Melinda Gates Foundation. (2012). *Gathering feedback for teaching: Combining high-quality observations with student surveys and achievement gains.* Measuring Effective Teaching (MET) Project Research Paper. Seattle, WA.

Borg, S. (2003). Teacher Cognition in Language Teaching: A Review of Research on What Language Teachers Think, Know, Believe, and Do. *Language Teaching, 2*, 81–109. https://doi.org/10.1017/S0261444803001903

Borg, S. (2010). Language Teacher Research Engagement. *Language Teaching 43*(4). https://doi.org/10.1017/S0261444810000170

Borg, S., & Burns, A. (2008). Integrating Grammar in Adult TESOL Classrooms. *Applied Linguistics, 29*(3), 456–482. https://doi.org/10.1093/applin/amn020

Brouwer, N., & Korthagen, F. (2005). Can Teacher Education Make a Difference? *American Educational Research Journal, 42*(1), 153–224.

Burn, K., & Mutton, T. (2018). Constructing the Curriculum of (Initial) Teacher Education: When Should New Teachers Be Encouraged to Ask Critical Questions? *Impact: Journal of the Chartered College of Teaching,* September. https://impact.chartered.college/article/constructing-curriculum-initial-teacher-education-when-new-teachers-encouraged-ask-critical-questions/

Byram, M., Gribkova, B., & Starkey, H. (2002). *Developing the Intercultural Dimension in Language Teaching: A Practical Introduction for Teachers.* http://www.coe.int/t/dg4/linguistic/source/guide_dimintercult_en.pdf

CEFR. (2013). *Common European Framework of Reference for Languages – Self-assessment Grid.* https://europass.cedefop.europa.eu/sites/default/files/cefr-en.pdf

Chevallard, Y. J. C. (1986). La Transposition didactique: du savoir savant au savoir enseigné. *Revue Française de Pédagogie, 76*(1), 89–91.

Clark, E., & Paran, A. (2007). The Employability of Non-native-speaker Teachers of EFL: A UK Survey. *System, 35*(4), 407–430. https://doi.org/10.1016/j.system.2007.05.002

Clarke, D., & Hollingsworth, H. (2002). Elaborating a Model of Teacher Professional Growth. *Teaching and Teaching Education, 18*, 947–967.

Cochran-Smith, M., & Lytle, S. L. (2009). *Inquiry as Stance: Practitioner Research for the Next Generation.* Teachers College Press.

Cochran-Smith, M., & Power, C. (2010). New Directions for Teacher Preparation. *Educational Leadership, 67*(8), 6–13.

Elliott, J. (2001). Making Evidence-based Practice Educational. *British Educational Research Journal, 27*(5), 555–574. https://doi.org/10.1080/01411920120095735

Ellis, R. (2005). Principles of Instructed Language Learning. *System, 33*(2), 209–224. https://doi.org/10.1016/j.system.2004.12.006

Ellis, R. (2010). Second Language Acquisition, Teacher Education and Language Pedagogy. *Language Teaching, 43*(2), 182. https://doi.org/10.1017/S0261444809990139

Ellis, V., & McNicholl, J. (2015). *Transforming Teacher Education : Reconfiguring the Academic Work*. Bloomsbury.

Ellis, V., & Orchard, J. (2014). Learning teaching 'from experience': Towards a history of the idea. In V. Ellis & J. Orchard (Eds.), *Learning Teaching from Experience: Multiple Perspectives and International Contexts* (pp. 1–18). Bloomsbury Academic. https://doi.org/10.5040/9781472593313.ch-001

Evetts, J. (2011). A New Professionalism? Challenges and Opportunities. *Current Sociology*, 59(4), 406–422. https://doi.org/10.1177/0011392111402585

Freeman, D. (2002). The Hidden Side of the Work: Teacher Knowledge and Learning to Teach. A Perspective from North American Educational Research on Teacher Education in English Language Teaching. *Language Teaching*, 35(1), 1–13. https://doi.org/10.1017/S0261444801001720

Freeman, D., & Johnson, K. E. (1998). Reconceptualizing the Knowledge-Base of Language Teacher Education. *TESOL Quarterly*, 32(3), 397–417. https://doi.org/10.2307/3588114

Hockly, N. (2000). Modelling and "Cognitive Apprenticeship" in Teacher Education. *ELT Journal*, 54(2), 118–125. https://doi.org/10.1093/elt/54.2.118

Hockly, N. (2018). Video-based Observation in Language Teacher Education. *ELT Journal*, 72(3), 329–355. https://doi.org/10.1093/elt/ccy022

John, P. D. (2006). Lesson Planning and the Student Teacher: Re-thinking the Dominant Model. *Journal of Curriculum Studies*, 38(4), 483–498. https://doi.org/10.1080/00220270500363620

Korthagen, F. (2016). Inconvenient Truths about Teacher Learning: Towards Professional Development 3.0. *Teachers and Teaching*, 23(4), 1–19. https://doi.org/10.1080/13540602.2016.1211523

Khine, M., & Lourdusamy, A. (2003). Blended Learning Approach in Teacher Education: Combining Face-to-Face Instruction, Multimedia Viewing and Online Discussion. *British Journal of Educational Technology*, 34(5), 671–675.

Kriewaldt, J., & Turnidge, D. (2013). Conceptualising an Approach to Clinical Reasoning in the Education Profession. *Australian Journal of Teacher Education*, 38(6). https://doi.org/10.14221/ajte.2013v38n6.9

Lange, D. L. (1983). Teacher Development and Certification in Foreign Languages : Where is the Future? *The Modern Language Journal*, 67(4), 374–381.

Lightbown, P. M. (2003). SLA research in the classroom/SLA research for the classroom. *The Language Learning Journal*, 28(February 2012), 4–13. https://doi.org/10.1080/09571730385200151

Llurda, E. (2005). *Non-native Language Teachers: Perceptions, Challenges and Contributions to the Profession*. Springer.

Lortie, D. (1975). *Schoolteacher: A Sociological Study*. University of Chicago Press.

Macaro, E. (2001). Analysing Student Teachers' Codeswitching in Foreign Language Classrooms: Theories and Decision Making. *The Modern Language Journal*, 85(4), 531–548. https://doi.org/10.1111/0026-7902.00124

Macaro, E., Graham, S., & Woore, R. (2016). *Improving Foreign Language Teaching: Towards a Research-based Curriculum and Pedagogy*. Routledge.

Maier, A. (2012). Doing Good and Doing Well: Credentialism and Teach for America. *Journal of Teacher Education*, 63(1), 10–22. https://doi.org/10.1177/0022487111422071

Malderez, A., Hobson, A. J., Tracey, L., & Kerr, K. (2007). Becoming a Student Teacher: Core Features of the Experience. *European Journal of Teacher Education*, 30(3), 225–248. https://doi.org/10.1080/02619760701486068

140   *Laura Molway*

Marsden, E., & Kasprowicz, R. (2017). Foreign Language Educators' Exposure to Research: Reported Experiences, Exposure via Citations, and a Proposal for Action. *Modern Language Journal, 101*(4), 613–642. https://doi.org/10.1111/modl.12426

Mayer, D. (2017). Professionalizing Teacher Education Accountability. *Oxford Research Encyclopedia of Education*, May 2017, 1–25. https://doi.org/10.1093/acrefore/9780190264093.013.96

McGraw, A., & Fish, T. (2018). Selection and Rejection in Teacher Education: Qualities of Character Crucial in Selecting and Developing Teacher Education Students. *Asia-Pacific Journal of Teacher Education, 46*(2), 120–132. https://doi.org/10.1080/1359866X.2017.1355048

McIntyre, D. (1995). Initial Teacher Education as Practical Theorising: A Response to Paul Hirst. *British Journal of Educational Studies, 43*(4), 365–383.

Moeller, A., & Nugent, K. (2014). Developing Intercultural Competence in the Language Classroom. *Faculty Publications: Department of Teaching, Learning and Teacher Education, 161*, 1–18. https://doi.org/10.1002/9781118784235.eelt0282

Molway, L., Arcos, M., & Macaro, E. (2020). Language Teachers' Reported First and Second Language Use: A comparative contextualized study. *Language Teaching Research*, 1–34. https://doi.org/10.1177/1362168820913978

Moodie, I. (2016). The Anti-apprenticeship of Observation: How Negative Prior Language Learning Experience Influences English Language Teachers' Beliefs and Practices. *System, 60*, 29–41. https://doi.org/10.1016/j.system.2016.05.011

Moussu, L. (2006). *Native and Nonnative English-Speaking English as a Second Language Teachers: Student Attitudes, Teacher Self-Perceptions, and Intensive English Administrator Beliefs and Practices.* Purdue University. https://doi.org/10.1007/s13398-014-0173-7.2

Mutton, T., Hagger, H., & Burn, K. (2011). Learning to Plan, Planning to Learn: The Developing Expertise of Beginning Teachers. *Teachers and Teaching: Theory and Practice, 17*(4), 399–416. https://doi.org/10.1080/13540602.2011.580516

Mutton, T., Woore, R., and Molway, L. (in press) Supporting Student Teachers' Practical Theorising via Written Assignments. In Mutton, T., Childs, A., and Burn, K. (Eds.) *Practical Theorising in Initial Teacher Education.* Routledge.

Nation, I., & Macalister, J. (2010). *Language Curriculum Design.* Routledge.

Newby, D., Allan, R., Fenner, A.-B., Jones, B., Komorowska, H., & Soghikyan, K. (2007). *The European Portfolio for Student Teachers of Languages.* Council of Europe. http://archive.ecml.at/mtp2/fte/pdf/C3_Epostl_E.pdf

Opfer, V. D., & Pedder, D. (2011). Conceptualizing Teacher Professional Learning. *Review of Educational Research, 81*(3), 376–407. https://doi.org/10.3102/0034654311413609

Peacock, M. (2001). Pre-service ESL Teachers' Beliefs about Second Language Learning: A Longitudinal Study. *System, 29*(2), 177–195. https://doi.org/10.1016/S0346-251X(01)00010-0

Schleicher, A. (2016). Teaching excellence through professional learning and policy reform: Lessons from around the world. In *International Summit on the Teaching Profession.* OECD Publishing. https://doi.org/http://dx.doi.org/10.1787/9789264252059-en

Shulman, L. (1986). Those Who Understand: Knowledge Growth in Teaching. *Educational Researcher, 15*(2), 4–14. https://doi.org/10.3102/0013189X015002004

Smith, S., & Conti, G. (2016). *The Language Teacher Toolkit.* CreateSpace Independent Publishing Platform.

Tedick, D. J. (2009). K–12 Language Teacher Preparation: Problems and Possibilities. *Modern Language Journal, 93*(2), 263–267.

Tinsley, T., & Board, K. (2017). *Language Trends 2016/17: Language Teaching in Primary and Secondary Schools in England*. British Council. https://doi.org/10.1016/j.pcl.2008.07.007

UCET. (2020). *Intellectual Base of Teacher Education Report*. https://www.ucet.ac.uk/11675/intellectual-base-of-teacher-education-report-updated-february-2020

Ur, P. (2013). Language-teaching Method Revisited. *ELT Journal, 67*(4), 468–474. https://doi.org/10.1093/elt/cct041

Winch, C., Orchard, J., & Oancea, A. (2013). *The Contribution of Educational Research to Teachers' Professional Learning – Philosophical Understandings*. BERA.

Wright, T. (2010). Second Language Teacher Education: Review of Recent Research on Practice. In *Language Teaching, 43*(3). https://doi.org/10.1017/S0261444810000030

Yook, C., & Lee, Y.-hun. (2016). Korean EFL Teachers' Perceptions of the Impact of EFL Teacher Education upon Their Classroom Teaching Practices. *Asia-Pacific Journal of Teacher Education, 44*(5), 522–536. https://doi.org/10.1080/1359866X.2016.1144171

8 Systemic in-service language teacher education

Simon Borg
(Western Norway University of Applied Sciences)

Introduction

It is now widely accepted that teacher quality is the most significant school-level influence on student outcomes (Opper, 2019). Improving teacher competence has, therefore, become a critical element in global efforts to enhance educational quality. While teachers can improve through professional development activities which are wholly autonomous and individual, in this chapter, I will focus on attempts to promote systemic change in teacher quality through formally organised in-service initiatives. Specifically, the discussion will examine, with reference to the teaching of English as a foreign language, central issues in the planning, implementation and evaluation of in-service programmes that are organised by educational authorities and which seek to promote change in the competence and practices of large numbers of teachers in a particular context. The issues I discuss will also be relevant to in-service work that is more modest and which operates, for example, at the level of individual institutions. However, given ongoing efforts around the world to improve English language teaching through systemic in-service programmes, and my experience of such programmes, they will be my main focus here. Table 8.1 lists a set of illustrative in-service initiatives I will refer to throughout the chapter.

These projects (all active in the last five years, apart from that in Oman which ended in 2009) sought to bring about changes in the work of practising teachers, mostly in primary contexts. Discussion of this work in the academic literature has been limited (EfECT is an exception: see Borg, Clifford, & Htut, 2018), though in-house publications for the Oman project were produced on its conclusion (for example, Atkins, Lamb, & Wedell, 2009) and evaluation reports from the other projects have in some cases been made available online (for example, for EfU: Borg, 2019a). In every case, the in-service training was delivered by an external organisation (most commonly the British Council) in partnership with local educational authorities. Broader discussions of a more sociolinguistic nature regarding the role of international organisations in systemic teacher professional development are beyond my scope here, but it is relevant to note criticisms of approaches which seek to supplant local educational practices with 'foreign' and often contextually unsuitable models of teaching and learning (Wedell, 2009)

DOI: 10.4324/9781003008361-10

Systemic in-service language teacher education   143

Table 8.1 Systemic in-service programmes

Project	Context	Scale
Tejas	India	16,000 primary teachers
SPEX	Azerbaijan	1500 primary/secondary teachers
NTTP	Egypt	22,000 primary teachers
PALTAGs	Occupied Palestine Territory	800 primary teachers
BA TESOL	Oman	920 primary teachers
EfECT	Myanmar	2000 college teachers
RETC	Thailand	17,000 primary/secondary English teachers
EfU	Ukraine	330 university ESP teachers
NTTP	Sudan	3230 primary school teachers

and which, in particular, posit simplistic dichotomies between teacher-centred and student-centred pedagogies (Hardman et al., 2016) in which the latter are unquestioningly superior and thus the goal of educational reform. Without in any way suggesting they were wholly unproblematic, though, the projects I focus on here have been carefully planned, delivered as partnerships with the support of, and with decision-making input by, local educational authorities, and driven by a concern (typically informed by a needs analysis) to support teachers, learners and educational systems more generally.

Drawing on these various in-service initiatives and also considering key themes in the contemporary literature on teacher professional development, the discussion that follows is organised around a number of themes that merit explicit consideration when in-service language teacher education is being planned.

Models of in-service teacher education

A fundamental decision when in-service programmes are being designed regards the model that the programme will adopt. Kennedy (2005) suggested nine models for the continuing professional development (CPD) of teachers as follows: training; award-bearing; deficit; cascade; standards-based; coaching/mentoring; community of practice; action research; and transformative. Some of these distinctions are problematic because they are not exclusive; an award-bearing programme may adopt an action research model; cascade models may also reflect a deficit orientation. Kennedy's definition of what she called the transformative model ('the combination of a number of processes and conditions ... drawn from the other models ... not a clearly definable model in itself' – p. 246) also emphasizes the overlaps in her typology. Kennedy (2014) revisited her original typology and proposed eight models of CPD; a key difference here was that action research and what she had called the transformative model were combined into 'collaborative professional inquiry models'.

I see action research as an example of a professional development strategy rather than a model, which is a broader concept defined by a range of principles. It is useful, therefore, to separate models of in-service work as a set of principles (closer to what Feiman-Nemser, 1990 called 'orientations') from the concrete

144 *Simon Borg*

Table 8.2 Models of in-service teacher education

Parameter	Transmission model	Constructivist model
Role of teachers	Acquiring and later applying propositional knowledge	Reflecting on received and experiential knowledge; learning with and from colleagues
Role of 'trainer'	Authoritative source of propositional knowledge	Facilitative guide for teacher learning
Nature of content	Propositional (received knowledge)	Propositional, practical, personal and experiential
Teacher learning processes	Input from the trainer	Dialogue with the teacher educator and colleagues; reflection; inquiry in the classroom
Site of teacher learning	Training room	Schools and classrooms
Dynamics	Individual: teachers learn primarily from the trainer	Collaborative: teachers learn together and from one another
Role of classroom practice	Propositional knowledge shapes classroom practice	Experience provides the basis for evaluating received knowledge

strategies through which such models can be implemented. As an example, Table 8.2 summarizes two contrasting models with reference to a number of underlying principles. These are theoretical extremes and in practice in-service programmes will not be so sharply defined. But the divisions highlighted here illustrate clearly the very different ways in which in-service teacher education can be conceptualized.

In common with Kennedy's analysis and, more recently, that of Hayes (2019), the first model sees professional development as the acquisition of propositional knowledge which teachers receive via input from an authoritative trainer. The in-service work often occurs at an off-site training venue and teachers are subsequently expected to put the knowledge acquired into practice when they return to their schools (often after the formal end of the training). On larger-scale initiatives, this model often utilizes a cascade mode of delivery, through which teacher educators first complete the in-service course themselves before subsequently delivering it to larger groups of teachers (for discussions, including criticisms of cascade training, see Bett, 2016; Hayes, 2000; Turner, Wilson, & Brownhill, 2016).

In contrast, a constructivist model sees teacher learning as a process of theorizing practice, enquiring, reflecting on experience, and learning with and from peers. The classroom is recognized as a key site for teacher learning and external support may come from facilitators or mentors who guide teachers rather than seeking to determine what and how they learn. Accounts of what makes professional development effective (for a recent analysis, see Weston & Hindly, 2019) tend to highlight such constructivist characteristics, as seen in the following summary of the literature.

Systemic in-service language teacher education   145

There is an emerging consensus that CPD 'works' better when it has these features:

- relevance to the needs of teachers and their students
- teacher involvement in decisions about content and process
- teacher collaboration
- support from the school leadership
- exploration and reflection with attention to both practices and beliefs
- internal and/or external support for teachers (e.g. through mentoring)
- job-embeddedness (i.e. CPD is situated in schools and classrooms)
- contextual alignment (with reference to the institutional, educational, social and cultural milieu)
- critical engagement with received knowledge
- a valuing of teachers' experience and knowledge.

(Borg, 2015, p. 6)

Such features are evident in a number of specific contemporary professional development strategies, such as mentoring (Davis, 2014), action research (Mills, 2014) and lesson study (Lewis & Hurd, 2011).

The projects in Table 8.1 illustrate the point made earlier that, in practice, in-service programmes will be located on a continuum between the transmission-constructivist extremes. Oman, EfECT, RETC, NTTP in Sudan and SPEX were all characterized by a series of trainer-delivered input sessions (and hence more transmission-oriented), but in all cases, participants were also given regular opportunities to reflect, discuss, learn from colleagues and make connections between input and classroom practice. Tejas, NTTP in Egypt and PALTAGs were more obviously constructivist; they utilized a community of practice Teacher Activity Group (TAG) approach through which teachers met once a month over a school year to talk and learn about teaching under the guidance of a facilitator[1]. In between the monthly meetings, the teachers interacted online using social media to share experiences from their classrooms. It is clear, too, from these examples, that decisions about models of in-service work are never made solely on theoretical grounds; factors such as the resources available (including budget), contextual feasibility, existing educational cultures (including approaches to CPD), and the wishes of local education authorities will also exert significant influence.

While constructivist models of professional development are strongly favoured in the contemporary literature, three caveats are necessary when general conclusions from this literature are being applied to the field of foreign language teaching.

1   The first is that empirical evidence specific to teacher learning in our field remains limited and conclusions in the literature about what 'works' come largely from other disciplinary areas. Caution is thus justified when, for example, using evidence from in-service work with science teachers in secondary schools in the USA to inform decisions about supporting teachers of English in primary schools in Sudan.

146   *Simon Borg*

2   The second caveat is that the potential contexts for in-service language teacher education vary so significantly that it is unrealistic to expect any one particular definitively superior model or approach to emerge. As Weston and Hindly (2019, p. 65) note, 'it seems particularly unlikely that any one standard design of professional development would be appropriate nor indeed practical in all contexts'.

3   Finally, it is important to avoid blind assumptions about the effectiveness of certain models of in-service teacher education simply because they are theoretically fashionable. Constructivist models assume that certain conditions are in place, such as skilled teacher educators, adequate levels of teacher autonomy, time, and reflective and inquiry skills among teachers. In many contexts, such conditions do not exist and this should be taken into account when in-service programmes are being designed. Compatibility between existing approaches to CPD and the proposed design for in-service work is also an important issue.

Thus while, overall, there is consensus in the literature about those broad features that will enhance the effectiveness of in-service programmes (see, for example, Popova et al., 2018, who focus in particular on at-scale in-service work internationally), one key over-riding principle in choosing a model of in-service teacher education – and the specific strategies for implementing it – is that it needs to be feasible in the target context. On the SPEX programme in Azerbaijan, for example, interactive workshops led by teacher educators alternated, over the course of a school year, with reflective sessions in which teachers shared their experiences of trying out ideas from the workshops in their classrooms. It had initially been envisaged that teachers could organize these sessions independently as collaborative dialogues, without the presence of the teacher educator. However, it was felt that, in that context, in-service teacher education was given credibility by the presence of a teacher educator and that teachers were unlikely to meet to discuss their teaching in a self-directed, less formally organised manner. The programme was thus modified, so that teacher educators led these reflective sessions. To take one further example, the NTTP programme in Sudan was characterized by several features of a transmission model: cascade training, input-based workshops (every weekend for 12 weeks) and no school-based component. While not theoretically ideal, this was a feasible model given the scale of the programme (over 3000 teachers), conditions in schools (modest support for professional development), a lack of mentors to provide school-based support, and teacher attributes (such as the limited experience of teacher-led and collaborative CPD).

Teacher autonomy and motivation

In her framework for CPD, Kennedy (2005) saw the move from transmissive to transformative models as being strongly linked with increasing levels of teacher autonomy. This notion has been conceptualized in many ways (for a review, see Parker, 2015), but for the purposes of this discussion, it refers to the

Systemic in-service language teacher education   147

independence which teachers can exercise in relation to professional development – for example, whether joining a course is voluntary or not; whether they have a say in when, how and what they learn on an in-service programme; and how much freedom they have to change what and how they teach.

It must be recognized that systemic in-service programmes may be limited in their ability to promote teacher autonomy by a range of factors: educational systems that are centralized (for example, where professional development is prescribed and autonomy is an emergent concept); the expertise of teacher educators (higher levels of competence are required for in-service work that promotes teacher autonomy) and even teachers' own expectations (that in-service work involves acquiring knowledge that is externally defined). Many of these factors will explain why, on most of the projects listed in Table 8.1, decisions about programme objectives, content and processes were largely centralized and applied across cohorts of teachers. In certain cases, though, teachers were able to assume some ownership. On Tejas, as noted earlier, teachers were encouraged to use experience from their classrooms as the content for discussions of pedagogical issues, while on PALTAGs, each monthly meeting involved presentations by teachers, in which they shared classroom experiences and discussed their attempts to implement ideas acquired during the in-service programme (British Council, 2019b).

An issue of particular relevance to teacher autonomy is whether participation by teachers in systemic in-service programmes should be voluntary or compulsory. In several projects I have worked on, Ministries of Education have nominated the teachers who are required to participate. While this would seem to contravene one principle for effective professional development – voluntary engagement by teachers (Lamb & Wyatt, 2019, for example, advise that in-service teacher education should not be forced on teachers) – it can be justified on the basis that systemic educational reform is unlikely if only a minority of the change agents participate in the activities that are meant to support the reform. It is also the case that, when given the option of joining an in-service programme – particularly one that is extended – not all teachers will do so. Various factors may contribute to such a situation such as workload concerns and previous negative experiences of in-service programmes. Regarding the latter, on the NTTP in Egypt, it was reported that some teachers were reluctant to join because they expected the training to be similar to what they had experienced before and found unproductive. A few months into this project, though, it was also reported that teachers' attitudes had become more positive when they realized that this was a novel programme (British Council, 2019a) and these positive dispositions were also confirmed by survey responses at the end of the project (Borg, 2020).

This perhaps highlights another reason why requiring teachers to join in-service programmes is not always a bad thing: the belief that initial resistance will wear off once the benefits of participating start to be evident. Well-designed programmes can proceed on such a basis in the knowledge that, as teachers become motivated to participate, a lack of teacher autonomy will become less of

148　*Simon Borg*

a concern (is I am enjoying a course and feel I am benefiting, should it bother me that I have no say in its design?). In this sense, it could be argued that teacher motivation trumps teacher autonomy in the hierarchy of factors that contribute to the effectiveness of in-service teacher education programmes. And while teacher autonomy will shape the extent to which teachers are able to modify their teaching during or after an in-service programme, such modifications are unlikely unless the motivation to change exists.

How best to motivate teachers to engage in and benefit from in-service programmes remains a matter of debate, though. Lamb and Wyatt (2019) argue for an intrinsic approach (CPD is motivating as a benefit in its own right) and it has also been noted that 'intrinsic drivers have a profound impact on teacher motivation' (UNESCO-IICBA, 2017, p. 13). I have certainly encountered many teachers who are highly motivated during mandated in-service programmes because they appreciate the opportunity to learn and to improve their teaching. A review of international professional development programmes, though, also concluded that these were more likely to be effective (that is, to lead to gains in student learning) when they were linked to incentives such as promotion or salary: 'without incentives, trainings may not have a meaningful impact' (Popova et al., 2018, p. 25). Understanding what is likely to motivate teachers in different contexts would seem to be key in increasing their engagement with in-service programmes.

Overall, while the principles of self-determination and voluntarism remain desirable, it must be accepted that in many contexts educational reform will be thwarted unless in-service programmes are compulsory. This does not imply, though, a complete absence of teacher autonomy. It is possible, for example, to conceive of centralized in-service work that also gives teachers some ownership of the programme and to allow them to shape it in a way that is beneficial for their professional learning and classroom practices (see, for example, Flessner & Stuckey, 2014, for a discussion of the implementation of a mandated action research scheme for teachers).

Programme objectives

Clearly defined objectives are essential for in-service work; they will drive programme content and processes and also provide a reference point for programme evaluation. Objectives will ideally be based on evidence, such as from a needs analysis which identifies areas of language teaching and learning that can be targeted.

A key question for programme designers, then, relates to WHO the target beneficiaries of an in-service programme are and WHAT specific impacts on these beneficiaries are envisaged. Teachers are the primary beneficiaries of in-service programmes and Table 8.3 lists a range of teacher objectives that such programmes may have.

In-service programmes may also specify objectives in relation to students. After all, as the literature regularly notes (for example, Guskey, 2000; Timperley, 2011), the ultimate purpose of teacher professional development is to enhance

Systemic in-service language teacher education   149

Table 8.3 Teacher objectives on in-service programmes

Focus	Description
Language proficiency	Teachers' command of the target language
Teaching knowledge	Background knowledge about educational theory, teaching and learning
Instructional skills	Teachers' ability to implement specific teaching strategies in training contexts (such as microteaching)
Knowledge of curriculum	Teachers' familiarity with a new curriculum or textbook
Attitudes and beliefs	Broad dispositions and specific views about what is true
Confidence	How well teachers feel they can achieve specific tasks
Classroom practice	Teachers' routine instructional behaviours in classrooms
Reflective competence	Teachers' capacity to analyze, evaluate and change their practices
Inquiry skills	Teachers' ability to conduct classroom research for professional development
Collegiality	Teachers' ability to collaborate effectively

Source: Adapted from Borg (2018a).

the learning experience and thus it is entirely reasonable to expect students to benefit from in-service programmes too. A focus on improving student achievement is also regularly cited as a feature of effective professional development for teachers (Weston & Hindly, 2019). While this is a theoretically sound argument, though, the sophisticated evaluation designs required to examine causal links between in-service programmes and student outcomes, particularly achievement, mean that such links are rarely systematically explored. Thus, while many of the in-service language teacher education programmes I have worked on have posited potential benefits for students, these have tended to focus on other outcomes (important in themselves) such as student attitudes, motivation and behaviour in the classroom rather than achievement. For example, on Tejas, one objective in relation to primary school students was that they would, as a result of the project, speak more English during lessons; this was assessed through classroom observations without, though, any attempt to measure changes in student achievement. The relatively short time scales of many in-service interventions also means that a focus on measuring improvements in student achievement is often not feasible. A longer-term (2008–2017) and well-funded (over £50 million) project such as *English in Action* in Bangladesh, does, however, illustrate how the formal measurement of learners' English proficiency can be incorporated into the evaluation of in-service language teacher education[2].

Finally, it can be noted here that systemic in-service teacher education programmes may also target changes at an institutional level. For example, a programme might seek to create a more collaborative school ethos, one where decisions are data-driven and based on inquiry, where student learning is a central concern or where professional development is valued and supported. The EfU project illustrates such concerns; teachers who attended the in-service programme were required, on return to their institutions, to organize seminars

150   Simon Borg

for colleagues through which they disseminated what they had learned; these regular events also encouraged the ongoing sharing and discussion of classroom practice within ESP departments. The national 'Quality for Competence' in-service programme in Norway also has as one of its objectives 'collective learning and development of professional community in each school' (Ministry of Education, 2015, p. 5).

Programme content

As noted above, objectives will drive decisions about programme content and here too various choices are available, not just in terms of the topics teachers will engage with during an in-service programme but also regarding how centrally defined this content is. For all the programmes in Table 8.1, decisions about content were made by the programme designers (typically on the basis of a needs analysis), and materials were then identified or designed to cover relevant topics. On Tejas and NTTP in Egypt, for example, these materials took the form of resource books that contained various practical units of work focused on language development and teaching methods, while on PALTAGs, teachers studied online teaching methodology modules related to areas of classroom practice with which teachers needed most support. The Oman project was award-bearing and content was chosen to provide adequate academic coverage of the field of primary ELT. There are several good reasons for working with standardized content on in-service programmes. For example, it allows for consistency across groups of teachers working simultaneously in different locations. It also reduces the demands on teacher educators, which is a significant factor when (a) this role is being fulfilled on a part-time basis (on Tejas and the NTTP in Egypt, for example, teacher educators were also full-time teachers); (b) teacher educators have limited experience of designing in-service materials; and (c) the in-service programme is being delivered intensively (as on the EfECT and RETC programmes). On large-scale systemic programmes, pre-defined materials greatly simplify programme management.

Another content-related decision relates to how localized the materials for an in-service programme will be. Localization adds face validity and increases teachers' perceptions of the relevance of a programme. However, high-quality localized content requires a budget. On EfECT, this was available and a set of modules (for details, see Borg et al., 2018) were designed specifically for this programme. In Oman, too, there was substantial investment in the development of bespoke materials linked to the teachers' context. On other programmes, budgets have constrained the extent to which localized materials could be developed. The original materials used on Tejas, for example, were often rather generic and not closely linked to the teachers' curriculum in Maharashtra. OETIS, a small online programme for teachers of English in Syria, also utilized a set of online language development and 'global' teaching methodology modules. While producing localized materials will enhance their relevance to the teachers, this is often not an option due to the resources required (including expertise and funding).

Systemic in-service language teacher education 151

A flexible approach to defining content during in-service work is more feasible when a school-based and teacher-led approach is adopted. For example, the Teacher Leadership and Learning Programme, supported by the Ontario Ministry of Education, helped teachers conduct self-directed professional development. Clearly, while this (voluntary) programme was regulated by an over-arching framework, the focus was on teacher-led, often collaborative, activity in schools (Lieberman, Campbell, & Yashkina, 2017). There was thus no standardized content for teachers to learn, and decisions were made locally depending on the focus of the teachers' projects. This is a feature of in-service work that utilizes action research and similar strategies, and while these are well-established in our field (Burns, 2010; Rebolledo, Smith, & Bullock, 2016), they have not in my experience been applied at a systemic level. The English Language Teacher Development project (Bowden, 2013) in Malaysia was, though, a large-scale initiative (1200 primary teachers in 600 schools, supported by 120 mentors) that eschewed formal workshops and adopted a mentoring model. There was no pre-determined package of content for the programme and mentors and teachers met regularly in schools and worked together on issues that were of immediate relevance to teaching and learning. Perhaps the single feature of this project that allowed it to implement mentoring on such a scale was the funding available; this made it possible for 120 full-time expatriate mentors to be employed, enabling a highly favourable ratio of one mentor for every ten teachers (on the ELISS mentoring programme in West India, in contrast, the ratio was 1:15, with mentors who continued to be full-time teachers of English and received a one-day reduction in their workload but no additional pay: see Borg & Parnham, 2020). It is clear from these examples that decisions about the model of an in-service programme (see section "Models of in-service teacher education") can have significant implications for its content, in particular the degree of standardisation (how far all teachers cover the same material), localization (the extent to which content is linked to teachers' specific contexts), individualization (how far the content is tailored to a teacher's specific needs) and ownership (teacher involvement in shaping the content).

Teacher educators

Just as the quality of learning that students experience is powerfully shaped by the competence of their teachers, teacher educator competence has a significant effect on the quality of in-service programmes, irrespective of their design principles. In other words, it is simplistic to argue that, for example, constructivist approaches such as mentoring will necessarily produce superior results to more conventional workshop-based in-service work – so much depends on the teacher educator. The importance of teacher educator competence in in-service programmes, therefore, cannot be over-stated. The specific competences that are required will vary across programmes depending on the model and specific strategy they adopt and their goals. However, it is possible to identify some broad competences which in-service teacher educators require.

152   *Simon Borg*

In education generally, Koster et al. (2005) defined a competence profile for teacher educators which consisted of four areas: content competencies, communicative and reflective competencies, organizational competencies and pedagogical competencies. Each area was broken down into specific sub-competencies. Similar frameworks appear elsewhere in the literature (for example, Goodwin & Kosnik, 2013) and, while they do provide interesting insight, their focus on university-based teacher educators working with prospective teachers means their relevance to systemic in-service programmes in developing contexts must be carefully assessed.

In language teaching, Malderez and Wedell (2007) and Wright and Bolitho (2007) discuss issues relevant to teacher educator competence (the latter for example, stress the importance of facilitation skills and building on participants' prior knowledge). Matei et al. (2007) focus in more detail on the following aspects of a language teacher educator's profile: background knowledge, organisation and presentation, training methodology, facilitation, observation, attitudes, and motivation. More recently, a framework proposed by the British Council (2015)[4] suggests that competent teacher educators require professional practices (such as understanding how teachers learn and supporting and mentoring teachers), enabling skills (such as communicating effectively and teamworking skills) and self-awareness features (such as openness and empathy). While this is not always made explicit in frameworks of teacher educator competences, it is also typically assumed that teacher educators will already have well-developed basic classroom teaching competences.

As noted above, the specific requirements of different in-service programmes will vary, but the general point here is that, given the impact teacher educators will have on teachers' learning experiences, it is vital that an analysis of the teacher educator competences required is carried out by those responsible for the programme. This can inform decisions about recruitment and about the kinds of preparatory and ongoing support teacher educators will need.

Recruiting teacher educators is more easily accomplished on smaller, more local programmes where, for example, the numbers required may be limited and their work will take place within a single institution or in geographically contiguous areas. For example, on TEDP in Malaysia, 100 teachers were supported by two teacher educators. The local availability of a pool of experienced teacher educators can also facilitate recruitment. However, on larger programmes, challenges can arise. On the NTTP in Egypt, 488 teacher educators were recruited against a target of 600 (Borg, 2020), while on Tejas, 207 were recruited against a target of 250 (Borg, 2019b). Scale was not the only challenge in these two cases; the criteria (teaching experience, English proficiency and teaching knowledge) were rigorous; teacher educators were also being recruited locally from amongst experienced teachers, who were expected to maintain their existing teaching workload in addition to working as teacher educators (for example, one day a week – sometimes at the weekend). Considering all of these factors, recruitment on both NTTP and Tejas was quite successful.

Systemic in-service language teacher education 153

In terms of preparation for their role, this will vary depending on teacher educators' entry profiles and the responsibilities they will be required to fulfil. On EfU, for example, experienced international trainers were engaged to deliver one-week courses and they were not required to undergo any formal preparation. On NTTP and Tejas, in contrast, local teacher educators attended 10 to 15 days of training before and during the project. Where programmes involve online work (see section "Online in-service teacher education"), teacher educators will require additional competences and, perhaps, preparation through some form of 'trainer training'. E-moderators (experienced teacher educators who had received training to support teachers online) on the OETIS programme in Syria, for example, provided online support to groups of teachers via Zoom and WhatsApp.

To conclude this section, therefore, there are several key questions that systemic in-service programmes need to address in relation to teacher educators:

- What competences will they require?
- How many of them will be needed?
- How will they be recruited?
- Will they be locally or externally sourced?
- What preparation will they need?
- What range of responsibilities will they be given?
- Will they be paid and/or receive any incentives?
- What ongoing support will they receive?
- How will the quality of their work be assessed?

Intensive and distributed in-service work

I have been asked on numerous occasions to give advice on whether an in-service programme should be organised intensively (for example, five consecutive days) or distributed (for example, one day a week for five weeks). As I have stressed throughout here, while this issue can be assessed theoretically, the decision will ultimately be determined by a number of more practical considerations. Ideally, I would always opt for a distributed approach because it allows teachers time to experiment in the classroom in between sessions where they are encountering new theoretical or practical ideas. This can take the form of a 'day release' model (for example, one non-teaching day a week for professional development), which, reflecting on experiences in Asia, Hayes and Chang (2012) claim is most likely to have an impact on teachers. In the Oman project, outside the intensive winter and summer schools held during the holidays, the programme adopted such a model, with teachers working with their teacher educators one day a week. In Azerbaijan, too, a cyclical approach was employed through which teachers met for three hours once or twice a week. Distributed programmes thus allow for the reciprocal interactions between theory and practice that intensive programmes do not. Additionally, distributed programmes conceptualize professional development as an extended process rather than a shorter-term event. This reflects the

154   *Simon Borg*

often-repeated advice in the literature that 'professional learning should be iterative, with opportunities to apply learning in real practice, reflect and improve over time' (Weston & Hindly, 2019, p. 64).

There will also be practical reasons why a distributed approach to in-service teacher education is preferable. Intensive programmes remove teachers from the classroom and this is both logistically inconvenient for schools (who may need to provide substitute teachers) and disruptive for students. Intensive programmes, though, can work at times when the disruption to schools and students will be minimal; for example, a number of countries have a tradition of intensive in-service summer schools and this is often a popular option because teachers feel they can focus entirely on professional development. However, such intensive programmes are more suited to input-based workshops which, while allowing for a range of practical activities (including perhaps peer teaching), cannot establish cyclical links with teachers' ongoing classroom experiences. The wishes of key stakeholders can also be a determining factor in how in-service programmes are organised; the RETC, for example, consisted of an intensive three-week training course which, while more aligned with the transmission model discussed earlier, was the approach favoured by local education authorities funding the project.

The EfU project in Ukraine (Borg, 2019a), though, did illustrate how the limitations of intensive in-service work can be addressed through effective follow-up institutional support. As part of this project, university teachers of English attended one-week workshops. When teachers returned to their departments, key messages from the workshops were reinforced in a number of ways: a new curriculum (which incorporated principles promoted in the workshops); support from department heads (who were committed to the changes promoted by the programme and who had themselves attended the workshops); dissemination sessions, at which trained teachers shared workshop content with those who had not attended; and regular meetings in which teachers discussed their classroom practices. So, despite the fact that the core of the in-service programme consisted of a rather conventional set of intensive workshops, the initiative succeeded in promoting changes in teachers' knowledge, skills and classroom practices because of effective post-training support. This was a good example of in-service teacher education being approached as a collective endeavour by institutions, departments and teachers. It also highlights the manner in which, as noted by Orr et al. (2013), workshops can be an effective component within a broader approach to in-service teacher education that provides other forms of job-embedded opportunities for professional development.

Online in-service teacher education

In the context of in-service language teacher education, 'on-line' refers to those components that are not conducted in face-to-face settings and these include a wide range of options such as pre-recorded lectures, live webinars, podcasts, online discussion forums, online self-study modules (possibly with support from e-moderators), e-mentoring, Massive Online Open Courses (MOOCs) and social

Systemic in-service language teacher education   155

media groups. A classification developed by the Online Learning Consortium in the US is widely used in describing online courses: these can be web facilitated (with up to 29% of the course being online), blended or hybrid (30% to 79%) and online (80% or more). Murray and Christison (2017), though, propose a taxonomy that focuses not on the volume of online work but on the form it takes; they thus describe language teacher education as being enhanced (largely face-to face with some online support), blended/hybrid, flipped and totally online (either with or without a synchronous component). Online in-service language teacher education work can clearly take multiple forms and this has been discussed through an extensive literature (for a recent review, see Murray & Christison, 2018).

In language teaching contexts, discussions of technology and online learning have often focused on online courses provided on postgraduate university programmes (for example, Son & Windeatt, 2017). However, advances in technology and a recognition of the practical (including cost) benefits that it offers mean that online components are an increasingly visible part of systemic in-service programmes for language teachers. In a recent account, Lightfoot (2019), for example, discusses these benefits in terms of the way online options enhance access, flexibility and choice for teachers, as well as how such technologies can promote collaboration, community and inclusion among teachers (see also Kiddle & Prince, 2019). It is also clear that online teacher education can create many challenges; Lightfoot (2019), for example, highlights five challenges related to access (the availability of infrastructure), skills (digital literacy), motivation (of teachers to engage with technology) and relevance and contextualization (in relation to teachers' local needs).

Some examples from programmes I have recently worked on illustrate the ways in which online components are being incorporated into systemic in-service language teacher education. On PALTAGs, teachers studied online teaching methods modules each month and then attended monthly face-to-face meetings. On the NTTP in Egypt and Tejas in India, teachers also attended monthly meetings during which they worked on the development of their English language and teaching skills. In between meetings, teachers interacted on WhatsApp groups that were co-ordinated by their teacher educators. The English for the Community project in Romania was not a systemic in-service programme (that is, not Ministry-sponsored and large-scale) but, here too, teachers studied teaching methods modules together each month, then used Facebook groups to share their experiences of applying ideas from the modules in their classrooms. The use of social media is a particularly useful way of maintaining a sense of community among a group of teachers whose physical meetings are periodic. These examples also illustrate the different levels of centrality that online components may assume on in-service programme: in PALTAGs they were core to the in-service programme while in Egypt, India and Romania they played a supporting role.

Wholly online in-service language teacher education programmes have also been implemented in contexts where conflict has limited the movement of teachers and teacher educators and required a more flexible remote approach to in-service work.

156 *Simon Borg*

In Syria, for example, the OETIS programme engaged teachers in the independent study of online language development and teaching modules, supported by regular Zoom sessions with e-moderators. In Libya, in-service courses for teachers in university language centres have been delivered via Skype.[3] In this model, teachers met in a training room and a remote teacher educator delivered the session through a video call; a local teacher educator was also available to provide support.

Of course, the decision to incorporate online elements into an in-service programme needs to be based on a sound feasibility analysis. For example, it cannot always be assumed that high-speed connections are available or that access to laptops and tablets is universal; in India, for example, most teachers access the internet via their mobile phone. Teachers may also need initial and ongoing technical support in order to engage effectively with the online components of in-service programmes. On one programme in Jordan, teachers were given access to VEO – an online platform that allows them to record lessons and share them with colleagues. Uptake of this opportunity varied, though, and an analysis of the reasons for this suggested five factors (see Table 8.4) which, while referring to in-service work that involves sharing videos online, will also be relevant to the use of technology in in-service language teacher education more generally (see also Mann, Crichton, & Edmett, 2020, for a discussion of the use of video by teachers involved in the RETC in Thailand). Table 8.4 suggests that while technical factors may hinder efforts to engage teachers in online teacher education, attitudes, professional knowledge, and local bureaucratic and regulatory issues may also intervene. I recall at least one programme, too, where attempts to encourage teachers to engage in critical debate through online forums failed because teachers were reluctant to make public and in writing anything that might be seen as being critical of the local educational authorities. This is another example of contextual issues that must be considered in decisions about online in-service teacher education.

One final point about the use of online components in in-service work is that their effectiveness needs to be evaluated rather than assumed. For example,

Table 8.4 Barriers to video-based online teacher education

Technical	Do teachers have the technical expertise to make good quality recordings of their lessons and to share them online? Is support available to help them with such matters?
Attitudinal	Are teachers positively disposed to the use of technology for their own professional development?
Professional	Do teachers have the understandings and skills to comment critically on their own videos and on those shared by their colleagues?
Bureaucratic	Are schools likely to discourage teachers in any way from videoing their lessons and sharing these online? Is clearance from school leaders (or other authorities) necessary before teachers record and share videos?
Regulatory	What child protection and privacy regulations need to be respected when teachers are making and sharing videos of their lessons?

Source: Adapted from Borg (2018b).

on projects which have used WhatsApp groups to foster teacher networks in between physical meetings, there has been limited analysis of the interactions that actually take place in those groups (but see Parnham, Gholkar, & Borg, 2018) and it is therefore difficult to make strong claims about the contributions such online mechanisms make to the process of teacher development. It should not be assumed that online components are automatically effective and, when utilized, these should be a focus of programme evaluations.

Programme evaluation

In-service programmes should also include an evaluation component which seeks to ascertain how far the objectives of the programme have been met. A substantial literature on the evaluation of development interventions more generally (for example, Görgens-Albino & Kusek, 2009; Markiewicz & Patrick, 2016), teacher professional development (such as Killion, 2018; Muijs & Lindsay, 2008) and language teacher education specifically (for example, Kiely, 2019) exists and this provides valuable direction for the evaluation of in-service teacher education programmes. Drawing on this material and on my practical experience of evaluating in-service programmes, Table 8.5 lists some criteria for conducting such evaluations.

While all these criteria are desirable, some are critical. For example, it is not possible to evaluate in-service programmes unless their objectives (i.e. hoped-for results) have been clearly specified. This allows evaluation procedures to be closely aligned with targets and minimizes the risk that, as I have witnessed

Table 8.5 Criteria for evaluating in-service programmes

Is the evaluation of impact	Questions
• Integral	Is impact evaluation built into the design of the programme?
• Objectives-driven	Is the evaluation of impact aligned with the objectives of the programme?
• Multi-staged	Are repeated/ongoing evaluation data collected?
• Rigorous	Are evaluation tools appropriate and well-designed and are data competently analyzed?
• Multi-method	Are a variety of qualitative and quantitative measures collected?
• Technology-enhanced	Is technology utilized appropriately to maximize the collection of evaluation data?
• Participatory	Are a range of stakeholders involved in decisions about the conduct and interpretation of the results?
• Formative	Are evaluation data used to inform decisions during a programme?
• Feasible	Is the approach to evaluating the impact of the programme feasible, given the availability of time, funding, expertise and other resources?

Source: Adapted from Borg (2018a).

158   *Simon Borg*

on some programmes, large volumes of evaluation data are collected which are related only peripherally to the programme's objectives and do not contribute to its evaluation. Aligning evaluation with objectives also has implications for when evaluation data are collected: if, for example, a programme seeks to promote sustained change in some aspect of teachers' work, it would be necessary to examine what teachers do in the medium-term, not just at the end of the programme.

Rigour is another non-negotiable feature of effective programme evaluation – data collection instruments must be technically appropriate (i.e. well-designed and fit for purpose) and data must be analyzed and interpreted systematically. Multi-staged evaluation is important when comparisons are to be made between pre- and post-programme measures (change cannot be measured without reference to a baseline). Another criterion which is indispensable is feasibility. There is little point in designing a sophisticated evaluation plan which requires expertise and other resources such as time and funding which are not available. As with all aspects of in-service programmes I have discussed here, theoretical desirability and feasibility will always need to interact in shaping what actually happens. For example, on the NTTP in Egypt and Tejas, it would have been desirable to collect extensive observational data from hundreds of teachers around the country in order to assess the impact of the programme on their classroom practices; in both cases, though, the resources to support such an undertaking were not available and it was necessary to rely on fewer observations supplemented by self-reports via teacher questionnaires. For its first cohort, SPEX in Azerbaijan performed better in this respect by observing almost all of the 500 teachers involved both at the start and end of the programme; the availability of a cadre of trained observers and the limited geographical spread (one city) of the teachers, in this case, facilitated such an undertaking.

Additional criteria mentioned in Table 8.5 are also essential but it would be wrong to claim that effective programme evaluation cannot occur unless they are met. For example, while a formative approach to evaluation provides information that can shape programme content and processes in an ongoing manner, this is not really feasible on large-scale intensive programmes. Similarly, while technology can contribute to effective programme evaluation (particularly on larger programmes and if this entails remote contact with teachers after the programme has ended), the absence of technology does not inherently limit the work of evaluators. Participatory evaluation is certainly desirable where it can be achieved; my experiences, though, suggest that while sponsors do sometimes shape the way programmes are evaluated, key participants such as teachers and teacher educators typically function as sources of data rather than contributing to the evaluation framework itself. For a discussion of engaging stakeholders in programme evaluations, see Bryson and Patton (2015).

Conclusion

My goal in this chapter has been to highlight some key issues which arise in the design of systemic in-service language teacher education programmes and to

Systemic in-service language teacher education   159

illustrate these issues with reference to a selection of programmes I have been involved in. While for analytical convenience I have discussed eight issues separately, they are inextricably linked; decisions about models of in-service work, for example, have implications for the way programmes are organised, their objectives, activities and for the roles of teachers and teacher educators. The interplay between theoretical desirability (as presented in the literature on teacher professional development) and contextual appropriateness and feasibility has also been a constant feature of the analysis presented here. This in no way implies that theoretical understandings of professional development are irrelevant to the design of real-world systemic in-service programmes. The key point I have tried to emphasize here, though, is that theoretical choices must be informed by close understandings of context – who the teachers are and their existing knowledge, beliefs, motivations and practices; the social, cultural and educational systems they work in; stakeholder expectations; and the resources (such as time, teacher educators and funding) available to support professional development. The systematic evaluation of in-service language teacher education – which remains an under-developed domain of activity in our field – is key in our ongoing attempts to understand how theoretical drivers and contextual parameters can be optimally reconciled to support effective professional development and sustainable educational reform.

Relating the issues raised in this chapter to your own context:

1 What kinds of in-service programmes for foreign language teachers are available in your context and how effective are they in improving teaching and learning?
2 Based on ideas discussed in this chapter, what changes could be made to the design, implementation and evaluation of these programmes to improve their effectiveness?

Notes

1 See https://www.youtube.com/watch?v=ao4AikxaIeo for a video about TAGs.
2 See https://www.eiabd.com/ for project evaluation reports.
3 For a webinar discussing this, see https://www.teachingenglish.org.uk/article/ben-gray-skype-based-teacher-training-solutions-libya
4 A revised version of this framework has been recently produced and will be available in 2022.

References

Atkins, J., Lamb, M., & Wedell, M. (Eds.). (2009). *The design and evolution of the BA educational studies (TESOL) programme: Perspectives from Leeds.* Muscat, Oman: Ministry of Education, Oman.

Bett, H. K. (2016). The cascade model of teachers' continuing professional development in Kenya: A time for change? *Cogent Education*, *3*, 1139439. Retrieved from https://www.cogentoa.com/article/10.1080/2331186X.2016.1139439.pdf

160 Simon Borg

Borg, S. (2015). Overview – beyond the workshop: CPD for English language teachers. In S Borg (Ed.), *Professional development for English language teachers: Perspectives from higher education in Turkey* (pp. 5–13). Ankara: British Council.

Borg, S. (2018a). Evaluating the impact of professional development. *RELC Journal, 49*(2), 195–216.

Borg, S. (2018b). *Teacher activity groups in MENA.* Unpublished report.

Borg, S. (2019a). *The impact of the English for universities project on ESP and EMI in Ukrainian higher education.* Retrieved from http://www.britishcouncil.org.ua/sites/default/files/efu_impact_report_.pdf

Borg, S. (2019b). *Tejas year 3 evaluation report.* Unpublished report.

Borg, S. (2020). *National teacher training programme: Year 1 evaluation report.* Unpublished report.

Borg, S., Clifford, I., & Htut, K. P. (2018). Having an EfECT: Professional development for teacher educators in Myanmar. *Teaching and Teacher Education, 72,* 75–86.

Borg, S., & Parnham, J. (2020). Large-scale teacher development through mentoring. *The Teacher Trainer, 34*(2), 2–7.

Bowden, R. (2013). Introduction to the English language teacher development project (ELTDP). In S. Borg (Ed.), *Narratives of teacher development: Reading and speaking* (pp. 5–8). Kuala Lumpur: British Council.

British Council. (2015). *Continuing professional development (CPD) framework for teacher educators.* Retrieved from https://www.teachingenglish.org.uk/article/cpd-framework-teacher-educators

British Council. (2019a). *National teacher training programme: Year 1 midline report.* Unpublished report.

British Council. (2019b). *Teaching for success: Occupied Palestinian Territories project report 2018–2019.* Palestine: The British Council. Retrieved from https://www.britishcouncil.ps/sites/default/files/tfs_report_online.pdf

Bryson, J. M., & Patton, M. Q. (2015). Analyzing and engaging stakeholders. In K. Newcomer, H. Hatry, & J. Wholey (Eds.), *Handbook of practical program evaluation* (Fourth ed., pp. 36–61). Hoboken, NJ: John Wiley & Sons.

Burns, A. (2010). *Doing action research in English language teaching. A guide for practitioners.* New York: Routledge.

Davis, E. (2014). *Making mentoring work.* New York: Rowman & Littlefield Education.

Feiman-Nemser, S. (1990). Teacher preparation: Structural and conceptual alternatives. In W. R. Houston (Ed.), *Handbook of research on teacher education* (pp. 212–233). New York: Macmillan.

Flessner, R., & Stuckey, S. (2014). Politics and action research: An examination of one school's mandated action research program. *Action Research, 12*(1), 36–51.

Goodwin, A. L., & Kosnik, C. (2013). Quality teacher educators = quality teachers? Conceptualizing essential domains of knowledge for those who teach teachers. *Teacher Development, 17*(3), 334–346.

Görgens-Albino, M., & Kusek, J. Z. (2009). *Making monitoring and evaluation systems work: A capacity development toolkit.* Washington, DC: World Bank.

Guskey, T. R. (2000). *Evaluating professional development.* Thousand Oaks, CA: Corwin Press.

Hardman, F., Stoff, C., Aung, W., & Elliott, L. (2016). Developing pedagogical practices in Myanmar primary schools: Possibilities and constraints. *Asia Pacific Journal of Education, 36,* 98–118.

Hayes, D. (2000). Cascade training and teachers' professional development. *ELT Journal, 54*(2), 135–145.

Systemic in-service language teacher education 161

Hayes, D. (2019). Continuing professional development/continuous professional learning for English language teachers. In S. Walsh & S. Mann (Eds.), *The Routledge handbook of English language teacher education* (pp. 155–168). London: Routledge.

Hayes, D., & Chang, K. (2012). Theoretical perspectives on and international practice in continuing professional development for English teachers. *English Teaching, 67,* 107–129.

Kennedy, A. (2005). Models of continuing professional development: A framework for analysis. *Journal of In-Service Education, 31*(2), 235–250.

Kennedy, A. (2014). Understanding continuing professional development: The need for theory to impact on policy and practice. *Professional Development in Education, 40*(5), 688–697.

Kiddle, T., & Prince, T. (2019). Digital and online approaches to language teacher education. In S. Walsh & S. Mann (Eds.), *The Routledge handbook of English language teacher education*. London: Routledge. [e-version].

Kiely, R. (2019). Evaluating English language teacher education programmes. In S. Walsh & S. Mann (Eds.), *The Routledge handbook of English language teacher education*. London: Routledge [e-version]

Killion, J. (2018). *Assessing impact: Evaluating professional learning* (Third ed.). Thousand Oaks, CA: Corwin.

Koster, B., Brekelmans, M., Korthagen, F., & Wubbels, T. (2005). Quality requirements for teacher educators. *Teaching and Teacher Education, 21*(2), 157–176.

Lamb, M., & Wyatt, M. (2019). Teacher motivation: The missing ingredient in teacher education. In S. Walsh & S. Mann (Eds.), *The Routledge handbook of English language teacher education*. [e-version]

Lewis, C. C., & Hurd, J. (2011). *Lesson study step by step: How teacher learning communities improve instruction*. Portsmouth, NH: Heinemann.

Lieberman, A., Campbell, C., & Yashkina, A. (2017). *Teacher learning and leadership of, by, and for teachers*. London, England: Routledge.

Lightfoot, A. (2019). ICT and English language teacher education opportunities, challenges and experiences. In S. Walsh & S. Mann (Eds.), *The Routledge handbook of English language teacher education* (pp. 52–67). London: Routledge.

Malderez, A., & Wedell, M. (2007). *Teaching teachers: Processes and practices*. London: Continuum.

Mann, S., Crichton, R., & Edmett, A. (2020). Evaluating the role of video in supporting reflection beyond inset. *System, 90.* https://doi.org/10.1016/j.system.2019.102195

Markiewicz, A., & Patrick, I. (2016). *Developing monitoring and evaluation frameworks*. Thousand Oaks, CA: Sage.

Matei, G. S., Bernaus, M., Heyworth, F., Pohl, U., & Wright, T. (2007). *First steps in teacher training: A practical guide*. Graz: ECML.

Mills, G. E. (2014). *Action research: A guide for the teacher researcher*. New York: Pearson.

Ministry of Education. (2015). *Competence for quality*. Oslo: Ministry of Education, Norway.

Muijs, D., & Lindsay, G. (2008). Where are we at? An empirical study of levels and methods of evaluating continuing professional development. *British Educational Research Journal, 34*(2), 195–211.

Murray, D. E., & Christison, M. (2017). Online language teacher education: Participants' perceptions and experiences. Retrieved from https://www.tirfonline.org/wp-content/uploads/2017/03/TIRF_OLTE_2017_Report_Final.pdf

162   Simon Borg

Murray, D. E., & Christison, M. (2018). *Online language teacher education: A review of the literature*. Norwich: Aqueduto.

Opper, I. M. (2019). *Teachers matter: Understanding teachers' impact on student achievement*. Retrieved from https://www.rand.org/pubs/research_reports/RR4312.html

Orr, D., Westbrook, J., Pryor, J., Durrani, N., Sebba, J., & Adu-Yeboah, C. (2013). *What are the impacts and cost effectiveness of strategies to improve performance of untrained and under-trained teachers in the classroom in developing countries? A systematic review.* London: EPPICentre, University of London.

Parker, G. (2015). Teachers' autonomy. *Research in Education, 93*(1), 19–33.

Parnham, J., Gholkar, R., & Borg, S. (2018). Using WhatsApp for peer support in a mentoring programme. *The Teacher Trainer, 32*(1), 1–7.

Popova, A., Evans, D. K., Breeding, M. E., & Aranciba, V. (2018). *Teacher professional development around the world: The gap between evidence and practice: Policy research working paper WPS 8572.* Washington, DC: World Bank Group.

Rebolledo, P., Smith, R., & Bullock, D. (2016). *Champion teachers: Stories of exploratory action research.* London: The British Council.

Son, J.-B., & Windeatt, S. (2017). *Language teacher education and technology: Approaches and practices.* New York: Bloomsbury Publishing.

Timperley, H. (2011). *Realizing the power of professional learning.* Milton Keynes: Open University Press.

Turner, F., Wilson, E., & Brownhill, S. (2016). The transfer of content knowledge in a cascade model of professional development. *Teacher Development, 21*(2), 1–17.

UNESCO-IICBA. (2017). *Teacher support and motivation framework for Africa: Emerging patterns.* Retrieved from http://unesdoc.unesco.org/images/0025/002599/259935e.pdf

Wedell, M. (2009). *Planning educational change: Putting people and their contexts first.* London: Continuum.

Weston, D., & Hindly, B. (2019). Professional development: Evidence of what works. In C. Scutt & S. Harrison (Eds.), *Teacher CPD: International trends, opportunities and challenges* (pp. 60–67). London: Chartered College of Teaching.

Wright, T., & Bolitho, R. (2007). *Trainer development*: Published online at http://www.lulu.com/content/554846.

Part II

Applying the debates to second language learning contexts

9 Implicit versus explicit grammar learning and teaching

Mirosław Pawlak

Introduction

Even though there is now a broad consensus that grammar instruction might be necessary or at least facilitative in some contexts, controversies abound about how this should most beneficially be done. Crucial in this respect is the distinction between explicit and implicit grammar teaching, which is related to learners' awareness that a particular grammar feature is the focus of the pedagogical intervention. The chapter provides theoretical support for explicit and implicit learning of grammar, shows how explicit and implicit teaching can be implemented in classroom practice, and synthesizes research findings which shed light on the effectiveness of these two options. While empirical evidence points to greater superiority of explicit instruction, it is argued that the two approaches should be adeptly combined in foreign language pedagogy in order to ensure that learners not only get to know relevant rules but also develop the ability to use them in spontaneous interaction.

When we overview different methods of teaching a second and foreign language (L2) that have held sway over the years, it becomes clear that all their proponents have felt compelled to take a position on how target language (TL) grammar should be learned and taught (e.g., Larsen-Freeman & Anderson, 2011). This situation should hardly come as a surprise since, as Nassaji (2017, p. 205) points out, "grammar is central to language and language learning". Indeed, grammar teaching (GT) has been the staple of L2 pedagogy in most educational settings and it has also remained largely traditional, with teachers typically relying on introducing and practising grammar as well as stressing the accuracy of learners' production of TL forms (cf. Larsen-Freeman, 2014; Pawlak, 2020). By contrast, the role of grammar instruction (GI) has generated heated discussions among second language acquisition (SLA) specialists, with some of them (e.g., Krashen, 1981) advocating that the teaching of this subsystem should be discontinued. On the whole, however, there is a consensus at present that if learners are expected to get to know and use TL grammar, pedagogical intervention is facilitative or even necessary, although controversies abound about how GI should most beneficially be provided (Ellis, 2018; Ellis & Shintani, 2014; Larsen-Freeman, 2014; Nassaji, 2017; Nassaji & Fotos, 2011;

DOI: 10.4324/9781003008361-12

166   *Mirosław Pawlak*

Pawlak, 2014, 2021). The present chapter is concerned with one of the most important and also perhaps the most enduring debates in this respect, that is, whether successful grammar learning and teaching should be explicit or implicit, or perhaps strive to adeptly integrate these two approaches (cf. Nassaji, 2017; Pawlak, 2013).

Knowledge, learning and teaching of L2 grammar

Before considering explicit and implicit options in GT, it is warranted to carefully distinguish between three constructs that are crucial for the present discussion, namely, the *knowledge of L2 grammar*, its *learning* and *teaching*. Whatever the theoretical provenance of the descriptions of the L2 grammatical system, be they minimalist, functional or cognitive, such pedagogical grammars are necessary because they provide a point of departure for classroom interventions (Larsen-Freeman, 2009). Their importance is not diminished by the fact that the rules and patterns they contain have little to do with the mental reality of learners' interlanguages and do not reflect processes involved in producing or understanding grammar structures. A comprehensive and theory-neutral definition of grammar is offered by Larsen-Freeman (2009, p. 521), who describes it as "a system of meaningful structures and patterns that are governed by particular pragmatic constraints". Based on her earlier work (e.g., Larsen-Freeman, 2003), she views this L2 subsystem as encompassing three interdependent dimensions: (1) *structural*, related to the way a specific TL feature, such as how the unreal past conditional, is formed, (2) *semantic*, connected with the meaning that the structure carries in a particular situation and (3) *use*, concerning occasions on which the feature should be employed (i.e., time cannot be taken back). Embracing this definition entails two assumptions. First, the word *structure* is understood broadly, referring not only to morphemes, function words or clauses but also patterned sequences, discourse-level and topological patterns. Second, grammar is regarded as a skill and therefore Larsen-Freeman (2003) introduces the notion of *grammaring* which denotes accurate, meaningful and appropriate use of grammar structures.

Regardless of the specific building blocks of grammar that are taught or whether instruction takes account of the three dimensions mentioned above, it should be underscored that the fact that such information is committed to memory does not mean that it will be available for use in real time. This brings us to the vital distinction between *explicit knowledge* and *implicit knowledge*, which lies at the heart of most contemporary SLA theories. These two types of grammar representation differ along several dimensions, that is, awareness, type of knowledge, systematicity, accessibility, conditions of use, self-report and learnability. More precisely, learners are conscious of the explicit knowledge they possess; it consists of facts about the L2 being learned, such as rules concerning the formation and use of a given structure, although these facts often lack precision and are frequently inaccurate. Such knowledge can be quite easily verbalized, which, however, does not have to involve reliance on metalanguage; it is not restricted by the lack of requisite processing mechanisms (Pienemann &

Implicit vs explicit grammar learning and teaching 167

Lenzing, 2015), nor is it subject to maturational constraints. A major limitation of explicit knowledge is that its employment requires controlled processing and therefore it is feasible only when learners are afforded sufficient time to access pertinent rules. By contrast, implicit knowledge is tacit and intuitive. It is procedural in the sense that it relies upon condition-action rules, and it does not lend itself to description. While it is constrained by learners' age and the ability to perform necessary syntactic operations, it is available for use in real-time processing, thereby providing a basis for fluent, spontaneous TL performance (Ellis, 2009). Importantly, as indicated by neurolinguistic research, the two types of representation are distinct because they are associated with different areas of the human brain (cf. Ullman, 2015).

While the distinction between explicit and implicit knowledge is crucial theoretically, and it has been routinely invoked in studies exploring the effects of different pedagogical interventions, it is not without its share of problems. DeKeyser (2010), for example, makes the point that labelling explicit knowledge as declarative and implicit knowledge as procedural may be an oversimplification, not least because procedural knowledge that is not fully automatized may still require falling back on consciously held rules. Another problem is that fully implicit knowledge may not be attainable for learners who are not children and have only scant exposure to the TL, which is the norm in many foreign language contexts. In such contexts, the initial stages of L2 instruction routinely involve the provision of explicit rules and these rules are unlikely to be forgotten, even when a learner becomes fluent in the TL. In effect, DeKeyser (2017) argues that it might make more sense to abandon the concept of implicit knowledge and focus instead on what he refers to as *highly automatized explicit knowledge*, which can also underpin fluent and accurate use of TL features in spontaneous communication. Incidentally, if this common-sense position is adopted, there are grounds to assume that studies investigating the effectiveness of various instructional options might as well confine themselves to determining learning outcomes in terms of explicit and highly automatized explicit knowledge, rather than seeking elaborate but often unreliable ways of measuring implicit knowledge (Pawlak, 2019).

Not less important is the essential question concerning the relationship between explicit and implicit knowledge, an issue that has far-reaching implications for pedagogy. While the *non-interface position* flatly denies the contribution of consciously known rules to fluent L2 performance (Krashen, 1981), the *weak-interface position* holds that such knowledge can be facilitative for the development of implicit knowledge if the learner is psycholinguistically ready to acquire a particular structure (Ellis, 1997). The *strong-interface position* is based on the assumption that rules can be automatized to such a degree that they can be employed effortlessly in real-time performance if the right kind of practice is provided (DeKeyser, 2007). Although not all specialists will be willing to accept this claim, it would seem that only the last option is a realistic proposition for most practitioners, in view of the fact that GT has been part and parcel of L2 pedagogy for decades.

168   *Mirosław Pawlak*

Finally, it is important to emphasize that L2 knowledge, whether explicit or implicit and whether it is the outcome of naturalistic, untutored acquisition or pedagogic intervention, should be seen in terms of a *product*, even if this product is in a state of constant flux. As such, it should be distinguished from the *processes* leading to its development, that is, learning and instruction, as well as its actual *use* in controlled and spontaneous situations. Since the processes that lead to the emergence of explicit and implicit (or highly automatized) knowledge of L2 grammar are the focus of this chapter, a few words of explanation are in order.

To quote Nassaji (2017, p. 206), "implicit learning is often defined as learning without awareness, taking place when learners are exposed to meaning-focused input, while explicit learning is conscious, taking place mainly through explicit instruction". He goes on to say that while implicit learning leads to the development of implicit knowledge, explicit learning contributes to the growth of explicit knowledge. However, things get more complicated when we consider the nature of different types of GT and its effects on the actual mastery of grammar. As Ur (2011, p. 510) explains, "implicit teaching means exposing students to, or getting them to use, grammatical forms and meanings but without actually discussing the rules, whereas explicit teaching involves verbal explanations of form and use". It is quite evident from this definition that implicit instruction does not have to be exclusively meaning-focused but can also rely on interventions that are more or less transparent to learners (e.g., input enhancement). On the other hand, somewhat contrary to this characterization, explicit instruction can often go beyond the provision of rules and fall back upon different types of practice, which, yet again, may involve different levels of awareness (e.g., text-creation activities; see section "Choices in explicit and implicit grammar learning and teaching"). Another issue is whether GT can ever be entirely implicit in situations when learners are familiar with relevant rules and can be expected to resort to them when performing different tasks (cf. DeKeyser, 2017). Equally important is the fact that implicit and explicit learning and instruction may feed into both implicit and explicit knowledge (see section "Choices in explicit and implicit grammar learning and teaching").

Theoretical support for explicit and implicit grammar learning and teaching

Despite the arguments advanced by the proponents of the non-interface position (e.g., Krashen, 1981), support for GI comes from a number of SLA theories and hypotheses, some of which do not seek to make any claims about its most beneficial types, while others place more store by either more explicit or more implicit pedagogical interventions. Only the most relevant theoretical positions are considered here and the discussion is confined to their key tenets.

It is only fitting to start this overview with the *noticing hypothesis* (Schmidt, 1990, 2001) since it constitutes an important point of reference for many other theoretical stances. The core assumption underlying this hypothesis is that L2 learning cannot successfully take place without a certain degree of attention to

Implicit vs explicit grammar learning and teaching 169

TL features in linguistic data. Such awareness at the level of noticing fosters access to form-meaning mappings, allowing learners to engage in internal comparisons and identify gaps in their interlanguage systems. Importantly, Schmidt (2001) also recognizes the beneficial role of metalinguistic awareness, particularly in the case of features that are redundant, less salient or cannot be learned from exposure alone (e.g., adverb placement, grammatical structures that are semantically close in the mother tongue and L2). Such premises provide unequivocal support for both explicit and implicit grammar learning and teaching, with the intention of triggering different levels of awareness.

The noticing hypothesis is closely tied to two other theoretical positions that underpin the cognitive-interactionist approach to SLA (Kim, 2017), that is, the *revised interaction hypothesis* (Long, 1996) and the *output hypothesis* (Swain, 1995). The former posits that negotiated interaction, be it the result of genuine communication breakdowns or errors in L2 use, allows learners to direct their selective attention to specific TL features. As a consequence, the salience of such features is increased, corrective feedback (CF) can be provided and opportunities for modified output arise. Closely related to the concept of *focus on form*, or "a kind of instruction that draws the learner's attention to linguistic forms in the context of meaningful communication" (Nassaji & Fotos, 2011, p. 10), this theoretical position favours implicit GI, in particular the provision of CF in the form of recasts (i.e., correct reformulations of erroneous learner utterances that preserve the initial meaning). If we examine the different interpretations of focus on form, however, it becomes clear that the interaction hypothesis has lent support to instructional techniques which entail different levels of implicitness (e.g., Loewen, 2011), not to mention the fact that even recasts can vary considerably in the extent to which their corrective function is apparent (Nassaji, 2015).

The output hypothesis claims that output production is indispensable to trigger syntactic processing (i.e., a focus on grammar), but learners should be encouraged to produce *pushed output*, which is accurate, precise and appropriate. Swain (1995) also points out that output production serves three important roles, namely: (1) it fosters noticing, (2) it enables testing hypotheses about how the TL works and (3) it allows conscious reflection on TL use, a function that is metalinguistic in nature. When these roles are considered, the output hypothesis justifies the use of a wide array of techniques, ranging from more explicit or implicit CF moves to grammar explanations to help learners reformulate their written texts.

Support for different variants of GT also derives from a number of other theoretical positions. One of the most important is *skill-learning theory* (DeKeyser, 2007, 2017), which builds upon Anderson's (1983) adaptive control of thought theory. It is predicated on the assumption that initial, declarative knowledge of L2 rules has to be proceduralized and automatized to such an extent that it can be used in spontaneous, time-pressured performance (see section "Knowledge, learning and teaching of L2 grammar"). For this to happen, learners need to be accorded opportunities for a suitable kind of practice. In line with the assumptions of transfer-appropriate processing (TAP), according to which conditions of

170 *Mirosław Pawlak*

learning should mirror conditions of use (Lightbown, 2008), such practice can be more controlled and explicit, when proceduralization of rules is the primary goal. However, it should also involve the use of targeted TL features in real-time communication, thereby offering justification for the employment of more implicit instructional options with the aim of automatizing the pertinent rules.

The remaining theories and hypotheses assuming a facilitative role of GT do not specify whether explicit or implicit instruction is more beneficial. According to *processability theory* (Pienemann & Lenzing, 2015), the development of implicit L2 knowledge is dependent on access to increasingly complex processing operations and, thus, pedagogical intervention should be geared to the developmental stage of the learner. Whether such intervention is explicit or implicit, however, is irrelevant because the theory only focuses on how grammar develops in the human mind.

Input processing theory (VanPatten, 2015) seeks to explain how learners process TL data in order to make form-meaning connections and provides a basis for *processing instruction*, intended to change non-optimal processing strategies transferred from the mother tongue. Such instruction involves both explicit and implicit components, and, besides, VanPatten (2015, p. 129) stresses that the theory "is neutral/agnostic on the issue of whether adults engage implicit or explicit processes when learning a second language".

Connectionism is based on the assumption that language is represented in the mind by means of constructions which are learned by making associations between form and meaning or function, a process that is reliant on the frequency of occurrence of specific TL features (Ellis & Wulff, 2015). While such learning is by definition implicit and inductive, involving extraction of regularities from linguistic data, it can be aided by pedagogical intervention which facilitates the acquisition of non-salient forms or constructions that represent new semantic or pragmatic concepts. Both explicit and implicit GI can be beneficial because "learners' language systematicity emerges from their history of interactions of implicit and explicit language learning" (Ellis & Wulff, 2015, p. 89).

Finally, the *delayed-effect hypothesis* states that the benefits of GI, whatever form it may take, need time to manifest themselves (Lightbown, 1998). This is because such instruction can speed up acquisition when the learner has reached the required stage of interlanguage development, it can have a priming effect by stimulating subsequent noticing, or it may enable deeper processing the next time the structure is encountered (Larsen-Freeman, 2003).

Choices in explicit and implicit grammar learning and teaching

This section offers an overview of classifications of techniques and procedures in GI, laying special emphasis on identifying instructional options that are more explicit or implicit. Before doing so, however, several caveats need to be mentioned. First, the criterion for distinguishing these two categories is the degree of learners' awareness of the pedagogical focus of the tasks and activities

Implicit vs explicit grammar learning and teaching   171

they perform. Ellis and Shintani (2014, p. 83) explain that "explicit language instruction caters to intentional language learning (...) it makes clear to the learner what is the instructional target and provides activities to assist them in learning it". Accordingly, implicit instruction is implemented with the aim of engaging implicit learning mechanisms in such a way that learners focus on understanding and producing messages (Nassaji, 2017). Such a neat distinction, though, is not always feasible, mainly due to contextual considerations, nor can the outcome in regard to the growth of explicit and implicit knowledge be taken for granted. Second, while some of the frameworks have been put forward specifically with GT in mind, others extend to broadly conceived *form-focused instruction*, where different subsystems are targeted. Third, some of the classifications are inclusive in that they adopt a very broad interpretation of pedagogical intervention, while others confine themselves to different options in *focus on form* (Long, 1991). Fourth, the overview is selective and some taxonomies are described in more detail than others.

The classification proposed by Doughty and Williams (1998) includes extremely varied instructional options. They are categorized in terms of whether pedagogic intervention is planned or responds to learner need (i.e., proactive or reactive), whether it occurs outside of communicative activity or is embedded in it (i.e., sequential or integrated), and whether it is explicit or implicit. A range of techniques and procedures are listed in the order of growing explicitness:

1 *Input flood* (i.e., exposing learners to texts containing multiple instances of the targeted feature);
2 *Task essentialness* (i.e., using communicative tasks that necessitate reliance on a given structure or *focused communication tasks*, Ellis, 2003);
3 *Input enhancement* (e.g., increasing salience through 'bolding' all instances of a structure in a text);
4 *Negotiation* (i.e., responding to errors in conversation by means of confirmation checks or clarification requests);
5 *Recasts* (i.e., corrective reformulations of erroneous utterances);
6 *Output enhancement* (e.g., reacting to errors concerning a specific structure with a clarification request);
7 *Interaction enhancement* (i.e., a combination of input enhancement, output enhancement and direct explanations);
8 *Dictogloss* (i.e., collaborative reconstruction of texts containing the targeted form);
9 *Consciousness-raising* (i.e., communication in small groups aimed at understanding a grammar structure);
10 *Input processing* (i.e., a procedure used to change default processing strategies);
11 *Garden path* (i.e., deliberately leading learners to make errors and notice them).

As empirical evidence kept accumulating, taxonomies of focus-on-form techniques became more detailed, specialized and sophisticated, zooming in on instructional options that direct learners' attention to TL features during the

172 *Mirosław Pawlak*

performance of communicative tasks. A good example is Loewen's (2011) division into *intensive* and *extensive focus on form*, where the former involves preselection of the structure to be targeted whereas the latter is unplanned and can concern a range of features. In both cases, pedagogic intervention can be *proactive* (e.g., the use of a focused communication task) and/or *reactive* (e.g., the provision of CF). When it comes to the issue of explicitness and implicitness, it yet again should be considered on a continuum. For example, intensive proactive focus on form can be achieved through activities that make learners more or less aware of their intended focus, such as input enhancement, focused communication tasks or even a dictogloss. By contrast, extensive proactive focus on form is by definition explicit (e.g., a question followed by an explanation), as it is hard to see how else the teacher could get learners to attend to a specific feature. Reactive focus on form, or the provision of CF can be implemented by means of corrective moves that can be *input-providing*, where no attempt at self-correction is expected, or *output-prompting*, where learners are encouraged to modify their utterance. Specific techniques range from *recasts*, which are implicit, to more or less explicit *prompts* (e.g., clarification requests vs. metalinguistic comments), to *direct correction*, which is unequivocally explicit (Ellis & Shintani, 2014; Nassaji, 2015; Pawlak, 2014). It should be emphasized once again that even recasts vary in implicitness, since enhanced stress or a rising intonation pattern is likely to alert learners to their corrective function (Nassaji, 2015).

Moving on to more comprehensive classifications of options in GI, Pawlak (2006), based on Ellis (1997), makes a key distinction between *learner-performance options* and *feedback options*. Since the latter have already been presented in some detail, suffice it to say that CF provided in controlled exercises can only be explicit, irrespective of whether the correct form is supplied or self-correction occurs. Otherwise, it would simply fail to achieve its main goal of furthering understanding of the targeted structure.

When it comes to learner-performance options, they are divided into *focused communication tasks*, which require the use of a feature in production or reception, and *activities focused on a specific TL feature*. One goal of such activities is *consciousness-raising*, or helping learners understand how a given structure works, either *directly* through *deduction* (i.e., direct rule provision) or *indirectly* by means of *induction* (i.e., rule discovery). The second goal is to provide learners with opportunities for practice. Such practice can be *input-oriented*, where learners do not have to produce the TL form but are guided to understand form-meaning mappings (e.g., through input-enhancement or processing instruction). Much more often, however, practice is *output-oriented*, whereby learners are required to employ the feature in different types of activities. Although these activities could be *error-inducing*, when learners are in a sense tricked into making errors (e.g., the garden path technique), they are mainly implemented to achieve the opposite, that is, they are *error-avoiding* in nature. In this case, a fundamental distinction is made between *text-manipulation* and *text-creation activities*. The former are controlled exercises, where learners produce sentences that can only be manipulated in limited ways by, for example,

Implicit vs explicit grammar learning and teaching 173

filling out gaps. The latter allow students much more freedom, since they can produce their own sentences, as when they are asked to come up with a speech involving different conditionals or narrative tenses.

A much more recent classification of options in form-focussed instruction has been put forward by Ranta and Lyster (2017), who relate them to the three stages of SLA, namely, input, intake and output. They talk about *input enhancement, metalinguistic explanations* or *consciousness-raising tasks* and different forms of *practice*, which are *proactive*, and *corrective feedback*, which is *reactive*, but the specific techniques these categories encompass mirror those discussed above.

When the instructional options included in such divisions are considered from the perspective of explicit and implicit grammar learning and teaching, some problems appear as well. On the one hand, it is indisputable that introducing grammar structures through the provision of metalinguistic information (e.g., deduction or induction) or using different types of controlled practice (e.g., text-manipulation or text-creation) are bound to make learners aware of the objective of the intervention. On the other, the status of such options as focused communication tasks, input flood or input enhancement is less clear, as it depends, for instance, on whether learners have recently practised the targeted structure and are thus somehow prepared to attend to it. In fact, the distinction between focused communication tasks and text-creation activities may become irrelevant if learners are cognizant that the aim in both cases is to freely practise a structure that was previously directly introduced (cf. Pawlak, 2014).

There is one more aspect of GI that deserves attention at this juncture. This is instruction in the use of strategies that can aid the process of learning and using TL grammar, or *grammar learning strategies* (GLS). Research into GLS is in its infancy and there have been few attempts to classify them or undertake relevant strategy training. A taxonomy of GLS has been proposed by Pawlak (2018, 2020), who divided them into *metacognitive, cognitive, affective* and *social*. Cognitive GLS are the most pertinent here, as they are related to techniques and procedures employed in GI. They are divided into *strategies used to assist production and comprehension of grammar in communication tasks, strategies used to develop explicit knowledge of grammar, strategies used to develop implicit knowledge of grammar*, and *strategies used to deal with corrective feedback on errors in the production of grammar*. It is obvious from this division that adept employment of GLS may not only aid the understanding of grammar rules or increase accuracy in controlled exercises, but it can also contribute to the use of the targeted structures in spontaneous communication, thus allowing the development of implicit or automatized knowledge (DeKeyser, 2017; Pawlak, 2019). Therefore, while GLS instruction would, by definition, have to be explicit and follow the general models and principles of strategy training, the activities used for this purpose as well as the resulting learning modes could be both explicit and implicit.

The above discussion allows several important observations. First, a division of options in learning and teaching grammar into explicit and implicit sometimes poses a daunting challenge, particularly in foreign language contexts where a

174 *Mirosław Pawlak*

mostly structural syllabus is adopted. In fact, even in the case of input flooding, input enhancement or unobtrusive feedback moves, learners are unlikely to remain oblivious to the pedagogic agenda if they consistently have their attention directed at a specific feature or if this feature has already been taught. Delivering implicit GI can also be a problem in predominantly meaning-focused modes of instruction. For example, incorporating the instructional sequence composed of noticing, awareness activity, guided and autonomous practice into content-based language teaching (Ranta & Lyster, 2017) is bound to sensitize students to the TL forms targeted. Second, it cannot be taken for granted that explicit and implicit instruction will respectively set in motion explicit and implicit learning processes, thus leading to the development of explicit and implicit knowledge. Who can be sure, for instance, that noticing bolded instances of the passive voice in a written text (i.e., input enhancement) will not spur the learner to recall pertinent rules, or that a metalinguistic comment from the teacher will not have a delayed effect by facilitating progression through developmental stages? Perhaps then, it would be more reasonable to talk about instructional options that are likely to contribute to the growth of highly automatized TL knowledge in accordance with TAP (Lightbown, 2008). Third, it is fair to say that many, if not most, teachers do not fall back on some of the techniques and procedures devised by specialists, not only because GT is often still quite traditional (Larsen-Freeman, 2014; Pawlak, 2020) but also because they are simply not familiar with them. Fourth, it should be emphasized that, in practice, the teaching of grammar typically relies upon constellations of instructional options, which can be aided by the application of different types of GLS (Nassaji & Fotos, 2011).

Evidence for the effectiveness of explicit and implicit grammar learning and teaching

Even though the effectiveness of explicit and implicit grammar learning and teaching has figured quite prominently in research on form-focused instruction (FFI), synthesizing the available empirical evidence presents a formidable challenge. This is because the sheer volume of relevant studies is enormous, some of the instructional options have been subject to intensive empirical investigation, whereas others have been blatantly neglected, and there are differences in how explicitness and implicitness have been operationalized. For these reasons, this overview will focus in the main on syntheses and meta-analyses of existing research, first in general and then in regard to more specific instructional options, in particular the provision of CF. Subsequently, emphasis will be shifted to research projects that have addressed less frequently examined techniques and procedures, the role of variables moderating the effects of different instructional options as well as methodological issues.

Generally speaking, the findings of research conducted thus far point to the superiority of more explicit instructional options. In their seminal meta-analysis, Norris and Ortega (2000) compared the effects of both types of GI in 49 experimental and quasi-experimental studies, operationalizing explicitness in terms of the presence of rule explanations or openly directing learners to pay attention to TL features. They concluded that, although all types of instruction were effective, explicit treatments led to better learning outcomes (mostly on measures of explicit knowledge) than implicit interventions, with the gains being largely maintained over time. Such findings were corroborated by Spada and Tomita (2010), who took into account 41 studies, as well as Goo et al. (2015), who considered 34 relevant research projects. However, the meta-analysis by Kang, Sok and Han (2019), based on the findings of 54 empirical studies, demonstrated that the difference between explicit and implicit instruction was less relevant than the outcome measures used, the instructional setting or initial L2 proficiency. The complexity of this issue is also underscored by the outcomes of the comparisons of instruction drawing upon the *focus on form* and *focus on forms* approach. The former is definitely more implicit (Long, 1991) and the latter is more explicit, since it usually entails the introduction of rules which initiate the presentation – practice – production (PPP) procedure. Similar to the outcomes of the meta-analysis conducted by Norris and Ortega (2000), more recent studies (e.g., Shintani, 2013; Valeo, 2013) have failed to provide evidence for the superiority of either approach, with the caveat that their operationalizations were quite disparate, involving combinations of various techniques, and the presence of explicit instruction in one form or another appeared to be advantageous. However, a recent study by Karimi and Abdollahi (2020) provided evidence that explicit instruction is indeed more beneficial for improved mastery of the targeted features but also underscored the effect of mediating factors.

When it comes to comparisons of the effectiveness of more specific explicit and implicit options in GI, the empirical evidence is the most extensive and compelling in the case of CF. Russell and Spada (2006), for example, synthesized 15 studies dealing with the effects of oral and written CF, failing to find a clear advantage for explicit or implicit corrective strategies. Such findings were by and large corroborated by Lyster and Saito (2010), who meta-analyzed 15 quasi-experimental, classroom-based studies, showing that the effects of explicit correction did not significantly differ from those of recasts or prompts. Somewhat by contrast, the meta-analysis of 33 primary studies conducted by Li (2010) demonstrated that although explicit CF was more effective in the short term, implicit CF was more likely to have a beneficial effect over time. A recent study by Zhao and Ellis (2020) offers further evidence for the comparable effectiveness of implicit and explicit CF in the acquisition of L2 English third person -*s* by Chinese university-level learners. The former was operationalized as a single corrective move in the form of an implicit recast and the latter as a dual corrective move that involved a prompt and a more explicit recast. Participants' performance on tests of declarative and procedural knowledge showed that although explicit CF generated more uptake and attempts at repair, it was no more efficacious in terms of overall accuracy than implicit CF. On the other hand, if we look at the results of specific studies, it is clear that even in cases when the effectiveness of explicit and implicit CF moves was comparable, the latter did not confer a greater advantage, which indicates that "covert error treatment can at best, under favourable conditions, work only

176 *Mirosław Pawlak*

as well as overt CF" (Pawlak, 2014, p. 211). This assumption is supported by the fact that most evidence shows the superiority of prompts over recasts, which can be attributed to the fact that the requirement for self-correction makes learners more likely to attend to the problematic TL feature (Lyster & Saito, 2010; Pawlak, 2014).

As regards comparisons of other instructional options that are more explicit or more implicit, the empirical evidence is scarce. In general, yet again, techniques and procedures that more overtly draw learners' attention to the targeted structure have more often proved to be more efficacious. For example, research has shown that input enhancement works better than input flooding alone (e.g., Jourdenais et al., 1995), input flood is more effective when accompanied by explicit GI (Trahey & White, 1993), more salient types of input enhancement produce better results (LaBrozzi, 2016; Simard, 2009), and explicit instruction may be needed to ensure the positive contribution of input enhancement (Indrarathne & Kormos, 2017; Winke, 2013). However, there is also evidence that more explicit instructional options do not always yield superior results. For instance, Loewen and Inceoglu (2016) did not find a difference between enhanced and unenhanced conditions with respect to the amount of attention and gains in the knowledge of the Spanish past tense. Broszkiewicz (2011), in turn, demonstrated that although focused communication tasks and contextualized practice activities had a similar effect on explicit knowledge of the English past counterfactual conditional, the former had a more beneficial impact on the development of implicit knowledge.

When considering research into the effects of explicit and implicit instructional options, we have to bear in mind that these effects are bound to be impacted by mediating variables, such as individual difference (ID) factors, the properties of the targeted feature, or the context in which GI occurs (Pawlak, 2017). For reasons of space, suffice it to say that there is evidence that the contribution of explicit and implicit GT is a function of the complexity of TL forms (e.g., Karimi & Abdollahi, 2020; Spada & Tomita, 2010), whether the predominant focus of instruction is on form or meaning (e.g., Sheen, 2004), or even specific types of classroom exchanges (e.g., Oliver & Mackey, 2003). When it comes to ID factors, a mediating effect has been found, among others, for working memory (e.g., Goo, 2016; Indrarathne & Kormos, 2018), learning style (e.g., Rassaei, 2015), anxiety (e.g., Sheen, 2008) or beliefs (e.g., Karimi & Abdollahi, 2020). It should be underscored, however, that research on the role of mediating variables is scant, both with respect to GI in general and the contribution of explicit and implicit GT in particular. This is unfortunate, because merely showing that some instructional options are more efficacious may be of little relevance if this efficacy hinges upon which grammar structures are taught, to whom they are taught, and under what circumstances.

Finally, the empirical evidence concerning the contribution of explicit and implicit GT should be taken with circumspection for methodological reasons. For one thing, some techniques have been examined in just a handful of studies and the meta-analyses include investigations in which explicitness and implicitness were sometimes operationalized in a disparate manner. This brings us to the more general issue of the implementation of a particular instructional option in a given study, the structures that are targeted, the length of the intervention or the characteristics of participants. For example, using recasts of the more explicit type targeting the passive voice in English in two treatment sessions with secondary school students may produce different outcomes than the employment of more implicit recasts following errors in the French past tense delivered over four weeks to a group of university students. The picture becomes exceedingly more complex if we take account of ID factors. There is also the crucial issue of how learning outcomes are measured, since there are wide-ranging differences between studies. Not all of them tap both explicit and implicit (highly automatized) knowledge, let alone their productive and receptive dimensions, and even when they do, a variety of disparate tasks are used for this purpose (cf. Ellis & Roever, 2018; Pawlak, 2019).

Pedagogical implications

Nassaji and Fotos (2011, p. 139) argue that "teachers should be eclectic in their pedagogical approach. That is, they should choose and synthesize the best elements, principles, and activities of different approaches to grammar teaching to attain success". This comment certainly also applies to the choice of more explicit and implicit instructional options, which does not mean that such options should be used in a haphazard, unprincipled manner. While any pedagogical recommendations have to be informed by the realities of a particular instructional setting, it is perhaps uncontroversial that the main aim of teaching grammar structures is to develop the ability to use them accurately, meaningfully and appropriately in communication (Larsen-Freeman, 2003). In other words, the predominant goal of GI is to help learners develop implicit knowledge, or much more realistically in many contexts, automatize the explicit knowledge that they have at their disposal.

Keeping this in mind, it is clear that even though explicit instructional options may be more effective than implicit ones, their employment should only be the first step rather than an instructional goal in itself. This indicates that while metalinguistic explanations, consciousness-raising tasks, controlled exercises as well as overt CF during such activities serve their purpose by helping learners understand, practice and proceduralize grammar rules, they have to be followed by tasks that allow the use of TL forms more spontaneously under time constraints. This is in accordance with the principles of TAP (Lightbown, 2008) and only by doing so can we hope to foster the development of automatized knowledge needed for everyday communication. This aim can be achieved by means of productive or receptive focused communication tasks and text-creation activities, and it is quite irrelevant whether learners become cognizant of the pedagogic focus of such activities or not. Obviously, there is also a place for input flood or input enhancement which can further sensitize students to the targeted feature but also provide a stimulus for its employment in interaction, as

178   *Mirosław Pawlak*

well as general communication tasks that require the use of a variety of TL structures. Particularly important is the provision of CF during real-time interaction because this can activate implicit learning mechanisms or contribute to automatization of TL knowledge. While more explicit CF types have been found to be more effective, the decision whether to draw upon direct correction, prompts or recasts must depend on the situation. For example, when the targeted feature has been recently introduced and practiced, implicit recasts might do their job, whereas when errors in a range of structures are corrected, it might be necessary to make CF more explicit. In most cases, though, a combination of various techniques will be an optimal solution. It would also be ideal if the choice of instructional options took into account the nature of the structure taught and individual learner profiles. However, despite appeals that L2 instruction should be individualized (e.g., Ellis & Shintani, 2014), it appears to be somewhat unrealistic to expect teachers to tailor their instructional practices to the characteristic of particular students.

The choice of explicit and implicit instructional options should also be considered not only in terms of isolated classes but also sequences of lessons as well as overall curricular goals. For instance, the PPP procedure should be interpreted broadly as extending beyond a single class, where the relevant rule is presented and then practiced in a controlled and then more communicative way (this third element is often absent anyway). Rather, one could envisage a situation where the TL feature is introduced by means of deduction or induction, consciousness-raising tasks, processing instruction or textual enhancement, depending on its nature. The following several classes could be dedicated to different types of practice, with a gradual shift from controlled exercises to focused communication. Different types of CF could be provided on errors in the use of the targeted feature depending on the activities used. Later on, the structure could be singled out for intervention during more general communication tasks that necessitate reliance on a variety of TL resources. In this case, different CF moves, whether more explicit or implicit, should be the default instructional options, although a need might also arise for reminding learners of relevant rules. The structure could also be revisited during review classes not necessarily by asking learners to perform controlled exercises but, rather, by resorting to the various focus-on-form activities discussed by Doughty and Williams (1998). How exactly GI is executed will surely depend on the specific educational context, out-of-school access to the TL, the objectives of the course, and the goals that learners wish to pursue (Pawlak, 2013).

Conclusion

In view of the consensus among theorists and researchers that some form of grammar teaching is beneficial, the crucial question is how such pedagogic intervention should be implemented. Without doubt, one of the most acute controversies is whether grammar learning and teaching should be more explicit or more implicit, or what combinations of these instructional options are the

Implicit vs explicit grammar learning and teaching   179

most favorable. Specialists have identified a number of possibilities concerning how such options can be operationalized and a number of studies have been conducted with the aim of appraising their effectiveness. However, there are two main problems with such research. The first is related to its scope and methodological issues because some techniques have been investigated much more intensively than others and little is known about the value of clusters of different options. In addition, there are clear differences in how apparently the same interventions are operationalized as well as in how the mastery of the targeted form is measured, and there is a paucity of research investigating the impact of mediating variables. The second problem is linked to disseminating research findings among teachers in an accessible way, as well as making sure that such proposals are realistic and geared to the needs of specific instructional contexts. These problems certainly need to be addressed if the chasm between research and teaching practice (Larsen-Freeman, 2014) is ever to be even partially bridged in the hope of making grammar instruction more effective.

Relating the issues raised in this chapter to your own context:

1   In your own context of foreign or second language learning, is grammar teaching predominantly explicit or implicit? Why should this be the case?
2   What are the most popular techniques for introducing and practicing grammar structures in your context?

References

Anderson, J. (1983). *The architecture of cognition*. Cambridge: Cambridge University Press.

Broszkiewicz, A. (2011). The effect of focused communication tasks on instructed acquisition of English past counterfactual conditionals. *Studies in Second Language Learning and Teaching, 1*, 335–363.

DeKeyser, R. (2007). The future of practice. In R. DeKeyser (Ed.), *Practice in a second language: Perspectives from applied linguistics and cognitive psychology* (pp. 287–304). Cambridge: Cambridge University Press.

DeKeyser, R. (2010). Cognitive-psychological processes in second language learning. In M. H. Long & C. J. Doughty (Eds.), *The handbook of language teaching* (pp. 117–138). Oxford: Wiley-Blackwell.

DeKeyser, R. (2017). Knowledge and skill in SLA. In S. Loewen & M. Sato (Eds.), *The Routledge handbook of instructed second language acquisition* (pp. 15–32). New York and London: Routledge.

Doughty, C. J., & Williams, J. (1998). Pedagogical choices in focus on form. In C. J. Doughty & J. Williams (Eds.), *Focus on form in classrooms second language acquisition* (pp. 197–261). Cambridge: Cambridge University Press.

Ellis, N. C., & Wulff. S. (2015). Usage-based approaches to SLA. In B. VanPatten & J. Williams (Eds.), *Theories in second language acquisition* (2nd ed., pp. 75–93). London: Routledge.

Ellis, R. (1997). *SLA research and language teaching*. Oxford: Oxford University Press.

180   *Mirosław Pawlak*

Ellis, R. (2003). *Task-based language learning and teaching*. Oxford: Oxford University Press.

Ellis, R. (2009). Implicit and explicit learning, knowledge and instruction. In R. Ellis, S. Loewen, C. Elder, R. Erlam, J. Philp, & H. Reinders (Eds.), *Implicit and explicit knowledge in second language learning, testing and teaching* (pp. 3–25). Bristol: Multilingual Matters.

Ellis, R. (2018). *Reflections on task-based language teaching*. Bristol: Multilingual Matters.

Ellis, R., & Roever, C. (2018). The measurement of implicit and explicit knowledge. *The Language Learning Journal*. https://doi.org/10.1080/09571736.2018.1504229

Ellis, R., & Shintani, N. (2014). *Exploring language pedagogy through second language acquisition research*. London and New York: Routledge.

Goo, J. (2016). Corrective feedback and working memory capacity in interaction-driven L2 learning. *Studies in Second Language Acquisition, 34*, 445–474.

Goo, J., Granena, G., Yilmaz, Y., & Novella, M. (2015). Implicit and explicit instruction in L2 learning: Norris & Ortega (2000) revisited. In P. Rebuschat (Ed.). *Implicit and explicit learning of languages* (pp. 443–482). Amsterdam: John Benjamins.

Indrarathne, B., & Kormos, J. (2017). Attentional processing of input in explicit and implicit conditions: An eye-tracking study. *Studies in Second Language Acquisition, 39*, 401–430.

Indrarathne, B., & Kormos, J. (2018). The role of working memory in processing L2 input: Insights from eye-tracking. *Bilingualism: Language and Cognition, 21*, 355–374.

Jourdenais, R., Ota, M., Stauffer, S., Boyson, B., & Doughty, C. J. (1995). Does textual enhancement promote noticing? A think-aloud protocol analysis. In R. Schmidt (Ed.), *Attention and awareness in second language learning* (pp. 183–216). Honolulu: University of Hawaii.

Kang, E. Y., Sok, S., & Han, Z. (2019). Thirty-five years of ISLA on form-focused instruction: A meta-analysis. *Language Teaching Research, 23*, 428–453.

Karimi, M. N., & Abdollahi, S. (2020). L2 learners' acquisition of simple vs. complex linguistic features across explicit vs. implicit instructional approaches: The mediating role of beliefs. *Language Teaching Research*. https://doi.org/10.1177/1362168820921908

Kim, Y. (2017). Cognitive-interactionist approaches to L2 instruction. In S. Loewen & M. Sato (Eds.), *The Routledge handbook of instructed second language acquisition* (pp. 126–145). New York and London: Routledge.

Krashen, S. (1981). *Second language acquisition and second language learning*. Oxford: Pergamon.

LaBrozzi, R. M. (2016). The effects of textual enhancement type on L2 form recognition and reading comprehension in Spanish. *Language Teaching Research, 20*, 75–91.

Larsen-Freeman, D. (2003). *Teaching language: From grammar to grammaring*. Boston: Thomson & Heinle.

Larsen-Freeman, D. (2009). Teaching and testing grammar. In M. H. Long & C. J. Doughty (Eds.), *The handbook of language teaching* (pp. 518–542). Malden, MA: Blackwell.

Larsen-Freeman, D. (2014). Research into practice: Grammar learning and teaching. *Language Teaching, 48*, 263–280.

Larsen-Freeman, D., & Anderson, M. (2011). *Techniques and principles in teaching grammar*. Oxford: Oxford University Press.

Li, S. (2010). The effectiveness of corrective feedback in SLA: A meta-analysis. *Language Learning, 60*, 309–365.

Lightbown, P. M. (1998). The importance of timing in focus on form. In C. J. Doughty & J. Williams (Eds.), *Focus on form in classrooms second language acquisition* (pp. 177–196). Cambridge: Cambridge University Press.

Implicit vs explicit grammar learning and teaching 181

Lightbown, P. M. (2008). Transfer appropriate processing as s model for classroom second language acquisition. In Z. Han (Ed.), *Understanding second language process* (pp. 27–44). Clevedon: Multilingual Matters.

Loewen, S. (2011). Focus on form. In E. Hinkel (Ed.), *Handbook of research in second language teaching and learning: Volume II* (pp. 576–592). New York and London: Routledge.

Loewen, S., & Inceoglu, S. (2016). The effectiveness of visual input enhancement on the noticing and L2 development of the Spanish past tense. *Studies in Second Language Learning and Teaching, 6,* 89–110.

Long, M. (1991). Focus on form: A design feature in language teaching methodology. In K. De Bot, R. Ginsberg, & C. Kramsch (Eds.), *Foreign language research in cross-cultural perspectives* (pp. 39–52). Amsterdam: John Benjamins.

Long, M. H. (1996). The role of the linguistic environment in second language acquisition. In W. C. Ritchie & T. K. Bhatia (Eds.), *Handbook of second language acquisition* (pp. 413–468). New York: Academic Press.

Lyster, R., & Saito, K. (2010). Oral feedback in classroom SLA: A meta-analysis. *Studies in Second Language Acquisition, 32,* 265–302.

Nassaji, H. (2015). *The interactional feedback dimension in instructed second language learning. Linking theory, research, and practice.* London: Bloomsbury.

Nassaji, H. (2017). Grammar acquisition. In S. Loewen & M. Sato (Eds.), *The Routledge handbook of instructed second language acquisition* (pp. 205–223). New York and London: Routledge.

Nassaji, H., & Fotos, S. (2011). *Teaching grammar in second language classrooms: Integrating form-focused instruction in communicative context.* New York and London: Routledge.

Norris, J. M., & Ortega, L. (2000). Effectiveness of L2 instruction: A research synthesis and quantitative meta-analysis. *Language Learning, 50,* 417–528.

Oliver, R., & Mackey, A. (2003). Interactional context and feedback in child ESL classrooms. *Modern Language Journal, 87,* 519–533.

Pawlak, M. (2006). *The place of form-focused instruction in the foreign language classroom.* Poznań – Kalisz: Adam Mickiewicz University Press.

Pawlak, M. (2013). Principles of instructed language learning revisited: Guidelines for effective grammar teaching in the foreign language classroom. In K. Droździał-Szelest & M. Pawlak (Eds.), *Psycholinguistic and sociolinguistic perspectives on second language learning and teaching: Studies in honor of Waldemar Marton* (pp. 199–220). Heidelberg: Springer.

Pawlak, M. (2014). *Error correction in the foreign language classroom: Reconsidering the issues.* Heidelberg: New York.

Pawlak, M. (2017). Individual differences variables as mediating influences on success and failure in form-focused instruction. In E. Piechurska-Kuciel & M. Szyszka (Eds.). *At the crossroads: Challenges of foreign language learning* (pp. 75–92). Heidelberg: Springer.

Pawlak, M. (2018). Grammar learning strategy inventory: Another look. *Studies in Second Language Learning and Teaching, 8,* 351–379.

Pawlak, M. (2019). Tapping the distinction between explicit and implicit knowledge: Methodological issues. In B. Lewandowska-Tomaszczyk (Ed.), *Contacts & contrasts in educational contexts and translation* (pp. 45–60). Cham: Springer Nature.

Pawlak, M. (2020). Grammar and good language teachers. In C. Griffiths & T. Tajeddin (Eds.), *Grammar and good language teachers* (pp. 219–231). Cambridge: Cambridge University Press.

Pawlak, M. (2021). Teaching foreign language grammar: New solutions, old problems. *Foreign Language Annals.* https://doi.org/10.1111/flan.12563.

Pienemann, M., & Lenzing, A. (2015). Processability theory. In B. VanPatten & J. Williams (Eds.), *Theories in second language acquisition* (2nd ed., pp. 159–179). London: Routledge.

Ranta, L., & Lyster, R. (2017). Form-focused instruction. In P. Garret & J. M. Cots (Eds.), *The Routledge handbook of language awareness.* New York and London: Routledge. https://www.routledgehandbooks.com/doi/10.4324/9781315676494.ch4

Rassaei, E. (2015). Recasts, field dependence-independence cognitive style, and L2 development. *Language Teaching Research, 19,* 499–518.

Russell, V., & Spada, N. (2006). The effectiveness of corrective feedback for the acquisition of L2 grammar: A meta-analysis of the research. In J. M. Norris & L. Ortega (Eds.), *Synthesizing research on language learning and teaching* (pp. 133–164). Amsterdam: John Benjamins.

Schmidt, R. (1990). The role of consciousness in second language learning. *Applied Linguistics, 11,* 17–46.

Schmidt, R. (2001). Attention. In P. Robinson (Ed.), *Cognition and second language instruction* (pp. 3–32). Cambridge: Cambridge University Press.

Sheen, Y. (2004). Corrective feedback and learner uptake in communicative classrooms across instructional contexts. *Language Teaching Research, 8,* 263–300.

Sheen, Y. (2008). Recasts, language anxiety, modified output, and L2 learning. *Language Learning, 58,* 835–874.

Shintani, N. (2013). The effect of focus on form and focus on forms instruction on the acquisition of productive knowledge of L2 vocabulary by young beginning-level learners. *TESOL Quarterly, 47,* 36–62.

Simard, D. (2009). Differential effects of textual enhancement forma on intake. *System, 37,* 124–135.

Spada, N., & Tomita, Y. (2010). Interactions between type of instruction and type of language feature: A meta-analysis. *Language Learning, 60,* 263–308.

Swain, M. (1995). Three functions of output in second language learning. In G. Cook & B. Seidlhofer (Eds.), *Principles and practice in applied linguistics. Studies in honor of H. G. Widdowson* (pp. 125–144). Oxford: Oxford University Press.

Trahey, M., & White, L. (1993). Positive evidence and preemption in the second language classroom. *Studies in Second Language Acquisition, 15,* 181–204.

Ullman, M. T. (2015). The declarative/procedural model. In B. VanPatten & J. Williams (Eds.), *Theories in second language acquisition* (2nd ed., pp. 135–158). London: Routledge.

Ur, P. (2011). Grammar teaching: Research, theory, and practice. In E. Hinkel (Ed.), *Handbook of research in second language teaching and learning: Volume II* (pp. 507–522). New York and London: Routledge.

Valeo, A. (2013). The integration of language and content: Form-focused instruction in a content-based language program. *Canadian Journal of Applied Linguistics, 16,* 25–50.

VanPatten, B. (2015). Input processing theory. In B. VanPatten & J. Williams (Eds.), *Theories in second language acquisition* (2nd ed., pp. 113–134). London: Routledge.

Winke, P. M. (2013). The effect of input enhancement on grammar learning and comprehension: A modified replication of Lee (2007) with eye-movement data. *Studies in Second Language Acquisition, 35,* 323–352.

Zhao, Y., & Ellis, R. (2020). The relative effects of implicit and explicit corrective feedback on the acquisition of 3rd person -s by Chinese university students: A classroom-based study. Language Teaching Research. https://doi.org/10.1177/1362168820903343

10 Vocabulary learning in theory and practice
Implicit and explicit mechanisms

Ron Martinez

Introduction: Evidence that one can learn vocabulary without explicit instruction

A putative distinction between 'explicit' and 'implicit' vocabulary learning (also sometimes referred to as 'intentional' and 'incidental' vocabulary learning[1]) can be traced back to at least Stephen Krashen's early writings (Krashen, 1976, 1981) on language 'learning' versus 'acquisition', which for decades proved so influential in Applied Linguistics. The idea behind this distinction, which was part of what Krashen ultimately termed the 'Monitor Model', was that language development is a natural and biologically endowed part of all humans. By contrast, 'conscious learning' of a (second) language is a mechanism available to people after a certain age (Bley-Vroman, 1988) but does not contribute to actual language development. According to the proposed model, language acquisition has its own natural and underlying course, and this development cannot be consciously accelerated by formal learning (e.g. of grammar rules), other than in a performative way (e.g. on a proficiency test). Krashen's ideas held that actual language acquisition occurs naturally, through meaningful exposure and interaction with a foreign language at a level the hearer/reader comprehends (providing so-called 'comprehensible input').

In theory, comprehensible input would have been sufficient for language acquisition to occur, supposedly activating an innate 'Language Acquisition Device', originally proposed by Noam Chomsky (1967). As evidence for this, Krashen pointed to a number of studies showing that vocabulary had been naturally 'picked up' through reading, without explicit attention to particular lexical items. One study often cited by Krashen (e.g. Krashen, 1989; Pitts, White & Krashen, 1989) looked at how much vocabulary readers could show knowledge of after reading the novel *A Clockwork Orange* by Anthony Burgess. In the book, Burgess's characters often pepper their speech with a kind of slang called 'nadsat' (adapted from Russian), thus making it possible to assume that these fictional vocabulary items are unknown prior to encountering them in the novel. Krashen cites Saragi, Nation and Meister (1978), who tested 20 native speakers of English on their knowledge of 90 nadsat items after reading the novel. Krashen enthusiastically reports that "subjects had picked up at least forty-five words simply by

DOI: 10.4324/9781003008361-13

184 *Ron Martinez*

reading a novel!" (Krashen, 1989, p. 446). Part of this enthusiasm was related to the fact that the participants were not told that they were going to be tested on their vocabulary after reading the book, but were simply asked to read – thus (for Krashen) adding evidence that acquisition is a naturally occurring mechanism that does not require formal learning. While there is little debate that lexical gains were demonstrated in the Saragi et al. study (and others that followed), the extent to which one can simply 'absorb' vocabulary through reading alone has been problematized (e.g. Elgort & Warren, 2014; Pellicer-Sánchez & Schmitt, 2010). In particular, a question can and has since been raised: Is it the case, then, that a teacher is superfluous in terms of acquiring vocabulary?

Evidence that teaching can make a difference

One of the most important contributions to better understanding the question posed at the end of the previous section comes from Warwick Elley's (1989) study on children learning vocabulary through listening to stories. This study helps us understand the complexity behind the vocabulary acquisition process, with insights into key variables such as level of interest, attention and repetition. Most important, Elley's seminal investigation provides evidence that a teacher can make a difference when it comes to vocabulary learning.

Elley conducted two different experiments to explore the extent to which elementary school children in New Zealand could 'pick up' vocabulary simply from being read to. For the first experiment, Elley asked seven teachers of 168 children to read aloud from a book, from which 20 vocabulary items had been identified as (likely) previously unknown to those pupils. A pre-test showed that, on average, fewer than half of participants knew each word before hearing the story. At post-test, however, the children were able to demonstrate a 15.4% mean increase in receptive knowledge of the items assessed. Such results would seem to support Krashen's 'input hypothesis', that is, vocabulary acquisition would simply occur naturally, as long as the input was at a level that students could comprehend.

However, Elley also conducted a second intervention, this time tweaking the independent variables. In Elley's (1989) second experiment, he wanted to explore whether explicitly drawing students' attention to particular vocabulary items would make a difference. He also endeavoured to better understand the possible influence of the content of the book itself (i.e. the interest level of the story being read). A total of 127 pupils were divided into two treatment groups, and a further 51 students were recruited as controls. Elley chose two different books to be read to all groups – *Rapscallion Jones*, a story which Elley judged likely to be interesting to the pupils, and *The White Crane*, a folktale with "a more serious tone" but that was "particularly well illustrated with large, attractive pictures" (p. 181). In the first treatment, students were read to, with teachers adding an extra explanation for lexis identified as previously unknown, and in the second treatment, teachers would read without any further elaboration or complementation. In addition, the book titles that received this added

Vocabulary learning in theory and practice 185

lexical explanation were counterbalanced, with one treatment group hearing *Rapscallion Jones* without explanation, and the other treatment group hearing it with explanation (and vice versa for the other title).

Of greatest relevance, for the purposes of the discussion being constructed here, is the analysis of the lexical items for which students gained the most receptive knowledge. Elley points to the following variables as notable:

- *frequency* – words that appeared more often in the story and/or were supported by illustrations, tended to be answered correctly by students on the post-test;
- *context facilitation* – words with rich contextual and co-textual environments were answered significantly more correctly by pupils on a post-test, especially those judged as being key to plot development.

However, there were other variables that influenced the results, including whether or not there was any teacher-directed explicit focus on meaning, and also the content matter of the book itself. In the case of both *Rapscallion Jones* and *The White Crane*, students showed significantly more lexical gains when the teacher explained the meanings of the new words. Yet here, too, there were differences. With the *Rapscallion Jones* book reading, the pupils showed a 14.8% increase in receptive knowledge of the words with no teacher explanations, and a full 39.9% with explanations. Interestingly, when students were read *The White Crane* book, they demonstrated only 4.4% gains without teacher explanations, and even with explanations, accuracy increased by a comparatively modest 17.1% – less than half as much as the other story.

Finally, after three months, Elley asked all pupils to take a delayed post-test to check how durable the gains in their vocabulary knowledge were, and there was very little attrition in knowledge shown by participants (reportedly between 2% and 3%).

In terms of the implications of this study as it pertains to this chapter, there are a number of important points to be taken from Elley's seminal study. First, it was clear that in all conditions, students were able to demonstrate vocabulary gains even without the teacher explicitly pointing the words out, or explaining their meaning. Thus, some might say that students indeed appear to be able to learn vocabulary *implicitly*, at least on the face of it. But does that necessarily mean that the students did not *explicitly* focus on those items?

Second, Elley's data showed that there seemed to be properties of certain words that contributed positively to their chances of being noticed and picked up by students, including word class (nouns tended to be more easily understood in the context of the story than verbs or adjectives), how often a word was repeated in the story (i.e. its frequency), and the quality and quantity of the contextual cues by which the participants' could work out the words' meanings. The preceding features can be subsumed under a broader umbrella of *salience*, that is, variables that contribute to the reader/hearer paying *attention* to a word. It is worth noting the types of words that students seemed to be able to pick up

186 *Ron Martinez*

on their own versus those which appeared to benefit most from explicit elaboration from the teacher. For example, students were able to show a 59% gain in receptive knowledge of the items *ne'er-do-wells* and *pizzazz* without any explicit complementation by the teachers. One might say that those items 'stick out' as being 'different' in form and even sound from other lexis. By contrast, the students benefited appreciably from the teachers' added explanation for the item *startling* (53% gain with explanation, and absolutely no gain without). Elley does not provide a detailed discussion of why that particular item may have shown such a contrast beyond its word class (students showed greater gains for nouns compared to adjectives and verbs). Nevertheless, it is not a leap to guess that its form is not as likely to stand out as a word like *pizzazz*, and in fact, may even be confused with *starting* if the word is not explicitly pointed out by the teacher.

Moreover, there was at least one more variable that may have been conducive to greater or lesser degrees of attention. Elley notes that a "distinguishing feature" of *The White Crane* folktale was that students seemed to lack "involvement" with the story's plot, with characters that were less than compelling, and little humour or action (p. 185). Elley was unable to provide any theoretical explanation for the possible influence of this feature – this level of "involvement" – but research has since built on this notion, and it will feature later in this chapter.

In summary, what the Elley study usefully illustrates is that

1 *word frequency is important* – repetition of an item, in context, appears to contribute positively to noticing and retention of lexis;
2 *input matters* – the content itself and the extent to which that content can 'involve' or otherwise engage the reader/listener seems to make a positive difference;
3 *teaching matters* – although Elley's study showed that even without explicit teaching, students are able to show some knowledge gains, the research also demonstrated that what the teacher does to help learners notice lexis can be of benefit.

In the remainder of the current chapter, I will elaborate on the key concepts outlined above, concluding by discussing what the practical implications are for the language educator and for language learning in general.

Matters of frequency

When I first visited Brazil, a country where I would end up spending a good number of years, one of the first language items I noticed in Portuguese was simply *Oi!*, which I also noticed was generally followed by *Tudo bem?* (meaning, respectively, 'Hello!' and 'How are you?'). There is a good reason why I 'noticed' these items: in social encounters, they are very common! They are also the first items I felt comfortable using in Portuguese, for the same reason. The reader may reflect upon similar experiences (s)he may have had when first coming into contact with a foreign language.

Vocabulary learning in theory and practice   187

It is a phenomenon that was well documented in a diary study in which Richard Schmidt (with colleague Sylvia Frota) analyzed his own development in Portuguese whilst living in Brazil for five months (Schmidt & Frota, 1986). One key element that emerged from their analysis was that Schmidt's competence in Portuguese had often developed as a function of consciously 'noticing' linguistic features in the L2. Key, however, was that once a gap between their existing L2 knowledge ('*i*') and a correct target form was noticed, then the unknown item ('+*1*') must also be met again by the language learner in order to be acquired:

> If the comparison between i and +1 shows a gap, the i+1 form becomes a candidate for acquisition. If it turns up in input with some minimum **frequency**, it can be confirmed and acquired.
>
> (p. 311, boldface added)

It is of relevance here to note that Schmidt was in large part also responding to his contemporary, Stephen Krashen, and his stance that conscious (i.e. explicit) learning had no important role. Schmidt arrives at a very different conclusion, and we will return to this point later.

In any case, what Schmidt seemed to have himself noticed was that frequency could be an important variable in language acquisition, and the literature has grown extensively since that early (1986) study to add strength to this notion. In vocabulary studies specifically, much has been written on what have been called 'vocabulary thresholds', that is, how much lexis one needs to know in a given language in order to be able to do particular things in that language (for example, read and adequately comprehend an academic article). What emerged from those studies on thresholds is that most texts actually have many words that repeat. In fact, as much as 80% of most texts (other than specialized ones, such as technical manuals) is composed of the 2,000 most frequent (i.e. common) words in English (Nation & Waring, 1997). Computerized analysis of large amounts of texts in the field of corpus linguistics has shown, time and again, that most known human languages follow a kind of distribution in which the most frequent words are doing most of the 'heavy lifting' in actual communication (for a recent review, see Vilkaitė-Lozdienė & Schmitt, 2019).

The fact that most discourse is actually mostly made up of very frequent words should come as encouraging news to most learners. After all, it has been estimated that educated native speakers of English possess at least a passive knowledge of over 20,000 words, plus the related forms of those words, or *word families* (Zechmeister, et al., 1995) – with similar estimates for other languages. To ask a foreign language learner to commit 20,000 words to memory would be bordering on the ridiculous.

On the other hand, knowledge of only the 2,000 most frequent words means, in practice, that a reader will have comprehension gaps for every one in five words in most texts. This raises another important question, one that has indeed

188 Ron Martinez

been asked and addressed by several researchers over the years (e.g. Bensoussan & Laufer, 1984; Huckin & Coady, 1999; Nassaji, 2003; Paribakht & Wesche, 1999): How good are foreign language learners at guessing the meaning of unknown words (a process also called *lexical inferencing*)? The answer to this question is actually fraught with complexity, but this complexity will prove useful in the current discussion.

What has emerged in the research on lexical inferencing is that the likelihood that a reader/listener will notice a word and then 'learn' it is not a binary issue (i.e. correct or incorrect guess), but rather, often tends to be a cumulative one, that is, sensitive to the number of encounters a learner has with that item. In the seminal *Clockwork Orange* (and related) studies cited earlier (e.g. Saragi, et al. 1978), it was asserted that a certain number of encounters (typically around ten) with an unknown word was often required before a learner was able to show that (s)he had gleaned its meaning, and L2 research (e.g. Waring & Takaki, 2003) has shown similar results. In other words, as in the Elley (1989) study involving reading to children, the likelihood of a pupil being able to demonstrate understanding of a vocabulary item seems to increase with the number of times that the pupil reads or hears that word or phrase. Further, and also of relevance to this chapter, any number of encounters with a particular item may precede the first occasion on which the reader/listener apperceives (i.e. notices) that word or phrase.

Yet, the Elley study also revealed that there were other important variables beyond frequency that contributed to the meaning of a word being successfully gained. Any notion that 'one need only encounter a word in context ten times for it to be acquired' (as an example) is clearly an oversimplification. Instead of focusing on the 'quantity' of frequency, more recent thinking has focused on the more *qualitative* aspects of that repetition. (Learners are humans, not machines!) This more 'human' aspect of learning, with respect to frequency and other variables, will be the focus of the next section.

Matters of input: How noticing happens

With so much talk of words and frequency, one might lose sight of the learner herself or himself in all this. Naturally, learning is inescapably a biological process; learning involves a change in the brain. When a person learns something new, it usually means that an existing neural network has somehow grown or been altered. For example, I remember when my son, at six years old, learned the word *chorus*. He was watching a children's animated television show on dinosaurs, with a catchy tune with a chorus that went "Tyrannosaurus, that's the chorus". The line repeated so often that he asked me, "What does *chorus* mean?" I then explained that it is the line of a song that repeats, and asked him if he could think of a chorus in a Beatles song. He quickly confirmed his understanding by enthusiastically belting out chorus after chorus, from *I Want to Hold Your Hand* to *Yellow Submarine*. For some time after, my son would say, "Daddy, that's the chorus" every time he heard the relevant part of a Beatles song.

Vocabulary learning in theory and practice   189

Hebbian learning theory would posit that my son already had a neural network for a number of Beatles songs. Further, within a stimulus that he was interested in and understood, he noticed that in a sequence of sounds (i.e. morphemes) that were familiar to him (*Tyrannosaurus, that's the...*) he picked out a novel morpheme that he wanted to understand, or whose meaning he wanted to confirm. This new string of phonemes that he was holding in his working memory – *chorus* – may have never found a home in his budding mental lexicon if not for the fact that (with my help) he was able to associate it with that existing neural network. He had made the connection needed to understand, establishing a new synapse (Zull, 2002).

Importantly, when that new synapse was formed, a new neuronal network was also established (T-rex song, *chorus* + Beatles songs). However, and of relevance here, a number of conditions during and after that first exposure can determine the success with which that network survives, and if ultimately *chorus* remains a permanent part of the lexicon. Of note:

- my son understood every word in that sentence (*Tyrannosaurus, that's the chorus*) except for the word *chorus* itself;
- that sentence repeated itself several times (it itself was the in chorus);
- he was interested in the input – it had his attention, and he wanted to know the meaning;
- I supplied the meaning when he was interested and ready to know it.

Before this incident occurred, I could have handed my son a shortlist of new words that included *chorus,* bribed him with a trip to the zoo if he learnt the meaning of the word, and it probably would not have been nearly as effective. All the above-mentioned conditions were important, i.e. sufficient background knowledge (both linguistic, and of other songs), and noticing a lexical gap at a state of attention to the input. Without them, the word *chorus* in that input may have never found its way into his long-term memory (Garagnani, Wennekers & Pulvermüller, 2008). Robinson (2003) provides a succinct summary of the attentional processes involved:

> Attention is the process that encodes language input, keeps it active in working and short-term memory, and retrieves it from long-term memory. [...] The focus of attention is a subset of short-term memory, and short-term memory is that part of long-term memory in a currently heightened state of activation.
>
> (p. 631)

Retrieval and spacing

One key part of Robinson's operationalization of the construct of 'attention' above is that short-term memory is key not only to the initial learning of a novel lexical item but also to its retrieval. It is this retrieval that can be a determinant of whether or not a newly learned word becomes one that stays learnt.

190   *Ron Martinez*

According to Baddeley (1990), every opportunity to retrieve a newly learned word – either receptively, in reading/listening, or productively, in writing/speaking – strengthens the memory (i.e. neural) connections and makes subsequent retrieval faster and easier.

Note, however, that while retrieving a lexical item can be an important part of making a new word or phrase a long-term fixture of one's vocabulary, the 'spacing' (i.e. time interval) between each retrieval is also important. And this brings us back to the notion of frequency and repetition. Often, the research that has pointed to a certain number of repetitions being a significant factor in determining whether or not a vocabulary item is learned implicitly is cited without also considering the time between exposures. It would seem unreasonable to imagine that by simply inserting ten instances of the same target vocabulary item in one paragraph, or asking a learner to repeat a word (e.g. through subvocalization) ten times, that exercise would automatically translate into long-term retention of that word. On the other hand, if a learner meets a new word and then does not see or hear it again for a few years, it would be equally unrealistic to assume its meaning would be easily retrieved – if remembered at all. As Nation (2013) summarizes:

> If too much time has passed between the previous meeting and the present encounter with the word, then the present encounter is effectively not a repetition but is like a first encounter with the word. If, however, a memory of the previous meeting with the word remains, then the present encounter can add to and strengthen that memory.
>
> (p. 108)

Thus, returning to my son's learning of the word *chorus*, although the repetition in the song may have contributed to him noticing the item in the first place – and piquing his interest enough to ask me for its meaning – that alone may not have sufficed for his ultimately being able to keep its form and meaning in long-term memory. It was encountering the item over time, on subsequent exposures to varied input sources, that most likely established that word as a fixture of his young lexicon.

Subject areas matter

This finally leads us to a key point about language input sources, and why they play a key role in both implicit and explicit learning of vocabulary. As mentioned in the previous section, it would be a herculean task to ask a language student to learn the 20,000 or so words that most people know in their first language, but it has been established that knowledge of the most common words in a foreign language (say the top 3,000), enables one to comprehend as much as 95% of the vocabulary in a text written in that language (Nation, 2006). Yet, it is that 5% of unknown vocabulary that is the elusive and more challenging aspect of vocabulary thresholds.

Vocabulary learning in theory and practice   191

While many of those 3,000 words that comprise the bulk of most texts will naturally recur if one reads and listens to enough of the target language – thus potentially providing regular opportunities to retrieve the meanings of those words and strengthen the automaticity of their recall – the vast majority of the words in that 5% will not repeat with the regularity needed to keep their meaning in long-term memory (Cobb, 2007; cf. McQuillan & Krashen, 2008).

Fortunately, most learners of a foreign language, especially once they reach a level of proficiency at which they have a knowledge of 2,000 to 3,000 words, also have more specific or specialized interests and needs in that language. It is certainly true that many foreign language learners report wanting to learn an L2 (or L3 etc.) because they want to use it when they travel, or for more general purposes such as reading novels or watching films in that language, and the 2,000 to 3,000 more common, 'general service' words (West, 1953) will largely meet those needs. However, many learners (adults in particular) will also report more specific needs in a foreign language, as in the case of learning English for Academic Purposes, for instance, or so-called 'Business English'. This is actually good news in terms of vocabulary development: it means that a learner need not worry about the 20,000 or so words that most educated native speakers would know, but instead focus on that (roughly) 5% of words that will likely be recurring lexical items in the specific subject area with which they need or want to engage. But how should they go about learning these subject-specific words?

A number of corpus-derived[2] vocabulary lists for specific purposes have emerged over recent years (e.g. Coxhead, 2000; Ward, 2009; Yang, 2015) and each shows how there are a number of discipline-specific words that recur in one area of knowledge that do not necessarily feature prominently in others. Thus, some have proposed that students could somehow endeavour to explicitly memorize these words to accelerate their lexical development (Cobb, 2007; Nation & Waring, 1997). Although there is no reason to question that memorizing words in lists, through various techniques, may be of some help, one may nonetheless wonder to what extent such an exercise contributes to the type of retrieval described earlier, which is important in order to actually learn a word. For such learning to occur, it is clear that repeated exposure to the target words, in their naturally occurring contexts, is the best way to incrementally strengthen and flesh out word knowledge.

Developing breadth and depth of vocabulary knowledge

By 'flesh out' in the preceding sentence, I am referring especially to the importance of countenancing vocabulary knowledge not as items that are either 'learned' or 'not learned', but rather as a spectrum of gradually acquired word knowledge: one's vocabulary consists of not only how many words one knows (i.e. vocabulary knowledge *breadth*) but also how much information about those words one possesses (i.e. vocabulary knowledge *depth*). This can include spelling,

192 *Ron Martinez*

Figure 10.1 An illustration of how 'vocabulary' is connected to more than individual words.

connotation, pronunciation, collocation,[3] and so on. Consider, for example, the knowledge required to complete the sentence in Figure 10.1, and how you came to possess that knowledge.

Most anyone would guess that the hidden word in Figure 10.1 is *inconvenience*, and feel quite confident about that guess. Yet, there are many lexical possibilities: *problem, issue, delay, frustration* would all be plausible candidates. If one were learning English, and wanted to learn the word *inconvenience*, simply attempting to explicitly commit that word and its meaning to memory would not likely lead to knowing that it fits perfectly well in the sentence shown in Figure 10.1. You, the reader, likely did not hesitate to guess *inconvenience*, because you were probably immediately able to identify the context (a supermarket), which may have activated your memory (including linguistically related memory) associated with supermarkets and similar social situations, of which you, as an adult, have much familiarity through hundreds if not thousands of personal encounters. And in some of those encounters, it is likely that you read or heard the word 'inconvenience' used in the same or a similar sentence. Moreover, you recognize that it is an appropriate word to be used in that context, and know that it may sound strange to use the same sentence in a different situation. (It might sound awkward to text *I apologize for any inconvenience* to one's partner, for instance, if one were running late.)

Hence, while explicitly trying to learn a new word by memorizing it (e.g. from a wordlist) may be a start, it is unlikely to contribute to the kind of depth of knowledge exemplified in the preceding discussion. Furthermore, it would be

Vocabulary learning in theory and practice 193

onerous to try to present or otherwise explicitly learn such semantic complexity (e.g. through a dictionary entry) and expect it to 'stick' or truly be a part of one's productive vocabulary. Instead, what research shows is that multiple encounters with previously encountered vocabulary can help deepen lexical knowledge. As Nation (2013) puts it:

> Is it possible to use context to keep adding small amounts of information about words that are not yet fully known? The answer to this question is clearly 'Yes'.
>
> (p. 354)

Not only can each new encounter with a not-fully-known word help flesh out one's knowledge of that word's meaning, but each instance also contains information around the word beyond the morpheme itself, including which words typically co-occur with it (i.e. collocates), and even which types of discourse or text (i.e. genres) in which one can expect to encounter, or not encounter, that word. This idea is the implicit learning mechanism held in *lexical priming* (Hoey, 2005):

> As a word is acquired through encounters with it in speech and writing, it becomes cumulatively loaded with the contexts and co-texts in which it is encountered, and our knowledge of it includes the fact that it co-occurs with certain other words in certain kinds of context.
>
> (p. 8)

As Hoey further points out, it is necessary for the word to have first been noticed, and "to have occurred twice (at least)" in naturally occurring input for this "cumulative" depth of knowledge to begin to grow. It can be reasonably assumed that the most important and useful words a learner needs will naturally recur in the target language input with which that learner engages. If important lexis does not recur in the input frequently enough to support its learning, it is likely because (a) the learner is not reading/listening in the target language frequently enough (see also the section on teaching below), and/or (b) the learner is not reading/listening to the right kind(s) of discourse. For example, a student that needs to learn French for culinary purposes is unlikely to encounter the specific vocabulary she or he needs if that student is only reading Proust!

The preceding point bears relevance to important conditions for vocabulary learning. According to Nation (2013, p. 117), the psychological conditions that favour the learning of a word involve *noticing a word, retrieving a word*, and *using the word creatively*. Here I have argued that noticing is sensitive to at least two variables: word frequency (i.e. the word stands out as important because of how often it appears), and because the learner is – for whatever reason – attentive to that lexical item at a particular moment. As we shall see in the following section, that apperception on the part of the student may arise from the student her- or himself, or maybe facilitated (e.g. by the teacher or textbook). In either case, if there is no initial noticing of the novel vocabulary item, then obviously, subsequent encounters with it are not likely to make any difference.

194   *Ron Martinez*

Thus, I would posit that *choice of language input matters greatly*, in at least two ways: (a) in its level of interest to students (promoting their attention), and (b) as a source of repetition. Language input that is more likely to heighten a learner's attention (i.e. desire to understand) will also more likely be conducive to noticing. Further – and this is good news to language learners – the lexis that is likely to be of most use to the learner will naturally recur in the input that is of greatest relevance to that learner. This in turn means that most learners will not have to concern themselves with trying to learn 20,000 or so words necessary to understand 98% of the words in a given text, the threshold at which 'adequate comprehension' is said to occur (Schmitt, Jiang & Grabe, 2011). As long as learners endeavour to engage meaningfully with written or spoken texts in the target language – and in the subjects or areas of discourse most relevant to them – then the most common and important lexis for that learner will naturally repeat. This will provide opportunities for regular retrieval, simultaneously contributing to both breadth and depth of vocabulary learning.

In the next section, I will address the third element of Nation's proposal, that is, the creative use of words.

Matters of teaching

The driving question for the discussion in this section is the following: What can the teacher do to facilitate both implicit and explicit learning of vocabulary? It is worth recalling the debate presented at the beginning of this chapter concerning the extent to which the acquisition of language can be said to occur through conscious learning mechanisms (i.e. intentional behaviours deployed by the student or teacher). The research overview provided in the previous section ('Matters of input') reveals the premise of the *implicit v. explicit* dichotomy to be dubious. Clearly, there is a dynamic interface between the two (Ellis, 2005), and one certainly does not detriment the other – in fact, quite the opposite (Ellis, 2006; Ender, 2016). As shown in Elley's (1989) research, students that simply listen to a story will pick up new vocabulary, and the extent to which they do so can depend on a number of variables, including whether (and how often) the lexis is repeated, the concreteness or imageability of the words, how important it is to understand the words in order to comprehend the greater context, and how much the student is interested in understanding the input in the first place. All of the aforementioned can make a difference, but what the Elley study also illustrates is that there are things that a teacher can do to enhance vocabulary learning further still. In short, teaching matters.

One important way the teachers ameliorated conditions for vocabulary learning in the Elley (1989) classroom research was through particular choices made prior to teaching. In the case of that study, there were at least two: (1) which book would most likely be met with interest by the pupils, and (2) which lexis would most benefit from extra explanation by the teacher. Thus, there was an implicit hypothesis that the book that featured animals, *Rapscallion Jones*, would be more engaging than its (apparently) duller folktale counterpart, *The White Crane*.

Vocabulary learning in theory and practice 195

Furthermore, teachers analyzed the lexis beforehand and assessed that there were certain words and phrases (e.g. *pizzazz, startling, ne'er-do-well*) that many pupils were unlikely to understand accurately on their own. As teachers, we have some control over both those aspects of vocabulary teaching – the themes and genres we focus on in class, and explicit attention to lexical items. In both cases, Elley's (1989) findings support the assertion that vocabulary learning is best kept focused on meaning, at least in the initial stages, and what we do as teachers may be merely a starting point to later deepening of that nascent vocabulary knowledge. We need to be aware of the limitations of what we can do during class time – if students limit their vocabulary learning to what they get during class alone, they are unlikely to achieve their learning goals. We can, however, do our part to encourage *engagement* with the target language inside and, especially, outside of class.

Although a number of different theories have been put forward over time, the construct of engagement is the one that best encompasses, in my view, the variables that can most influence both implicit and explicit vocabulary learning. Schmitt (2010) asserts that "it is a commonsense notion that the more a learner engages with a new word, the more likely she/he is to learn it" (p. 26) and "it seems that virtually anything that leads to more exposure, attention, manipulation or time spent on lexical items adds to their own learning" (p. 28). What a teacher does during class should aim to enhance students' engagement with the language – not only in the class itself but also beyond it Therefore, whatever vocabulary learning activities we do with our students should be seen as having a secondary aim, namely, contributing to their training as lifelong autonomous learners who will have the tools – and desire – to engage with words as often as possible.

Nation (2007) has suggested that a teacher aiming to develop students' lexical knowledge need to consider four 'strands': *meaning-focus input* (i.e. implicit learning), *language-focused learning* (i.e. explicit), *meaning-focused output* (need for retrieval), and *fluency development* (basically, leisurely or extensive activities to practice the skills of reading and listening). According to Nation and Webb (2011), planning for a good balance among these strands is the first and "most important job of the vocabulary teacher" (p. 1). In the Elley (1989) study, the teachers that read the stories to their pupils can be said to have attended to at least three of these strands. After all, the pupils in that study were asked to listen to stories; they were focused on meaning before anything else. The teachers had singled out particular lexical items worth explicitly teaching or explaining, and so there was a language focus as well. Finally, the very fact that students were read to regularly, and from two different books, can be said to have possibly contributed to their fluency development. We do not know if there were opportunities for meaning-focused output later, but those could have occurred via, for example, simply asking students to tell each other about their favourite parts of the stories.

However, Nation and Webb (2011) also claim that there is another important job of the vocabulary teacher: "The second most important job of the vocabulary teacher is to train learners in the use of vocabulary strategies" (p. 2). One good way to integrate strategy awareness in the classroom is to use language-focused learning moments as training opportunities. Martinez (2021), for example, had non-native English students in a higher education setting in the United States read academic research articles in their respective disciplines (engineering, design, business, and so on) – a meaning-focused activity. Students had also been taught about how to use electronic resources to check the meaning and frequency of words during class. Students then delivered brief presentations on the articles they had read, and taught other students the lexis they (the students) had themselves identified as being particularly interesting or useful – i.e. language-focused learning. However, in addition, after students had delivered their presentations and taught the vocabulary, the instructor (Martinez) would often elaborate on certain items which he deemed to deserve more attention. This elaboration did not so much involve the instructor 'explaining' the vocabulary *per se*, but contextualizing it further and showing additional examples through the use of online corpora[2], web searches, and even *Google* images. This complementing by the instructor had two aims: in the short term, to point out important features of the lexis already presented by the students; in the longer term, to model certain tools and techniques that students could later employ when reading or listening on their own.

Finally, with respect to what teachers can do to optimize vocabulary learning, I would add that we need to aim to be student-centred. As exemplified in the Martinez (2021) study just described, the task was set by the instructor (read a research article), but students were afforded the choice of whatever theme they preferred. This is also common sense: whatever a teacher can do to heighten students' interest (i.e. attention) may also increase their chances of noticing potentially important lexis in the input. This is a phenomenon I observed recently in the context of training university lecturers in Brazil to deliver their subjects through English (also known as English Medium Instruction, or EMI). One important focus of the EMI training course I teach is to steer lecturers away from the idea that they must always 'lecture'. Instead, I show them how nearly any given lesson can benefit from student contributions, with lessons thus being co-constructed with students. It is not an easy paradigm to shift, but by the end of the course, most lecturers are able to demonstrate some change. I had the opportunity to observe a short course in Crop Science delivered in English by four different lecturers, two of whom did not take my EMI training course (Martinez, Fogaça & de Figueiredo, 2019). Unsurprisingly, the two lecturers that took the course asked more questions, and waited longer for students to give a considered response. Moreover, the two that took the EMI training also engaged students in more student-centred activity, requiring them to discuss points before being asked to answer content-focused questions. At the end of the Crop Science course, students were interviewed, and reported that they preferred the teaching styles of the teachers that engaged them more with questions and pair or group work. Many students complained about one professor in particular ('Victor'), who almost never asked questions, and lectured for the entire duration of the class. Separately, I also asked students to transfer the words they had learned, organized by 'Day' (there had been four straight days of tuition, each by a different lecturer). The collected notes showed that students had written down many new vocabulary items for nearly all the lecturers, especially the ones who had allowed students time to contribute. Interestingly, but again not surprisingly, those were not the lecturers who had supplied the most linguistic volume (i.e. largest number of words); indeed, the relationship between words noticed and volume of lecturer speech was almost an inverse one. It was Victor, who had spoken the most but involved students least, who had been least successful in terms of supplying input that encouraged students to notice and engage with lexis.

Conclusion

In this chapter, I have tried to show that, in a way, the distinction between 'implicit' and 'explicit' vocabulary learning is one that is interesting on a theoretical level, but in practice, somewhat of a red herring. In reality, these are essentially metaphors for complex learning mechanisms that are sensitive to myriad variables inherent to the language input, learner, teacher and teaching. I would propose a different metaphor: learning a new vocabulary item is like growing a plant from a seed. When a new word is explicitly taught – or is otherwise noticed by the learner – that is planting the seed. Connecting the written and/or spoken form of that word to a meaning is like putting that seed in a kind of soil. Furthermore, in a garden, some seeds are planted intentionally (i.e. explicitly), and other times plants may appear where none were intentionally planted, but nonetheless a seed somehow found its way into the soil (i.e. implicitly). However, a seed planted in soil on its own, without sufficient water and sunlight, will not thrive. If left without these elements, it will simply wither. In vocabulary learning, the garden itself is one's existing lexicon, and the repeated encounters with a new word are the water and sunlight the seed needs. Just the right amount of each, at regular intervals, increases the chance of growth and long-term survival. As teachers, we can plant seeds, and help students find more seeds, and we can even supply some of the water and sunlight. Moreover, we can help prepare the soil and raise the awareness of our 'gardeners' regarding those things that help nature take its course. Ultimately, however, gardening requires patience – growth cannot be forced. It requires regular and explicit attention in order to truly flourish.

Relating the issues raised in this chapter to your own context:

1 Think about your own teaching context. What do you (or your curriculum) do to foster more autonomous vocabulary-building practices among learners?
2 Reflect on the issues raised in the chapter (for example, 'spacing', 'attention', 'engagement'). How could the current teaching approaches you (and/or your institution) adopt better incorporate them?

198   *Ron Martinez*

Notes

1   Hulstijn (2003) draws a theoretical distinction between *implicit/incidental* versus *explicit/intentional* with respect to vocabulary, arguing that implicit learning is a broader construct of learning (e.g. gradually acquiring a rule-based competence without intention). Similarly – according to Hulstijn – explicit learning entails intentionally trying to understand rules and language systems, whereas intentional learning of vocabulary is more of an item-based kind of learning, typically aiming to commit lexical items to memory. While I largely agree with Hulstijn's distinction, here no such theoretical line will be drawn, as for practical purposes, they do not further the aim of this chapter.
2   Corpus-linguistic research usually involves the computerized analysis of large amounts of text to understand its lexical or grammatical features. For example, an analysis of a corpus of English newspapers might reveal that the word *report* is more common in that genre than in a similarly sized corpus of cookbooks or song lyrics.
3   Here, 'collocation' refers to the natural phenomenon whereby certain pairings or strings of words tend to recur. For example, the word 'friend' in English can be premodified by any number of adjectives, but there are some *collocates* that are particularly common, such as 'close', 'good', and 'old', and likewise it may be postmodified frequently by 'from school', 'from work' and 'of mine'. These sequences ('close friend', 'good friend', 'friend from school', 'friend of mine') are often called collocations, and research (especially in corpus linguistics – see Note 2) has shown their central importance to vocabulary knowledge (e.g. Sinclair, 1991).

References

Baddeley, A. (1990). *Human memory*. London: Lawrence Erlbaum Associates.
Bensoussan, M., & Laufer, B. (1984). Lexical guessing in context in EFL reading comprehension. *Journal of Research in Reading*, *7*(1), 15–32.
Bley-Vroman, R. (1988). The fundamental character of foreign language learning. In W. Rutherford and M. Sharwood Smith (Eds.) *Grammar and second language teaching: A book of readings*, New York: Newbury House, 19–30.
Chomsky, N. (1967). Recent contributions to the theory of innate ideas. *Synthese*, *17*, 2–11.
Cobb, T. (2007). Computing the vocabulary demands of L2 reading. *Language Learning & Technology*, *11*(3), 38–63.
Coxhead, A. (2000). A new academic word list. *TESOL Quarterly*, *34*(2), 213–238.
Elgort, I , & Warren, P. (2014). L2 vocabulary learning from reading: Explicit and tacit lexical knowledge and the role of learner and item variables. *Language Learning*, *64*(2), 365–414.
Elley, W. B. (1989). Vocabulary acquisition from listening to stories. *Reading Research Quarterly*, 174–187.
Ellis, N. C. (2005). At the interface: Dynamic interactions of explicit and implicit language knowledge. *Studies in Second Language Acquisition*, *27*(2), 305–352.
Ellis, N. C. (2006). Selective attention and transfer phenomena in L2 acquisition: Contingency, cue competition, salience, interference, overshadowing, blocking, and perceptual learning. *Applied Linguistics*, *27*(2), 164–194.
Ender, A. (2016). Implicit and explicit cognitive processes in incidental vocabulary acquisition. *Applied Linguistics*, *37*(4), 536–560.
Garagnani, M., Wennekers, T., & Pulvermüller, F. (2008). A neuroanatomically grounded Hebbian-learning model of attention–language interactions in the human brain. *European Journal of Neuroscience*, *27*(2), 492–513.

Vocabulary learning in theory and practice   199

Hoey, M. (2005). *Lexical priming: A new theory of words and language*. Oxford: Routledge.

Huckin, T., & Coady, J. (1999). Incidental vocabulary acquisition in a second language: A review. *Studies in Second Language Acquisition, 21*(2), 181–193.

Hulstijn, J. H. (2003). Incidental and intentional learning. In C. J. Doughty and M. H. Long (Eds.) *The handbook of second language acquisition*, Oxford: Blackwell Publishing, 349–381.

Krashen, S. D. (1976). Formal and informal linguistic environments in language acquisition and language learning. *TESOL Quarterly, 10*(2), 157–168.

Krashen, S. D. (1981). *Second language acquisition and second language learning*. Hoboken, NJ: Prentice Hall.

Krashen, S. (1989). We acquire vocabulary and spelling by reading: Additional evidence for the input hypothesis. *The Modern Language Journal, 73*(4), 440–464.

Martinez, R., Fogaça, F., & de Figueiredo, E. H. D. (2019). An instrument for English medium instruction (EMI) classroom observation in higher education. *Caderno de Letras*, (35), 221–234.

Martinez, R. (2021). A student generated vocabulary syllabus in an English for academic purposes (EAP) context. In P. Szudarski & S. Barclay (Eds.) *Vocabulary theory, patterning and teaching*, Bristol: Multilingual Matters, 211–236.

McQuillan, J., & Krashen, S. D. (2008). Commentary: Can free reading take you all the way? A response to Cobb (2007). *Language Learning & Technology, 12*(1), 104–108.

Nassaji, H. (2003). L2 vocabulary learning from context: Strategies, knowledge sources, and their relationship with success in L2 lexical inferencing. *TESOL Quarterly, 37*(4), 645–670.

Nation, I. (2006). How large a vocabulary is needed for reading and listening?. *Canadian Modern Language Review, 63*(1), 59–82.

Nation, P. (2007). The four strands. *International Journal of Innovation in Language Learning and Teaching, 1*(1), 2–13.

Nation, I. S. P. (2013). *Learning vocabulary in another language*. Cambridge: Cambridge University Press.

Nation, I. S. P. & Webb, S. (2011). *Researching and analyzing vocabulary*. Boston: Heinle Cengage.

Nation, P. & Waring, R. (1997). Vocabulary size, text coverage and word lists. In N. Schmitt & M. McCarthy (Eds.) *Vocabulary: Description, acquisition and pedagogy*, Cambridge: Cambridge University Press, 6–19.

Paribakht, T. S., & Wesche, M. (1999). Reading and 'incidental' L2 vocabulary acquisition: An introspective study of lexical inferencing. *Studies in Second Language Acquisition*, 21(2), 195–224.

Pellicer-Sánchez, A., & Schmitt, N. (2010). Incidental vocabulary acquisition from an authentic novel: do 'things fall apart'?. *Reading in a Foreign Language, 22*(1), 31–55.

Pitts, M., White, H., & Krashen, S. (1989). Acquiring second language vocabulary through reading: A replication of the Clockwork Orange study using second language acquirers. *Reading in a Foreign Language, 5*(2), 271–275.

Robinson, P. (2003). Attention and memory during SLA. In C. J. Doughty & M. H. Long (Eds.) *The handbook of second language acquisition*. Oxford: Blackwell Publishing, 631–678.

Saragi, T., Nation, P., & Meister, G. (1978). Vocabulary learning and reading. *System*, 6, 70–78.

Schmidt, R., & Frota, S. N. (1986). Developing basic conversational ability in a second language: A case study of an adult learner of Portuguese. In R. R. Day (Ed.) *Talking to learn: Conversation in second language acquisition*. Rowley, MA: Newbury House, 237–326.

200   *Ron Martinez*

Schmitt, N. (2010). *Researching vocabulary: A vocabulary research manual*. London: Palgrave Macmillan.

Schmitt, N., Jiang, X., & Grabe, W. (2011). The percentage of words known in a text and reading comprehension. *The Modern Language Journal, 95*(1), 26–43.

Sinclair, J. (1991). *Corpus, concordance, collocation*. Oxford: Oxford University Press.

Vilkaitė-Lozdienė, L., & Schmitt, N. (2019). Frequency as a guide for vocabulary usefulness. In S. Webb (Ed.), *The Routledge handbook of vocabulary studies*. Abingdon: Routledge, 81–96.

Ward, J. (2009). A basic engineering English word list for less proficient foundation engineering undergraduates. *English for Specific Purposes, 28*(3), 170–182.

Waring, R., & Takaki, M. (2003). At what rate do learners learn and retain new vocabulary from reading a graded reader?. *Reading in a Foreign Language, 15*(2), 130.

West, M. (1953). *A general service list of English words*. London: Longman, Green and Co.

Yang, M. N. (2015). A nursing academic word list. *English for Specific Purposes, 37*, 27–38.

Zechmeister, E. B., Chronis, A. M., Cull, W. L., D'anna, C. A., & Healy, N. A. (1995). Growth of a functionally important lexicon. *Journal of Reading Behavior, 27*(2), 201–212.

Zull, J. E. (2002). *The art of changing the brain: Enrichng teaching by exploring the biology of learning*. Sterling, Virgina: Stylus Publishing, LLC.

11 The L2-only versus the multilingual debate

Ernesto Macaro

Introduction

In this chapter, we begin by examining one of the key debates in Second Language Acquisition (SLA): whether the use of the students' first language (L1) is beneficial for second language (L2) learning. We examine the debate in terms of: the way it has been carried out by authors in the field, their terms of reference, and their use of citations of previously published literature.

We then examine some of the research evidence focusing on three main areas: measurements and descriptions of classroom interaction in which the two languages feature; the beliefs of teachers and learners; and the effect of using the L1 on vocabulary learning.

Defining our terms

Before we begin, we need to define our terms. When referring to the use of the languages available for learning in formal settings such as classrooms, researchers and practitioners in the field express this use in a variety of ways. They talk about: first language use; native language use; own-language use; L1 translation; second language use; target language use (the L2 being taught); codeswitching or code-mixing, when both the L1 and L2 are being used in a variety of ways; code-choice, translanguaging (usually when the use of both languages is being considered from a socio-cultural as well as an educational standpoint); the monolingual or bilingual approach.

In this chapter, I will be employing the terms 'L1 use/L2 use' unless I am attempting to make a particular distinction or elaborate on the complexities of the terms themselves (see below). Furthermore, I define an 'L2 classroom' as one where the prime objective of the teacher (or the curriculum on which that teaching is based) is to teach an L2. I use the term Medium of Instruction (MOI) or EMI (English Medium Instruction) when discussing those classrooms where academic content (e.g. science, geography, mathematics) is the prime objective of the teaching and learning, even though there may be an additional objective – that of promoting L2 learning (see Lasagabaster, this volume).

DOI: 10.4324/9781003008361-14

202   *Ernesto Macaro*

A great debate?

Perhaps in no other field of Second Language Education do we find research and commentary so frequently peppered with the words 'debate' and 'controversy' as we do in the field that has examined L1 use in the L2 classroom. Even the research on the implicit and explicit learning of morphology and syntax (see Pawlak, Chapter 9, this volume) does not initiate its background sections so frequently with an outright reference to heated debate or seemingly unresolved controversy. The following opening statements by authors in the field are typical in the literature:

> The use of learners' L1 is a controversial issue in L2 education.
> (Storch & Wigglesworth, 2003: 760)

> The issue of whether language teachers should use the L1 whilst teaching the L2 has always been a controversial one.
> (Üstünel & Seedhouse, 2005: 304)

> The use of the first language by teachers and/or learners in the second or foreign language classroom remains a controversial issue.
> (Moore, 2013: 239)

> There is an on-going debate about the extent to which NNSTs [non-native speaker teachers] should use learners' L1 in classroom instruction
> (Zhao & Macaro, 2014: 75)

> There is a continuing matter of debate on whether L1 contributes to or precludes the learning of a second language (L2).
> (Debreli & Oyman, 2016: 148)

> Since the 1980s, there has been a serious conflict between two schools of thought concerning the use of the native language
> (Hussein et al., 2020: 61)

It is therefore of some importance to look at the nature of that debate itself. Thus we now turn to statements made by authors in the early sections of their publications which suggest that the debate stems from a system of beliefs that have been imposed on the L2 teaching profession. Whether these can also be considered the authors' own 'initial stances' on the debate, it is not possible to say with certainty. The following kinds of statements are, once again, not uncommon:

> (...) long-held anti-L1 attitudes (...) have dominated foreign language (FL) pedagogy for several decades
> (Scott & De La Fuente, 2008: 100)

The L2-only versus the multilingual debate   203

[Codeswitching].... would probably go unmentioned and unnoticed in classroom contexts...were it not for the fact that language policies imposed from above are imbued with and influenced by pervasive and persistent monolingual ideologies

(Wei & Martin, 2009: 118)

There is widespread agreement among administrators in China that the native language (L1) should not be used in foreign language (L2) classrooms

(Van der Meij & Zhao, 2010: 396)

(...) deep rooted ideologies of linguistic purism combined with dominant TESOL knowledge claims have made it difficult to develop locally appropriate methodologies

(Lin, 2013: 521)

Among lay folk, attitudes towards CS [codeswitching] are often negative. Negative attitudes towards CS may stem partly from the belief about language standardisation and standard language ideology

(Chen & Rubinstein-Avila, 2018: 228–229)

We can also gather insights from authors' concluding statements, which often appear to concur with the perspectives iterated at the start of their papers, as in the following examples:

Despite the overwhelming force of the arguments and evidence in favour of bilingual language teaching in a globalised multilingual world, many curricula, institutions, syllabus and materials designers, as well as teachers, parents – and, of course, students – remain committed to monolingual teaching.

(Hall & Cook, 2012: 297)

In conclusion, our paper confirms that irrespective of institutional policies that advocate no (or minimal) use of students' L1 in L2 and foreign language classrooms, most teachers use CS, most likely—purposefully—to accomplish several important pedagogical strategies to reach the learning objectives in their language classrooms

(Chen & Rubinstein-Avila, 2018: 237)

A student new to the field, in 2020, and limiting themselves to publications, say, post-2000, would find themselves in a quandary. On the one hand, she would understand that there exists a consensus that the debate is ongoing with regard to whether the L1 should be used in the L2 classroom. On the other hand, it would appear to her that there is an overwhelming consensus among the student's academic predecessors that there is in fact no longer a debate to be had. They all appear to be holding the same opinion: promoting an L2-only

204   *Ernesto Macaro*

pedagogy is a bad idea. She would get the impression from careful reading that there are dark forces in the background still resolutely attempting to undermine this academic consensus. These forces appear to include: policymakers, syllabus and material designers, teachers, parents and students – so, quite a substantial group of stakeholders in the L2 education process. Nonetheless, the academic consensus, no doubt built on rigorous research evidence (our student would assume), is that the L1 has a rightful place in L2 learning. So, she assumes, the debate must be between academics and most other interested or affected stakeholders. Moreover, the debate seems to have stayed constant over time, because she observes that Chen & Rubinstein-Avila (2018), referring back 26 years to an opinion piece by Phillipson (1992), conclude that, "The general view is that English is best taught and learned – as a medium of instruction either in English subject classes or across all subjects – *monolingually*" (p. 231, my emphasis).

Our student wonders what the roots of this controversy are and notes that Moore (2013: 239) follows his statement (above) with the assertion that "both cognitive second language acquisition (SLA) theory (e.g. Duff & Polio, 1990; Polio & Duff, 1994) and Communicative Language Teaching (CLT) methodologies have been cited as providing empirical support for the 'English only' classroom, where use of the L1 is seen as a 'problem' to be avoided". Our student therefore assumes that Duff and Polio are examples of key authors who are promoting an L2-only pedagogy.

As our student is someone with a sharp and enquiring mind, she decides to delve deeper into the issue. She therefore starts to read papers and books from the 1980s and the 1990s to see where this pernicious anti-L1 ideology comes from. She locates Duff & Polio (1990) and reads the following statement: "Several researchers have underscored the need for high quantity, high quality foreign language input from teachers" (p. 154). These authors do not appear to her to be advocating total exclusion of the L1, or suggesting that 'high quantity' means 'exclusive use'.

So, if it isn't all researchers from 30 years previously advocating the exclusion of the L1, might it be national agencies, as suggested by some of the above citations? She therefore goes online to try to extract language policies in different countries but struggles to find any currently arguing for the exclusion of the L1. She notes that Swain, Kirkpatrick & Cummins (2011) are able to cite a 2004 Hong Kong Curriculum Development Council policy (2004: p. 109) which states:

> in all English lessons and beyond: teachers should teach through English and encourage learners to interact with one another in English

The student therefore wonders if 'teaching through English', and encouraging learners to interact in the language they are supposed to be learning, means that Cantonese at that time had to be totally excluded from the English classroom in Hong Kong, or whether some notional high percentage of L2 use was expected. From Liu et al. (2004: 605), she learns that the "South Korean

The L2-only versus the multilingual debate 205

Ministry of Education requested that English teachers maximise their English use". She assumes that 'maximize' does not necessarily imply the total exclusion of the L1.

She notes that Van der Meij and Zhao (2010: 396) claim that "there is widespread agreement among administrators in China that the native language (L1) should not be used in foreign language (L2) classrooms". Yet, these authors argue that "the norm is seldom spelled out officially" (p. 396) and that they have been unable to locate written statements with regard to English courses in Chinese universities. Our student, however, does have some success with regard to the secondary sector and obtains 'Guidelines for Teaching English in Secondary Schools' published by the Ministry of Education of People's Republic of China'. These state:

> **No.4.4: Use English as much as possible**. In order to help students establish the direct link between English expressions and their referred objects or concepts, and to improve the effectiveness of English teaching, *teachers should use English as much as possible* when teaching English. Beginners could be taught with the help of some tools like pictures, PowerPoint slides, or through performance, so as to facilitate their understanding. With an increase in students' knowledge of English and in their ability to use English, *teachers should use increasingly more English in their teaching*. Teachers should also use English in a way that students can understand based on their current English levels, and use the English expressions that students have already learned to explain new words or phrases, or other aspects of English. They can also provide students with examples of how to use certain English expressions they have learned in a certain context. *For the content which could not be taught by using the English expressions that have already been learned by the students, teachers could use Chinese to assist their teaching*. (My emphasis)

Thus it seems to her that, at least in the secondary sector in China, there is no dogmatic imposition of an L2-only policy and that in the tertiary sector, it may, at most, be implicit.

In a study on primary level students in Hungary (Nagy & Robertson, 2009), she reads that the national curriculum for that country "takes a pragmatic approach to the use of the first language in the foreign language classroom, acknowledging that it is unrealistic to expect young learners not to use the first language [although] the teacher is expected to use the target language most of the time" (p. 66).

In a study by Doiz & Lasagabaster (2017: 176), she finds a description of the language policy of the University of the Basque Country (UBC) and reads that: "Hence, it may be concluded that there is no official language policy concerning translanguaging or code-switching practices at the UBC". So, clearly, our student concludes, there are no dogmatic L2-only attitudes at the tertiary level in this autonomous region of Spain.

206   *Ernesto Macaro*

In a case study by Humphries (2014: 65), she reads that: "the Japanese Ministry of Education, Culture, Sports and Science and Technology (MEXT) introduced policies that focus on using English predominantly in the classroom for practical communication". Although she feels unsure what 'predominantly' might mean in percentage terms, once again, she wonders where these dogmatic and ideologically driven policies are to be found.

Undaunted, our student digs deeper and now discovers (thanks to Macaro, 1997, 2001) that the Department for Education (for England & Wales) some 30 years ago was arguing quite strongly for exclusion or near exclusion of the L1: "from the outset, the foreign language rather than English should be the medium in which classwork is conducted and managed" (Department of Education and Science, 1988: 12) and that: "the National Curriculum extends opportunities and experiences for pupils by promoting *maximum use of the target language*". The guidelines from Northern Ireland appear to have gone even further, arguing that by the near exclusion of the L1, learners would avoid interference from the sounds and the "syntactical patterns of the mother tongue (and) lessen any desire (they) may have to engage in the process of translation" (Department for Education for Northern Ireland, 1985, paragraph 3.1). Yet, thanks to the same author, she reads that, during the same period, the French national curriculum was taking a more measured approach to the teaching of foreign languages, stating that the learner must be "led gradually towards distancing himself/herself from the mother tongue" (Ministère de L'Education Nationale, 1993: 11).

Our student therefore ponders the fact that, in the vast majority of non-Anglophone countries, the most taught foreign language is English, whereas in the UK, clearly English is not a foreign language. On further enquiry, she finds out that in the early 1990s in the UK, the most taught foreign languages were French and German. She therefore hypothesizes that the status of English as a world language might constitute an influential factor, even in the 1980s and 1990s, with regard to policy on L1/L2 use. Might it be, she wonders, that because English is the international lingua franca, there was, and is still, more resistance to the drive to exclude the L1 from the classroom in non-Anglophone countries, for fear of this undermining the home language? Conversely, might it be that, given that languages such as French and German are not international languages to the same degree, and learners have limited exposure to them outside the classroom, there is no threat to the home language in the UK by attempting to exclude (L1) English from the L2 classroom? Therefore, she reasons, it should be the case that teachers in the UK would welcome and follow a strong recommendation on 'predominant' L2 use. She therefore wonders, as a result of those strong governmental recommendations for maximum L2 use in the UK in the late 1980s and early 1990s, whether the L1 has by now been mostly eradicated from L2 classrooms. So she consults a study by Chambers (2013: 44) and is surprised to read that the government inspectorate of schools (England & Wales), with regard to Modern Languages, "was critical of teaching and learning in general" and specifically, "use of the TL [target language] was too limited so that pupils heard less than they might have and did not practise

The L2-only versus the multilingual debate 207

the language sufficiently". Thus, it appears to her that government policies in the UK seem to have had little impact on practice with regard to L1/L2 use.

Still with the idea in mind that EFL and learning L2s other than English might entail different attitudes to L2 use, our student turns her attention to Üstünel and Seedhouse (2005). These authors provide a list of references supporting their statement about the controversial nature of L1 use (see above). These references come from papers published in the 1980s and early 1990s, of which the following are research papers or commentaries of EFL: Willis (1981) and Kharma & Hajjaj (1989). This list is then followed by supporting citations from the UK 'Modern Foreign Language' context (Chambers, 1991; Macdonald 1993), where, as we have noted, English is *not* taught as an L2. Üstünel and Seedhouse use these references to nonetheless observe that: "The conclusion to be drawn from these studies is that it is better to teach the language of English through the medium of English" (p. 305). Our student therefore feels that it remains unclear whether it is the status of the L2 being taught that is the key factor in the debate.

She now turns to some of the most recent publications on the topic of L1 use. She notes that El-Dakhs et al. (2018:26) state that "early and strong versions of the communicative teaching approach advocate the sole use of the target language". These authors reference Ramachandran and Abdul Rahim (2004) in support of their statement. So, our student decides that she had better follow up the latter study in order to get a clear understanding of their seemingly uncompromising position. To her surprise, she realizes that sole use of the target language is *not* being advocated by the latter authors in 2004. Their discussion, centring on the teaching of vocabulary, posits that implicit or incidental vocabulary teaching entirely through the L2 may have its limits. What they are in fact putting forward is a nuanced argument that some reference to the L1, within a general communicative approach, will be beneficial in vocabulary learning.

Our student finds a similar problem with a recent research paper published by Debreli and Oyman (2016). They cite authors who have claimed the L1 to be beneficial whereas "some have considered it [L1] to be a hindrance" (p. 148). They reference Cianflone (2009) as someone who apparently considers it to be a hindrance. Our student sleuth tracks down Cianflone (2009) and decides that, in her view, he in fact presents a balanced perspective with both advantages and disadvantages and, indeed, actually concludes in favour of 'principled use' (p. 4) with recognition of the L1 as 'an important learning device' (p. 3).

In another very recent paper (Hussein et al., 2020), our student notes that the authors reference Macaro (2005) as someone "who can be taken as an advocate of the elimination of code-switching use among FL learners [and] is not in favour of the use of code-switching on the following grounds" (Hussein et al., 2020, pp. 61–62). Apparently, among these 'grounds' is the following: "code-switching is not politically endorsed as it may allow native speakers of English to dominate the English language teaching scene at the expense of non-native English teachers" (Hussein et al., 2020, p. 62). The student is particularly confused by this statement and therefore decides to read the paper by Macaro (2005). She concludes that by no means is he against the use of code-switching

208   *Ernesto Macaro*

Table 11.1 Arguments in favour of L1 use

The bilingual teacher's brain is more closely aligned with that of the L2 learner than the
   monolingual teacher – they can understand what the learner is going through
Neurological research says: all languages known to a person are activated by a single
   stimulus; it's difficult to stop learners thinking in their L1
The bilingual teacher acts as a good role model by demonstrating that an L2 can be
   learnt well
It's not the just quantity of exposure that is important but the quality and whether
   students use the L2
Fairly low levels of teacher L1 use should not result in an increase in students' L1 use
Extensive L2 input modification (e.g. in order to explain a new word) may result in
   teachers doing all the talking and not leaving space for learner talk; quickly explaining in
   a shared L1 can be much quicker
Codeswitching occurs naturally among bilinguals, so why exclude it from the classroom?
Quite a lot of L1 can be delivered in a short space of time, so it should not detract too
   much from L2 exposure
Miming a word or a phrase in order to avoid the L1 takes the focus away from the language
L1 use reduces working memory constraints

and that he has been misunderstood by Hussein et al. (2020). Rather, Macaro
(2005) provides two sets of arguments, some in favour of L1 use and some
against. Our student makes some brief written notes of these arguments in the
form of two tables (Tables 11.1 and 11.2).

As a result of this last piece of investigation with regard to the 'debate', our
student is in a state of utter confusion and decides to go to the cafe for a coffee
and a large piece of cake, comforting items that we will now leave her to enjoy.

I have not described the above scenario in order to dismiss or condemn
researchers working in the field, many of whom I know and admire. Indeed,
some of the implied criticisms above might be attributed to some of my own
work on the topic. Nevertheless, I do think it important to make the point that
the debate has become messy. In my concluding section of this chapter, I make
some recommendations of how we could improve the debate.

Table 11.2 Arguments against L1 use

L1 use to give the meaning of a word or phrase may inhibit a learner from developing
   inferencing strategies (ability to guess from the context)
L1 use undermines the possibility of 'negotiation of meaning' in classroom interaction
L1 use may lead to the use of grammatical structures in L2 which the learner is not
   conceptually ready to learn
Too much L1 use cuts down on exposure to the TL, which provides the necessary input
   for learning
Learners in pair and group work tasks use the L1 instead of L2. Some teachers feel this is
   a problem.
L1 use leads to a non-communicative kind of pedagogy. Used extensively, L1 use is often
   associated with a grammar-translation way of teaching
Although codeswitching occurs naturally among bilinguals, they are not necessarily trying
   to learn a language in the same way as learners are in formal settings such as a classroom

Researching the debate

We will now turn our attention to individual pieces of empirical research to see if there is any substantial evidence for the inclusion of the L1 or its converse, L2-only teaching and learning. Due to lack of space, I am limiting myself to L1 use in the whole-class interaction between teachers and learners.

How much L2 are students being exposed to?

We begin by considering studies which have measured the amount of L1/L2 used by teachers in classroom interaction. This gives us an indication of the exposure to the L2 that students in their classes might have.

It is not difficult to see from Table 11.3 that what we have is a huge array of practice in terms of L1 use. This practice does not appear to produce any recognizably stable patterns according to country, continent, language, curriculum type, or educational phase. In other words, none of the following potential variables would seem to have a clear and consistent impact on teacher L1/L2 talk in the classroom: the L2 being taught; the sociolinguistic context in which it is being taught; the educational context in which the L2 is being taught, the proficiency level, or the instructional status of the students. Moreover, there is little evidence in this aspect of the literature that it is teachers with a low proficiency in the L2 who are using more L1: see, for example, Raschka et al. (2009: 169) or Macaro (2001) in two very different contexts.

Table 11.3 L1 use in a selection of research

Publication	Percentages (range) of L1 use by teachers recorded	Education Level & L2 taught	Country/jurisdiction of study
Duff & Polio (1990)	0%–90%	University (variety of languages)	USA
Kong & Zhang (2005)	2%–5%	University (English)	China
Macaro (2001)	4%–12%	Secondary (French)	England and Wales
Rolin-Ianziti & Brownlie (2002)	0%–18%	University (French)	Australia
Liu, Ahn, Baek & Han (2004)	10%–90%	Secondary (English)	Korea
Guo (2007)	8%–37%	University (English)	China
De la Campa & Nassaji (2009)	9%–13%	University (German)	Canada
Jafari & Shokrpour (2013)	3%–5%	University (English ESP)	Iran
Nagy & Robertson (2009)	9%–47%	Primary (English)	Hungary
Tien & Li (2014)	6%–30%	University (EMI)	Taiwan
Tian & Kunschak (2014)	9%–11%	University (EMI)	China
Humphries (2014)	72%–90%	University (EMI)	Japan
Tayjasanant & Robinson (2014)	32%–82%	University (EMI)	Thailand and Bhutan

210 *Ernesto Macaro*

It should also be noted that it is very problematic to do any kind of systematic aggregation of teacher L1 use, even if one wanted to do so across such different contexts because the following different analysis systems have been adopted:

- *Timed analysis.* This is when a researcher identifies which language is being spoken, say, on every fifth second (Macaro, 2001) or which language is being 'mostly' spoken during a five-second interval (Tian & Kunschak, 2014). Some researchers have used longer intervals, for example, Jafari & Shokrpour (2013), who describe their method as follows: "every fifteen seconds the language of the utterance being spoken at that time was noted" (p. 94).
- *Word analysis.* This is when individual words are counted in each of the two languages (De la Campa & Nassaji, 2009).
- *Utterance analysis.* Copland and Neokleus (2011) used this method, describing it as follows: "Whenever a Greek [L1] word was spoken, an utterance ensued. The utterance finished either when the teacher next spoke in English or when a student spoke".

All these different measurement methods have their advantages and disadvantages and indeed would provide different percentages if used on the same data. For example, it is highly likely that a five- second sampling technique will produce comparatively lower levels of teacher L1 use than word analysis, because the rate of speech for the L1 tends to be faster than that for L2, the latter being often characterized by repetitions, slower articulation and longer pauses. However, this technique does arguably provide the most precise measurement in terms of time in a lesson that students are exposed to the L2. Word analysis is relatively quick and easy to calculate but runs into difficulties with languages such as Chinese, where the definition of what a word is problematic, and languages with large numbers of compounds (e.g. German). Utterances have the advantage of, generally, being linked to idea units but become problematic when they contain a switch of a single word to the opposite language (also known as intra-sentential codeswitching). A further problem is that not all researchers provide percentages of L1/L2 use. For example, Copland and Neokleus (2011) give only raw figures – although these are still very interesting, in that one of the four teachers they recorded produced only one L1 utterance, whereas another produced 634!

We also have to be careful in distinguishing between observed L2/L1 use and self-reported use. For example, Van der Meij & Zhao (2010) explored the practices and attitudes of 40 teachers in two Chinese universities with various levels of (self rated) proficiency in English, using questionnaires and observation of classes. The teachers claimed that their aim was 'limited use of codeswitching' (p. 400) and that generally, they were quite satisfied with the amount of codeswitching they were using. Yet, the researchers found that codeswitching was "seven times more prevalent than these teachers believed" (p. 405) and took up ten times more of the classroom interaction time than the teachers thought. The students' attitudes were also investigated and they reported a more accurate estimation of the teachers' L1 use than the teachers themselves did.

The L2-only versus the multilingual debate   211

So we have a great deal of variance: variance even within contexts as well as variance in how we have measured L1/L2 use. This variance in the available research evidence does contribute to the difficulty of providing any secure foundations on which to base pedagogical arguments in favour of, or against, the use of the L1. What can be concluded with reference to the above variability is that to talk, as some commentators (and indeed some of the above policy documents) do, of 'maximizing use of the L2' is quite meaningless (see Macaro, 2013). What would that maximizing look like against such an array of practice? How could an observer possibly judge that a teacher had used the L2 to its maximum? We return to this issue later in our discussion of what optimal use of the L1 might entail. For now we turn to another avenue of related research: the language functions to which the L1 and the L2 is put.

For what pedagogic purposes do teachers use the L1?

The functions of South Korean high school teachers' codeswitching were investigated by Liu et al. (2004). Thirteen high-school classes with thirteen different teachers produced the following functions in L1: greetings; procedural instructions; questions (e.g. checking comprehension); explanations of words; explanations of grammar; giving background information to a text; behaviour management; compliments or confirmation; and jokes or personal talk (p. 616).

Raschka et al. (2009) investigated the functions to which L1 use was put in adult education 'cram schools' in Taiwan, using as sources of data two classes at around intermediate level. Both teachers who were observed and recorded had at least seven years of teaching experience. The level of codeswitching for both teachers is described as 'fairly high' by the authors. They found that teachers switched to L1 in order to: socialize with their students; to elicit students' answers in L2; to switch to another topic; for classroom management (e.g. for admonishing); and for metalinguistic explanations (e.g. grammar points). Functions were complex and overlapping. What is also interesting about the two schools investigated is their advertising material: "one of the schools claimed to teach through the first language, while the other claimed to provide an 'English-only' learning environment" (p. 160). Yet, the functions to which the L1 was put were very similar in both.

In an Australian university, Rolin-Ianziti and Brownlie (2002) investigated beginners' French classes of four teachers, two of whom were native speakers of French and two were non-native. They found that the teachers switched to L1 for: translation (of lexis); metalinguistic purposes (to comment on form); highlighting of contrasts between L1 forms and L2 forms; and communicative purposes – most of the last being for managing the lesson. Across the four teachers, there was a similarity of use across the categories, with no apparent variance between the native-speaking teachers (NST) and non-native speaking teachers (NNST). Hobbs, Matsuo and Payne (2010) report, on the contrary, that there were considerable differences in their case studies of NNSTs (English L1) and NSTs (Japanese L1) teaching Japanese as an L2 in England, with the latter,

212   *Ernesto Macaro*

surprisingly, using more English than the NNSTs. The authors attribute this to differences in educational cultures and past teaching and learning experiences.

A study which attempted to differentiate L1 use by the experience level of the teacher was carried out by De la Campa and Nassaji (2009) with German L2 in a university in Canada. The authors state that 'the course objectives described in the course syllabus were acquiring oral language proficiency, increasing leaners' lexical and syntactic skills, and providing insights into the L2 culture' (p. 744). The researchers found quite important differences between the two instructors involved in their study, in terms of the functions for which they used L1: inter-sentential equivalents and administrative issues were provided in L1 more by the novice teacher. The experienced teacher used the L1 more for intra-sentential information on lexis and for personal comments. The novice teacher spoke fast and then translated when students did not understand. The more experienced teacher spoke more slowly and paraphrased more frequently, suggesting that TL use may be a skill which can be developed over time. However, as this research was limited to a case study of only two teachers it could not be generalized to, say, larger populations of novice and experienced teachers.

In order to investigate whether different countries generally had different practices with regard to L1 use, Molway, Arcos and Macaro (2020) compared the self-reported practices of teachers teaching English as an L2 in Spain and teachers teaching languages other than English (LOTE) in the UK. They found evidence that teachers of English in Spain claimed to use more L2 (and for different functions) than teachers of LOTE in the UK.

In a very different context (university classes in Canada, of which one was an Applied Linguistics class taught in German), we have a study by Dailey-O'Cain and Liebscher (2009). They used a socio-cultural approach to examine the functions of L1 use, demonstrating that both sets of participants – teachers and students – were involved in effecting these functions of L1. They divide the L1 switches into 'discourse-related functions' (such as a topic switch) and 'participant-related functions' which the authors describe as "switches that correspond to the preferences of either the person performing the switch or his or her fellow conversation participants, such as momentarily forgetting a word or a phrase" (p. 137). The essential difference in this approach taken by these authors is to demonstrate that L1 use is co-constructed among the teacher and the students in the interaction (see also Üstünel & Seedhouse, 2005), rather than being simply teacher-imposed. Nonetheless, the different functions for L1 use are not dissimilar to those identified in other studies.

We can now summarize the functions of L1 use in L2 classrooms around the world, in all phases of education, as follows:

- contrasting L1 and L2 forms
- providing metalinguistic information/commentary
- Translating lexical items
- giving L1 explanations of previously used L2 utterances
- topic switching

The L2-only versus the multilingual debate   213

- providing instructions for carrying out tasks
- prompting L2 use
- commenting on social events
- eliciting learner participation
- lesson management
- behaviour management

In other words, L1 use can permeate all aspects of classroom interaction. Apart possibly from 'greetings at the start of a lesson', it is difficult to find a function in the literature that is *always* carried out in L2 by all teachers.

Teacher and student attitudes to L1 use

Before describing studies which have looked at attitudes by classroom stake-holders (teachers and students) to L1 use, I would like to outline a theoretical framework in which to consider the attitudes of teachers. This is one I developed some 20 years ago (Macaro, 2001) and, as it seems to have stood the test of time in terms of other researchers using it, I feel justified in offering it again here. The framework argues that teachers hold one of three positions with regard to L1 use for the purposes of teaching the L2:

- The *Virtual* position. There is no pedagogical value in L1 use. You learn or 'acquire implicitly' the L2 *only through* the L2. The L1 can be excluded from the L2 classroom as long as the teacher is skilled enough. The classroom needs to become 'virtual' in the sense that it becomes 'like the target country'. A teacher might summarize this as: 'I think the best way to teach a language is entirely through the L2 and it's perfectly possible to do so'.
- The *Maximal* position. There is no pedagogical value in L1. The best way to learn the L2 is *only through* the L2. However, perfect teaching and learning conditions do not exist and therefore teachers have to resort to the L1. A teacher might summarize this as: 'I wish I could use L2 all the time but I can't. They're not good enough and maybe I'm not skilled enough either'.
- The *Optimal (or principled)* position. There is *some* pedagogical value in L1 use. Some aspects of learning may actually be enhanced by making L1 connections. There should therefore be a constant exploration of pedagogical principles (underpinned if possible by research evidence) regarding whether and in what ways L1 use is justified. A teacher might summarize this as: "I could use the L2 all the time if I wanted to but I don't think that would be the best way for my students to learn".

(Adapted from Macaro, 2001, 2009)

I have argued, and continue to maintain, that the virtual and optimal positions are the only ones that can be justified through evidence: that is, they are the only ones *that can be tested* through research. The maximal position cannot be tested through research because of the huge variety of practice that I have

214 *Ernesto Macaro*

outlined above, as well as the variety in belief systems, which I will address shortly. Moreover, the maximal position can engender feelings of personal deficit and guilt.

A question that could be asked is whether teachers' attitudes to L1 use differ according to the kind of course that they are teaching. For example, at the tertiary level, Jafari and Shokrpour (2013) carried out a study in an Iranian medical university with two teachers of English for Specific Purposes, collecting data through classroom observations, interviews and questionnaires (with both students and teachers). The qualitative data revealed that both teachers considered a bilingual approach to be appropriate and more effective than communicative language teaching. However, we should note (see above) that the amount of L1 recorded was quite limited and, importantly, the teachers' ideal percentage of 'less than 10%' concurred with what was observed. This adds to the notion that what practitioners consider 'maximum L2 use' or 'appropriate L1 use' is a very movable feast.

Another contextual variable that might affect L1 use relates to classrooms where the L2 is the Medium of Instruction, rather than the subject being taught. Doiz and Lasagabaster (2017) investigated the beliefs and self-reported practices of 13 EMI teachers in universities in the Basque Country who had all fulfilled the requirement of C1 level English (CEFR). The authors use the Macaro (2001, 2009) framework of how teachers position themselves: virtual, maximal and optimal. The researchers found that most teachers were in the 'virtual position', whereby they believed that all interactions should be in L2. Moreover, there was little doubt in the minds of the teachers that L2 should be the main language used, whilst realizing that outside the classroom, the L1 countered the effect of the immersion they were trying to achieve in the classroom. One teacher, in particular, saw a problem with L1 use because of the impact it had on the students' L1 use: "The problem I see with using Spanish or Basque to resolve a comprehension problem is that once you do that, they are going to do the same thing and it is hard to maintain the use of their L2" (p. 167). In contrast, another appeared to adopt the maximal position: "using the students' L1 is not great but it is not the end of the world" (p. 167).

The studies cited above represent three different types of higher education classrooms: ones where the L2 is the main teaching aim (EFL); ones where the focus is on language but for the purpose of facilitating content learning (ESP); ones where content learning is the primary focus and the L2 is the medium of instruction (EMI). Despite some variation in teacher attitudes to L1 use in terms of what amount is acceptable, by far the most fall into the category of maximal use of the L2.

Space does not allow further descriptions of studies on teacher beliefs but in general, teachers accept that L1 use is either desirable or unavoidable (Macaro, 2001; Wang, 2003). With regard to student attitudes, many come to the same conclusions (Lee, 2018; Tian & Kunschak, 2014). This holds true for the secondary phase of education as well, although there is some evidence that adults are more prepared to accept an L2-only approach than young learners

The L2-only versus the multilingual debate 215

(Lee & Macaro, 2013) and that students are accepting of a need for some L1 use, particularly in lexical explanations (Tian & Hennebry, 2016). The issue of vocabulary learning is one to which we now turn.

L1/L2 use and vocabulary learning

The research area we have been looking at so far contains one major gap: L1/L2 effectiveness studies. Does use of the L1 lead to better learning than L2-only use? One of the few clusters of studies that have explored this dimension is that of vocabulary acquisition. Given the importance of acquiring vocabulary in both breadth and depth for SLA (Nation, 2001), it is unsurprising that researchers should have focused on this aspect in relation to the two (or more) languages available to the learners.

Tian and Macaro (2012), using a randomized design, explored whether teacher codeswitching (CS) in providing information about a lexical item was more effective than L2-only information (Non-CS) in learning that vocabulary item. The context was Chinese university EFL students and the research questions were operationalized in relation to a listening comprehension activity. After listening to a recorded text, the CS group was provided by the teacher with information about some of the lexical items in the text in L1, while the Non-CS group was provided with L2 information. The researchers found that both groups made lexical gains against a control group which did not receive any lexical information, with the CS group statistically outperforming the Non-CS group. Similar results were obtained by Zhao & Macaro (2014), also with university students (non-majors) in China. It is therefore useful to compare these findings with a different context (secondary school learners of French in England) but using a very similar research design (Hennebry et al., 2017). Once again, greater gains were observed for the group which received the L1 equivalent over the L2 definition group and this held true for both higher- and lower-proficiency students. As a point of comparison, Lee & Levine (2020) recently explored the effect of providing L1 information about phrasal verbs during a listening activity with undergraduates when compared to providing L2-only information and found that it made a significant difference, and particularly benefited intermediate learners compared to advanced learners.

It appears, therefore, that learning an L2 word may benefit from it being associated with L1 information. Indeed, a further insight into this aspect is provided by Kim, Lee and Lee (2020), who carried out a meta-analysis of the effectiveness of L1 versus L2 glosses on vocabulary learning. Although this analysis was in the context of glosses provided in reading comprehension activities (i.e. not oral language use by the teacher), nevertheless, it supports the above trend in suggesting that L1 information with regard to lexical items is beneficial – and particularly so for lower-proficiency level students. Moreover, it is not impossible to transfer the 'glosses in reading comprehension context' to the pedagogical context of teacher talk. Here, the teacher can be seen not only as a 'walking dictionary' (providing the information) but also as a dictionary designer, making decisions

216　*Ernesto Macaro*

about whether and when to provide lexical information in L1 or L2 or, for that matter, both (see Macaro et al., 2009, for further discussion of this concept).

Even though teacher L1 use to provide lexical information about new L2 words does seem a promising area of research to explore further, we do have to apply some caution in promoting it. Macaro (2017) aimed to discover what strategies students were using in response to a teacher attempting to explain new words through L2 only. Again, these were students in secondary schools in England after some three years of learning French. This qualitative study suggested that students were continually relying on a strategy of looking at the cognate nature of the target word (how much the word was like an L1 word) or of cognate words in the explanation given in L2. This 'cognate spotting' was a default strategy and was not used in combination with other strategies, such as inferencing from context, segmenting the speech stream or trying to recall if the L2 word had been previously encountered or, indeed, learnt. The study concluded that, if the teacher always gives L1 equivalents or explanations, or advises students to look for words which look like L1 words (where this is possible), then students may narrow down the range of potential strategies they can use. Students may then not be able to deploy these strategies subsequently, when L1 information is not available to them, as in an 'outside the classroom' situation.

Conclusions

I began this chapter by describing the 'debate' that has been frequently alluded to by researchers in this field of SLA. It is not difficult to see that this debate could be improved in the future. I would propose that this improvement could be achieved by:

1　Authors ensuring that they do not begin their papers by giving the impression of having already made up their minds about the value of the L1 in learning an L2. Rather they should do so from the empirical evidence they have collected, and in comparison to the evidence provided by others;
2　Authors being less selective about which previous publications they rest their arguments on;
3　Authors being less categorical in their statements that policymakers impose an L2-only policy, unless they can provide clear evidence that this is the case;
4　Authors who write strong statements about 'the debate' avoiding giving the impression that other authors, to whom they refer, hold clear views in favour or against the statement, whereas in fact they do not;
5　Authors being more helpful to their readers with regard to timelines in research, policy and practice. They should identify changes over the decades in relation to these sources;
6　Authors being more wary of conflating EFL and the learning of other L2s without articulating any potential problems therein.

The L2-only versus the multilingual debate   217

On the last point, Hall & Cook (2012) argue strongly that SLA research has not been helpful in that respect: "In our view, this failure to differentiate [between English and other languages being taught] is a considerable weakness; while the psycholinguistic aspects of language learning may indeed have some universal features, the sociolinguistic factors vary considerably" (p. 272).

A second aspect which would greatly improve the debate would be the provision by researchers of some hard evidence with regard to *learner outcomes*, obtained using sound comparative designs. We can carry on describing the interaction in the classroom, and we can further extend the database on teacher and student attitudes, but until we have some notion that use of the L1 (to whatever degree) or of L2-only produces better learning in a given context, then we will not be able to move the field forward and make clear recommendations to pre-service teachers, in-service teachers and policymakers. I have suggested that there is some evidence that L1 use in relation to vocabulary learning is beneficial, but we need more evidence.

We need to look at percentages of L2 interaction and whether the research tells us that various aspects of learning are enhanced by reference to the L1. For example, we may find that some teacher L1 talk does indeed lead to greater student L2 talk, for example, in a subsequent group task. Or it may be that allowing some L1 use by students in some group tasks eventually leads them to use *more L2* in subsequent tasks (see, for example, Macaro et al., 2014; Vrikki, 2009). This would give us some fairly hard evidence of beneficial outcomes. Another promising area, and related to the previous one, involves observing the interaction between teachers and learners in EMI contexts and the effect that excluding the L1 has on the quality of questioning by the teacher (Pun & Macaro, 2019).

I return to the value of the 'optimal and principled position', based on research evidence – and yes, of course, also teacher judgement in his/her own educational context. Moreover, that optimal position *needs to take into account what the aims of the course being taught are*. If the aims are to prepare students for the four skills with an emphasis on interaction and communication, then one would expect the interaction to consist *predominantly* of the L2. Earlier, we looked at a study by Copland and Neokleus (2011). A telling quote from them is the following: "Tina's lesson was conducted almost wholly in English [L2], while Lisa's was conducted almost wholly in Greek" (p. 272). These teachers were teaching students (aged 14) in after-school classes in Cyprus. It is hardly possible, from the nature of the interaction in their classrooms, to conceive that they were adopting comparable pedagogical techniques and in fact extracts from the researcher's transcriptions (p. 273) prove that point. From these transcriptions, Tina appears to be adopting a communicative approach based on negotiation of meaning but allowing students to ask questions in L1; Lisa is adopting a translation approach. We need to identify which approach, if any, led to better student learning.

Another, more global, research approach we might take is to look at world rankings of second language learning (e.g. The EF English Proficiency Index 2019). We could select the top five countries and the bottom five countries, but

218   *Ernesto Macaro*

ensure that these had similar broad features in terms of gross domestic product and stage of development. Then, a study could be carried out of these ten countries to ascertain what broad pedagogical approach was being taken by the majority of teachers and how much L1/L2 was being used and for what functions. Clearly, this would be a major research project!

I am aware that I have hardly touched on another aspect of the debate: the socio-political impact of English on the languages of non-Anglophone countries and that debate's relationship with L1/L2 use. Especially I have not discussed the potential discriminatory effect that the English-only position might have on the value of NSTs versus NNSTs (Mahboob & Golden 2013; Moussu & Llurda 2008). But that debate deserves a chapter all to itself.

Relating the issues raised in this chapter to your own context:

1 In your own second language education context, are there national or institutional policies or recommendations for the use of the L1 by teachers and students?
2 To what extent is there a consensus among practitioners, in your own context, about the use of the L1 when teaching the second language?

References

Chambers, F. (1991) Promoting use of the target language in the classroom. *Language Learning Journal*, 4, 27–31.

Chambers, G. (2013). The target language revisited. *Teaching and Teacher Education*, 36, 44–54.

Chen, Y. & Rubinstein-Avila, E. (2018). Code-switching functions in postcolonial classrooms. *The Language Learning Journal*, 46:3, 228–240, doi:10.1080/09571736.2015. 1035669

Cianflone, E. (2009). L1 use in English courses at university level. *ESP World, Issue 1* 8:22, 1–5, http://www.esp-world.info.

Copland F. & Neokleus, G. (2011). L1 to teach L2: Complexities and contradictions. *ELT Journal* 65:3, 270–280.

Dailey O'Cain, J. & Liebscher, G. (2009). Teacher and student use of the first language in foreign language classroom interaction: functions and applications. In M. Turnbull & J. Dailey-O'Cain. (eds.). *First Language Use in Second and Foreign Language Learning.* pp. 131–144. Bristol: Multilingual Matters.

De La Campa, J.C. & Nassaji, H. (2009). The amount, purpose, and reasons for using L1 in L2 classrooms. *Foreign Language Annals*, 42, 742–759. http://dx.doi.org/10.1111/j.1944-9720.2009.01052.x

Debreli, E. & Oyman, N. (2016). Students' preferences on the use of mother tongue in English as a foreign language classrooms: Is it the time to re-examine English-only policies? *English Language Teaching*, 9:1, 148–162.

Department of Education and Science. (1988). *Modern Languages in the School Curriculum: A Statement of Policy.* London: Her Majesty's Stationery Office.

Department of Education for Northern Ireland. (1985). *Good Practice in Education. Paper 2: Modern Languages Teaching in Northern Ireland.* Bangor, Northern Ireland: Department of Education for Northern Ireland.

The L2-only versus the multilingual debate   219

Doiz, A. & Lasagabaster, D. (2017). Teachers' beliefs about translanguaging practices. In Catherine M. Mazak & K. S. Carroll (eds.). *Translanguaging in Higher Education: Beyond Monolingual Ideologies*. pp. 157–176. Cleveland: Multilingual Matters.

Duff, P. A. & Polio, C. G. (1990) How much foreign language is there in the foreign language classroom? *The Modern Language Journal*, 74, 154–166.

EF English Proficiency Index, (2019). A Ranking of 100 Countries and Regions by English Skills. www.ef.com/epi

El-Dakhs, D. A. S. ElHajj, H. & Jawaher & Al-Haqbani, J. N. (2018) The effect of word type on the L1 support for L2 vocabulary learning: The case of Arab EFL learners. *International Journal of English Linguistics*, 8:4, 25–38.

Guo, T. (2007). A case study of teacher's codeswitching behaviours in mainland China's university EFL classrooms and students' reactions to the codeswitching. Unpublished Doctoral dissertation, University of Oxford, UK.

Hall, G. & Cook, G. (2012). Own-language use in language teaching and learning. *Language Teaching*, 45:3, 271–308.

Hennebry, M., Rodgers, V. Macaro, E. & Murphy, V (2017). Direct teaching of vocabulary after listening: Is it worth the effort and what method is best? *The Language Learning Journal*, 45:3, 282–300.

Hobbs, V. Matsuo, A. & Payne, M. (2010). Code-switching in Japanese language classrooms: An exploratory investigation of native vs. non-native speaker teacher practice. *Linguistics and Education* 21, 44–59.

Humphries, S. (2014). Codeswitching in two Japanese contexts. In R. Barnard & J. McLellan (eds.). *Codeswitching in University English-Medium Classes: Asian Perspectives*. pp. 65–91. Bristol: Multilingual Matters.

Hussein, R. F., Saed, H. A. & Haider, A. S. (2020). Teachers and students code-switching: The inevitable evil in EFL classrooms. *International Journal of Learning, Teaching and Educational Research*, 19:2, 60–78.

Jafari, S. M. & Shokrpour, N. (2013). The role of L1 in ESP classroom: A triangulated approach. *International Journal of English and Education*, 2:3, 90–104.

Kharma, N. N. & Hajjaj, A. H. (1989). Use of the mother tongue in the ESL classroom. *International Review of Applied Linguistics*, 27, 223–235.

Kim, H.-S. Lee, J. H. & Lee, H. (2020). The relative effects of L1 and L2 glosses on L2 learning: A meta-analysis. *Language Teaching Research*. doi:10.1177/1362168820981394

Kong, H. & Zhang, P. (2005). An investigation on teacher talk in an extensive reading classroom for English majors. *Education and Modernization*, 76:3, 38–43. [n.b. Article is in Chinese]

Lee, J. H. (2018). Exploring relationships between second language learners' attitudes towards classroom language and variables that motivate their learning. *Language Awareness*, 27:3, 243–258.

Lee, J. H. & Levine, G. S. (2020). The effects of instructor language choice on second language vocabulary learning and listening comprehension. *Language Teaching Research*, 24:2, 250–272.

Lee, J. H. & Macaro, E (2013). Investigating age in the use of L1 or English-only instruction: Vocabulary acquisition by Korean ESL learners. *The Modern Language Journal*, 97:4, 887–901.

Lin, A. (2013). Toward paradigmatic change in TESOL methodologies: Building plurilingual pedagogies from the ground up. *TESOL Quarterly*, 47:3, 521–545.

Liu, D., Ahn, G., Baek, K. & Han N. (2004). Questions and Challenges in the drive for maximal use of English in teaching. *TESOL Quarterly*, 38:4, 605–638.

220   *Ernesto Macaro*

Macaro, E. (1997). *Target Language Collaborative Learning and Autonomy*. Clevedon: Multilingual Matters.

Macaro, E. (2001). Analysing student teachers' codeswitching in foreign language classrooms: theories and decision making. *The Modern Language Journal*, 85, 531–548.

Macaro, E. (2005). Codeswitching in the L2 classroom: A communication and learning strategy. In E. Llurda (ed.). *Non-Native Language Teachers: Perceptions, Challenges, and Contributions to the Profession*. pp. 63–84. Boston, MA: Springer.

Macaro, E. (2009). Teacher use of codeswitching in the second language classroom. In M. Turnbull & J. Dailey-O'Cain (eds.). *First Language Use in Second and Foreign Language Learning*. Clevedon: Multilingual Matters.

Macaro. E. (2013). Overview: Where should we be going with classroom codeswitching research? In R. Barnard & J. McLellan (eds.). *Codeswitching in University English-Medium Classes*. Bristol: Multilingual Matters.

Macaro. E (2017). Students' strategies in response to teachers' second language explanations of lexical items. *The Language Learning Journal*, 45:3, 352–367.

Macaro. E., Guo, T. Chen, H. & Tian, L. (2009). Can differential processing of L2 vocabulary inform the debate on teacher codeswitching behaviour: the case of Chinese learners of English. In B. Richards, M. Daller, D. Malvern, P. Meara, J. Milton & J. Treffers-Daller (eds.). *Vocabulary Studies in First and Second Language Acquisition: The Interface between Theory and Application*. pp. 125–146. London: Palgrave Macmillan.

Macaro, E, Nakatani, Y., Hayashi, Y. & Khabbazbashi, N. (2014). Exploring the value of bilingual language assistants with Japanese English as a foreign language learners. *Language Learning Journal*, 42:1, 41–54.

Macdonald, C. (1993). *Using the Target Language*. Cheltenham: Mary Glasgow.

Mahboob A. & Golden, R. (2013). Looking for native speakers of English: Discrimination in English language teaching job advertisements. *Voices in Asia Journal*, 1:1, 72–81.

Molway, L. Arcos, M. & Macaro, E. (2020). Language teachers' reported first and second language use: a comparative contextualised study of England and Spain. *Language Teaching Research*. doi:10.1177/1362168820913978

Moore, P. (2013). An emergent perspective on the use of the first language in the EFL classroom. *Modern Language Journal*, 97:1. doi:10.1111/j.1540-4781.2013.01429.x

Ministère de L'Education Nationale (1993). Anglais: Classes de Collèges, 6e, 5e, 4e, 3e [English: Classes in lower secondary school, 1st, 2nd, 3rd, 4th year]. Paris: Centre Nationale de Documentation Pédagogique.

Ministry of Education, Peoples Republic of China (retrieved January 2020) http://www.pep.com.cn/xkzthyd/peixun/xkpx/peixun_1_1/kbjd/jiedu/201009/t20100927_915085.htm

Moussu, L. & Llurda, E. (2008) Non-native English-speaking language teachers: History and research. *Language Teaching*, 41, 315–348.

Nagy, K. & Robertson, D. (2009). Target language use in English classes in Hungarian primary schools. In M. Turnbull & J. Dailey-O'Cain (eds.). *First Language Use in Second and Foreign Language Learning*. pp. 66–86, Bristol: Multilingual Matters.

Nation, I. S. P. (2001). *Learning Vocabulary in Another Language*. Cambridge, UK: Cambridge University Press.

Polio, C. & Duff, P. (1994). Teachers' language use in university foreign language classrooms: A qualitative analysis of English and target language alternation. *Modern Language Journal*, 78, 313–326.

Phillipson, R. (1992). *Linguistic Imperialism*. Oxford: Oxford University Press.

The L2-only versus the multilingual debate 221

Pun, J. & Macaro, E. (2019) The effect of first and second language use on question types in English medium instruction science classrooms in Hong Kong, *International Journal of Bilingual Education and Bilingualism*, 22:1, 64–77.

Ramachandran, S. D., & Abdul Rahim, H. (2004). Meaning recall and retention: The impact of the translation method on elementary level learners' vocabulary learning. *RELC Journal*, 35:2, 161–178.

Raschka, C. Sercombe, P. & Huang C.-L. (2009). Conflicts and tensions in codeswitching in a Taiwanese EFL classroom. *International Journal of Bilingual Education and Bilingualism*, 12:2, 157–171.

Rolin-Ianziti, J. & Brownlie, S. (2002). Teacher use of learners' native language in the foreign language classroom. *Canadian Modern Language Review*, 58, 402–426.

Scott, V. M. & De La Fuente, M. J. (2008). What's the problem? L2 learners' use of the L1 during consciousness-raising form-focused tasks. *Modern Language Journal*, 92:1, 100–113.

Storch, N. & Wigglesworth, G. (2003). Is there a role for the use of the L1 in an L2 setting? *TESOL Quarterly*, 37, 760–770.

Tayjasanant, C. & Robinson, M. G. (2014). Codeswitching in universities in Thailand and Bhutan. In R. Barnard & J. McLellan (eds.). *Codeswitching in University-Medium Classes: Asian Perspectives.* pp. 92–103. Bristol: Multilingual Matters.

Tian, L. & Hennebry, M. (2016). Chinese learners' perceptions towards teachers; language use in lexical explanations: A comparison between Chinese-only and English-only instructions. *System*, 62, 77–88.

Tian, L. & Kunschak, C. (2014). Codeswitching in two Chinese universities. In R. Barnard & J. McLellan. (eds). *Codeswitching in University English-Medium Classes: Asian Perspectives* pp. 43–64. Bristol: Multilingual Matters.

Tian, L. & Macaro, E. (2012). Comparing the effect of teacher codeswitching with English-only explanations on the vocabulary acquisition of Chinese university students: A Lexical Focus-on-Form study. *Language Teaching Research*, 16:3, 361–385.

Tien, C.-Y. & Li, D. (2014) Codeswitching in a university in Taiwan. In R. Barnard & J. McLellan (eds.). *Codeswitching in University-Medium Classes: Asian Perspectives.* pp. 24–42. Bristol: Multilingual Matters.

Swain, M., Kirkpatrick, A. & Cummins, J. (2011). *How to Have a Guilt-Free Life Using Cantonese in the English Class: A Handbook for the English Language Teacher in Hong Kong.* Hong Kong: Research Centre into Language Acquisition and Education in Multilingual Societies. Hong Kong Institute of Education.

Üstünel, E. & Seedhouse, P. (2005). Why that, in that language, right now? Codeswitching and pedagogical focus. *International Journal of Applied Linguistics*, 15:3, 302–325.

Van der Meij, H. & Zhao, X. (2010). Codeswitching in English courses in Chinese universities. *Modern Language Journal*, 94:3, 396–410.

Vrikki, M. (2009). Comparing teachers' perceptions towards classroom codeswitching with empirical data in primary EFL classroom in Cyprus. Unpublished doctoral dissertation, university of Oxford.

Wang, J.-J. (2003). A facilitator or barrier: A survey on the role of the mother tongue in English class. *Modern Foreign Languages (Quarterly)*, 26:4, 394–402.

Wei, L. & Martin, P. (2009). Conflicts and tensions in classroom codeswitching: an introduction. *International Journal of Bilingual Education and Bilingualism*, 12:2, 117–122.

Willis, J. (1981). *Teaching English through English.* Harlow: Longman.

Zhao, T. & Macaro, E. (2014). What works better for the learning of concrete and abstract words: Teachers' L1 use or L2-only explanations? *International Journal of Applied Linguistics*, 26:1, 76–98.

12 Teaching phonics in a second language

Robert Woore

Introduction

This chapter explores some of the empirical and theoretical underpinnings of phonics instruction in a second language (L2) context. By phonics instruction, I mean explicit teaching of the systematic relationships between letters and sounds in an alphabetic L2 writing system. I will address a series of questions which may be helpful for practitioners and policymakers to consider when making decisions about instructional approaches in this area. Although the chapter will be relevant to the teaching of an L2 in any context, the principal focus will be on settings where the L2 is taught as a discrete subject in countries where that language is not an official or majority language (sometimes referred to as 'foreign language' contexts).

The overarching question addressed in this chapter is whether phonics instruction should form part of teaching an L2 – that is, whether teaching L2 phonics is a worthwhile endeavour. To answer this question, several sub-questions will be explored:

1 How well do learners master L2 letter-sound correspondences in the absence of phonics instruction? Do they develop proficiency in this area without explicit teaching?
2 If learners do not acquire proficiency in this area, does it matter? In other words, how important is mastery of letter-sound correspondences in L2 learning?
3 What evidence is there that explicit L2 phonics instruction is effective? What impact does phonics instruction have on other aspects of L2 learning?
4 If phonics should be taught in L2 contexts, then *how* should it be taught? What promising instructional approaches have been identified?

The answers to these questions may differ from those that would hold in the context of early first language (L1) literacy instruction. This is because L2 learners are often older and cognitively more mature; they may already be literate in their L1; their motivation for learning to read and write in the L2 will be

DOI: 10.4324/9781003008361-15

different; and so on. Furthermore, L2 learners are a heterogeneous group: for example, they begin learning the L2 at different ages, ranging from childhood to adulthood; they have various L1 backgrounds; and they may have experienced a diverse range of approaches to early literacy instruction in their L1. Thus, it is also possible that the above questions will have a range of different answers according to the individual educational context.

Background: The rise of phonics

Phonics instruction has been the subject of long and intense controversy in English-speaking countries such as the UK and the US. In a period of 'reading wars' lasting several decades (Pearson, 2004), some people have advocated phonics as the most effective way to teach young children to read and write in their L1; others have argued for a 'whole language' approach, where children use a range of different cues to discover the meanings of words which they encounter while reading texts for interest and enjoyment. As with many polarized debates, the truth is unlikely to lie at the extremes; Castles et al. (2018) call for 'an end to the reading wars' with a balanced, evidence-informed approach to early literacy instruction (p. 5). Nonetheless, as they note, a large body of research has led to a clear consensus that 'coming to appreciate the relationship between letters and sounds is necessary and non-negotiable when learning to read in alphabetic writing systems and that this is most successfully achieved through phonics instruction' (*ibid.*). Phonics also plays an important role in learning to spell, but the centre of gravity in phonics research has been reading, an emphasis which is also reflected in this chapter.

In the 2000s, official reviews of evidence commissioned by national governments in the US (National Institute of Child Health and Human Development (NICHD), 2000), the UK (Rose, 2006) and Australia (Rowe, 2005) similarly concluded that a planned, systematic programme of phonics instruction, delivered in the first few years of schooling, was the most effective way of teaching children to read. Subsequently, the teaching of phonics has been strongly pushed at the policy level in several Anglophone countries (though not without continuing controversy). In the UK, for example, the government pledged that all pupils would be taught 'systematic synthetic phonics[1] as the proven best way to teach early reading' (Department for Education, 2010, pp. 22–23).

Perhaps influenced by research, policies and practices in L1 English settings, phonics also appears to be gaining traction in L2 contexts around the world, from primary schools to universities. Cao (2017), based on a search of the Chinese national research database (CNKI), documents a steady rise in academic publications relating to phonics in English as a Foreign Language (EFL) settings since the first recorded mention of this term in that database in 2005. Further, Huo and Wang (2017) report that phonics is now included in government-endorsed school English curricula in many countries, such as Malaysia and Taiwan, and anecdotal evidence also suggests a rise in phonics teaching in EFL classrooms

224   Robert Woore

in other countries, including Saudi Arabia and Spain. Meanwhile, in the UK, an influential review of L2 pedagogy in schools (Bauckham, 2016) emphatically advocated the 'direct and systematic teaching of phonics' in languages which use an alphabetic writing system (p. 12). The questions addressed in this chapter need to be seen against this backdrop of growth in L2 phonics teaching, and its advocacy by influential actors. To what extent are these developments supported by research evidence?

Some key concepts

Grapheme-phoneme correspondences

Before continuing, let us define and explore some key concepts. A basic definition of phonics instruction was given above, but this might be stated more precisely as 'explicitly teaching the systematic relationships between graphemes and phonemes in an alphabetic writing system' – in other words, teaching the language's grapheme-phoneme correspondences (GPC). If a phoneme is a 'minimal sound unit … capable of contrasting word meaning' (Katamba, 1989, p. 21), then a grapheme can then be defined as the written unit corresponding to a phoneme in a particular word[2]. To illustrate this, Table 12.1 shows four English words, each composed of three phonemes and, in written form, three graphemes. As Table 12.1 makes clear, graphemes are not simply 'letters'. Rather, they are sometimes composed of two or more letters – and these letters can even be discontiguous, as in the English word 'shape' with its so-called 'split digraph' <a – e>, representing the sound /ɛɪ/. They can also include diacritics (as in English café, Zoë, soupçon).

References to grapheme-phoneme correspondences are well established in the literature on phonics. However, beginner readers may also make links between larger written units and the sounds they represent (Ziegler & Goswami, 2005). These larger units may include the orthographic rime (the string of letters representing a vowel plus any final consonants in a syllable, such as <at> in 'cat' and <ight> in 'light') and even whole words. This involvement of larger orthographic units is particularly true of 'deep' orthographies like English, where individual graphemes may have multiple pronunciations (e.g. <ou> in out, pour and through). Therefore, rather than referring to GPC, I prefer the more flexible term 'symbol-sound correspondences' (or 'spelling-sound correspondences') (SSC).

Table 12.1 Phonemes and graphemes in four English words

Word	Sip			ship			sheep			shape		
Phonemes	s	ɪ	p	ʃ	ɪ	p	ʃ	i	p	ʃ	ɛɪ	p
Graphemes	s	i	p	sh	i	p	sh	ee	p	sh	a-e	p

Teaching phonics in a second language 225

Phonological decoding

Another key term is 'phonological decoding' (also known as 'phonological recoding' or simply 'phonological coding'). This may be defined as 'convert[ing] the visual print into its corresponding spoken form' (Nassaji, 2014, p. 9). It is useful to distinguish between the phonological decoding of two different categories of words, which may be decoded using different mechanisms. On the one hand are words which are familiar to the reader. These may be recognized as wholes and mapped onto existing phonological representations (pronunciations) of these words, which are already stored in the reader's long-term memory. This route can be used to pronounce words accurately, even if they have irregular or inconsistent SSC, as in words like *have* (which does not rhyme with 'wave') or *of* (where the <f> is not pronounced/f/). On the other hand, there are unfamiliar words which the reader has not previously encountered in written form. This will frequently happen for novice readers, but even expert readers encounter low-frequency words and proper nouns which they have not seen before. Yet, expert readers can generally pronounce these words, at least in an alphabetic writing system whose SSC they know well. This can be demonstrated using so-called 'pseudowords', strings of letters which could be words of a given language, but happen not to be. If you are reading this chapter, you can probably pronounce (and feel confident in your pronunciation of) English pseudowords like *screaf, brank* and *flaced,* even though, by definition, you have not seen them before (because I made them up). You do this by applying your knowledge of the English SSC which make up these words at a 'sub-lexical' level (that is, using orthographic units smaller than the word as a whole). The above two mechanisms or 'routes' for pronouncing words – (a) retrieving the pronunciation as a whole; (b) assembling the pronunciation via knowledge of sub-lexical SSC – form the basis of a highly influential model of skilled word reading known as the 'dual route' model (Coltheart, 2005).

For our current purposes, the key point is that learners of an alphabetic L2 may be able to recognize familiar written words and pronounce them accurately, without actually having mastered the SSC of which they are composed (see Woore, 2018 for an example). For this reason, unfamiliar words have an important role to play in both teaching and assessing phonics, because they force learners to attend to symbol-sound mappings at a sub-lexical level. This is why widely used tests of English decoding include pseudowords in the items that children are asked to read aloud (e.g. Woodcock, 2011; and the UK government's *Phonics Screening Check* for first-grade pupils: Standards and Testing Agency, 2019). Similarly, several of my own studies with L2 learners have used Reading Aloud Tests comprising low-frequency words, likely to be unfamiliar to the participants (e.g. Woore, 2009).

Synthetic and analytic phonics

The term 'phonics teaching' encompasses various different approaches. A key distinction is between 'synthetic' and 'analytic' phonics. In the former, children

226 *Robert Woore*

are taught the sounds of individual graphemes, pronounce these in isolation and then 'blend' them together into overall word pronunciations (e.g. sounding out the individual phonic values of <c>, <a>, <t> and combining these to give /kat/, 'cat'). In analytic phonics, by contrast, children are helped to analyze groups of words which they have already encountered and to identify patterns within them: for example, *cat, cake* and *cup* all start with the phoneme/k/, represented by the grapheme <c>. This pattern-spotting could also be done with larger written units such as orthographic rimes (e.g. *cake, rake* and *bake* all end with/eɪk/, spelt <ake>).

In either approach, being able to map individual phonemes onto individual graphemes requires 'phonemic awareness', that is, the ability to identify and manipulate the sounds of individual phonemes in spoken words. Research suggests that, while children may spontaneously develop an awareness of larger phonological units at an early age (whole words, syllables and onset-rimes), it is only when they learn to read and write an alphabetic language that they develop phonological awareness at the finest 'grain size' of individual phonemes (Ziegler & Goswami, 2005). This may have important implications for L2 learners moving from one writing system to another: for example, Russian learners of English will be helped in their learning of L2 GPC by the fact that they have already developed phonemic awareness in their alphabetic L1 (even though the alphabet is a different one).

In another important distinction, phonics instruction may be 'systematic', following a clear, pre-planned sequence, or 'embedded' within a wider literacy programme. In the latter approach, teachers draw learners' attention to particular SSC incidentally, as the need arises in the course of their reading. Shanahan (2005) warns that the terms 'synthetic' and 'systematic' have sometimes – wrongly – been used interchangeably, leading to confusion in interpreting research evidence and policy recommendations. In fact, synthetic and analytic phonics can both be taught either systematically or 'responsively, based on teacher observations of student need' (*ibid.*, page 12). In an L1 context, the major reviews of evidence mentioned earlier (see section "Background: The rise of phonics") find consensus in supporting systematic phonics instruction over the embedded, ad hoc variety. By contrast, the debate between synthetic and analytic phonics remains less clearly resolved (e.g. NICHD, 2000; Torgerson et al., 2006)[3].

Should we teach L2 phonics?

I turn now to this chapter's overarching question: when teaching an L2, should we teach L2 phonics? I begin by exploring learners' L2 phonological decoding outcomes in the absence of explicit phonics instruction. Do they master the language's SSC incidentally (and rapidly), simply through exposure to the written and spoken forms of the language? If so, then L2 phonics instruction would be redundant.

Without phonics

Progress in phonological decoding

My interest in L2 phonics began when, as a teacher of French and German in an English secondary school, I noticed that many of my students – even after years of studying the language – frequently mispronounced words when reading them aloud. They seemed to flounder when attempting to read unfamiliar words, and complained that French or German spelling was crazy, illogical or 'back to front'. This seemed to me paradoxical, given that their point of reference, English, is an unusually complex and inconsistent orthography (Share, 2008). The students' complaints might be likened to a platypus finding it strange that other mammals do not lay eggs.

Subsequently, a series of studies based in L2 classrooms in English secondary schools investigated this issue more systematically (Erler, 2003; Erler & Macaro, 2011; Woore, 2009, 2014). These studies confirmed my experiences as a teacher: they concluded that, in the absence of explicit phonics instruction, many students had low proficiency in decoding L2 French and made little progress in this area, even over a period of several years. Participants in these studies tended to rely on what Erler (2003, p. 166) called the 'heuristic of English': that is, they used their knowledge of English SSC to decode French words, resulting in anglicized pronunciations. This problem has been observed in other contexts, too: for example, in a study by Sparks (2015), US school students showed a recurring influence of English when pronouncing words in L2 Spanish.

What of higher proficiency L2 learners? Do they eventually develop knowledge of L2 SSC and the ability to apply these successfully? Evidence suggests that even at more advanced levels of language study, after extensive experience with the target language, many students do not become proficient L2 decoders. For example, Li (2019) found that students majoring in English at three Chinese universities were highly inaccurate when reading English words aloud, performing at similar levels to native-speaking children in Grade 1. Further, many of the students' mispronunciations appeared to reflect the SSC of *pinyin* (the official Roman-alphabetic representation of Chinese). Alghamdi (2020) found similar deficiencies in English decoding amongst foundation year university students in Saudi Arabia: on a reading aloud test, they performed equivalently to native-speaking children in grades 2–3.

For all the above-mentioned studies, the levels of decoding proficiency which I have reported here are average ones across their samples as a whole. There was considerable variation within these samples: some learners were more or less proficient than others. Therefore, the evidence does not say that learners *cannot* acquire phonological decoding proficiency in an alphabetic L2 without phonics instruction. However, it does suggest that, in the absence of explicit instruction, *many* learners do not become proficient L2 decoders.

228　*Robert Woore*

'Transfer' and beyond

The influence of L1 SSC on L2 decoding is often described in terms of cross-language 'transfer' (Odlin, 1989). Where the two languages share the same alphabet (e.g. English and Spanish), this can be understood as the result of L1-based symbol-sound associations being automatically activated or 'triggered' by L2 input (Koda, 2007). Of course, many graphemes (particularly consonantal ones) have similar pronunciations in various European orthographies, thus aiding accurate L2 decoding; by contrast, the pronunciations of vowels more often differ. To give an example, an English speaker naïve to French SSC and faced with the French word 'voilé' ('veiled',/vwale/) is likely to decode the <v> and the <l> correctly, but the <oi> and <é> incorrectly. Thus, L1 transfer in L2 decoding can be both facilitative and disruptive, with the extent and nature of its influence varying according to the specific pair of languages involved.

The learner's task is then to retune her L1 decoding processes as necessary, to suit the needs of the L2. However, this can be difficult. Woore (2010) argued that a key first step in this process of retuning L1-based decoding is for learners to become aware of which shared written symbols are pronounced differently in the L2 compared to their L1. They can then consciously disrupt the automatic activation of these 'unhelpful' L1-based symbol-sound associations. In turn, this may provide space for new, L2-based mappings to become established – and, eventually, automatized through practice.

The challenge of learning to decode an L2 will, of course, be very different for those whose L1 and L2 writing systems are typologically more distant. Several studies have explored this issue. Researchers have compared the decoding of L2 English (Roman alphabetic) by learners with various L1 backgrounds, such as Spanish (also Roman alphabetic), Korean (non-Roman alphabetic) and Chinese (logographic or 'morphemic') (e.g. Koda, 1999; Hamada & Koda, 2008; Muljani, Koda & Moates, 1998; Wang & Koda, 2005). Drawing together work in this area, Koda (2005) proposed an 'Orthographic Distance Effect', whereby the ease of learning to decode an L2 depends (at least partly) on how similar the writing system is to that of the learner's L1. Highly congruent L1-L2 pairs are predicted to result in faster and easier mastery of the L2 writing system because, there is more potential for positive transfer of existing L1 knowledge. Whilst this may be so, we need to keep in mind the above-mentioned studies conducted in English secondary schools. These show that even for highly congruent pairs of L1-L2 writing systems (e.g. English and French), learning to decode the L2 can be far from trivial.

The importance of SSC knowledge

The previous section has documented some of the problems that learners encounter in developing and applying knowledge of L2 SSC. But does this matter, and if so, why? There is not space here for a comprehensive discussion of this question, so I have selected five areas which I consider particularly salient: reading, spelling, vocabulary acquisition, oral communication and affective issues.

Teaching phonics in a second language 229

Reading

We have seen that, in L1 contexts, the main focus of phonics research and policy has related to the teaching of reading. Teaching phonics helps children learn to read L1 by enabling them to sound out words which they have not seen before in print, and thus to 'discover' their meanings. For example, by sounding out <cat>, an English-speaking child can recognize the resulting spoken form as denoting the small furry animal that sleeps on the sofa at home. This works because, in L1, children approach the task of learning to read already proficient in the spoken language: they have a large bank of oral vocabulary knowledge (and other linguistic knowledge) onto which they can map the written words they sound out. This is the basis of the well-established 'Simple View of Reading' (SVR), which sees reading comprehension as the product of (a) decoding and (b) general language comprehension, often measured by a listening comprehension test (Gough & Tunmer, 1986; Hoover & Gough, 1990).

What of L2 contexts? There are important differences between L1 and L2 learners in terms of the role of phonological decoding in learning to read. In many L2 classrooms, learners encounter written words and texts at the very start of learning the language itself. Thus, as Grabe and Stoller (2011) argue,

> one benefit of developing accurate letter-sound correspondences is lost in most L2 settings; that is, L2 students cannot match a sounded-out word to a word that they know orally because they do not yet know the word orally.
>
> (pp. 36–37)

Echoing this argument, studies of immigrant L2 learners (e.g. 'English Language Learners' in US schools; see also Chalmers and Murphy, this volume) have found that, whilst their L2 decoding skills may develop relatively quickly, they lag behind L1 peers in oral language knowledge. This, in turn, forms the main impediment to their successful reading comprehension (Melby-Lervåg & Lervåg, 2014). In terms of the 'Simple View of Reading', these learners can accurately decode words from written into spoken forms but do not then understand what they have decoded. An important implication of this, Melby-Lervåg & Lervåg argue, is that 'unless specific decoding problems are detected, interventions that aim to ameliorate reading comprehension problems among second-language learners should focus on language comprehension skills', rather than on decoding (*ibid.*, p. 409).

On the other hand, there is some evidence that decoding *can* be important for L2 reading comprehension. For example, Erler & Macaro's (2011) large, nationally representative study of English secondary school students found that two-thirds of respondents agreed with the statement, 'When I can't read a French word easily, I sound it out in my head'. However, even if a learner does know a target word orally, sounding it out may not help much if their decoding is defective. Indeed, several participants in an earlier study by Erler (2003) – investigating English secondary school students' experiences of reading

230 *Robert Woore*

in French – complained about exactly this problem. As one participant put it, after practising words orally in class then seeing them written down, 'they look like a different word than what you've been repeating' (p. 165). Interestingly, very similar comments were made by participants in Alghamdi's (2020) study, in the very different educational context of Saudi university students learning L2 English. For example, one student complained that, although she might know a word orally, 'when I read it, it doesn't come to my mind. I read it like it's a new word to me'.

Finally, even if learners' L2 decoding is accurate, it may be slow and effortful at the beginning stages. This will use up limited working memory capacity, leaving fewer resources available for 'higher level' comprehension processes (Stanovich, 1980), such as making inferences and integrating textual information with existing world knowledge. In turn, this will impede comprehension. Overall, then, whilst decoding might not have the same impact on learning to read in an L2 as it does in L1, its importance should certainly not be discounted.

Spelling

> When thinking about phonic work, what most people have in mind is the teaching and learning of reading. However, phonic work is also essential for the development of writing, especially spelling.
>
> (J. Rose, 2006, p. 4)

Despite Rose's argument, in L1 settings, research into the effects of phonics on children's spelling is much more limited than research relating to reading. For example, Torgerson et al.'s (2006) systematic review identified only three Randomized Controlled Trials (RCTs) that examined the impact of phonics instruction on spelling, with no evidence for any effect being found; but in the same review, 12 studies contributed to the conclusion that phonics had a positive effect on reading accuracy. There is even less evidence on phonics and spelling in L2 contexts. Clearly, however, knowledge of the systematic mappings between written symbols and sounds in an alphabetic writing system can be bidirectional – that is, taking the form of *sound-to-symbol* mappings (sometimes called Phoneme-Grapheme Correspondences, or PGC) as well as *symbol-to-sound* mappings (or GPC). This can help learners to spell words which they know orally, without having to rely on retrieving the whole written form intact from memory.

As in the case of print-to-sound decoding, in the absence of explicit instruction, L2 spelling patterns tend to be influenced by L1 transfer. Both positive and negative effects may arise, depending on the relationship between the L1 and L2 writing systems (Figueredo, 2006). Such influence may be overcome with effort: that is, beginner L2 learners might spell a word wrongly when writing in a hurry, but spell it correctly if they really think about it. Again, however, within limited capacity theories of writing (e.g. McCutchen, 1996), this may interfere with 'higher-level' processes, such as generating ideas and translating these into language.

Vocabulary acquisition

Vocabulary knowledge is a central component of L2 learning and use, strongly predicting performance in all four language skills (Milton, 2013; see also Martinez, this volume). Accurate SSC knowledge can be seen as important for vocabulary learning because it helps form strong links between the orthographic and phonological representations of words, making these coherent and mutually reinforcing. It also allows missing information in one of these nodes to be filled in. For example, if you were reading a text about an imaginary creature called a 'quisk' (Figure 12.1)[4], your knowledge of English SSC would immediately tell you that its spoken form is /kwɪsk/. If you subsequently heard me say, 'Look at that quisk!', you would know what I was talking about; you would have learnt the phonological form of this new word. Conversely, if you first heard me say 'quisk' without seeing it written down, your English SSC knowledge would give you a good idea of how to spell the word.

These processes are likely to be particularly important in instructed L2 contexts, where a learner's first encounter with many words may be in written form. As noted above, in such a situation, sounding these words out will not help learners to 'discover' their meanings. However, the other side of this coin is that L2 learners with good SSC knowledge can sound out new words to 'discover' their pronunciations. Of course, in the case of a real word that you did not know, you could always check the pronunciation in a dictionary (increasingly facilitated by audio playback in apps and online dictionaries). Nonetheless, the ability to derive this pronunciation quickly and confidently for yourself from the written form gives you greater autonomy and efficiency as a learner. A relatively recent line of research has indeed found evidence of a link between L2 decoding proficiency and success in L2 vocabulary learning (Hamada & Koda, 2008; Li, 2019).

The above-described processes rely on accurate SSC knowledge. Without this, learners will derive incorrect pronunciations (or, working in the reverse direction, incorrect spellings) for unfamiliar words, perhaps based on the transfer of L1 SSC. Learners may then store the resulting 'spelling pronunciations' in long-term memory and subsequently produce them when speaking, even in

Figure 12.1 An imaginary creature.

232   *Robert Woore*

the absence of any written stimulus. For example, Bassetti (2017) found that Italian learners of L2 English produced a longer medial consonant sound in words like 'kitty' (where it is spelt with a double letter) than in words like 'city' (single letter). This, she argues, is because Italian orthography uses single and double consonant letters to contrast short and long consonant phonemes (e.g. *nono*,/nɔno/, 'ninth' versus *nonno*,/nɔnno/, 'grandpa'). Her participants then transferred this L1-based SSC knowledge to the L2.

Some might argue that a possible pedagogical response to the problem of spelling pronunciations in L2 would be to teach new words orally first, withholding the written forms until the phonological forms are securely learned. Anecdotally, this approach has been popular in L2 classrooms in England in recent years. When the written forms are then introduced, the idea is that learners can link these to the pre-stored pronunciations as wholes without needing to analyze them sub-lexically. However, a concern with such an approach is that it might actually impede learners from mastering L2 SSC. It could be likened to giving learners ready-built Lego® toys, rather than teaching them how to combine the individual blocks for themselves – a skill which ultimately will allow them to build a wide variety of other shapes and structures.

Oral communication

If inaccurate SSC knowledge affects vocabulary acquisition, this may in turn have implications for using the language when speaking and listening. Italians who pronounce 'kitty' with a lengthened medial consonant may not have much difficulty making themselves understood, but English learners of French who think that *blanc* (/blã/, 'white') is pronounced like the English word 'blank' may not recognize this word when they hear it spoken, and may pronounce it incomprehensibly to other users of the language.

Further, because of the interconnections between orthographic and phonological representations in long-term memory (Frost & Ziegler, 2012), accurate (and fluent) SSC knowledge may also facilitate L2 listening. It may help learners to segment the auditory input and to recognize words in the stream of connected speech – a key challenge of L2 listening comprehension (Field, 2008). Field (2004) further argues that L2 learners who are faced with an unfamiliar but salient word in a spoken text may find it useful to visualize the word's orthographic form in order to help identify it. Visualizing a word based on incorrect SSC will prevent this strategy operating efficiently.

Affective issues

In a study investigating the phonological decoding of beginner learners of French in an English secondary school (Woore, 2011), I audio-recorded students as they read aloud a series of unfamiliar French words. Listening back to the recordings afterwards, I found – in amongst the pronunciations of the test items themselves (the focus of my analysis) – a number of *sotto voce* comments

Teaching phonics in a second language   233

in which students verbalized their feelings about the task they were completing. Some typical examples were:

They're like really weird words, like they don't exist.
These words get more ridiculous as we go along!
Some of these don't even look like real words. I reckon you're just trying to trick me.
I don't know because most of them look like gibberish basically.

On one level, these comments are amusing, but they also contain an important message. For these learners, the L2 writing system is something alien and unfathomable. Their lack of understanding of this system is therefore attributed to something external and beyond their control (see Weiner, 1986), and so they will have little incentive to try to master it. Thus, an important early goal of phonics instruction (in my view) is to help learners gain a better understanding of the learning challenges they face. French SSC, for example, whilst they may be complex, are actually much more consistent than English ones, at least when moving from print to sound. Understanding this fact may help learners to see the L2 writing system as something that they can master, provided they invest sufficient time and effort. Conversely, for L2 English learners whose L1 writing system has much more transparent and consistent SSC (e.g. Italian or Spanish), it may help them to gain a realistic understanding of the challenges posed by English orthography, rather than blithely (and incorrectly) assuming that its SSC will be easy to learn.

There is also evidence that poor decoding can impact on learners' wider motivation for learning an L2. Erler's (2003) investigation of reading in L2 French led her to conclude that students who lack this foundational literacy skill – and yet who are expected to engage with reading and writing as a core part of their French curriculum – 'are bound to take offence and become disaffected learners' (p. 308). Indeed, in their later, large-scale study of students learning French in English schools, Erler & Macaro (2011) found that those with greater proficiency and confidence in French decoding were also more likely to want to continue learning the language in the future.

Is teaching L2 phonics effective?

If SSC knowledge is important for L2 learning, and if many learners do not develop this knowledge 'incidentally', does it follow that we should teach it explicitly, as in a programme of phonics instruction? Not necessarily: learners do not always learn what we teach them, and the effects of teaching are not always those that we foresee. Therefore, it is important to look for evidence on whether explicit teaching of L2 phonics can be effective, and what its effects (if any) may be on wider L2 learning.

Whilst phonics instruction has been extensively researched in relation to early L1 literacy (particularly in English), very few phonics studies have been conducted

234 *Robert Woore*

in L2 contexts where the L2 in question is not an official or majority language (i.e. those which might traditionally be labelled 'foreign language' contexts). In particular, in such 'non-majority L2' settings, there have been few high-quality experimental studies, in which the outcomes of an intervention group, who receive phonics instruction, are compared to those of a control group – a research design sometimes seen as the 'gold standard' for evaluating pedagogical interventions (e.g. Moore, Graham & Diamond, 2003). I will therefore begin by looking at evidence in a related and more widely researched L2 context: that of school pupils from immigrant families, whose L2 is the majority language of the community in which they are living and being educated. I will then move on to studies conducted specifically in non-majority L2 contexts. Given the limited scope of this chapter, my review is necessarily selective, highlighting a few of what I consider the more significant studies.

Migrant second language learners

Migrant second language learners – such as 'English Language Learners' (ELLs) in US schools and 'English as an Additional Language' (EAL) pupils in the UK – are a large and growing demographic in many Anglophone countries (Adesope et al., 2011). Several recent reviews have sought to synthesize evidence on how best to support these learners in the crucial task of learning to read and write. For example, Adesope et al. (2011) conducted a meta-analysis of 20 experimental studies evaluating the teaching of literacy to immigrant ESL (English as a Second Language) students, from kindergarten to Grade 6, in English-speaking countries. Their findings align with the evidence relating to L1 English-speaking children: namely, systematic phonics instruction is an effective approach for teaching English literacy to young ESL learners. However, to put this finding into context, both (a) cooperative reading (where pairs or small groups of learners work together on tasks such as reading aloud and story comprehension) and (b) the writing of reflective diaries by learners, were found to have a slightly greater effect than phonics instruction. There was also considerable variation in the effectiveness of the literacy interventions included in the review, perhaps reflecting contextual differences at the school level or individual differences amongst the learners themselves (e.g. their L1 background).

Another important review in this area was conducted by the US National Literacy Panel on Language-Minority Children and Youth, which was charged with synthesizing evidence on these learners' English literacy development. The panel's final report (August & Shanahan, 2006a) noted the limited amount of experimental research available in this area; however, a later update (August & Shanahan, 2010) identified various additional, relevant studies, and found that these confirmed the findings of the original report. Three of the panel's key conclusions are highlighted here, since they seem likely to have particular relevance for non-majority L2 contexts as well. First, systematic, explicit instruction in the key components of reading – including phonics – was found to be beneficial for ELLs, just as it is for L1 English-speaking pupils. Second, in an important caveat

Teaching phonics in a second language 235

to the previous point, instruction in basic literacy skills was found to be necessary, but not in itself sufficient, for ELLs to become proficient readers and writers in English. This is because (as noted above) ELLs often lag behind their L1 peers in general language comprehension, despite having well-developed decoding and spelling skills. A more specific systematic review by Purewal (2008), focussing on the effects of teaching synthetic phonics to young EAL pupils in the UK, reached a similar conclusion. Thus, for these learners, 'extensive oral English development must be incorporated into successful literacy instruction' (August & Shanahan, 2006b, p.4). Third, August and Shanahan emphasize that 'language-minority students are not blank slates. They enter classrooms with varying degrees of oral proficiency and literacy in their first language' (*ibid.*, p. 5). Accordingly, the effectiveness of literacy instruction for ELLs can be enhanced by making adjustments based on their L1 knowledge. For example, there is little point in re-teaching letter-sound correspondences which learners have already mastered in their L1, if these are the same as in English: it would be more valuable to focus on those SSC which differ between their L1 and L2.

Phonics in non-majority L2 contexts

Whilst evidence from ELLs in English-dominant societies may shed valuable light on the teaching of phonics in non-majority L2 classrooms (i.e. those traditionally labelled as 'foreign language' settings), caution is also needed when transferring findings between these contexts. Non-majority L2 learners differ in important respects: for example, they may have far less exposure to the L2, both inside and outside school; their motivational profiles and attitudes towards the L2 may be different; and many will be learning alongside classmates with similar levels of L2 proficiency and perhaps a shared L1. I therefore turn now to studies conducted specifically in L2 contexts of this latter kind. I have organized these studies by age group.

YOUNG LEARNERS

A recent review by Huo & Wang (2017) investigated the effectiveness of 'phonological-based instruction' (including phonics) for young EFL learners from Kindergarten to Grade 6. However, of the 15 studies included in the review, only three were judged sufficiently rigorous to give confidence in their findings. Further, only one of these more rigorous studies related specifically to phonics teaching, which was Dixon et al.'s (2011) study of 500 Year 1 children based in 20 primary schools in slum areas of Hyderabad, India[5]. In this study, pupils who followed a six-month programme of synthetic phonics made greater improvements in reading and writing than a control group who received their regular instruction (largely based on the rote learning of texts). The authors conclude that even L2 learners in disadvantaged circumstances, 'many with illiterate parents even in their mother tongue, are able to decode and blend English words successfully when taught using a synthetic phonics programme' (p. 473).

236   *Robert Woore*

They do, however, acknowledge that the phonics intervention was more engaging and interactive than the traditional teaching experienced by the control group, creating a 'novelty effect' which may have influenced the findings.

Looking across the studies in their review more broadly, Huo & Wang (2017) find consistently positive effects of explicitly teaching phonics and phonological awareness on EFL pupils' reading subskills (such as phonemic awareness and phonological decoding), with a medium-sized effect. However, a smaller impact (or in some cases no significant impact) of such instruction was found on real word reading. On this basis, the authors argue that 'the effectiveness of phonological-based instruction may be constrained by the limited exposure to oral and written English in the EFL context'. Developing pupils' wider knowledge of the L2 is therefore crucial: 'it is very important that phonics should be supplementary to general L2 instruction not a replacement for it' (p. 10). These conclusions clearly echo those reached by August and Shanahan (2006a) and Purewal (2008) in relation to minority language pupils in English-speaking countries.

SECONDARY SCHOOL STUDENTS

Moving to the secondary school phase of education, Coates et al. (2017) conducted an experimental study of Italian students (aged 17–18) learning L2 English. A trial group of 24 students followed a 20-hour programme of L2 phonics instruction (spread over 10 weeks) in addition to their regular English lessons. A control group of 14 students also followed an additional English course for the same length of time, focussing on examination practice but without any phonics. Following the intervention, the phonics group performed better than the control group at both spelling and decoding English words. They also performed better on measures of English lexis, pronunciation and discourse (but not grammar), as assessed in a short interview. However, whilst this study is described as an RCT, it appears that random allocation to the two groups was conducted previously as part of the school's administrative procedures, rather than being done specifically for the experiment, thus introducing a risk of bias. Further, the authors acknowledge that their findings could have been influenced by teacher effects.

In the context of L2 classrooms in England, Woore et al. (2018) conducted a 'cluster' RCT in which 36 intact French classes (each in a different school) were allocated to three different groups. Over 16 weeks, one group received systematic phonics instruction for around 10 minutes every lesson, focussing on certain French SSC known to pose problems for English-speaking learners. The students also read eight texts containing plentiful examples of the target SSC. These texts, which were somewhat above participants' productive L2 level, covered engaging cultural topics and were intended to encourage reading for genuine interest and pleasure. The second group received explicit instruction in reading strategies, with the same texts providing opportunities to practise the strategic approaches they were taught. The third ('Texts') group worked with the same eight texts as the other two groups but received neither phonics nor strategy instruction. Students' outcomes on a range of variables were measured at three points: before, immediately after and six months after the intervention; however, due to considerable attrition between time points 2 and 3, only the immediate effects of the intervention can be assessed with confidence.

For current purposes, I will focus on the three main linguistic variables that were measured in the study: phonological decoding, reading comprehension and vocabulary knowledge. On all three of these variables, there were no significant differences between the groups at time 1. The key findings were as follows. First, on a descriptive level, the Phonics group made the most progress in phonological decoding; the authors hypothesize that a more robust, statistically significant advantage for the phonics group might have been observed, had it been possible to use a more sensitive measure of decoding (such as a reading aloud test). Second, in reading comprehension, no group outperformed the others at time 2; all three groups made substantial progress on this variable over the course of the study, perhaps helped by their engagement with the challenging texts. Third, in terms of vocabulary knowledge, an advantage was observed at time 2 for both the Strategies group and – most clearly – the Phonics group over the Texts group. All three groups recorded significant increases in vocabulary knowledge between times 1 and 2, but with different effect sizes: small for the Texts group, small-medium for the Strategies group and medium-large for the Phonics group. Overall, the authors conclude that 'an integrated approach to French reading instruction – combining explicit instruction in both Strategies and Phonics with the use of appropriately challenging, engaging texts – is more likely to be beneficial than any of these approaches in isolation' (p. 7).

UNIVERSITY STUDENTS

Turning to university-level learners, Cihon et al. (2013) conducted three small-scale interventions in which short phonics sessions were taught to US undergraduate students, enrolled on an L2 Italian language course (1 hour per week) in preparation for a cultural visit to Italy. The approach to phonics teaching involved the use of hand signals to represent individual phonemes in combination with their written representations, developed by the International Communication Learning Institute[6] for deaf and hard of hearing students. A single-subject research design was used (with no comparison group), in which each participant's outcomes after the intervention were compared to their performance beforehand. The authors found that even a short phonics session, targeting sounds which participants decoded incorrectly at baseline, resulted in marked improvements in decoding accuracy. However, the number of participants in each intervention was small (between 5 and 10 in each case); further, given that they were preparing for an L2 immersion experience in Italy, their motivation to learn the target SSC may have been particularly high, and not necessarily typical of L2 learners in other contexts. Finally, Italian SSC are

238   *Robert Woore*

extremely consistent (Seymour et al., 2003); thus, the findings may not necessarily transfer to other L2s.

In another university-based study, Sturm (2013) investigated the impact of a phonetics and pronunciation course on undergraduate students of L2 French in the United States. Though the course was not labelled as a phonics intervention as such, it did include 'learning grapheme-to-phoneme equivalents'. Eleven students who received the phonetics training were compared to an equal number who followed a range of other courses, but without explicit instruction in French pronunciation. The phonetics group showed a larger improvement in accuracy when reading connected French text aloud, with a large effect size. However, the researcher herself taught the phonetics group but not the other students, introducing the possibility of a teacher effect. Further, participants were not randomly allocated to conditions: those in the phonetics group chose to enrol in this course, so may have been particularly keen to improve their French pronunciation in the first place.

A larger-scale study involving university undergraduates by Li (2019) investigated the impact of L2 phonics instruction on both phonological decoding and vocabulary learning. One class of English majors in each of three Chinese universities followed a systematic, twelve-week programme of synthetic phonics, covering 101 English GPC. These classes were compared with three matched classes in the same universities, who followed an English phonology course but received no phonics instruction. After the intervention, the phonics group performed significantly better than the comparison group on a phonological decoding test, with a medium effect size (whereas at baseline, both groups had performed equivalently). On a task requiring participants to memorize a set of unfamiliar English words, the phonics group also showed significant advantages, at post-test, in their ability to (a) recall the words' spoken forms, (b) recall their written forms and (c) recognize their spoken forms. Reflecting arguments made earlier in this chapter, these findings suggest that phonics instruction did indeed improve these participants' L2 vocabulary learning. Nonetheless, the study has some limitations. The lack of delayed post-tests makes it impossible to gauge whether the advantages for the phonics group were maintained over time. Further, the researcher herself taught all participants in both conditions. Whilst this eliminates a possible confound caused by different teachers, it does mean that the evaluation of the phonics intervention was not independent of its implementation.

SUMMARY

Surveying the body of experimental research described above as a whole, what conclusions can be drawn? Consistently positive effects of L2 phonics teaching on L2 phonological decoding seem to have been found. However, in contrast to L1 research, there is (as yet) little indication that L2 phonics improves L2 reading comprehension. On the other hand, emerging evidence supports the hypothesis that L2 phonics instruction may facilitate L2 vocabulary acquisition.

How should we teach L2 phonics?

What the above research cannot tell us is *how* L2 phonics can best be taught; that is, which pedagogical approaches appear (on average) to be most effective. A number of factors need to be considered in this regard.

First, in terms of the synthetic/analytic debate, there is insufficient evidence to recommend one over the other. Most of the L2 research to date has trialled synthetic phonics instruction, with only a few studies – for example, three of those in Huo & Wang's (2017) review – adopting a more analytic approach. This issue remains contested even in L1 phonics research, but it is worth noting that the optimal approach may be different in an L2 context, where learners are usually older, cognitively more advanced and perhaps already literate in their L1. All of these characteristics may facilitate the analysis of L2 written forms, helping learners to identify sub-lexical patterns within them (i.e. consistent with an analytic phonics approach). More research is needed on this topic.

Second, whereas some studies have taught a comprehensive programme of L2 SSC (e.g. Li, 2019), others have adopted a more focussed approach, targeting 'tricky' SSC likely to pose problems for learners (e.g. Woore et al., 2018). Again, no studies (to my knowledge) have directly compared these two approaches. Often, existing (including commercial) English phonics schemes are used in L2 contexts, which are comprehensive in their SSC coverage and work through a sequence designed for young L1 learners. However, as has been noted, many L2 learners are already literate in their L1. It may well be beneficial to capitalize on this existing knowledge, for example, by drawing learners' attention to similarities and differences between the SSC of their L1 and L2 (where these use the same alphabet). Certainly, it would seem wasteful to re-teach SSC which they have already mastered in their L1; conversely, they may need help in overriding automatic but inappropriate L1-based associations, in order to allow knowledge of L2 SSC to gain a foothold.

Third, we have discussed L2 phonics in general terms, but all writing systems are different. Some are much more phonologically transparent, with more consistent SSC, than others. Therefore, the design principles of optimal programmes of phonics instruction will depend not only on the learners' L1 but also on the particular L2 they are learning.

Fourth, there may be other problems in 'implanting' L1-based phonics schemes into L2 contexts. One issue is that, being designed for young children, they may be poorly suited to older, cognitively more advanced L2 learners: for example, their content and visual appearance may be perceived as 'childish'. Second, such resources may need to be adapted to L2 learners' world knowledge and cultural norms. For example, an image of a *sled* might be used to exemplify the English grapheme <e>, but this object will be more familiar in some cultures (such as Anglophone ones with snowy winters!) than others[7]. Third, interesting questions arise concerning the phonological norms espoused in any phonics programme, particularly from a 'Global Englishes' perspective (see Rose & Galloway, 2019). Who determines the phonological value that a given grapheme

240   *Robert Woore*

should represent? Should this be based on a 'native speaker' variety of English (and if so, which one) or on a local L2 variety (e.g. Hong Kong English)? Unfortunately, there is no room to explore this question further here, but it is one which will confront any EFL teacher seeking to implement phonics instruction. To teach phonics is inescapably to teach pronunciation as well (see Kennedy & Trofimovich, Chapter 13, this volume).

Finally, decisions must be made about assessment. If phonics should be taught, then logically, learners' outcomes should also be monitored (even if only informally), both to evaluate past teaching and to inform future planning. This might be done via tasks such as transcription (to assess sound-to-print mappings) and reading aloud (print-to-sound mappings). Both can target specific SSC and, through analysis of learners' errors, provide diagnostic insight into their current understandings and misconceptions. Individual reading aloud tasks are time-consuming to administer and mark, and not necessarily practicable in whole class contexts; creative solutions may need to be explored, such as the use of speech recognition software, 'speaking homework' (see Shanks, 2019[8]) or paired tasks in class, where the teacher can circulate and 'eavesdrop'.

Drawing on arguments made earlier in this chapter, any tasks designed to assess L2 decoding or spelling should include unfamiliar real words or pseudowords, if insight is to be gained into learners' knowledge of sub-lexical symbol-sound mappings. Consideration must also be given to time limits. I argued above that learners may automatically apply L1-based knowledge to L2 decoding and spelling tasks, with conscious intervention being needed to override these automatic connections, where they differ from the L2. Indeed, both Erler (2003) and Li (2019) found that some of the more accurate L2 decoders in their studies were actually slower at reading the target words aloud. Thus, to assess learners' *accuracy* in L2 decoding, an unspeeded test may be most appropriate (at least at beginner levels), because it gives learners time to reflect and to apply any explicit L2 SSC knowledge that they may have gained through phonics instruction. Eventually, it is of course important for L2 decoding and spelling to become fluent (automatized) through repeated practice. Thus, speeded tests may become more appropriate as learners progress. However, accuracy must be achieved first; it is no good automatizing incorrect connections.

Conclusions

The overarching question addressed in this chapter is whether phonics should be taught to L2 learners; whether this is a worthwhile endeavour. In contrast to the wealth of literature dedicated to phonics teaching in L1 (particularly English), research on L2 phonics is still at an early stage. Many questions remain unanswered. Broadly, however, I believe that the answer to the chapter's overarching question is 'Yes, probably'. I have added 'probably' because all classrooms are different: ultimately, it is individual teachers who must decide the answer to this question in their own contexts, based on a careful diagnostic assessment of their learners and their own professional judgment.

Teaching phonics in a second language 241

To gain more detailed understanding of L2 phonics teaching, this chapter has also explored a series of sub-questions, the answers to which may be summarized as follows.

Do learners acquire knowledge of L2 SSC without explicit phonics instruction?

Some learners may master L2 SSC for themselves, simply through exposure to the language. However, many learners appear not to do so, even where their L1 and L2 writing systems are highly congruent. Without explicit instruction, many learners continue to rely on L1-based knowledge as a 'heuristic' to decode and spell L2 words, even though this may lead to incorrect outcomes.

How important is knowledge of L2 SSC?

In an L1 context, phonics has been framed chiefly in terms of learning to read and spell (particularly the former). In an L2, however, its impact may be much wider. Phonics instruction – where this results in more accurate and fluent knowledge of L2 SSC – may benefit various other aspects of L2 learning. In particular, emerging evidence suggests benefits for the crucial task of L2 vocabulary acquisition, as well as motivation for learning the language.

Is teaching L2 phonics effective?

The research evidence on this question remains limited in quantity, and the studies that do exist have various methodological limitations. However, consistently positive effects of phonics instruction on L2 decoding have been found across various phases of formal education (primary school, secondary school and university): it appears that L2 learners who are taught phonics are more likely to develop more accurate SSC knowledge than those who are not. Experimental evidence is also emerging of an impact on L2 vocabulary learning. However, much more research is needed in this area.

If L2 phonics should be taught, how should it be taught?

Once again, the available evidence does not support a firm answer to this question. However, a carefully planned, systematic phonics programme is more likely to ensure coverage of key SSC than an ad-hoc approach. It also seems highly likely that the optimal form of L2 phonics instruction will depend on the specific learning context, including the particular L1-L2 combination and the age and cognitive maturity of the learners. Teachers should capitalize on any existing L1 literacy knowledge their learners may have, taking account of similarities and differences between the L1 and L2 writing systems: for example, some SSC may not need to be taught, because they are the same as in the L1; others may need particular attention, in order to prevent the automatic triggering of incorrect,

242 *Robert Woore*

L1-based pronunciations or spellings. Finally, integral to phonics instruction is the effective monitoring of learners' outcomes. Identifying their current strengths and weaknesses will help tailor future teaching more effectively to their needs.

Relating the issues raised in this chapter to your own context:

1 How proficient are your own L2 learners at phonological decoding in the target language? How accurately and how fluently can they read aloud both familiar and unfamiliar words in the L2?
2 What L1 literacy knowledge do your learners already have, which may help them or hinder them when learning to decode words in the L2?
3 Based on your learners' existing L1 literacy knowledge, are there any L2 letters or letter combinations which are likely to need particular attention when teaching L2 phonics? Conversely, are there any symbols which may need less attention?
4 In practical terms, how might it be possible to systematically monitor learners' phonological decoding in your own context?

Notes

1 The meaning of 'synthetic' phonics will be covered later in this chapter.
2 Note that 'grapheme' is sometimes also used in a broader sense, essentially as a synonym for written symbol (Cook & Bassetti, 2005), including Chinese characters.
3 The UK's 'Rose Review' (J. Rose, 2006) pronounced in favour of synthetic phonics, but this has been contested (e.g. Wyse & Styles, 2007).
4 This pseudoword and its imaginary referent (Figure 12.1) come from the UK government's *Phonics Screening Check* (Standards and Testing Agency, 2019).
5 Note that although Huo & Wang (2017) include this study in their review of 'EFL' instruction, Dixon et al. (2011) themselves do not describe English as a 'foreign' language for their participants.
6 http://seethesound.org/
7 Thanks to Dr Naomi Flynn of Reading University (personal communication) for this example.
8 https://resources.ncelp.org/concern/parent/6q182k142/file_sets/8g84mm259

References

Adesope. O. O., Lavin, T., Thompson, T., & Ungerleider, C. (2011). Pedagogical strategies for teaching literacy to ESL immigrant students: A meta-analysis. *British Journal of Educational Psychology*, 81(4), 629–653. https://doi.org/http://dx.doi.org/10.1111/j.2044-8279.2010.02015.x

Alghamdi, H. (2020). *L2 Decoding and Reading Comprehension in Saudi Foundation Year ESL Students: An Investigation into Readers' Decoding Abilities, Outputs, Experiences, and Processes, and the Contribution of Their L2 Decoding Proficiency to Their L2 Reading Comprehension*. University of Oxford.

August, D. E., & Shanahan, T. E. (2006a). *Developing Literacy in Second-Language Learners: Report of the National Literacy Panel on Language-Minority Children and Youth*. Lawrence Erlbaum Associates Publishers.

Teaching phonics in a second language   243

August, D. E., & Shanahan, T. E. (2006b). *Executive Summary: Developing Literacy in Second-Language Learners: Report of the National Literacy Panel on Language-Minority Children and Youth.* Lawrence Erlbaum Associates Publishers.

August, D., & Shanahan, T. (2010). Response to a review and update on developing literacy in second-language learners: Report of the national literacy panel on language minority children and youth. *Journal of Literacy Research, 42*(3), 341–348. https://doi.org/10.1080/1086296X.2010.503745

Bassetti, B. (2017). Orthography affects second language speech: Double letters and geminate production in English. *Journal of Experimental Psychology: Learning, Memory, and Cognition, 43*(11), 1835–1842. https://doi.org/10.1037/xlm0000417

Bauckham, I. (2016). Modern foreign languages pedagogy review. A review of modern foreign languages teaching practice in key stage 3 and key stage 4. Teaching Schools Council: London. https://tscouncil.org.uk/wp-content/uploads/2016/12/MFL-Pedagogy-Review-Report-2.pdf

Cao, M. (2017). An analysis of phonics teaching in mainland China. *Journal of Language Teaching and Research, 8*(2), 286–290. http://dx.doi.org/10.17507/jltr.0802.09

Castles, A., Rastle, K., & Nation, K. (2018). Ending the reading wars: Reading acquisition from novice to expert. *Psychological Science in the Public Interest, 19*, 5–51. https://doi.org/10.1177/1529100618772271

Cihon, T. M., Morford, Z., Stephens, C. J., Morrison, D., Shrontz, R., Kelly, K. L., Morford Stephens, Christopher J., Z., Morrison, D., Shrontz, R., & Kelly, K. L. (2013). The effects of large-group instruction, modeling, or see the sound/visual phonics on undergraduate students learning to read Italian. *Reading in a Foreign Language, 25*(1), 26–51. https://search.proquest.com/docview/1373091246?accountid=13042

Coates, R. A. G., Gorham, J., & Nicholas, R. (2017). The efficacy of phonics-based instruction of English as a second language in an Italian High School: A randomised controlled trial TT – La eficacia de la Instrucción Basada en Pronunciación en una Clase de Inglés como Segunda Lengua en una escuela secund. *GiST, 15*, 29. https://search.proquest.com/docview/2303718383?accountid=13042

Coltheart, M. (2005). Modeling reading: The dual route approach. In M. J. Snowling & C. E. Hulme (Eds.), *The Science of Reading: A Handbook* (pp. 6–23). Blackwell Publishing Ltd.

Cook, V., & Bassetti, B. (2005). An introduction to researching second language writing systems. In V. Cook & B. Bassetti (Eds.), *Second Language Writing Systems* (pp. 1–70). Multilingual Matters.

Department for Education (2010). The importance of teaching: The schools white paper 2010. https://assets.publishing.service.gov.uk/government/uploads/system/uploads/attachment_data/file/175429/CM-7980.pdf

Dixon, P., Schagen, I., & Seedhouse, P. (2011). The impact of an intervention on children's reading and spelling ability in low-income schools in India. *School Effectiveness and School Improvement, 22*(4), 461–482. https://doi.org/http://dx.doi.org/10.1080/09243453.2011.625125

Erler, L. (2003). *Reading in a Foreign Language – Near-Beginner Adolescents' Experiences of French in English Secondary Schools.* University of Oxford.

Erler, L., & Macaro, E. (2011). Decoding ability in French as a foreign language and language learning motivation. *Modern Language Journal, 95*(4), 496–518. https://doi.org/10.1111/j.1540-4781.2011.01238.x

Field, J. (2004). An insight into listeners' problems: Too much bottom-up or too much top-down? *System, 32*(3), 363–377. https://doi.org/10.1016/j.system.2004.05.002

244 Robert Woore

Field, J. (2008). Revising segmentation hypotheses in first and second language listening. *Systema*, 36(1), 35–51. https://doi.org/10.1016/j.system.2007.10.003

Figueredo, L. (2006). Using the known to chart the unknown: A review of first-language influence on the development of English-as-a-second-language spelling skill. *Reading and Writing*, 19(8), 873–905. https://doi.org/10.1007/s11145-006-9014-1

Frost, R., & Ziegler, J. C. (2012). Speech and spelling interaction: The interdependence of visual and auditory word recognition. In G. Gaskell (Ed.), *The Oxford Handbook of Psycholinguistics* (pp. 1–14). Oxford University Press. https://doi.org/10.1093/oxfordhb/9780198568971.013.0007

Gough, P. B., & Tunmer, W. E. (1986). Decoding, reading, and reading disability. *RASE*, 7(1), 6–10.

Grabe, W. & Stoller, F. L. (2011). *Teaching and Researching Reading*. Second Edition. Longman: Harlow.

Hamada, M., & Koda, K. (2008). Influence of first language orthographic experience on second language decoding and word learning. *Language Learning*, 58(1), 1–31. https://doi.org/10.1111/j.1467-9922.2007.00433.x

Hoover, W. A., & Gough, P. B. (1990). The simple view of reading. *Reading and Writing: An Interdisciplinary Journal*, 2, 127–160. https://doi.org/10.1145/504412.504413

Huo, S., & Wang, S. (2017). The effectiveness of phonological-based instruction in English as a foreign language students at primary school level: A research synthesis. *Frontiers in Education*, 2(May), 1–13. https://doi.org/10.3389/feduc.2017.00015

Katamba, F. (1989). *An Introduction to Phonology*. https://doi.org/10.1016/s0095-4470(19)30628-x

Koda, K. (1999). Development of L2 intraword orthographic sensitivity and decoding skills. *The Modern Language Journal*, 83(1), 51–64. https://www.jstor.org/stable/330406

Koda, K. (2005). Learning to read across writing systems. In V. Cook and B. Bassetti (Eds.), *Second Language Writing Systems* (pp. 311–334). De Gruyter.

Koda, K. (2007). Reading and language learning: Crosslinguistic constraints on second language reading development. *Language Learning*, 57(Suppl. 1), 1–44. https://doi.org/10.1111/0023-8333.101997010-i1

Li, S. (2012). Decoding ability and vocabulary acquisition in second language English- A study of Chinese advanced EFL learners. Unpublished MSc dissertation. University of Oxford.

Li, S. (2019). The effects of phonics instruction on L2 phonological decoding and vocabulary learning [University of Oxford (United Kingdom)]. In *PQDT – UK & Ireland*. https://search.proquest.com/docview/2307401128?accountid=13042

McCutchen, D. (1996). A capacity theory of writing : Working memory in composition. *Educational Psychology Review*, 8(3), 299–325.

Melby-Lervåg, M., & Lervåg, A. (2014). Reading comprehension and its underlying components in second-language learners: A meta-analysis of studies comparing first- and second-language learners. *Psychological Bulletin*, 140(2), 409–433. https://doi.org/10.1037/a0033890

Muljani, D., Koda, K. and Moates, D. R. (1998). The development of word recognition in a second language. *Applied Psycholinguistics*, 19(1), 99–113. https://doi.org/10.1017/S0142716400010602

Nassaji, H. (2014). The role and importance of lower-level processes in second language reading. *Language Teaching*, 47(1), 1–37. https://doi.org/10.1017/S0261444813000396

Teaching phonics in a second language   245

National Institute of Child Health and Human Development (NICHD). (2000). Report of the National Reading Panel. Teaching children to read: An evidence-based assessment of the scientific research literature on reading and its implications for reading instruction: Reports of the subgroups (NIH Publication No. 00-4754). Washington, DC: U.S. Government Printing Office. https://www.nichd.nih.gov/sites/default/files/publications/pubs/nrp/Documents/report.pdf

Odlin, T. (1989). *Language Transfer: Cross-linguistic Influence in Language Learning.* Cambridge University Press.

Pearson, P. D. (2004). The reading wars. *Educational Policy, 18*(1), 216–252. https://doi.org/10.1177/0895904803260041

Purewal, S. (2008). *Synthetic phonics and the literacy development of second language young learners. A literature review of literacy ideologies, policies, and research.* Unpublished Master's Dissertation, University of Leeds. https://esoluk.co.uk/beginners/docs/synthetic-phonics.pdf

Rose, H., & Galloway, N. (2019). *Global Englishes for Language Teaching.* Cambridge University Press.

Rose, J. (2006). Independent review of the teaching of early reading final report. In *Department for Education and Skills* (Issue March). www.standards.dcsf.gov.uk/phonics/report.pdf

Rowe, K. (2005). *Teaching reading: Report and recommendations. National Inquiry into the Teaching of Literacy.* Australian Government, Department of Education, Science and Training. https://research.acer.edu.au/cgi/viewcontent.cgi?article=1004&context=tll_misc

Seymour, P. H. K., Aro, M., Erskine, J. M., Wimmer, H., Leybaert, J., Elbro, C., Lyytinen, H., Gombert, J. E., Le Normand, M. T., Schneider, W., Porpodas, C., Ragnarsdottir, H., Tressoldi, P., Vio, C., De Groot, A., Licht, R., Iønnessen, F. E., Castro, S. L., Cary, L., … Olofsson, Å. (2003). Foundation literacy acquisition in European orthographies. *British Journal of Psychology, 94*(2), 143–174. https://doi.org/10.1348/000712603321661859

Shanahan, T. (2005). The National Reading Panel report. Practical advice for teachers. *Learning Point Associates/North Central Regional, 1,* 41–47. http://eric.ed.gov/ERICWebPortal/recordDetail?accno=ED489535

Shanks, D. (2019). National Centre for Excellence for Language Pedagogy (NCELP). https://resources.ncelp.org/concern/parent/6q182k142/file_sets/8g84mm259

Share, D. L. (2008). On the Anglocentricities *Spoken homework* of current reading research and practice: The perils of overreliance on an 'outlier' orthography. *Psychological Bulletin, 134*(4), 584–615. https://doi.org/10.1037/0033-2909.134.4.584

Sparks, R. L. (2015). Language deficits in poor L2 comprehenders: The simple view. *Foreign Language Annals, 48*(4), 635–658. https://doi.org/10.1111/flan.12163

Standards and Testing Agency (2019). Key stage 1 phonics screening check: Pupils' materials. Retrieved from www.gov.uk/government/publications/phonics-screening-check-2019-materials, 18.02.2021.

Stanovich, K. E. (1980). Toward an interactive-compensatory model of individual differences in the development of reading fluency. *Reading Research Quarterly, 16*(1), 32. https://doi.org/10.2307/747348

Sturm, J. L. (2013). Explicit phonetics instruction in L2 French: A global analysis of improvement. *System, 41*(3), 654-662. https://doi.org/10.1016/j.system.2013.07.015

Torgerson, C. J., Brooks, G., & Hall, J. (2006). *A Systematic Review of the Research Literature on the Use of Phonics in the Teaching of Reading and Spelling.* Nottingham: DfES Publications.

246 Robert Woore

Wang, M. and Koda, K. (2005). Commonalities and differences in word identification skills among learners of English as a second language. *Language Learning*, 55(1), 71–98. https://ezproxy-prd.bodleian.ox.ac.uk:2102/10.1111/j.0023-8333.2005.00290.x

Weiner, B. (1986). *An Attributional Theory of Motivation and Emotion*. Springer-Verlag.

Woodcock, R. W. (2011). *Woodcock Reading Mastery Tests: WRMT-III*. Pearson.

Woore, R. (2009). Beginners' progress in decoding L2 French: Some longitudinal evidence from English modern foreign languages classrooms. *Language Learning Journal*, 37(1), 3–18. https://doi.org/10.1080/09571730902717398

Woore, R. (2010). Thinking aloud about L2 decoding: An exploration of the strategies used by beginner learners when pronouncing unfamiliar French words. *Language Learning Journal*, 38(1), 3–17. https://doi.org/10.1080/09571730903545210

Woore, R. (2011). *Investigating and Developing Beginner Learners' Decoding Proficiency in Second Language French: An Evaluation of Two Programmes of Instruction*. University of Oxford. https://search.proquest.com/docview/1798407755?accountid=13042

Woore, R. (2014). Beginner learners' progress in decoding L2 French: Transfer effects in typologically similar L1-L2 writing systems. *Writing Systems Research*, 6(2), 167–189. https://doi.org/10.1080/17586801.2013.838536

Woore, R. (2018). Learners' pronunciations of familiar and unfamiliar French words: What can they tell us about phonological decoding in an L2? *Language Learning Journal*, 46(4), 456–469. https://doi.org/10.1080/09571736.2016.1161062

Woore, R., Graham, S., Porter, A., Courtney, L., & Savory, C. (2018). *Foreign language education: Unlocking reading (FLEUR)-A study into the teaching of reading to beginner learners of French in secondary school*. https://ora.ox.ac.uk/objects/uuid:4b0cb239-72f0-49e4-8f32-3672625884f0

Wyse, D., & Styles, M. (2007). Synthetic phonics and the teaching of reading: The debate surrounding England's 'Rose Report'. *Literacy*, 41(1), 35–42. https://doi.org/10.1111/j.1467-9345.2007.00455.x

Ziegler, J. C., & Goswami, U. (2005). Reading acquisition, developmental dyslexia, and skilled reading across languages: A psycholinguistic grain size theory. *Psychological Bulletin*, 131(1), 3–29. https://doi.org/10.1037/0033-2909.131.1.3

13 What kind of pronunciation learning should teachers expect of their learners?

Sara Kennedy and Pavel Trofimovich

Introduction

When it comes to second language (L2) pronunciation, both L2 teachers and learners might find it easy to set out an ultimate goal of instruction: to sound like a native speaker. It is important, though, to ask ourselves some questions about this goal: Generally, is it a good idea? How feasible is this goal for learners to attain? How necessary is this goal to teachers' and learners' purposes for L2 instruction? Are there other objectives for L2 pronunciation learning – ones which might be crucial for learners in specific contexts and also more attainable by learners? In this chapter, we present two general approaches for setting instructional goals for L2 pronunciation: nativeness and intelligibility (Levis, 2005, 2020). In the words of Levis, "[t]he nativeness principle holds that it is both possible and desirable to achieve native-like pronunciation in a foreign language", while the intelligibility principle "holds that learners simply need to be understandable" (2005, p. 370).

Derwing and Munro (1997) and Munro and Derwing (1995) explored the notion of being understandable and found that, for listeners, L2 speakers' pronunciation could be differentiated into three aspects: intelligibility (measures of listeners' actual understanding), comprehensibility (listeners' judgements of how easy or difficult L2 speech is to understand) and accentedness, which has most recently been defined as "[p]erceived differences in pronunciation as compared with a local [language] variety" (Derwing & Munro, 2015). L2 pronunciation teaching which emphasizes lack of accentedness, or nativelike pronunciation, as its goal is associated with the nativeness principle, while teaching, which emphasizes intelligibility and/or comprehensibility is associated with the intelligibility principle.

Before discussing possible goals of instruction, we first review research findings about some of the variables that influence L2 pronunciation learning and about the success (or lack of success) by learners in L2 pronunciation development. After summarizing the evidence for the adoption of the intelligibility principle, we lay out general expectations for L2 pronunciation learning based on the research evidence presented. These expectations have implications for the ways that teachers design and implement their teaching and learning activities.

DOI: 10.4324/9781003008361-16

248 *Sara Kennedy and Pavel Trofimovich*

Variables Influencing L2 pronunciation learning

As with any complex skill, the learning of L2 pronunciation can be influenced by many different variables. These variables include those which are more individual (cognitive and affective) and those which are more related to the context for L2 learning and use (e.g., nature of L2 input; community perceptions of L2 learners).

Age

One common finding about L2 pronunciation learning is that learners who speak a first language (L1) different from the language of their schooling and who start school as children (not as adolescents or adults) tend to learn what seems to listeners to be nativelike L2 pronunciation (e.g., Abrahamsson & Hyltenstam, 2009; Bongaerts et al., 1997; Tahta et al., 1981), whereas the pronunciation of the children's parents tends to retain influence from their L1, even if parents have had extensive exposure to the L2. This type of situation is typical of migrants to a country or jurisdiction, where these migrants speak an L1 that is different from the official or school language. Generally speaking, the older an L2 learner is when arriving in an L2-rich environment, the stronger the L1 influence on the learner's L2 pronunciation (Flege et al., 1999). Some L2 learners who arrive as children may eventually speak the L2 with nativelike pronunciation (Winitz et al., 1995), but even children who arrive in an L2 environment at a young age (6–9 years old) may retain some L1 influence in their L2 pronunciation as adults, particularly if they continue to regularly use their L1 into adulthood (Flege et al., 2006; Piske et al., 2002).

Other children live in environments where L2 exposure is infrequent, apart from limited L2 instruction. These environments are often referred to as foreign language (FL) learning contexts because they contrast with contexts where the target (second) language is widely spoken in the community. Findings on different starting ages for children receiving FL instruction are mixed. In Lecumberri and Gallardo (2003), Spanish children who started FL English instruction at age 11 were rated less accented in English than children who started FL English instruction at the age of 4 or 8, suggesting that there was an advantage for those who started learning the language later. This finding implies that older children might be cognitively more ready to acquire L2 pronunciation compared to younger children (e.g., Fullana, 2006). Alternatively, in an eight-year study on Croatian children learning one of four different FLs, children who began FL instruction at 6–7 years of age were significantly better at L2 pronunciation than children who began FL instruction at age 10–11, but the researchers noted that this difference depended on "the quality of exposure, which in the FL context is dependent on the quality of teaching" (Nikolov & Mihaljević Djigunović, 2006, p. 247). The early learners in this study received FL instruction which, from Grades 1–4, was more intensive (more instructional hours) than typical FL instruction, with only 10–15 learners per class (Mihaljević Djigunović, 2015). Clearly, L2 learners' cognitive capacity as well as instructional and input factors (in terms of the nature and intensity of language instruction) might determine how strongly age influences L2 pronunciation learning for learners in FL contexts.

Cross-language perceptual similarity

Another variable which can influence an L2 speaker's pronunciation learning is the speaker's ability to perceive how the pronunciation of the L2 is similar to or different from the pronunciation of their L1. For example, when L1 Japanese learners of English were asked to listen to the English/l/sound (as in *led*) and to choose the Japanese sounds most similar to it, they associated English/l/with Japanese/ɾ/ (a "tapped r" sound) (Guion et al., 2000). What is more striking, however, is that this type of L2–L1 perceptual mapping, whereby English/l/ was identified as an excellent example of a similar, "competing" L1 sound, predicted Japanese learners' difficulty in discriminating between the two English sounds/ɹ/and/l/ (as in *red* vs. *led*). If L2 speakers cannot accurately perceive when (and how) an L2 sound is different from a similar, competing sound in their L1, they will have difficulty perceiving (and very likely producing) differences between that L2 sound and other, similar L2 sounds, leading to persistent L1-influenced accent in their speech. This difficulty has been found to increase with the age of learning, such that L2 learners who are children are better than adults at identifying sounds that are different between their L1 and L2 and at differentiating between related L2 sounds (Baker et al., 2008). This perceptual difficulty, whereby learners struggle to differentiate L2 sounds from competing L1 sounds, highlights the importance of "noticing" – which, in the context of L2 instruction, can take the form of teachers explicitly drawing learners' attention to specific perceptual or acoustic features of L2 sounds that clearly distinguish them from similar sounds in both the learners' L1 and their L2.

Motivation

Motivation is a construct that is many-faceted and dynamic, and it is only recently that researchers have started to rigorously explore how L2 learners' motivation, their will, and effort to reach their goals might be related to their L2 pronunciation learning. Nagle (2018), who treated motivation as dynamic, measured the motivation of adult low-proficiency L2 Spanish learners multiple times over a year of university Spanish courses and related these measures to listener-assessed accentedness and comprehensibility for the same learners. Generally, learners' motivation decreased slightly over the year, though individual learners varied in their pattern of increase and decrease; Nagle explained this in terms of learners' processes in "allocat[ing their] motivational resources as efficiently as possible" (p. 211) towards different pronunciation learning goals such as travelling in Spanish-speaking countries. Over the course of the year, learners whose effort increased consistently showed less accented pronunciation over time, while learners whose effort remained the same or decreased showed

250   Sara Kennedy and Pavel Trofimovich

flat trajectories for accentedness ratings. No relationship was found between comprehensibility ratings and motivation measures, which may be explained by the possible positive effects of the communicative instruction on learners' comprehensibility. Put differently, changes in learners' comprehensibility were likely driven by instruction and, compared to changes in accentedness, depended less on dynamic variation in individual learners' motivation. Nagle also notes that motivation interacts with other variables such as identity (including ethnic identity) and learner autonomy, which will be discussed next.

Ethnic identity

One way to define ethnic identity is through reference to a person's subjective experience of being part of an ethnic group (Ashmore et al., 2004). The link between ethnic identity and L2 pronunciation is related to an L2 learner's feelings about his or her own (ancestral) ethnic group and about the community of speakers which claims the L2 as their group's language. For example, in Gatbonton et al. (2005), L1 French university students studying English at a university in majority French-language Quebec, located within majority English-speaking Canada, completed a questionnaire exploring their affiliation to their ethnic group. They then listened to samples of L2 English recorded by L1 French speakers and rated those speakers for accentedness, for the speakers' presumed affiliation to their ethnic group, and for the listeners' own desire to collaborate with the speakers in hypothetical scenarios such as working on a community project. When listeners rated the speakers as having low levels of L1 French accent in English, those same speakers were also rated with low affiliation to their ethnic groups. This implies that the strength of the speakers' accents was linked to the degree to which they were judged as representative members of their ethnic group. In addition, listeners who reported high levels of affiliation to their ethnic group were less likely to accept, as a representative of their project group, a fellow francophone who sounded least accented in L2 English (i.e., who sounded least "French"). Thus, speaking non-accented L2 English may have been seen as showing less loyalty to francophones, prompting at least some listeners to choose a speaker who sounded more accented in L2 English and who was thus likely considered to be more loyal. Clearly, L2 pronunciation learning is not value-neutral for L2 learners, and issues of pronunciation, belonging, identity and group membership are tightly intertwined, leading not only to accent-based judgments (e.g., with some speakers considered more loyal members of a particular ethnic group than others) but also to accent-driven behaviours (e.g., listeners choosing who to work with based on the speaker's L2 accent).

Autonomy in learning

Just as L2 learners have their own feelings about being (or not being part) of a particular group, L2 learners can choose to act autonomously, without guidance from teachers, to deepen their pronunciation learning. Pronunciation learning strategies are a subset of learning strategies, defined by Oxford (1990) as "specific actions taken by the learner to make learning easier, faster, more enjoyable, more self-directed, more effective, and more transferable to new situations" (p. 8). The pronunciation learning strategies reported by L2 learners have been categorized in different ways, such as metacognitive (e.g., seeing opportunities to practice), cognitive (e.g., rehearsing), affective (e.g., consciously relaxing when stressed), or social (e.g., practising with others) (Pawlak, 2010). Few researchers have explored the links between the use of pronunciation learning strategies and L2 pronunciation learning. However, Sardegna (2011) found that after university-level L2 learners were trained on pronunciation learning strategies in a pronunciation course over one semester, the learners were noticeably more accurate in reading aloud texts containing the pronunciation features targeted in the course, even months after the course had ended. In this case, the L2 learners had likely learned how to be autonomous in learning.

Amount of experience

As demonstrated above in research on age, in FL environments, starting L2 instruction earlier for young learners (resulting in a longer period of instruction) does not always result in more nativelike pronunciation compared to young learners who started instruction a few years later (Lecumberri & Gallardo, 2003). Similarly, for adult L2 speakers who live in an environment where the L2 is the main language, or one of the main languages, used in public life, their length of residence in that environment (which is often considered a proxy for the amount of experience) is not always related to the degree to which their L2 pronunciation is nativelike (Aoyama et al., 2008; Flege et al., 2006). For just-arrived adult L2 speakers, their level of L2 accentedness may lessen over their first six months of residence (Munro & Derwing, 2008). However, long-time residents do not demonstrate such a straightforward relationship between the length of residence and L2 pronunciation. Simply put, L2 speakers with relatively more experience of L2 instruction, or who are in an L2 environment, do not always acquire pronunciation which is relatively more nativelike (Aoyama et al., 2008).

Nature of instruction

One clear and consistent finding from meta-analyses and reviews of research on L2 pronunciation instruction is that, overall, L2 learners who receive pronunciation instruction improve in their pronunciation, whether the instruction targets individual sounds or suprasegmental features such as rhythm, stress and intonation (Lee et al., 2015; Thomson & Derwing, 2015). Generally, both instruction which focusses on communication and freer L2 use, and instruction which focusses on specific, formal elements of pronunciation (e.g., word stress) can lead to improved pronunciation. The nature of the improvement depends on the measures used to assess improvement. In the most recent meta-analysis of L2 pronunciation instruction, Saito and Plonsky (2019) found that improved pronunciation was found for controlled production tasks which measure specific elements of L2 pronunciation (such as individual sounds or rhythm, stress, or intonation), but not for tasks where L2 learners speak spontaneously and where speech is assessed through global ratings such as accentedness or listeners' own ease of understanding the L2 speech (comprehensibility).

The above finding does not mean that pronunciation instruction is ineffective for global measures of L2 pronunciation. What this finding suggests is that the meta-analyses and reviews drew on instructional studies which predominantly used measures focussing on specific elements of L2 pronunciation, not global measures. Saito and Plonsky (2019) note that when L2 learners start learning specific aspects of L2 pronunciation, they tend to produce more nativelike pronunciation in tasks which are more controlled and restricted than in tasks which require spontaneous speech. It may be that more studies on L2 pronunciation instruction need to include speaking tasks which elicit freer speech. More studies also need to focus on young L2 learners' pronunciation, as the participants in many published studies are adults (Thomson & Derwing, 2015).

There are a few published studies on the effects of FL pronunciation instruction for children. However, as we saw above, in Nikolov and Mihaljević Djigunović's (2006) large-scale Croatian study, the difference in L2 pronunciation results for young learners starting at different ages depended on L2 instruction being more intensive than usual, as well as on the teachers being given the freedom to engage in teaching which focussed both on students' needs and on their own style and intuitions (Mihaljević Djigunović, 2015). Lecumberri and Gallardo (2003) suggested that their early starting young learners in Spain did not develop more nativelike L2 pronunciation than their later-starting young learners because, even after years of FL instruction, the overall L2 exposure was still limited, and the non-native teachers for all young learners used L2 pronunciation which had noticeable L1 influence.

These findings are general ones and not about the nature of specific instructional approaches in specific teaching and learning contexts. This is because few research studies have explored instruction based on a coherent set of principles about how L2 speakers learn pronunciation. Among several notable exceptions are studies drawing on form-focussed instruction, which use techniques such as input enhancement to draw learners' attention to pronunciation features while learners are communicating meaningfully. Saito and Lyster (2012) and Saito (2013), for instance, showed that L2 learners of English who received form-focussed instruction and corrective feedback significantly improved their pronunciation of specific L2 sounds.

Instruction in contexts of increased L2 exposure

A number of educational programmes have been designed to increase the amount of L2 exposure in FL instruction. One popular approach, which in Europe is generally termed Content and Language Integrated Learning (CLIL), combines the study of academic subject matter with the use of the L2. Results for CLIL

Kinds of pronunciation learning of learners   253

students with respect to L2 pronunciation have been mixed. In a number of studies in Spain, comparisons between teenage students in CLIL programmes and in regular FL programmes found that CLIL students did not differ from regular students in the accentedness ratings they received, but CLIL students improved significantly in comprehensibility (Gallardo et al., 2009; Rallo Fabra & Juan-Garau, 2010) or in speech fluency (Gallardo & Lacabex, 2013).

Another approach to increasing L2 exposure used most often with post-secondary students, is study-abroad programs. Students spend a period ranging from several weeks to a year living and studying in a country or region where the L2 is a language used in daily and institutional life. Findings for these programmes are again mixed in terms of their effects on pronunciation. Students may improve in specific aspects of L2 pronunciation even after a short six-week stay (Nagle et al., 2016), but students generally did not develop more nativelike pronunciation (Martinsen et al., 2010), except for those who spent two years in an L2 environment for a service learning programme (Martinsen et al., 2014). Clearly, L2 instruction which massively increases L2 exposure, either by teaching subject matter in the L2 and/or by moving the student into an L2-rich environment, does not necessarily lead to a general improvement in pronunciation, particularly in the case of accent.

Quantity and quality of L2 use

As Moyer (2014) notes, abundant exposure to and use of the L2 outside of instructional settings is a common theme for what she called exceptional adult learners, those who have begun learning an L2 after the age of 10, yet whose pronunciation is rated nativelike by native speakers of the L2. This exposure and use include a conscious effort by these L2 learners to avoid using their more dominant languages, even in home environments, and consistent attempts to meet and communicate with native speakers of the L2, even in unfamiliar settings.

Even for L2 speakers who are not rated nativelike in their pronunciation (and notwithstanding the points above about the limitations of CLIL and study abroad contexts), the influence of L2 exposure and use is well established. For adult L2 speakers coming to an L2-rich environment as immigrants or as post-secondary students, those speakers who report more exposure to, or use of, the L2 outside of instructional settings are typically rated easier to understand or more nativelike than speakers who report comparatively less L2 exposure and use (Derwing & Munro, 2013; Moyer, 2011). Research on the influence of L2 exposure and use on pronunciation is set primarily in environments where the L2 is used in daily and institutional life. In FL or heritage language environments, where opportunities for L2 exposure and use are less frequent, the relationship between these variables and L2 speakers' pronunciation is less well established. However, in several studies, children who had only overheard the target language used around them (e.g., in conversations between adults), or who had extensively listened to L2 speech in instructional settings, were judged to have more nativelike pronunciation than L2 adult learners or children who had received more traditional instruction with speaking practice (Au et al., 2008; Trofimovich et al., 2009).

254 *Sara Kennedy and Pavel Trofimovich*

One area increasingly being explored in FL environments is the use of social media. The use of Twitter to provide out-of-class pronunciation information and models for challenging words has been successful in improving university students' pronunciation of those words in Spain (Fouz-González, 2017), in Turkey, along with the use of Youglish[1] for modelling language use in context (Kartal & Korucu-Kis, 2020), and in Iran, where adult learners' pronunciation of specific words also improved after Telegram[2] was used to provide models and additional instructional input (Xodabande, 2017). The use of mobile applications and social media to increase FL learners' L2 exposure and use continues to be a quickly growing area for researchers, teachers and learners to explore.

Setting instructional goals for L2 pronunciation

As discussed previously, many variables besides instruction can influence L2 pronunciation development. In addition, there is no single pedagogical approach which has been shown to be generally effective for L2 pronunciation development. Therefore, in this section, we outline and critically evaluate potential pronunciation models and pedagogical norms (i.e., pronunciation forms identified as learning targets) which teachers and learners may adopt, depending on their contexts of language teaching, learning and use.

Generally speaking, there are two approaches for setting instructional goals for L2 pronunciation: the nativeness principle and the intelligibility principle. The nativeness principle sets nativelike L2 pronunciation as an attainable and appropriate learning objective, while the basic tenet of the intelligibility principle is that while L2 learners need to be understandable, nativelike pronunciation is not necessary (Levis, 2005, 2020). From the research findings set out previously, it is clear that very few people who start learning an L2 after adolescence ever attain a nativelike accent in the L2, and even some children who arrive and stay in an L2-rich environment may retain some L1 influence in their L2 pronunciation. Therefore, it is not reasonable for L2 teachers or learners to expect that learners can develop nativelike pronunciation in the L2 as a result of instruction. If nativelike L2 pronunciation is set as the main pedagogical goal for L2 pronunciation learning, the great majority of learners will never attain the goal, which would seem to be a negative outcome.

We, therefore, advocate the adoption of the intelligibility principle. This does not mean that teachers and learners must go no further than the absolute minimum state of L2 pronunciation necessary for listeners' basic understanding. We agree with Derwing and Munro (2015) that teachers and learners should aim for L2 learners to use pronunciation which is "comfortably intelligible" (p. 389) and can be understood by a range of proficient listeners, an approach similar to that described in Jenkins's (2000) work on the pronunciation of English as a lingua franca.

However, as noted in Tokumoto and Shibata (2011), among others, some L2 students would prefer to work towards nativelike pronunciation rather than accepting L1-influenced pronunciation as appropriate and even desirable.

Kinds of pronunciation learning of learners   255

Tokumoto and Shibata recommend that in Japan, Japanese pre-service teachers should complete courses which examine the diversity of different language varieties, including non-native varieties. In this way, the authors suggest, teachers might develop positive attitudes towards L1-influenced L2 use and convey these attitudes to their students.

Depending on the L2 which is being learned, some teachers and learners may have access mainly or solely to materials which are based on a native variety of the L2. This variety can be considered a pronunciation model – understood broadly as an overall set of reference points for pronunciation in the L2. However, this model *does not need to be* the direct source for pedagogical norms for teachers and L2 learners but can be used because of its consistency or utility for providing reference points for teachers and learners. For example, in a model of North American English, verbs like *to suspect* may be pronounced with an initial schwa sound in the first unstressed syllable of the verb (/sə.ˈspɛkt/). However, teachers may decide that an acceptable pedagogical norm may be for learners to produce primary stress on the appropriate (second) syllable, but the unstressed first syllable may be produced with an unreduced vowel (/sʌ.ˈspɛkt/).

Murphy (2014) took a more expansive approach to pronunciation models, exploring the possibility of using samples of comprehensible L2 speech, regardless of whether the speech was L1-influenced. Using multiple models which include speakers of different target language varieties (e.g., Australian English, Hong Kong English) as well as non-native speakers of the target language might provide learners with realistic targets for L2 pronunciation learning and might show that teachers (and fellow learners) with L1-influenced accents can be legitimate and respected pronunciation models.

The pedagogical norms for a given context for L2 pronunciation instruction might be determined by a state educational authority, by the administrators of an institution, by teachers, or through negotiation between teachers and learners. Decisions about pedagogical norms can depend on many elements: learners' age and the purpose of instruction, the expectations and importance of any standardized assessments, the (in)flexibility of curricula and syllabi, the expertise and experience of teachers, the relative similarity or dissimilarity between the L2 and learners' L1(s), the motivation and wishes of learners. All of these will differ across different L2s and learning contexts, with the important consequence that there is no one set of pedagogical norms which will apply to all L2 pronunciation learning. However, drawing on the evidence covered earlier in this chapter, there are several expectations about L2 pronunciation learning that can be fairly confidently held by teachers, and these expectations have implications for the way teachers design or implement teaching and learning activities. The expectations are the following:

1 Very few people who start learning an L2 after adolescence attain native-like pronunciation in the L2. *Most L2 learners will speak an L2 with a non-native accent!* Learners can develop L2 pronunciation which is comprehensible, even with a noticeable non-native accent.

2 *Learners can only learn elements of L2 pronunciation which they notice.* This noticing can happen through explicit, form-focussed instruction, which refers to instruction where teachers pre-plan how to draw learners' attention to specific elements during a communicative activity. Examples of pre-planned noticing activities include input enhancement and priming by an interlocutor (e.g., Trofimovich et al., 2014).

3 Even after noticing specific elements of L2 pronunciation, learners need extensive practice in using these elements appropriately. It is very optimistic to think that most learners will acquire specific elements of L2 pronunciation only through periodic corrective feedback (e.g., Martin, 2020; Saito, 2013). *If they do not have extensive practice, whether inside the classroom or outside it, learners are unlikely to show or maintain changes to their pronunciation* (e.g., Derwing & Munro, 2013). Learners who find or who are provided with additional opportunities for L2 exposure or use tend to develop comparatively more comprehensible or less accented L2 pronunciation than learners who do not take such opportunities (e.g., Foote & McDonough, 2017; Moyer, 2011). Teachers can immediately increase learners' exposure and use of L2 pronunciation by integrating a focus on pronunciation into other teaching activities (Darcy, 2018).

4 *Learners' L2 pronunciation is influenced not only by instruction or by L2 exposure or use but also by learners' own beliefs and cognitions.* Their levels of motivation will vary (e.g., Nagle, 2018), and their reactions may be linked to the social and political context for L2 learning and use (e.g., Gatbonton et al., 2005; Trofimovich & Turuševa, 2020).

5 *Differences or similarities between the L2 and a learner's L1 or dominant language(s) will partially affect the learning challenges for that learner.* Some elements of L2 pronunciation may remain problematic even after intense effort or instruction (Takagi, 2002; Wiener et al., 2020).

The expectations listed above have implications for the way teachers and educational administrators should think about designing and implementing instructional activities and assessing learners. Some possible implications follow:

1 Except in very specific circumstances, such as L2 instruction for diplomats or academic phonetics courses for particular language varieties, it is not realistic or reasonable for teachers to set a pedagogical norm of nativelike pronunciation for L2 learners.

2 Teachers should not expect L2 learners to "just pick up" L2 pronunciation in class. A focus on particular elements of pronunciation should be planned and implemented through the design of activities or explicit instruction, ideally in a communicative framework (Darcy, 2018). This means a focus on form during communicative activities so that learners can notice the particular elements in focus.

3 Long-term L2 pronunciation learning requires repetition or recycling of activities and opportunities to use L2 pronunciation, again ideally in a communicative context. This is particularly important because pronunciation is often

taught with a focus on isolated forms (such as individual sounds or pronunciations of specific words), which does not help L2 learners integrate and transfer what they have learned into their subsequent spontaneous production. Teachers who design lessons or draw attention to opportunities which help learners to use and re-use L2 pronunciation will boost the effects of the initial instruction.

4 Teachers cannot compel learners to develop more comprehensible L2 pronunciation, especially if some learners' beliefs and goals do not include L2 pronunciation learning as a priority. However, teachers can ask learners about their own beliefs and goals and try to teach and advise in ways that respect learners' personhood and autonomy while presenting opportunities for learners to better manage their own pronunciation learning.

5 Teachers who are non-native speakers themselves could serve as excellent role models for those learners who are sceptical or apprehensive about adopting a non-native pronunciation model as their learning goal. Teachers often already know about challenging aspects of L2 pronunciation learning for learners of different L1s, especially if teachers have themselves learned the L2 as an additional language (see, for example, Gordon, 2020). Learners would benefit from particular attention and encouragement from teachers in addressing these challenges.

Conclusion

In this chapter, we have not provided a set of directives or guidelines for teachers to use when teaching L2 pronunciation. Instead, we have made a case, using empirical support, for adopting comfortable intelligibility (L2 speech which can be understood by a range of proficient listeners) as a pedagogical norm, and we have set out general expectations for L2 pronunciation learning, as well as pedagogical implications for activity design, teaching and assessment. Teachers have a great deal of knowledge about their own teaching and learning context and the characteristics of their learners. We hope these expectations and implications can serve to enhance language teaching and learning in teachers' own contexts.

Relating the issues raised in this chapter to your own context:

1 In your own second language education context, what are the advantages and disadvantages to adopting a pedagogical goal of intelligibility for learning L2 pronunciation? What are the implications for teachers, learners, education administrators and other stakeholders?

2 Here are some traditional ways that teachers help learners notice and practice different aspects of L2 pronunciation: teachers give explicit instruction to learners (e.g., tell learners how an L2 vowel sound is different from L1 vowel sounds), and have learners practice that aspect of pronunciation while receiving feedback from the teacher (e.g., learners repeat the L2 vowel sound in a limited set of word or phrases while the teacher gives corrective feedback). What additional techniques could you use in your educational context help learners to notice and practice L2 pronunciation?

Notes

1 YouGlish (https://youglish.com) is a website that indexes extracts of authentic videos from YouTube where specific words, names, or phrases are used. More than 15 languages are supported.
2 Telegram (https://telegram.org) is a popular online messaging application.

References

Abrahamsson, N., & Hyltenstam, K. (2009). Age of onset and nativelikeness in a second language: Listener perception versus linguistic scrutiny. *Language Learning, 59*, 249–306. https://doi.org/10.1111/j.1467-9922.2009.00507

Aoyama, K., Guion, S. G., Flege, J. E., Yamada, T., & Akahane-Yamada, R. (2008). The first years in an L2-speaking environment: A comparison of Japanese children and adults learning American English. *International Review of Applied Linguistics in Language Teaching, 46*, 61–90. https://doi.org/10.1515/IRAL.2008.003

Ashmore, R. D., Deaux, K., & McLaughlin-Volpe, T. (2004). An organizing framework for collective identity: Articulation and significance of multidimensionality. *Psychological Bulletin, 130*, 80–114. https://doi.org/10.1037/0033-2909.130.1.80

Au, T. K. F., Oh, J. S., Knightly, L. M., Jun, S. A., & Romo, L. F. (2008). Salvaging a childhood language. *Journal of Memory and Language, 58*, 998–1011. https://doi.org/10.1016/j.jml.2007.11.001

Baker, W., Trofimovich, P., Flege, J. E., Mack, M., & Halter, R. (2008). Child-adult differences in second-language phonological learning: The role of cross-language similarity. *Language and Speech, 51*, 317–342. https://doi.org/10.1177/0023830908099068

Bongaerts, T., van Summeren, C., Planken, B., & Schils, E. (1997). Age and ultimate attainment in the pronunciation of a foreign language. *Studies in Second Language Acquisition, 19*, 447–465. https://doi.org/10.1017/S0272263197004026

Darcy, I. (2018). Powerful and effective pronunciation instruction: How can we achieve it? *The CATESOL Journal, 30*, 13–45.

Derwing, T. M., & Munro, M. J. (1997). Accent, comprehensibility and intelligibility: Evidence from four L1s. *Studies in Second Language Acquisition, 19*, 1–16. https://doi.org/10.1017/S0272263197001010

Derwing, T. M., & Munro, M. J. (2013). The development of L2 oral language skills in two L1 groups: A 7-year study. *Language Learning, 63*, 163–185. https://doi.org/10.1111/lang.12000

Derwing, T. M., & Munro, M. J. (2015). *Pronunciation fundamentals. Evidence-based perspectives for second language teaching and research.* John Benjamins.

Flege, J. E., Birdsong, D., Bialystok, E., Mack, M., Sung, H., & Tsukada, K. (2006). Degree of foreign accent in English sentences produced by Korean children and adults. *Journal of Phonetics, 34*, 153–175. https://doi.org/10.1016/j.wocn.2005.05.001

Flege, J. E., Yeni-Komshian, G. H., & Liu, S. (1999). Age constraints on second-language acquisition. *Journal of Memory and Language, 41*, 78–104. https://doi.org/10.1006/jmla.1999.2638

Foote, J. A., & McDonough, K. (2017). Using shadowing with mobile technology to improve L2 pronunciation. *Journal of Second Language Pronunciation, 3*, 34–56. https://doi.org/10.1075/jslp.3.1.02foo

Fouz-González, J. (2017). Pronunciation instruction through Twitter: The case of commonly mispronounced words. *Computer Assisted Language Learning, 30*, 631–663. https://doi.org/10.1080/09588221.2017.1340309

Kinds of pronunciation learning of learners   259

Fullana, N. (2006). The development of English (FL) perception and production skills: Starting age and exposure effects. In C. Muñoz (Ed.), *Age and the rate of foreign language learning* (pp. 41–64). Multilingual Matters.

Gallardo, F., & Lacabex, E. G. (2013). The impact of additional CLIL exposure on oral English production. *Journal of English Studies*, 11, 113–131.

Gallardo, F., Lacabex, E. G., & Lecumberri, M. L. G. (2009).Testing the effectiveness of content and language integrated learning (CLIL) in foreign language contexts: The assessment of English pronunciation. In Y. R. de Zarobe & R. M. J. Catalan (Eds.), *Content and language integrated learning: Evidence from research in Europe* (pp. 63–80). Multilingual Matters.

Gatbonton, E., Trofimovich, P., & Magid, M. (2005). Learners' ethnic group affiliation and L2 pronunciation accuracy: A sociolinguistic investigation. *TESOL Quarterly*, 39, 489–511. https://doi.org/10.2307/3588491

Gordon, J. (2020). Implementing explicit pronunciation instruction: The case of a nonnative English-speaking teacher. *Language Teaching Research*. Published online 20 August 2020. https://doi.org/10.1177/1362168820941991

Guion, S. G., Flege, J. E., Akahane-Yamada, R., & Pruitt, J. C. (2000). An investigation of current models of second language speech perception: The case of Japanese adults' perception of English consonants. *The Journal of the Acoustical Society of America*, 107, 2711–2724. https://doi.org/10.1121/1.428657

Jenkins, J. (2000). *The phonology of English as an international language*. Oxford University Press.

Kartal, G., & Korucu-Kis, S. (2020). The use of Twitter and Youglish for the learning and retention of commonly mispronounced English words. *Education and Information Technologies*, 25, 193–221. https://doi.org/10.1007/s10639-019-09970-8

Lecumberri, M. L. G., & Gallardo, F. (2003). English FL sounds in school learners of different ages. In M. D. P. G. Mayo & M. L. G. Lecumberri (Eds.), *Age and the acquisition of English as a foreign language* (pp. 115–135). Multilingual Matters.

Lee, J., Jang, J., & Plonsky, L. (2015). The effectiveness of second language pronunciation instruction: A meta-analysis. *Applied Linguistics*, 36, 345–366. https://doi.org/10.1093/applin/amu040

Levis, J. M. (2005). Changing contexts and shifting paradigms in pronunciation teaching. *TESOL Quarterly*, 39, 369–377. https://doi.org/10.2307/3588485

Levis, J. M. (2020). Revisiting the intelligibility and nativeness principles. *Journal of Second Language Pronunciation*, 6, 310–328. https://doi.org/10.1075/jslp.20050.lev

Martin, I. A. (2020). Pronunciation can be acquired outside the classroom: Design and assessment of homework-based training. *The Modern Language Journal*, 104, 457–479. https://doi.org/10.1111/modl.12638

Martinsen, R. A., Alvord, S. M., & Tanner, J. (2014). Perceived foreign accent: Extended stays abroad, level of instruction, and motivation. *Foreign Language Annals*, 47, 66–78. https://doi.org/10.1111/flan.12076

Martinsen, R. A., Baker, W., Dewey, D. P., Bown, J., & Johnson, C. (2010). Exploring diverse settings for language acquisition and use: Comparing study abroad, service learning abroad, and foreign language housing. *Applied Language Learning*, 20, 45–69.

Mihaljević Djigunović, J. (2015). Context and structure of the study. In J. Mihaljević Djigunović & M. Medved Krajnović (Eds.), *Early learning and teaching of English: New dynamics of primary English* (pp. 1–9). Multilingual Matters.

Moyer, A. (2011). An investigation of experience in L2 phonology: Does quality matter more than quantity? *Canadian Modern Language Review*, 67, 191–216. https://doi.org/10.3138/cmlr.67.2.161

260 *Sara Kennedy and Pavel Trofimovich*

Moyer, A. (2014). Exceptional outcomes in L2 phonology: The critical factors of learner engagement and self-regulation. *Applied Linguistics, 35*, 418–440. https://doi.org/10.1093/applin/amu012

Munro, M. J., & Derwing, T. M. (1995). Foreign accent, comprehensibility, and intelligibility in the speech of second language learners. *Language Learning, 45*, 73–97. https://doi/10.1111/j.1467-1770.1995.tb00963.x

Munro, M. J., & Derwing, T. M. (2008). Segmental acquisition in adult ESL learners: A longitudinal study of vowel production. *Language Learning, 58*, 479–502. https://doi/10.1111/j.1467-9922.2008.00448.x

Murphy, J. M. (2014). Intelligible, comprehensible, non-native models in ESL/EFL pronunciation teaching. *System, 42*, 258–269. https://doi.org/10.1016/j.system.2013.12.007

Nagle, C. (2018). Motivation, comprehensibility, and accentedness in L2 Spanish: Investigating motivation as a time-varying predictor of pronunciation development. *The Modern Language Journal, 102*, 199–217. https://doi.org/10.1111/modl.12461

Nagle, C. L., Moorman, C., & Sanz, C. (2016). Disentangling research on study abroad and pronunciation: Methodological and programmatic considerations. In D. M. Velliaris & D. Coleman-George (Eds.), *Handbook of research on study abroad programs and outbound mobility* (pp. 673–695). IGI Global.

Nikolov, M., & Mihaljević Djigunović, J. (2006). Recent research on age, second language acquisition, and early foreign language learning. *Annual Review of Applied Linguistics, 26*, 234–260. https://doi.org/10.1017/S0267190506000122

Oxford, R. (1990). *Language learning strategies: What every teacher should know.* Newbury House.

Pawlak, M. (2010). Designing and piloting a tool for the measurement of the use of pronunciation learning strategies. *Research in Language, 8*, 1–14.

Piske, T., Flege, J. E., MacKay, I. R., & Meador, D. (2002). The production of English vowels by fluent early and late Italian-English bilinguals. *Phonetica, 59*, 49–71. https://doi.org/10.1159/000056205

Rallo Fabra, L., & Juan-Garau, M. (2010). Intelligibility and foreign accentedness in a context-and-language-integrated-learning (CLIL) setting. In K. Dziubalska-Kołaczyk, M. Wrembel, & M. Kul (Eds.), *New Sounds 2010: Proceedings of the Sixth International Symposium on the Acquisition of Second Language Speech* (pp. 373–378). Federal Adam Mickiewicz University.

Saito, K. (2013). Reexamining effects of form-focused instruction on L2 pronunciation development: The role of explicit phonetic information. *Studies in Second Language Acquisition, 35*, 1–29. https://doi.org/10.1017/S0272263112000666

Saito, K., & Lyster, R. (2012). Effects of form-focused instruction and corrective feedback on L2 pronunciation development of /ɹ/ by Japanese learners of English. *Language Learning, 62*, 595–633. https://doi.org/10.1111/j.1467-9922.2011.00639.x

Saito, K., & Plonsky, L. (2019). Effects of second language pronunciation teaching revisited: A proposed measurement framework and meta-analysis. *Language Learning, 69*, 652–708. https://doi.org/10.1111/lang.12345

Sardegna, V. G. (2011). Pronunciation learning strategies that improve ESL learners' linking. In J. M. Levis & K. LeVelle (Eds.). *Pronunciation and intelligibility: Issues in research and practice. Proceedings of the 2nd pronunciation in second language learning and teaching conference* (pp. 105–121). Iowa State University.

Tahta, S., Wood, M., & Loewenthal, K. (1981). Foreign accents: Factors relating to transfer of accent from the first language to a second language. *Language and Speech, 24*, 265–272. https://doi.org/10.1177%2F002383098102400306

Takagi, N. (2002). The limits of training Japanese listeners to identify English/r/and/l: Eight case studies. *The Journal of the Acoustical Society of America, 111,* 2887–2896. https://doi.org/10.1121/1.1480418

Thomson, R. I., & Derwing, T. M. (2015). The effectiveness of L2 pronunciation instruction: A narrative review. *Applied Linguistics, 36,* 326–344. https://doi.org/10.1093/applin/amu076

Tokumoto, M., & Shibata, M. (2011). Asian varieties of English: Attitudes towards pronunciation. *World Englishes, 30,* 392–408. https://doi.org/10.1111/j.1467-971X.2011.01710.x

Trofimovich, P., Lightbown, P. M., Halter, R. H., & Song, H. (2009). Comprehension-based practice: The development of L2 pronunciation in a listening and reading program. *Studies in Second Language Acquisition, 31,* 609–639. https://doi.org/10.1017/S0272263109990040

Trofimovich, P., McDonough, K., & Foote, J. A. (2014). Interactive alignment of multi-syllabic stress patterns in a second language classroom. *TESOL Quarterly, 48,* 815–832. https://doi.org/10.1002/tesq.156

Trofimovich, P., & Turuševa, L. (2020). Language attitudes and ethnic identity: Examining listener perceptions of Latvian-Russian bilingual speakers. *Journal of Language, Identity, and Education, 19,* 9–24. https://doi.org/10.1080/15348458.2019.1696682

Wiener, S., Chan, M. K., & Ito, K. (2020). Do explicit instruction and high variability phonetic training improve nonnative speakers' Mandarin tone productions? *The Modern Language Journal, 104,* 152–168. https://doi.org/10.1111/modl.12619

Winitz, H., Gillespie, B., & Starcev, J. (1995). The development of English speech patterns of a 7-year-old Polish-speaking child. *Journal of Psycholinguistic Research, 24,* 117–143. https://doi.org/10.1007/BF02143959

Xodabande, I. (2017). The effectiveness of social media network telegram in teaching English language pronunciation to Iranian EFL learners. *Cogent Education, 4.* https://doi.org/10.1080/2331186X.2017.1347081

14 Teaching the language or teaching the process

Peter Yongqi Gu

Introduction

In both curriculum and pedagogy, there exists a perennial debate between teaching the content or knowledge versus teaching the process or skills. Some contend that the precious school time should be devoted to "core knowledge"; others argue that the rapid growth of human knowledge makes the teaching of knowledge-making skills more important than knowledge itself. Still, others reject the debate, arguing that both are necessary for successful learning and teaching (Oates, 2018). In the meantime, research on self-regulated learning and learning-to-learn has always presumed the absolute importance of human agency in the learning process without questioning the need for content teaching.

In teaching second languages, teaching the language has always remained the implicit and explicit focus of research attention, although a robust line of research on language learning strategies has produced numerous insights over the last 40 years. The same debate as described above has also persisted, with some scholars insisting that teaching strategies may not be as profitable as focusing on the language skill itself (Renandya, 2012), while others argue for the usefulness of strategy instruction (Gu, 2019).

This chapter will summarize this debate in terms of the major arguments put forward by each camp. A review of empirical research will help comb through the evidence for each argument. It will be argued that the debate itself is meaningless in that teaching the process is meant to fundamentally enhance the teaching of the language.

The issue under debate

For curriculum developers, teachers and learners alike, an unavoidable choice to make at various points of the learning journey is between the *What* and the *How*. In other words, the choice is between content on the one hand and skills for learning the content on the other. In a task as laborious as language teaching and learning, the debate is even more conspicuous. It is manifested in dilemmas like: should I teach the language or should I teach the process of language learning?

DOI: 10.4324/9781003008361-17

Or, put another way, should I spend my precious curriculum time on teaching grammar, vocabulary, the four skills or even functional use, or should I spare some time for teaching/learning how to learn?

As I will attempt to demonstrate, this is a perennial issue that has existed since antiquity. One would think that it is such a straightforward question with a straightforward answer: that both are important and that both should be taught and learned. Yet, the very fact that the dilemma has persisted for centuries speaks for the complexity of the issue. We often hear scholars (e.g., Krashen, 2011) and teachers saying, "take care of the content, the skills will take care of themselves" or vice versa. Other variations of the debate include which comes first and which comes next. In language teaching, teachers and learners spend so much time covering textbook units and preparing for high-stakes exams that they find it hard to spend time on language learning strategies.

Relevance of the debate to everyday classrooms

The following anecdote illustrates how pertinent the debate still is in today's classrooms. I have been involved in a large-scale project in China that focuses on a web-based diagnostic language assessment platform. The project involved diagnostic tests of English for secondary schools. In addition to language assessment, we included the assessment of language learning strategies. The thinking behind the decision is intuitive: when a language test helps diagnose a language problem, it may well be a learning issue rather than a language issue. Diagnosing learning strategies will therefore help pinpoint the potential sources of the language problem and inform instructional decisions thereafter (Gu, 2017). Tens of thousands of students and teachers participated in the project. A year later, when we reviewed the project, we realized that many teachers and students either chose not to complete the learning strategy assessment or reluctantly did it but saw it as a redundant and time-consuming task.

Do learners really need to learn how to learn? Another example will make it more explicit. A few years ago, a mature student on our English proficiency programme made an appointment with me after learning that I am a learning strategy expert. He was a brilliant artist and had a conditional offer for a PhD programme and was desperately trying to complete the English proficiency programme to satisfy English language entry requirements. He said that he had failed the reading component of the exit test twice but could not figure out how he could possibly finish reading so much text within the given time. I took out a piece of text and asked him if he could finish reading it within 5 minutes and tell me what it was about. He said it was impossible but started reading anyway, verbalizing silently every sound and every word in his mind. I told him that nobody could finish reading the text his way within 5 minutes, but I could tell him within 1 minute what the author was talking about and that I even disagreed with the author. I then told him that reading academic texts is not about decoding from strings of words, sentences, paragraphs and texts, but about being informed about something or about seeing the authors' argument

264   *Peter Yongqi Gu*

and that the structures of these ideas follow very simple patterns. I was able to tell him what the article was about because I was looking at the title, the subtitles and sections, and the topic sentences for major paragraphs and sections. I was then using the information as constants, as it were, and coupled with my world knowledge and topical knowledge; I was able to fill in the information slots that I did not capture from the text. The experience was an eye-opener for the student. He said he did something similar when he was reading in his native language, Chinese, but never thought he could do the same thing in English.

What I was showing the student was the importance of reading strategies, i.e., my intentional actions beyond simple decoding of the text in order to maximize what I wanted to gain from reading. In doing so, I was using my knowledge of the topic (by inferring from the title) and my knowledge of text structure (of topic sentences and one theme per paragraph) to guess and predict what the text was about. I was also monitoring my comprehension by checking if my decoded meaning was congruent with my existing knowledge of the topic. I was even able to go beyond comprehension and engage in a dialogue with the author in places where my understanding of the topic did not concur with the author's exposition.

Reading strategies such as the above do not necessarily transfer from the native language when we learn a second language, and they need to be explicitly developed while we acquire reading ability in another language. In fact, we cannot ever take it for granted that all children acquire the right strategies in the first place for language processing in their native language.

The argument on both sides

Content over skills

The idea that foundational knowledge and skills are crucially important in learning is not at all new. A popular motto among Chinese learners, which warns people against shortcuts to learning and has lasted for 1,200 years, goes like this: "Diligence is the only way to the mountain of knowledge; perseverance is the only boat in the sea of learning" (Han Yu, 768~824 AD). The same idea is also an age-old tradition in apprenticeship models of learning, where the beginner goes through a prolonged period of training in basic skills before they are allowed to practice their trade in innovative ways.

In modern education, E. D. Hirsch (1987) has often been credited as the flag bearer of a "knowledge-based curriculum". Hirsch believed that schools were not teaching facts systematically and this was thought to be preventing children from succeeding at school. It was argued that conceptual knowledge and domain knowledge allow fluent processing of reading, and chunking of the relevant knowledge distinguishes between experts and novices (Hirsch, 2003). Without the basic accumulation of knowledge, the teaching of reading skills such as decoding or inferencing does not help improve children's reading. In fact, as Hirsch shows convincingly, many times it is the lack of background knowledge, rather than the lack of reading skills, that prevents children from understanding:

Teaching the language or teaching the process   265

"If the relevant prior knowledge is lacking, conscious comprehension strategies cannot activate it" (Hirsch, 2003, p. 22).

Similarly, Kolligian and Sternberg (1987) also suggest that researchers have paid too much attention to cognitive and metacognitive strategies and not enough attention to some other basic factors that influence the comprehension of students with learning difficulties. These other factors included knowledge of vocabulary, text structure and the topical background which were found to be crucially important. In addition, other factors such as fluency in reading were also shown to be as important as reading strategies (Gersten et al., 2001). Indeed, Helen Abadzi (2008) compellingly argues for the importance of automaticity of reading and writing in early primary schools, which serves as the foundation of success in later schooling. From a neuropsychology perspective, the automaticity of basic decoding (see Woore, this volume) will free up working memory for comprehension and make other higher-order strategic processing possible.

These ideas have been reiterated time and again, and many scholars attribute the failure of students at school to their deficiency in background topic knowledge. Lemov (2017) explicitly claimed that "prior knowledge affects comprehension—in many cases, far more than generic 'reading skills' do" (p. 11). Interestingly, Hirsch himself actually never disqualified the importance of learning skills. By emphasizing the importance of knowledge, he was simply saying that we should "kill several birds with one stone when we teach skills by teaching stuff" (Hirsch, 2003, p. 28). Hirsch explicitly mentioned that "facts and skills are inseparable" and that children should be empowered with the basic knowledge before they can make use of this knowledge with the help of learning skills (Severs, 2015).

In the field of second language teaching, the argument centres on the importance of foundational language knowledge and skills such as reading, listening, grammar and vocabulary versus strategies for learning these aspects of language competence. For scholars such as Stephen Krashen (2011), reading is best learned through reading, and listening is best learned through listening, not through strategies for reading or listening. Michael Swan (2008) also argued that lower-level decoding skills in reading need to become automatic first before a reader can make use of higher-level processing skills. Before this is done, "much of the work that is done in classrooms in order to 'teach' reading skills or strategies is more or less a waste of time" (p. 267). Lao and Krashen (2000) compared a class of Hong Kong university students who self-selected free voluntary reading for enjoyment with another class who went through academic skills training. The reading for enjoyment class outperformed the academic skills class on measures of vocabulary and reading rate.

Similarly, a number of scholars (e.g., Buck, 1995; Renandya, 2012; Renandya & Farrell, 2011) have pointed out that the major hurdles to listening comprehension for beginner level English as a foreign language (EFL) learners are their lack of ability to decode rapidly disappearing speech sounds, rather than their lack of strategies for listening. For these learners, "an overemphasis on strategy

266 *Peter Yongqi Gu*

training may undermine the value of practice, which plays a critical role in the acquisition of procedural knowledge in language learning like listening skills" (Renandya & Farrell, 2011, p. 55). Like the previously mentioned experts who argued for the importance of narrow reading and extensive reading, these scholars also suggest extensive listening as the most appropriate use of class time: "the bulk of our classroom time should be used to provide our students with lots of listening practice, the kind of practice in which they actually listen to a lot of meaningful, enjoyable, and comprehensible spoken text" (p. 58).

Interestingly, some scholars in this camp would argue that certain strategies do not need to be taught because they are what Swan (2008) would call "normal reading skills". Krashen (2011) and Smith (1975) even regard these skills as "our innate mental equipment" that we can automatically transfer from our native language. This is, however, debatable, as there is no evidence for either the automatic transfer of or the innateness of strategies such as prediction or comparison and contrast.

Skills over content

It is interesting to see how educational policymakers and teachers make simplistic interpretations of educational research. Convincing arguments often sway educational practices to extremes (Severs, 2015). After reviewing a vast body of research evidence on the usefulness of learning to learn, Hattie and Donoghue (2018) lamented "an over dominance on how to teach content and less focus on the methods of learning this content" and observed that "the teaching of 'learning' has diminished to near extinction in many teacher education programs" (p. 98).

The fact is, "domain knowledge is necessary but not sufficient for expert performance" (Collins & Kapur, 2014, p. 111). Indeed, beyond the basics of domain knowledge, skills of learning make a significant difference, so much so that strategic learning competence becomes a defining feature of success. From Confucius to the modern scholarship on learning strategies, the emphasis on strategic performance has dominated human thinking in the content versus skills debate for well over two millennia.

In a world of growing uncertainty and faced with the exponential growth of knowledge, defining basic knowledge in any domain is becoming increasingly difficult. Even when it is defined to a certain extent, new knowledge replaces or changes existing knowledge rapidly. Price (1963) studied the exponential growth of scientific knowledge and discovered that it took about 20 years to double the number of important discoveries and 15 years to double the number of chemical compounds known. Paradoxically, new scientific knowledge overturns old truth, and the decay of truth happens exponentially as well. It was found, for example, that the half-life (time taken for half of the knowledge to be overturned) in physics is about ten years, and that in psychology, it is about seven years (Arbesman, 2013). Instead of adding to the school curriculum, which is already much more crammed than decades ago, educators have shifted to a growing emphasis on the open and flexible abilities of adaptation and

Teaching the language or teaching the process 267

generic problem-solving. Lifelong learning has become a must for modern citizens. Learning to learn is now taken as one of the most needed educational goals (Perkins, 2014; Scott, 2015). In fact, Ackerman and Perkins (1989) saw content and skills as complementary to each other and referred to a "futuristic alternative" that involves "curriculum" (content) and "meta-curriculum" (strategies).

This side of the debate is supported by decades of robust empirical evidence across domains of learning. In a well-quoted dart-throwing experiment (Zimmerman & Kitsantas, 1997), all participants received training in dart-throwing. Participants were assigned to eight experimental groups and one control group. The experimental groups were characterized by four different "goal" conditions, each of which contained two groups: one group where participants recorded their scores, the other where they did not. The four goal conditions were as follows. First, participants in a "product" group were told to focus on getting the best score. Second, those assigned to a "process" condition were told that they could do well if they could focus on the final two strategies in training (1, keeping the arm vertical; 2, finger extension towards the target). A third group (a "transformed goal" condition) were told to adjust the two strategies following each throw by examining where the dart hit the bull's-eye (above or below; left or right). The fourth group (shifting goals from process to product) were told to focus on throwing strategies first, and to shift their focus to getting the best score after about 12 minutes when they had achieved automaticity during the process phase. The control group were simply asked to practice as much as they could within the given time after initial training. All eight experimental groups outperformed the control group at the end. The best performing group was the group that were told to shift halfway through from process (practicing the trained strategy) to product (focusing on getting the best score) while recording the result of each trial. On the other hand, training plus practice only (which is the equivalent to most school learning situations) was the least effective. Apparently, recording each trial fostered monitoring of practice and raised the participants' awareness of their state of learning. Strategies such as goal setting and a reflective, metacognitive regulation of strategy use (shifting from focusing on a skill to focusing on getting the best performance) seemed to work not just in improving dart-throwing but also in self-efficacy, interest and overall satisfaction of the learning experience.

Hattie and Donoghue (2016) summarized 228 meta-analyses on learning strategies with a combined sample size of more than 13 million students. Despite a wide range of results reported in these studies, the average effect size (Cohen's d) of 0.53 carries a message that learning strategies, in general, are moderately useful. In general, an effect size of 0.53 is normally interpreted as a medium difference between the experimental groups and the control groups (Cohen, 1988; Cumming & Calin-Jageman, 2016). Hattie and Donoghue explain the differential effects of learning strategies by examining whether the learning is related to knowledge at the surface, deep or transfer levels. At each of these levels, learning strategies differ in terms of the timing of learning (first acquiring versus consolidating learning). The effectiveness of learning strategies also depends on the

268 *Peter Yongqi Gu*

learners' skill (knowledge and ability), will (dispositions that affect learning), and thrill (motivations and emotions), both at the initial stage of learning (inputs) and at the product stage of learning (outputs). It is interesting to note that when the authors explained the relative ineffectiveness of problem-based learning ($d = 0.15$), they attributed the low effect to using problem-based learning before the students had attained sufficient surface knowledge: "It is likely that problem based learning works more successfully when students engage in forward reasoning and this depends on having sufficient content knowledge to make connections" (p. 11). In other words, a learning strategy such as problem-based learning will not be very useful unless the students already have enough basic knowledge of what they are learning.

Within the field of second language acquisition, research on language learning strategies has remained a major endeavour for over four decades. Most early empirical research was exploratory, producing a vast amount of correlational evidence relating various learning strategies to a host of learning outcomes and to "group differences" and other independent variables. Despite an over-cautious attitude to strategy instruction, more and more research is being conducted in this area (Gu, 2019). Plonsky's (2019) latest meta-analysis incorporated his earlier meta-analysis (Plonsky, 2011) and aggregated effects from 77 primary studies, including 112 experimental samples (N = 7,890). This meta-analysis of strategy instruction experiments obtained an overall weighted mean effect size of 0.66. This meant that after strategy instruction, scores in the experimental groups are on average "approximately two-thirds of a standard deviation higher than control groups" (Plonsky, 2019, p. 8). A wide range of moderator variables was synthesized as well. In general, focusing on a single strategy or a small set of strategies produces higher effects ($d = 0.86$) than teaching multiple strategies ($d = 0.58$). Metacognitive strategies have higher effects ($d = 1.00$) than cognitive strategies ($d = 0.56$). Students in higher proficiency levels benefit more ($d = 0.74$) than their beginner proficiency counterparts ($d = 0.39$). Instruction programmes that last more than two weeks produce better instruction results ($d = 0.65$) than those that are less than two weeks long ($d = 0.49$). Second language contexts are more conducive to strategy instruction ($d = 0.84$) than "foreign language contexts" ($d = 0.57$). Strategy instruction that focusses on pronunciation ($d = 2.07$), strategy use ($d = 1.11$), speaking ($d = 1.00$), reading ($d = 0.82$), grammar ($d = 0.75$), vocabulary ($d = 0.63$) or writing ($d = 0.59$) are more effective than strategy instruction that focus on listening ($d = 0.06$) and general proficiency ($d = 0.05$).

The massive amount of empirical evidence in these meta-analyses of strategy instruction has reassured us about the usefulness of strategies. In fact, as early as the 1960s, Hatcher (1968) was seriously concerned with the fragments of knowledge being taught in schools *vis-a-vis* "the knowledge explosion" (p. 14). He proposed that "education must also concern itself with the processes by which the knowledge or the structure of a discipline might be gained" (p. 15). "The challenge is here, and now is the time for this challenge to be met" (p. 16). Half a century later, an impressive amount of research has been done. And yet, we are still very much in the midst of this debate.

Teaching the language or teaching the process 269

This is hardly surprising. When we look at the importance of content, we will always see the influence of process factors; and when we focus on the strategies and skills of learning, we see the importance of basic content. When Bruner (1960) conceptualized the curriculum for American schools and emphasized on the "process" of education, he was talking about both the transfer of specific skills for immediate use after school and what he called "nonspecific transfer" of "principles and attitudes" (pp. 17–18) that go beyond basic knowledge and skills. In other words, an integrated and more nuanced perspective is in order.

The integration

Both sides of the debate seem to have stressed one thing at the expense of the other, although most scholars will not go to the extreme of rejecting the importance of the other altogether. In general, we do see a consensus: namely, that content and domain knowledge or basic language skills should be the primary focus at the beginning stage of learning and that learning how to learn or strategies and skills for learning become increasingly important as learning goes on. Table 14.1 summarizes the arguments on both sides.

The summary in Table 14.1 is simplistic in multiple ways. First, there is no clear delineation of levels of proficiency. Indeed, this may well be assessed on a case by case basis. Second, there is no clear indication of how important each side is at each level of proficiency. And, of course, it does not show how, exactly, instructional efforts should be allocated when we shift our emphasis from something important to something more important or *vice versa*. Nevertheless, one thing is clear: that going to the extremes is not the right option. Taking care of one side will not necessarily take care of the other. For those who believe that the ultimate aim of education is learning how to learn, my advice is that this lofty aim is best achieved one step at a time and that basic knowledge and skills in a domain are the foundations of any learning. On the other hand, even at the very beginner level, teachers need to start to cultivate learning skills because no learning skills are innate. Contrary to the claims of a few scholars, there is no evidence that some strategies are inborn. For second language learners, there is no evidence that all skills for first language acquisition or use will automatically transfer to the learning and use of a second language. Even when some get transferred, there is no guarantee that they are the right strategies for learning and using the second language.

Table 14.1 A simplistic summary of the debate

	Lower proficiency level	Higher proficiency level
Domain knowledge, concepts, content, or basic language skills	Very important	Important
Learning how to learn, or strategies and skills for learning	Important	Very important

270   *Peter Yongqi Gu*

There is evidence that fundamental language skills such as automaticity in decoding help facilitate strategic processing and learning how to read, listen and learn (Clarke, 1980). In Plonsky's (2019) meta-analysis of strategy-based language instruction, the average effect size for beginners is only 0.39, while the effect for intermediate and advanced learners is 0.74, showing the potential existence of a threshold level of language proficiency below which teaching and learning should concentrate on honing basic automaticity skills. "The linguistic means to use strategies properly" (Kellerman, 1991, p. 159) is what teachers are focusing on in classrooms and what has been highlighted by scholars but has so far evaded the empirical researcher's radar.

Empirical research on learning to learn in the field of second language education has concentrated on language learning strategies. While the evidence accumulated so far points to the usefulness of strategic language learning in general, the large variation in intervention effects demonstrates the complexity of the issue. Among a wide array of moderator factors, I would highlight the following that I believe should be given immediate attention: (1) the assessment and diagnosis of strategies before instruction, (2) closer attention to the link between language competence and strategic learning; and (3) more exploration of transformative epistemological and methodological innovations in research. Below, I will explore each of these factors in turn.

Assessment of current strategy needs, task demands and current language competence should produce finer evidence leading to the usefulness of strategy instruction. Assessment of learners – their "skill, will, and thrill" at various stages and levels, their cognitive flexibility and metacognitive agility; assessment of tasks and their demands; assessment of learning environments, in terms of their support and constraints: all these should help teachers decide what to do next in order to help their students move closer to the target of learning. We already know that some strategies are for beginner level learning, and some are not. Different strategies should be encouraged based on a diagnosis of different stages of learning and strategy competence. As the basic content/skills are learned, strategies such as relating new knowledge to existing knowledge are no longer needed; but new strategies become more important, such as those for elaborating and applying the new knowledge/skill to real-life situations and for transferring the strategy to other, similar tasks (Hattie & Donoghue, 2016). And of course, if a sizable proportion of students in a class are already using certain strategies, strategy instruction with a whole class approach will not be warranted.

Another fundamental issue for language teachers lies in the nature of language competence itself. It is easy to say that the basics are crucially important, without which students will not be able to benefit from learning strategies. However, it is not clear from research evidence or theory what these basics in language learning actually are. Basic knowledge? What knowledge? Basic skills? What skills? To use one example, knowledge of words in a foreign language has been shown to be so basic that the first 3000 most frequent words in English cover about 90% or more of all texts; and that anything less than 98% known words in any text (written or aural) would prevent a reader from understanding and from learning

Teaching the language or teaching the process 271

from the text independently (Nation, 2006, 2013). Researchers in other areas have not produced similar findings to inform teachers about, for instance, the basics of grammar that learners absolutely need before they can benefit from the use of strategies. I have repeatedly mentioned decoding as a basic skill in listening and reading. There is a limited amount of research on the bare essentials of reading automaticity. For example, school pupils are suggested to reach "45–60 words per minute by the end of grade 2 and 120–150 words per minute for grades 6–8" (Abadzi, 2008, p. 581). Beyond this, however, researchers have not clearly delineated the threshold level of the decoding skill and other basic language skills that have to be reached before students can benefit from strategic reading and listening.

Discerning readers must have realized that I have so far treated empirical findings, especially meta-analysis patterns that have usually summarized results from experimental studies, as more convincing than pure argumentation. In fact, convincing evidence does not have to come from experimental or correlational studies of the positivist tradition. Nevertheless, I have to admit that a deficit model, which focusses on experimentation and external "intervention", has been the dominant research paradigm. There has rarely been any evidence reported showing the usefulness of transformative approaches to strategy instruction that take learning strategies as empowering tools which are co-constructed with teachers and peers, embedded within specific tasks, situated in specific contexts, and associated with emotional entailments that accompany human learning. More humanistic research along the lines of mediated learning experience and dynamic assessment (Feuerstein et al., 2010; Kozulin & Garb, 2002; Kozulin & Presseisen, 1995) can add more insights to the debate and may move us closer to the truth. These approaches aim at finding the "learning potential" (Feuerstein et al., 2010) or the "zone of proximal development" (Vygotsky, 1978) of learners before providing scaffolding and working with the learners to explore the best strategies to complete the learning tasks and achieve learner growth. Until more research evidence is seen from this more interpretive and transformative epistemological perspective, however, some evidence is still infinitely better than no evidence.

That being said, it is now important to remind consumers of our research that, in today's world –which is increasingly pulled to dogmatic extremes with evangelical zeal – anything that goes with the flow to either side is to be taken with a large pinch of salt. That applies equally to the epistemological stances of researchers and to the debate between basic domain knowledge/skill versus learning to learn.

Summary

Most of the debate that is the focus of this chapter boils down to a matter of emphasis. Scholars stressing the fundamental importance of basic knowledge and skills often focus on the fact that learning builds on previous learning and that without a foundation of basic knowledge and skills, higher-order learning and strategic learning do more harm than good if done too early for too long.

272   Peter Yongqi Gu

On the other hand, scholars working on learning to learn often assume that the basics have already been obtained and that success depends on the students getting on their own feet to decide on what to learn, how to learn, when to learn, in what way and to what extent.

A general consensus is, however, in sight: namely, that foundational knowledge/skills in any domain are crucially important for further knowledge and skills to be built upon and for clearing working memory space so that higher-level thinking and strategic learning become possible. However, basic knowledge and skills will not automatically lead to higher-level knowledge and skills. Skills in learning to learn and learning to problem-solve should be carefully cultivated throughout the schooling years so that children can grow up being able to independently face the explosion of knowledge and the challenges and uncertainties of the future.

Sensible as it sounds, this consensus alone is nonetheless not sufficiently useful. The real problem which teachers are confronting is not knowing exactly what those basic knowledge and skills are or where the threshold point is before they can move to a focus on learning strategies for further growth. On the other side of the debate, the real problem does not lie in the lack of evidence showing the effectiveness of teaching students to learn in efficient ways. Rather, it lies in making teachers and learners aware of the research and in showing them how the research findings can be translated into teaching and learning practices inside the classroom. This will mean popularizations of research findings beyond academic journals and an emphasis on teachers as researchers in pre-service teacher education and teacher professional development programmes. For an applied field such as language education, it is the researcher's social responsibility to engage in less debate and more teacher-friendly applicable research.

Relating the issues raised in this chapter to your own context:

1 To what extent is the debate on content versus skills relevant to your own second language education context?
2 Within your context of second language education, which side are teachers on in this debate? Why?

References

Abadzi, H. (2008). Efficient learning for the poor: New insights into literacy acquisition for children. *International Review of Education*, 54(5), 581–604. https://doi.org/10.1007/s11159-008-9102-3

Ackerman, D., & Perkins, D. N. (1989). Integrating thinking and learning skills across the curriculum. In H. H. Jacobs (Ed.), *Interdisciplinary curriculum: Design and implementation* (pp. 77–95). Association for Supervision and Curriculum Development.

Arbesman, S. (2013). *The half-life of facts: Why everything we know has an expiration date*. Penguin Group (USA) Inc.

Bruner, J. (1960). *The process of education*. Vintage Books.

Buck, G. (1995). How to become a good listening teacher. In D. J. Mendelsohn & J. Rubin (Eds.), *A Guide for the teaching of second language listening* (pp. 59–73). Dominie Press.

Teaching the language or teaching the process 273

Clarke, M. A. (1980). The short circuit hypothesis of ESL reading – or when language competence interferes with reading performance. *The Modern Language Journal, 64*(2), 203–209. https://doi.org/10.1111/j.1540-4781.1980.tb05186.x

Cohen, J. (1988). *Statistical power analysis for the behavioral sciences* (2nd ed.). Routledge.

Collins, A., & Kapur, M. (2014). Cognitive apprenticeship. In R. K. Sawyer (Ed.), *The Cambridge handbook of the learning sciences* (2nd ed., pp. 109–127). Cambridge University Press.

Cumming, G., & Calin-Jageman, R. (2016). *Introduction to the new statistics: Estimation, open science, and beyond.* Routledge.

Feuerstein, R., Feuerstein, R. S., & Falik, L. H. (2010). *Beyond smarter: Mediated learning and the brain's capacity for change* (annotated edition). Teachers College Press.

Gersten, R., Fuchs, L. S., Williams, J. P., & Baker, S. (2001). Teaching reading comprehension strategies to students with learning disabilities: A review of research. *Review of Educational Research, 71*(2), 279–320. https://doi.org/10.3102/00346543071002279

Gu, Y. (2017). Formative assessment of language learning strategies. 英语学习（教师版）*English Language Learning (Teacher Edition), 2017*(9), 16–24.

Gu, Y. (2019). Approaches to learning strategy instruction. In A. U. Chamot & V. Harris (Eds.), *Learning strategy instruction in the language classroom: Issues and implementation* (pp. 22–37). Multilingual Matters.

Hatcher, T. E. (1968). Content versus methodology: A critical analysis. *Peabody Journal of Education, 46*(1), 14–17.

Hattie, J. A. C., & Donoghue, G. M. (2016). Learning strategies: A synthesis and conceptual model. *NPJ Science of Learning, 1*, https://doi.org/10.1038/npjscilearn.2016.13

Hattie, J. A. C., & Donoghue, G. M. (2018). A model of learning: Optimizing the effectiveness of learning strategies. In K. Illeris (Ed.), *Contemporary theories of learning* (2nd ed., pp. 97–113). Routledge.

Hirsch, Jr., E. D. (1987). *Cultural literacy: What every American needs to know.* Houghton-Mifflin.

Hirsch, Jr., E. D. (2003). Reading comprehension requires knowledge – of words and the world: Scientific insights into the fourth-grade slump and the nation's stagnant comprehension scores. *American Educator, 27*(1), 10–29, 44, 48–49.

Kellerman, E. (1991). Compensatory strategies in second language research: A critique, a revision, and some (non-)implications for the classroom. In R. Phillipson, E. Kellerman, L. Selinker, M. Sharwood Smith, & M. Swain (Eds.), *Foreign/second language pedagogy research: A commemorative volume for Clause Faerch* (pp. 142–161). Multilingual Matters Ltd.

Kolligian, J., & Sternberg, R. J. (1987). Intelligence, information processing, and specific learning disabilities: A triarchic synthesis. *Journal of Learning Disabilities, 20*(1), 8–17. https://doi.org/10.1177/002221948702000103

Kozulin, A., & Garb, E. (2002). Dynamic assessment of EFL text comprehension. *School Psychology International, 23*(1), 112–127. https://doi.org/10.1177/0143034302023001733

Kozulin, A., & Presseisen, B. Z. (1995). Mediated learning experience and psychological tools: Vygotsky's and Feuerstein's perspectives in a study of student learning. *Educational Psychologist, 30*(2), 67. https://doi.org/10.1207/s15326985ep3002_3

Krashen, S. (2011). Academic proficiency (language and content) and the role of strategies. *TESOL Journal, 2*(4), 381–393. https://doi.org/10.5054/tj.2011.274624

Lao, C. Y., & Krashen, S. (2000). The impact of popular literature study on literacy development in EFL: More evidence for the power of reading. *System, 28*(2), 261–270. https://doi.org/10.1016/S0346-251X(00)00011-7

274 *Peter Yongqi Gu*

Lemov, D. (2017). How knowledge powers reading. *Educational Leadership*, *74*(5), 10–16.

Nation, I. S. P. (2006). How large a vocabulary is needed for reading and listening? *The Canadian Modern Language Review/La Revue Canadienne Des Langues Vivantes*, *63*(1), 59–81.

Nation, I. S. P. (2013). *Learning vocabulary in another language* (2nd ed.). Cambridge University Press.

Oates, T. (2018). Skills versus knowledge: A curriculum debate that matters – and one which we need to reject. *Impact: Journal of the Chartered College of Teaching*, *4*. https://impact.chartered.college/article/skills-versus-knowledge-curriculum-debate-matters-one-need-reject/

Perkins, D. N. (2014). *Future wise: Educating our children for a changing world*. Jossey-Bass.

Plonsky, L. (2011). The effectiveness of second language strategy instruction: A meta-analysis. *Language Learning*, *61*(4), 993–1038. https://doi.org/10.1111/j.1467-9922.2011.00663.x

Plonsky, L. (2019). Language learning strategy instruction: Recent research and future directions1. In A. U. Chamot & V. Harris (Eds.), *Learning strategy instruction in the language classroom: Issues and implementation* (pp. 3–21). Multilingual Matters.

Price, D. J. de S. (1963). *Little science big science*. Columbia University Press.

Renandya, W. A. (2012). Five reasons why listening strategy instruction might not work with lower proficiency learners. *ELTWorldOnline.Com*, *4*. http://blog.nus.edu.sg/eltwo/files/2014/06/Five-Reasons-Why-Listening-Strategy-Instruction-Might-Not-Work-With-Lower-Proficiency-Learners_editforpdf-o13kt9.pdf

Renandya, W. A., & Farrell, T. S. C. (2011). 'Teacher, the tape is too fast!' Extensive listening in ELT. *ELT Journal*, *65*(1), 52–59. https://doi.org/10.1093/elt/ccq015

Scott, C. L. (2015). *The futures of learning 2: What kind of learning for the 21st century? (ERF Working Papers Series No. 14; UNESCO Education Research and Foresight)*. UNESCO. http://repositorio.minedu.gob.pe/handle/123456789/3709

Severs, J. (2015). 'I've been misinterpreted from Day 1'. *The Times Educational Supplement*, *5171*, 24–29.

Smith, F. (1975). The role of prediction in reading. *Elementary English*, *52*(3), 305–311.

Swan, M. (2008). Talking sense about learning strategies. *RELC Journal*, *39*(2), 262–273. https://doi.org/10.1177/0033688208092188

Vygotsky, L. S. (1978). *Mind in society: The development of higher psychological processes*. Harvard University Press.

Zimmerman, B. J., & Kitsantas, A. (1997). Developmental phases in self-regulation: Shifting from process goals to outcome goals. *Journal of Educational Psychology*, *89*(1), 29–36. http://dx.doi.org.helicon.vuw.ac.nz/10.1037/0022-0663.89.1.29

Reflections

Ernesto Macaro and Robert Woore

Introduction

In this edited volume, we set ourselves a double challenge through its title and its aims. The first challenge was to broaden the scope from an earlier volume in the 'Debates' series, published by Routledge in 2014, by using the term *'Second* Language Education' rather than *'Modern* Language Education'. As we noted in our introduction, the term 'Modern Language' was originally coined to make a distinction with 'classical languages' such as Latin or Ancient Greek. This distinction did not seem relevant to us, given that people may choose to learn all kinds of languages for all kinds of reasons: why should we discriminate simply based on a particular language's antiquity? We also felt uncomfortable with the term 'foreign language' because of its sometimes negative connotations of otherness and difference, and because of the tight interconnections which exist between multiple languages, both at the national and international levels, and indeed within the mind of the individual user. 'Foreign' seems to imply fixed boundaries that do not necessarily exist in reality. We noted that some scholars have proposed the term 'additional language' to encompass 'second, foreign, indigenous, minority, or heritage languages' learnt by 'school-aged children, adolescents, and adults' in a wide range of contexts (e.g. Douglas Fir Group, 2016:19). We intended the current volume to have a similarly broad frame of reference, but we preferred to use the term 'Second Language' (henceforth 'L2') because of its wide currency.

We also enjoyed the breadth of scope afforded to us by the term 'education', allowing us to look beyond the direct teaching and learning of languages themselves to the development of L2 teaching expertise. In light of the above, we invited contributions on, for example:

- multilingual learners of an L2 which is the majority language of their education, such as 'English as an Additional Language' (EAL) pupils in the UK (Chalmers and Murphy);
- the learning of L2 English as a phenomenon within a plurilingual world and the impact that this phenomenon may have on the first or 'home language' of students (Di Sabato & Kirkpatrick);

DOI: 10.4324/9781003008361-18

276 *Ernesto Macaro and Robert Woore*

- Content and Language Integrated Learning and English Medium Instruction, where educating students in a second language is, to varying degrees, promoted alongside content learning (Lasagabaster);
- The preparation of language teachers (Molway) and their continuing professional development (Borg).

We felt that these different educational frameworks were all part and parcel of the whole research endeavour of Second Language Education.

The second challenge offered by the title was to treat all second language learning as worthy of research and commentary, rather than providing a privileged position for English as an L2. We noticed that some of the edited books that we listed in Chapter 1 (Woore and Macaro) discuss language education solely in terms of teaching English (e.g. Richards & Renandya, 2002), even though the book title purports to be about teaching languages in general (*Methodology in Language Teaching*). However, despite our initial aspirations to include a broad range of L2s, we were not surprised to receive many contributions which did, nonetheless, focus on English. This is understandable, given the global importance of this language and the fact that the great majority of SLA research has turned its spotlight, one way or another, on the learning of English. Nonetheless, some chapters in this volume do include a focus on learning Languages Other Than English (LOTE: e.g. Woore; Graham; Macaro).

In this final chapter, we now wish to take a step back and offer some personal reflections on current debates in L2 education – both those covered by the chapters in this book and more broadly. We have grouped our reflections into four main categories. First, we will look at the debate between explicit and implicit teaching approaches, which we think is a key area underlying a number of other debates in L2 education. Second, we will consider the 'grain size' of debates: that is, whether these are operating at the holistic level of an overall pedagogical approach, or whether they concern the teaching of particular aspects of an L2, such as vocabulary or grammar. Third, we will consider the importance, in teaching and learning an L2, of context; how research might respond to contextual differences; and what the implications of this are for teachers and learners. Finally, we will consider some ways in which L2 education is changing as a result of technological developments, and the implications this may have for SLA research.

The implicit/explicit debate

One debate which came out strongly in our survey of stakeholders' views (Chapter 1) concerns the degree of 'explicitness' in L2 instruction. Indeed, our respondents indicated that this was a polarized question, often expressed in terms of a dichotomy – explicit *versus* implicit. We do not have space, in this brief final chapter, to expand upon the nuanced and contested definitions of these terms; we will settle for a loose distinction between (a) an approach where the teacher draws learners' attention to a specific aspect of the language, and tells them about it (explicit teaching), and (b) an approach where the teacher simply uses

Reflections 277

the language without drawing learners' attention to its forms (implicit teaching). Since the current volume does not have a chapter dedicated specifically to this debate in generalized form, we wished to comment on it a little further here.

We do have two chapters which refer directly to the explicit/implicit dichotomy (Martinez on vocabulary and Pawlak on grammar) – although for Martinez, the distinction, at least as relating to vocabulary learning, is one that is 'interesting on a theoretical level, but in practice somewhat of a red herring'. However, beyond Pawlak's and Martinez's contributions, it could be argued that many chapters in this volume relate, in some way, to the explicit/implicit distinction. For example, the use of the L2 in classroom interaction to put across information (Macaro) is more likely to reflect an 'implicit' orientation to L2 teaching and learning. By contrast, use of the L1 is more likely to be associated with an explicit comparison of languages, the teaching of grammar or, of course, a translation approach. The 'younger the better' notion (see Pfenninger & Singleton) reflects an inherent belief that children 'absorb language like sponges' (e.g. EL Gazette 2021a), whereas in fact older learners may have an advantage as a result of better-developed explicit learning mechanisms. Implicitness or explicitness featured in Graham's exposition of different components of aptitude, learners' reaction to feedback and motivational attitudes to grammar learning. The distinction also arises in the question of whether language learning strategies should be taught explicitly by teachers, or whether we can expect students to transfer their strategies, through some kind of implicit process, from their L1 (Gu). Similarly, can the symbol-sound correspondences of an L2 be learnt simply through exposure to the language, or is explicit instruction needed in this area – at least for some, if not for all, learners (Woore)? To what extent is explicit instruction helpful for the development of 'comfortably intelligible' L2 pronunciation (Kennedy & Trofimovich)?

Clearly, then, the explicit/implicit debate is an important one in L2 education, but we also need to consider it in terms of the context in which the L2 learning is happening. In some cases, learners are exposed to large amounts of input in the L2, creating conditions more favourable for implicit (or at least, incidental) learning. This is the case, for example: for multilingual migrant learners who find themselves in a school setting where the majority language is not their L1; for students learning subject content through the medium of another language (as in EMI settings); and in cases where learners create their own immersive context, for example by watching TV box sets or playing online games in their L2. As language learning in these kinds of contexts expands, perhaps the 'implicit/explicit' debate will become more constrained in its reach, applying most clearly to more traditional L2 classrooms (those sometimes labelled 'foreign language' settings). Among these 'input poor' learner populations, a research question arises as to whether explicit teaching of the L2 entails learners being exposed to less L2 input, and if so, what the effects of this may be (see below). However, in light of the burgeoning possibilities for informal language learning afforded by technology such as the internet and social media, perhaps the traditional loci of language learning are in any case becoming less fixed.

278 *Ernesto Macaro and Robert Woore*

If it is true that 'explicitness' and 'implicitness' are at the heart of many debates in classroom-based L2 education (which is, after all, still very widespread), then how are teacher educators expected to position themselves when summarizing research evidence to cohorts of beginner or experienced teachers? Should they declare their own beliefs (recognizing that these are likely to be influential); should they allow cohort participants to infer their views through the stances they take during the course of the programme; or should they present a range of different views and encourage participants to form their own opinions, through critical appraisal of relevant evidence? A 'practical theorizing' model of teacher education, such as that advocated by Molway, might be seen as more resilient in this respect, in that it does not rely on teacher educators 'telling' teachers what to think or do. Nonetheless, it needs to be borne in mind that this model is highly demanding on the teachers themselves, who are expected to make sense of a huge amount of potentially conflicting evidence.

Holistic versus fragmented debates

In our survey of stakeholders' views on key debates in L2 education (Woore & Macaro), by far the most popular broad category of concerns related to 'L2 pedagogy' – 'broadly speaking, how an L2 is best taught and assessed'. But how should this question be addressed – in terms of a holistic approach to pedagogy or a more fragmented approach? Molway notes, in relation to Initial Teacher Education, that 'there is an ongoing debate surrounding the ideal balance between the development of communicative competence and the development of knowledge about the workings of the language'. Can the development of the latter be associated with a 'method' or even an 'approach' to teaching an L2, in the way that the former usually is; or is it in fact a series of foci on individual aspects of language (morphosyntax, lexis, pronunciation, pragmatics), which can be dwelt on at will? This brings us back to the historical developments that we (Woore and Macaro) traced in Chapter 1, where edited books, over time, seem to have become less concerned with describing, researching or promoting an overarching method of teaching, focusing instead on specific aspects of language acquisition or its social context.

It appears we are caught, as applied linguists and teachers, in a dilemma. On the one hand, of course we want research to provide us with some answers as to whether this or that aspect of L2 teaching is effective. Yet, especially if we are teacher educators, we need research to provide evidence beyond these fragments of understanding, because, in a crowded curriculum where limited time is available for L2 learning, teachers need to make decisions about how best to allocate finite resources. Choosing to teach X may mean choosing *not* to teach Y; and choosing to focus explicitly on any specific aspects of a language must be balanced against overall exposure to, and interaction in, that language. Put differently, teachers constantly have to ask themselves: at what cost do I focus on this specific activity? If I teach phonics, or a particular grammar rule, or learning strategies, what am I thereby squeezing out of the curriculum?

A rather different kind of solution is perhaps embodied in the rise of CLIL teaching and EMI across the world. In the decisions that lead policymakers to promote (or even mandate) such approaches, might we detect an assumption that more traditional L2 classrooms have somehow failed to deliver adequate language learning for a sufficient number of students? If so, we may then want to ask what has led to such a state of affairs. Is it merely a lack of hours available in the school curriculum, and therefore unreasonable expectations of what can be achieved in formal learning contexts? Or is it because there has been a gradual shift from more communicative pedagogies to focusing on the individual components of language? And to what extent has that shift (if indeed it has occurred) been facilitated by a research interest in those components of language? If, as Lasagabaster suggests, there is some (albeit contested) evidence that CLIL does improve language learning, then might this be related to the fact that it is espousing an essentially communicative approach within a 'plentiful input' context, based on input and interaction to convey interesting academic content, which is therefore motivating for students? This debate is, of course, also related to the question of explicit/implicit approaches which we outlined in the previous section.

If CLIL is effective, could it ever completely replace classes where language is the principal focus (as in more traditional 'foreign language' classrooms)? Whilst this might currently seem unlikely, if it were to happen, we would argue that teachers within such programmes would, by necessity, have to embrace their roles as teachers of language as well as of subject content, drawing on appropriate SLA research to inform their pedagogical decision-making. This is not an easy undertaking, even for the most committed; and even then, there may be a cost of embracing CLIL. We should recall that in language classes, an often-stated (and in our view laudable) aim is to bring students into contact with the culture of the target country or countries, broadening students' perspectives beyond that of their own language and culture. Indeed, the opening statement in the national curriculum for England and Wales proclaims, 'Learning a foreign language is a liberation from insularity and provides an opening to other cultures' (DfE, 2013:1). Correspondingly, a recent survey of L2 teachers in England by Woore et al. (2020) found that the overwhelming majority saw a key aim of their teaching as being to develop 'students' knowledge of other cultures and a positive, tolerant attitude towards these' (p. 4). Can CLIL ever deliver this exposure to other cultures in similar ways? In its current forms, this seems unlikely, given the focus on delivering academic content.

In summary, it seems to us that more research is needed which looks at L2 teaching and learning 'in the round', focusing on the overall approach taken rather than individual aspects of it, and taking a more holistic view of learners' outcomes.

Debates in context

Reflecting our aim of broadening the scope of this volume, the preceding chapters have sought to apply their research and arguments across a variety of L2 education contexts. This raises interesting questions about the extent to which language learning and teaching involve universal processes, and the extent to which these processes vary according to the context. Indeed, this dilemma is clearly reflected in Borg's exposition of a variety of models of teacher professional development adopted in different educational settings.

The issue of universals versus contextual variations may also be asked about the debates themselves which arise in relation to L2 teaching and learning. We suggest that these can be ranged along a continuum: at one end are debates which are tightly bound to a particular, circumscribed context; at the other are those which are applicable across a wide range of contexts, and possibly even universally. To take a couple of examples, our analysis of stakeholders' views (Woore & Macaro) revealed a particular concern with exam difficulty and uptake of languages amongst respondents involved in teaching Languages Other Than English (LOTE) – respondents who, in fact, largely comprised teachers of 'Modern Foreign Languages' in the UK. This concern reflects the particular features of the educational context in which these respondents are operating. By contrast, both the explicit/implicit debate and the L1/L2 debate were frequently cited by respondents across our sample, irrespective of whether they were involved in teaching English or LOTE.

In our opening chapter (Woore & Macaro), we attempted to draw a distinction between 'issues' and 'debates' in L2 education. Whilst this is obviously not a clear-cut or watertight distinction, we proposed that 'debates' have 'been subjects of long-standing discussion and/or systematic inquiry', whereas 'issues' have not – even though they may well be problematic areas which arise on a daily basis in L2 classrooms. Another way of looking at this might be to say that debates reflect questions that apply across multiple contexts, whereas issues – whilst they may be important in a particular setting – are more narrowly bound to that context, and are unlikely to be debated more widely.

As we pointed out in Chapter 1, we can see contextual effects in L2 education as operating at various levels, which are also nested and overlapping. First, at the most general, 'macro' level, there are broad, socio-political factors, such as the dominant status of English as a global lingua franca. Then, there are decisions taken at national or institutional level: for example, which languages must or can be taught to children of which ages; which languages are actually taught in a given school; and how much time is made available for them (Di Sabato & Kirkpatrick). Third, there are contextual factors determined by the learners themselves, such as the various developmental, cognitive and affective correlates of age (Pfenninger & Singleton) as well as their L1 background. Finally, there are 'micro-contextual' factors affecting individual classrooms and learners (e.g. student X has not had breakfast; one member of this language class for refugees has had their application for residency refused).

Given the range of contextual factors outlined above, what is the role of research? How can we expect it to inform classroom practice? One response to this question perhaps lies in an increasing sensitivity of research to the effects of context at various levels. As Pfenninger and Singleton note in their chapter, studies have begun to investigate L2 learning and teaching as a 'complex dynamic system', in which 'many internal states (cognitive ability, motivation, attitude, emotions,

Reflections 281

and so on) and external states or events (the general context in which a language is learned, a particular teacher, an illness, a particular usage event, and so on) at any given moment may have an effect on the developmental path'. Consequently, 'it is only through the close and repeated tracking of language within individuals or groups that the essence of development will be made observable'. In fact, we would observe that the perspectives and understanding of the researcher, under such an approach, begin to align with those of a skilled teacher: someone who is able to draw not only on a critical understanding of learning theories and processes but also on detailed knowledge of individual students' circumstances, in order to form a holistic view of her or his development at any given moment in time (and to select the optimal instructional approaches going forwards). Therefore, we believe that the rich, contextualized knowledge of the teacher is powerful knowledge, central to the effective functioning of any education system. It should not necessarily be subordinated to knowledge derived from research and theorizing; rather, each should constructively inform and challenge the other.

In noting the above developments in research approaches, we certainly do not wish to denigrate the value of more traditional, quantitative paradigms, which seek to uncover universal processes or broad principles of L2 learning, and to find out what is likely to be the most effective pedagogical approach for the greatest number of learners. This case is made powerfully by Chalmers and Murphy, who call for more Randomized Controlled Trials to determine 'convincing causal evidence' for the effectiveness of multilingual pedagogy, rather than rushing to embrace it (and investing time and money in it), only to find out later that it has not delivered the hoped-for results. Obviously, evidence concerning the effectiveness of particular pedagogical approaches 'on average' is particularly important where these approaches are being advocated, or even mandated, by policymakers.

Returning to our earlier point about holistic versus fragmented approaches, however, we need to be mindful that any educational intervention (however effective) will always be 'at a cost': that is, by doing X, we choose not to do Y, and this is problematic if there is value in Y. Further, it is possible that a given pedagogical intervention does turn out to be 'effective', but in different ways than those envisaged; hence our suggestion (above) of the need for more research which attempts to evaluate overall methods or approaches to L2 teaching, and which takes a more holistic view of a learners' outcomes. For example, there is little point in a learner becoming more proficient in a given language if they simultaneously develop a more negative attitude towards that language and its speakers.

Furthermore, we are once again brought back to the importance of context and teachers' knowledge of that context. Just because a particular intervention has been shown to be effective 'on average' does not mean that it will be so for all learners all the time. As Mitchell, Myles and Marsden (2013) wisely advise,

> teaching is an art as well as a science, and irreducibly so, because of the constantly varying nature of the classroom as a learning community. There can be 'no one best method', however much research evidence supports it, which applies at all times and in all situations, with every type of learner. (p. 290)

282   *Ernesto Macaro and Robert Woore*

This implies that it is important for policymakers not to be dogmatic in their pronouncements of what should and should not be done in the classroom; rather than expecting research to tell us 'what works and why' (Blunkett, 2000), we might be better to ask for evidence concerning what is *likely* to work, and why. It is also very important (in our view) for teachers to feel empowered to systematically evaluate the effects of a given pedagogical approach on the individual learners in their classrooms, and to adjust this approach accordingly.

New contexts, new debates

Our exploration of the different layers of contextual factors affecting L2 learning also indicates that there are different spheres of influence in terms of who is able to change those factors. Clearly, some features cannot be changed (e.g. a learner's age or L1), but others are within the remit of national policymakers or institutional leaders and managers. However, for the vast majority of individual language learners, who are school students, there is little choice. Almost all of the 'whether to learn a language', 'which language', and 'how many hours per week' decisions are made for them. This lack of control over which language to learn could contribute to variable levels of motivation for language learning (specifically within expectancy-value models, as explored by Graham). There appears to be a huge appetite for language learning worldwide for a range of reasons – see, for example, the latest annual report on Duolingo (Blanco, 2020), which in 2020 had around 40 million active users per month worldwide. However, there is not necessarily such motivation amongst school children, where language learning is imposed on them without choice.

However, for both children and adults (at least, for those who have suitable access), technology creates the potential for much greater agency over the L2 learning process. Using freely available language learning apps, people may, for example, choose to learn: Spanish, because they have an ambition to visit Latin America; German, in order to study on an Erasmus programme in Austria; Italian, to better enjoy Italian opera; Swedish, to help them integrate into Swedish society following migration; or Mandarin, simply as 'brain training' during the pandemic lockdown (La Repubblica 2021; EL Gazette 2021b). Further, as we have noted, leisure activities such as watching films or online gaming in L2 may also provide multiple affordances for high-quality, informal language learning (see Sockett, 2014). In such ways, more of the contextual factors affecting L2 learning are being brought under the learners' control: for example, which language? How much time? When? Which approach to learning? These changes could have big implications for motivation and, ultimately, perhaps for learners' outcomes, too.

Might it be possible to bring together the complementary affordances of informal learning and classroom-based teaching, thus creating an integrated whole which is more effective than either of those domains in isolation (and also greatly increasing the total time spent engaging with the language)? For example, online viewing or gaming could provide opportunities for intensive,

Reflections 283

immersive engagement with the L2. The classroom could provide complementary teaching, guiding learners in how to engage with the L2 extramurally, how to choose appropriate materials, and helping them to develop the foundations of linguistic knowledge and strategic behaviour they need in order to make the most of this informal language engagement. An integrated L2 learning environment of this kind would require some rethinking of the role of the L2 teacher, who would need to consider how to optimize the learning process across the different domains.

Is there also scope to bring in more freedom of choice for school-based L2 learners, in terms of which language(s) they pursue? After all, both language learning apps and the internet now bring an enormous wealth of opportunities to engage with the material in all kinds of languages. Further, in the wake of the enforced adaptations that L2 learners and teachers have made to online teaching during the Covid crisis, perhaps some of the affordances of this approach can be preserved post-pandemic. For example, might virtual classrooms be envisaged, in which learners of a given language (say, Polish or Japanese), drawn from a number of different schools, can be taught by a specialist in that language? This might be financially viable where smaller, in-person classes in a given school are not.

Finally, where individuals are learning an L2 autonomously – such as through an app or via engagement with video content or gaming – we might wonder what role research has to play in this endeavour. Much ink has been spent on the question of L2 teachers' engagement with SLA research and how to increase it (e.g. Marsden & Kasprowicz, 2017). However, where control passes to individual learners and teachers are not there as mediators between research findings and pedagogy, how can research intervene in the L2 learning process, in order to make it more effective? Of course, at one level, research might inform the development of apps and other learning platforms. These learning platforms themselves generate huge amounts of data, giving potential for unprecedented insight into the language learning process (see, for example, http://burrsettles.com/). Again, however, there is perhaps a case for teachers to develop their role as facilitators of L2 learning which takes place not only in the classroom but also beyond it.

Conclusion

This book has contributed to the 'Debates' series by attempting to bring the notion of second language learning much more into the third decade of the 21st century. It is likely that the debates discussed in this book will remain topical for many years to come, but those new ones will also gain prominence as L2 learning itself continues to evolve. Because of the diverse contexts in which L2 learning takes place, we have made clear that we do not think research can provide 'the complete answers' to these debates, at least in terms of prescribing what a particular teacher should do at time X in classroom Y. Nonetheless, as we argued in Chapter 1, we believe that research is vital in providing 'guiding lights, points on the horizon towards which effective practice can be steered'.

284 *Ernesto Macaro and Robert Woore*

Our hope is that this book has helped to illuminate those points. It has sought to enhance practitioners' and policymakers' understanding of some of the key current debates in the field, thus enabling better-informed decisions to be made about various aspects of L2 education.

As the topics in this book and others continue to be debated and researched, we very much hope that these debates can be conducted in a spirit of collaboration and shared endeavour within the community of practice of L2 education. This community comprises teachers, teacher educators, policymakers, second language acquisition researchers – and indeed, learners themselves. All of these stakeholders are ultimately seeking the same thing: effective and enjoyable L2 learning. In all the glorious challenges and complexities of this process, for many of us working in this field, there is nothing like the moment of satisfaction when a learner (or their teacher) feels that real progress has been made!

A final word

We would like to stress our great appreciation to the authors of chapters in this book who, despite the great hardships, both professional and personal, caused by the Coronavirus pandemic of 2020–2022, managed to provide us with such excellent contributions to this volume. Thank you to you all.

References

Blanco, C. (2020) 2020 Duolingo Language Report: Global Overview. Retrieved from https://blog.duolingo.com/global-language-report-2020/, 17.02.2021.

Blunkett, D. (2000) Influence or irrelevance: Can social science improve government? Reprint of speech to a meeting convened by the ESRC on 2 February. *Research Intelligence*, *71*, pp. 12–21.

DfE (Department for Education) (2013) Languages programmes of study: Key stage 3. National Curriculum in England. Retrieved from https://assets.publishing.service.gov.uk/government/uploads/system/uploads/attachment_data/file/239083/SECONDARY_national_curriculum_-_Languages.pdf, 23.02.2021.

Douglas Fir Group (2016) A transdisciplinary framework for SLA in a multilingual world. *The Modern Language Journal*, *100*(S1), pp.19–47.

EL Gazette (2021a) https://www.elgazette.com/dual-language-learning-gets-a-lift/

EL Gazette (2021b) https://www.elgazette.com/lockdown-language-learning-rockets-in-uk/

LaRepubblica(2021)https://www.repubblica.it/cronaca/2021/01/26/news/dai_prof_influencer_ai_corsi_online_i_lockdown_risvegliano_interesse_per_le_lingue_straniere-284203860/ [tr. From teachers as influencers to online courses, lockdowns reawaken interest in foreign languages]

Marsden, E. & Kasprowicz, R. (2017) Foreign language educators' exposure to research: Reported experiences, exposure via citations, and a proposal for action. *Modern Language Journal*, *101*(4), 613–642. https://onlinelibrary.wiley.com/doi/abs/10.1111/modl.12426

Mitchell, R., Myles, F. & Marsden, E. (2013) *Second Language Learning Theories*, 3rd edition. London: Routledge.

Richards, J. C. & Renandya, W. A. (eds.) (2002) *Methodology in Language Teaching: An Anthology of Current Practice*. Cambridge: Cambridge University Press.

Sockett, G. (2014) *The Online Informal Learning of English*. Palgrave Macmillan.

Woore, R., Graham, S., Kohl, K., Courtney, L. & Savory, C., 2020. Consolidating the evidence base for MFL curriculum, pedagogy and assessment reform at GCSE: an investigation of teachers' views. Retrieved from https://ora.ox.ac.uk/objects/uuid:1f797d25-98b4-4b89-863a-779b2348ae20, 17.02.2021.

Index

Page numbers in **bold** denote tables. Page numbers followed by n denote notes.

Aaronson, D. 55
Abadzi, H. 265
Abdollahi, S. 175
Abdul Rahim, H. 207
accentedness 247, 249–253
Ackerman, D. 267
Adesope, O. O. 234
adolescent(s): immigrants 55; and language learning 21, 29
age/ageing: and cognition 54; L2 acquisition attainment in 56; and L2 pronunciation learning 248–249
Age and Immersion (AIM) study 59
age for second language learning 52–60; age as socio-cultural variable 53–54; age factor as a potentially dynamic entity 59–60; introduction 52–53; optimal age of onset across different L2 settings 55–59
age of onset (AO). *see* age for second language learning
Aguilar, M. 97, 99, 100, 101
Ahn, G. 204–205, 211
Alghamdi, H. 227, 230
American Council on the Teaching of Foreign Languages (ACTFL) 125
analytic phonics 225–226
Anderson, J. 169
Andrews. S. 124
anxiety in language learning 21, 112
Applied Linguistics 183
aptitude. *see* language aptitude
Arcos, M. 212
Association of Southeast Asian Nations (ASEAN) 32, 34
associative memory 108
attention 56, 189

Attitude/Motivation Test Battery (AMTB) 113
attitudes: anti-L1 202; language learners' 69, 91, 99, 107, 112–113, 117; L2-only 205, 207, 235, 255; to L1 use 213–215; motivational attitudes to grammar learning 277; of second language teachers 124, 130, 147, **149**, 156, 210; towards codeswitching 203
auditory acuity 56
August, D. E. 235, 236
Australia 111, 112
Austria 41
autonomy: in L2 pronunciation learning 250–251; teacher autonomy and motivation 146–148
Azerbaijan 42, 146, 153, 158

Bacon-Shone, J. 33, 36
Baddeley, A. 190
Baecher, L. 134
Baek, K. 204–205, 211
Bahasa Indonesia 36
Bale, J. 125, 133
Bangladesh **37**, 149
Bangla (language) 66
Barcelona European Council Recommendation 41
Basic Interpersonal Communicative Skills (BICS) 74
Bassetti, B. 232
Baumert, J. 57, 58
Belgium 41
beliefs: about language aptitude 112; expectancy 116; of second language teachers **12**, 82, 97, 111, 130–131, 135–136, 147, **149**

Benati, A. 10
Beyond Age Effects (BAE) study 57–58
bias: native speaker 25; towards native speakers of English 125
Bilingual Education Act 73–74
Bilingual Education Policy (BEP) 35–36
Birdsong, D. 54
BISTA 57, 58
Blackledge, A. 71
Blanco, C. 56
Bolitho, R. 152
Bolton, W. 33–34, 36
Borg, S. 280
Botha, A. 33–34
British Commonwealth 66
British Council 152
British Nationality Act 66
Brooks, G. 230
Broszkiewicz, A. 176
Brownlie, S. 211
Brunei 37
Bruner, J. 269
Burgess, A. 183
Business English 191

Cammarata, L. 102
Canada 57, 129
Cañado, P. 94
Cantonese (language) 36, 204
Cao, M. 223
Carroll, J. B. 108, 113
Castles, A. 223
causal evidence 72, 281
CEFR (Common European Framework of Reference) level 99, 214
Celic, C. 78
Cenoz, J. 92
CF. see corrective feedback (CF)
Chalmers, H. 80, 81–82, 281
Chan, S. H. 115
Chen, Y. 204
child immigrants 55
Chile 114
China: administrators in 203, 205; CNKI 223; English language education in 33–34; knowledge of English in 38; language education policy of 36; languages 36, 77, 204, 210, 228, 264; living languages in 32; Ministry of Education 205; secondary sector in 205; universities 205, 210, 215, 227, 238; university students in 175, 215; on web-based diagnostic language assessment 263

Chinese national research database (CNKI) 223
Chomsky, N. 183
Chostelidou, D. 97, 100
Chou, M.-H. 98, 101
Christison, M. 155
Chuang, H.-K. 77
Chumak-Horbatsch, R. 78
Cianflone, E. 207
Cihon, T. M. 237
Clarke, D. 130
Classical Greek 42
A Clockwork Orange (Burgess) 183, 188
Coates, R. A. G. 236
code-mixing. see codeswitching (CS)
codeswitching (CS) 202; amount of 210; attitudes towards 203; elimination of 207–208; intra-sentential 210; limited use of 210; non-CS group 215; practices at UBC 205; South Korean high school teachers 211; teacher 215
Codina Camó, A. 81
cognate spotting 216
Cognitive/Academic Language Proficiency (CALP) 75–77
cognitive control capacity 56
cognitive grammar learning strategies (GLS) 173
Cohen, A. D. 73
collegiality of second language teachers **149**
collocation, defined 198n3
Common European Framework Reference for languages 125, 214
common underlying proficiency theory 72, 76
communicative language teaching (CLT) 13, 122, 204, 207
competence of second language teachers 134, **149**, 152
complex dynamic systems theory (CDST) 59–60
comprehensibility 183, 247, 249–250, 253
confidence of second language teachers **149**
Confucius 39
connectionism 170
Connor, D. 134
conscious learning, of second language 183
consciousness-raising activities 171–173, 177, 178
constructivist models 146

288 *Index*

Conteh, J. 70
content, importance of 264–269
content and language integrated learning (CLIL) 9–10, 16, 43, 59–60, 252–253, 276, 279; and English as foreign language 90–92, 94; English-medium instruction *vs.* 90; features of 90; form-focused instruction into 101; implementation 92, 94, 95, 100; effects of CLIL on language learning 92–97; literature 92–93; overview 89–90; principles 90
content-based instruction (CBI) 16, 18, 25
content knowledge 123–124
contextual and co-textual environments, words with 185
continuing professional development (CPD) of teachers 143–147
Cook, G. 54, 217
Copland F. 210, 217
corpus-derived vocabulary lists 191, 198n2
corrective feedback (CF) 12, 28, 169, 252, 256–257; effects of CF on errors in production of grammar 173; explicit and implicit, effectiveness of 175–176; and form-focussed instruction 172, 252; provision of 169, 172, 174, 178; types of 178
Costley, T. 66
Courtney, L. 236
Creative Europe (funding programme) 43
Creese, A. 71
critical period hypothesis (CPH) 53
Croatia 41, 42
cross-language perceptual similarity 249
CS. *see* codeswitching (CS)
Csizér 114, 117
C-test 95, 96
Cummins, J. 44–45, 71, 72–77, 78, 204
Cunningham, C. 69
curriculum 56; course designers 127; design templates 132–133; elementary school 56; in Europe 45; influence exerted by tests and examinations on 22, 24; knowledge of second language teachers 149; L2 18–19; SLTE courses 122, 124, 131, 135
Cyprus 41, 80
Czechia 42

Dailey O'Cain, J. 212
Dallinger, S. 93, 95

Dalton-Puffer, C. 93
debates in L2 education 9–29; basic approaches 10; broad areas of 15–16; changing historical context 10, 13; chronological overview of edited volumes in L2 education 11–12; closed questions 25, 27; debate according to the language taught 16, 18; debates, defined 9–10; debates presented in the closed questions 14; key current debates 13; perceived importance of eleven debates in L2 education 26; specific issues according to the language taught 23–25
Debates in Modern Languages Education (Driscoll, Macaro and Swarbrick) 10
Debreli, E. 207
declarative knowledge 167, 169, 175
DeKeyser, R. 167
De La Campa, J. C. 212
delayed-effect hypothesis 170
Denmark 42
Derwing, T. M. 247, 254
Dewey, D. P. 113, 114–115
didactic transposition 123
Dixon, L. Q. 77
Dixon, P. 235, 242n5
Doiz, A. 205, 214
Donoghue, G. M. 266, 267
Dörnyei, Z. 113, 114, 116–117
Doughty, C. J. 10, 171, 178
Driscoll, P. 10
Duff, P. A. 204

EAL. *see* English as an additional language (EAL)
EAP (English for academic purposes) 92
Early, M. 71
East and Southeast Asia, learning and teaching of English and other languages in 32–39; and ASEAN Charter 34; difficulties associated with English learning 38–39; English as only foreign language education 38–39; historical background 33; language education policy 34–38
Education for All by 2015 38, 40
EfECT 145, 150
EFL. *see* English as a foreign language (EFL)
EfU project 149–150, 153, 154
Egypt 145, 147, 150, 152, 155, 158
Ehrman, M. 112
El-Dakhs, D. A. S. 207

Index   289

elementary school: children in New Zealand 184; language learning in 57, 129; teachers 129

ElHajj, H. 207

elitism 94, 95

Elley, W. 184–186, 188, 194, 195

Ellis, R. 53, 124, 171, 172, 175

ELT programme 150

e-moderators 153, 156

England: L2 learning in 21; multilingual pupils 68; *School Direct* (school-based models of Initial Teacher Education) 126; secondary school learners in 111

English: accentedness 250; acquisition of L2 175; English-speaking countries 2, 4, 18, 21, 111, 206, 218, 223, 234, 239; explicit knowledge of 176; impact of English on languages of non-Anglophone countries 218; as L2 in Spain 212; L1 Japanese learners of 249; L2 pronunciation learning 249; non-native English students 196; passive voice in 177; proficiency in 210, 263; progress in phonological decoding 227; pseudowords 225; secondary school students 229–230; spelling-sound correspondences 227, 231; status of 206; teaching 204–205; words 224

English as an additional language (EAL) 68–69, 74, 78, 234, 235, 275

English as a foreign language (EFL) 214, 265; Chinese university EFL students 215; commentaries of 207; and content and language integrated learning (CLIL)/English-medium instruction (EMI) 90–92, 94; learners 23; and learning L2s 207; phonics in 223–224, 235–236

English as a Second Language (ESL) 69, 234

English for Academic Purposes (EAP) 191

English for specific purposes (ESP) 92

English for the Community project 155

English GCSE (General Certificate of Secondary Education) 22

English in Action project 149

English as a lingua franca (ELF) 39

English language learners (ELLs) 16, 20, 229, 234–235

English Language Teacher Development project 151

English-medium instruction (EMI) 25, 89, 196, 201, 214, 217, 276, 279;

benefits 101; content and language integrated learning (CLIL) *vs.* 90; English as a foreign language (EFL) and 90–92; form-focused instruction in 102; implementation 101; effectiveness for language learning 97–99

English-only learning environment 211

English Proficiency Index (EPI) 37

environmental stimuli and language acquisition 55

Erasmus+ (funding programme) 43

Erler, L. 117, 227, 229, 233, 240

error(s): analysis of learners' 240; avoiding activities 172; in French past tense 177; inducing activities 172; in L2 use 169; in production of grammar 173

ethnic identity and L2 pronunciation learning 250

Europe, linguistic diversity in 39–47; content and language integrated learning 43; Council of Europe guidelines 44; language patrimony of the EU 40; languages of schooling in 43–44; multilingualism 44–45; non-EU "foreign" languages 42; plurilingual and intercultural education in school 43, 46–47; second foreign language, disappearance of 42; teaching of regional or minority languages in 42–43; unequal level of English competence across 42–43

European Economic Community (EEC) 67

European Union (EU) 67

Expanding Circle countries 33, 36, **37**

expectancy-value equation 116

experiential learning 133, 212

explicit knowledge: development of 173, 174; of grammar 173; highly automatized 167; implicit *vs.* 166–168; limitation of 167; *see also* grammar learning and teaching

explicit vocabulary learning *vs.* implicit 183, 198n1

Facebook groups 155

feedback: corrective **12**, 28, 110, 169, 252, 256–257; and language learning motivation 117–118

Ferring, D. 74

Fiege, C. 93, 95

Field, J. 10, 232

field-based mentors 128

Filipino (language) 35

Finland 42

290 *Index*

first language (L1), use of: arguments against 208; arguments in favour of 208: in L2 classroom 202–208, 212–213; pedagogic purposes 211–213; in selection of research 209–211; teacher and student attitudes to 213–215; and vocabulary learning 215–216

FL. *see* foreign language (FL)

FLE certification 126

fluency development 195

focused communication tasks 172, 173, 176, 177

focus on form(s): during communicative activities 256; comparisons of instruction 175; concept of 169; intensive and extensive 172; reactive 172; taxonomies of 171–172

foreign language (FL): classroom 56, 202–208; common words in 190; contexts 167, 222, 234, 268; environments 251, 253, 254; instruction 252–253; knowledge of words in 270; learning 248–249, 279; level of proficiency 191; methods of teaching 165; native-like pronunciation in 247; pronunciation instruction for children 252; public examinations in 22; teaching content in 18; in tertiary education 42; in UK 279, 280; *see also* English as a foreign language (EFL); second language (L2)

form-focused instruction (FFI) 102, 171, 174

Fotos, S. 177

France 41, 42–43

Freeman, D. 126

French language 41; accent 250; beginner learners of 232; English learners of 232; in English schools 233; and German 206; national curriculum 206; pronunciation course 238; reading in 117–118, 229–230, 237; symbol-sound correspondences 228, 233, 236; teacher of 211, 227

Frota, S. 187

Gallardo, F. 248, 252

Ganschow, L. 113

gao kao (entrance exam) 33

García, O. 71

Gardner, R. 113

Gatbonton, E. 250

Gené-Gil, M. 96

Germain, C. 91

German 41, 206, 212, 227, 282

Germany 89, 129

GI. *see* grammar instruction (GI)

Gibbons, P. 78

Goethe Institute 39

Goldstein, H. 81

Gonzales, A. 35

Goo, J. 175

Google images 196

Google Translate 78

Gorham, J. 236

GPC. *see* grapheme-phoneme correspondences (GPC)

Grabe, W. 229

Graddol, D. 92

Graham, S. 115, 236

grammaring, notion of 166

grammar instruction (GI): benefits 170; classifications of options in 172; explicit and implicit 169, 170, 174, 175, 176; goal of 177; role 165; support for 168; techniques and procedures in 170, 173; types 174

grammar learning and teaching, implicit *vs.* explicit 277–279; choices in 170–174; evidence for effectiveness 174–177; L2, knowledge, learning and teaching of 166–168; overview 165–166; pedagogical implications 177–178; theoretical support for 168–170

grammar learning strategies (GLS) 173, 174

grammar teaching (GT) 15, 23, 124, 165, 167; contribution 176; different variants of 169; explicit and implicit options in 166; facilitative role of 170; and language aptitude 110; types of 168

grammatical knowledge development 109

grammatical sensitivity 108

Granena, G. 175

grapheme-phoneme correspondences (GPC) 224, 226

Greece 41, 42

Griva, E. 97, 100

Guidelines for Teaching English in Secondary Schools 205

Guilloteaux, M. J. 116

Gunderson, L. 80

Haider, A. S. 208

Hajjaj, A. H. 207

Hall, G. 217

Hall, J. 230

Han, Z. 175

Index 291

Handbook of Language Teaching (Long & Doughty) 10
Han N. 204–205, 211
Harley, B. 109
Hart, D. 109
Hatcher, T. E. 268
Hattie, J. A. C. 266, 267
Hayes, D. 143
Hensch, T. K. 54
Hernández-Nanclares, N. 99, 100–101
Hindi (language) 66
Hindly, B. 146
Hirsch, E. D. 264–265
Hiver, P. 114, 117
Hobbs, V. 211
Hockly, N. 133
Hoey, M. 193
Hollingsworth, H. 130
Hollm, J. 93, 95
Hong Kong 36, **37**
Hong Kong Curriculum Development Council policy 204
Horwitz, E. K. 107
How languages are learned (Spada and Lightbown) 106
Hsieh, P. H. P. 115
Hu, G. 98, 99, 100
Hu, S. 71, 78
Huang C.-L. 57, 209, 211
Huennekens, M. E. 80
Humphries, S. 206
Hungary 41, 42, 112, 117, 205
Huo, S. 223, 235, 236, 239, 242n5
Hussein, R. F. 208
Hüttner, J. 92
Hyderabad (India) 235

Ideal L2 Self 114–115
identity texts, notion of 71
IELTS 38, 98
implicit knowledge: development of 170, 173, 174, 176, 177; explicit *vs.* 166–168; growth of 171; *see also* grammar learning and teaching
implicit vocabulary learning *vs.* explicit 183, 198n1
Inceoglu, S. 176
incidental vocabulary learning 183, 198n1
India **37**, 38, 155, 156
indigenous languages in education 35
individual difference (ID) factors 176, 177
Indonesia 34; knowledge of English in 38; language education in 36;

promotion of English as lingua franca in 39; young learners of English in 114
inductive learning ability 108
information: amounts of 193; as constants 264; intra-sentential 212; L1 and L2 215–216; lexical 215, 216; metalinguistic 173
input: enhancement 171, 172, 173, 174, 176, 177; flooding 171, 173, 174, 176, 177; hypothesis 184; processing theory 170
input, matters of 188–194; retrieval and spacing 189–190; subject areas matter 190–191;
inquiry skills of second language teachers **149**
instruction, L2 pronunciation learning 251–253
intelligence quotient (IQ) 106
intelligibility principle 247, 254, 257
intentional vocabulary learning 183, 198n1
interaction hypothesis, revised 169
intercultural competence 123
International Communication Learning Institute 237
intra-group variability 59
intra-sentential codeswitching 210
Iran 114
Issues in Modern Foreign Language Teaching (Field) 10
Issues in Second Language Teaching (Benati) 10
Italian language 41, 43, 232, 236, 237–238, 282
Italy 41, 42

Jackson, C. W. 81
Jafari, S. M. 210, 214
Japan 33, 38
Japanese 211–212, 249, 255; English as a foreign language 114–115; MEXT 206
Jawaher & Al-Haqbani, J. N. 207
Jenkins, J. 254
Jia, G. 55
Jiménez-Muñoz, A. 99, 100–101
Job, R. 81–82
job-embeddedness 145
John, P. D. 132
Johnson, C. 13, 54
Jonkmann, K. 93, 95
Jordan 156
Joshi, R. M. 77
Juan-Garau, M. 96

292 *Index*

Kachru, B. 33
Kang, E. Y. 175
Karimi, M. N. 175
Kennedy, S. 143, 147
Kharma, N. N. 207
Kiddle, T. 114
Kim, H.-S. 215
Kinsella, C. 55
Kirkpatrick, A. 35, 38, 204
Kiss, C. 112
knowledge: declarative 167, 169, 175; knowledge-based curriculum 264; lexical 193, 195; of L2 grammar 166–168; procedural 167, 169, 170, 175, 177, 266; of spelling-sound correspondences 228–233; of vocabulary 185, 191–194; *see also* explicit knowledge; implicit knowledge
Koda, K. 228
Kolligian, J. 265
Korea 112
Kormos 111, 114, 117
Koster, B. 152
Krashen, S. 183–184, 187, 265, 266

Lamb, M. 114, 148
Lambert, W. E. 73
Lange, D. L. 126
language: analytic ability 109; diversity in European continent 40; factor 75; input 194; knowledge enhancement activities 125; language-focused learning 195, 196; patrimony of the EU 40; politics 25; proficiency of second language teachers **149**
language acquisition device (LAD) 183
language aptitude 106–116; explained 108–110; impact on learners of 111–118; introduction 106–107; and language classroom 110–111; and language learning motivation 107–108, 112–118
language learning: apps 282; effectiveness of content and language integrated learning for 92–97; effects of English-medium instruction on 97–99; motivation 107–108, 112–118
Language-Minority Children and Youth 234
languages other than English (LOTE) 18, 23–25, 212, 280; teaching 27; in UK 16, 24–25
language teacher education. *see* second language teacher education (SLTE);

systemic in-service language teacher education
Lao, C. Y. 265
Larsen-Freeman, D. 166
Larson-Hall, J. 113, 114–115
Lasagabaster, D. 96, 205, 214, 276, 279
Latin 42
Latvia 41
Lavin, T. 234
L1 classrooms, homogenous 20
learner-performance options *vs.* feedback options 172
learning: acquisition *vs.* 183, 184; conscious, of second language 183; content and language integrated learning (CLIL) 252–253, 276, 279; grammar learning strategies (GLS) 173, 174; language-focused 195, 196; language learning apps 282; of L2 grammar 166–168; *see also* grammar learning and teaching; pronunciation learning; vocabulary learning
learning languages other than English (LOTE) 32–48; East and Southeast Asia 32–39; Europe 39–47
Lecumberri, M. L. G. 248, 252
Lee, H. 215
Lee, J. H. 81, 215
Lee, J. H.-W. 112
Lei, J. 98, 99, 100
Le Luong Minh 34
Lemov, D. 265
Lendl, J. 58
Lervåg, A. 229
leveraging language to leverage learning 72–78
Levine, G. S. 215
lexical approach to L2 teaching 19, 184, 185, 192, 198n2
lexical gap 189
lexical inferencing, research on 188
lexical items: analysis of 185; explicit attention to 183, 193, 195; information about 215, 216; initial learning of 189; recurring 191; retrieving 190
lexical priming 193
lexicon 189, 190, 197
Li, S. 108, 109, 110–111, 112–113, 175, 227, 238, 240
Libya 156
Liddicoat, A. 35, 38
Liebscher, G. 212
Liechtenstein 41
Lightbown, P. M. 106

Index   293

Lightfoot, A. 155
limited English proficiency (LEP) 69
linguistic cognition 56
linguistic competence 117
linguistic-cultural identity 55
linguistic interdependence, notion of 73
Linguistic Interdependence Hypothesis (Cummins) 72
listening to stories, vocabulary learning through 184–186
Lithuania 42
Liu, D. 204–205, 211
Li Wei 70
LLAMA aptitude test 108, 115
Llinares, A. 96
Loewen, S. 172, 176
Long, M. 10
L2-only *vs.* multilingual debate 201–221, 277, 279–282; definition 201; first language in foreign language classroom 202–208; L1/L2 use and vocabulary learning 215–216; L1 use, pedagogic purposes of 211–213; research into 209–216; teacher and student attitudes to L1 use 213–215
Lotto, L. 81–82
L2 (second language) 253–254; *see also* grammar learning and teaching; L2-only *vs.* multilingual debate; phonics, teaching; pronunciation learning
Lugo-Neris, M. J. 81
Luxembourg 41, 42
Lyster, R. 173, 175, 252

Macaro, E. 81, 82, 90, 93, 117, 207–208, 209, 212, 214, 215, 216, 229, 233
Macau 36
Mackey, A. 10, 13
Magid, M. 250
Malaysia 32, **37**, 38, 151, 152
Malda, M. 76
Malderez, A. 152
Malta 41
Mandarin (language) 36, 77
Markus, P. 71, 78
Marsden, E. 281–282
Martin, R. 74
Martinez, R. 196
Massive Online Open Courses (MOOCs) 154–155
Matei, G. S. 152
Matsuo, A. 211
maturational effects 61n1
maximal position, teachers position 213–214

May, S. 70
Mayer, D. 135
meaning-focused output 195, 196
meaning-focus input 195, 196
Measures of Effective Teaching (MET) project 134–135
medium of instruction (MOI) 133, 201, 214
Meier, G. 70
Meister, G. 183, 184
Melby-Lervåg, M. 229
Merino, J. A. 96
Mesman, J. 76
metalinguistic explanations 173, 177, 211
Mexico 112
migrant second language learners 234–235
migrants' linguacultural heritage in Europe 44
Mihaljevic Djigunovic, J. 252
Mitchell, R. 112, 281–282
modern language aptitude test (MLAT) 108–109, 112
Molway, L. 212
Mongolian (language) 36
Monitor Model 183
monolingual paradigm 44
Montero, M. K. 71, 78
Moore, P. 204
Morford, Z. 237
morphemes 166, 189, 193
Morrison, D. 237
mother tongue-based multilingual education (MTBMLE) 35–36
motivation: and language learning outcomes 107–108, 112–118; L2 pronunciation learning 249–250; and teacher autonomy 146–148; *see also* language aptitude
Moyer, A. 253
Muir, C. 116–117
multicausality 60
multilingual pupils in linguistically diverse classrooms: basic interpersonal communicative skills (BICS) 74; cognitive/academic language proficiency (CALP) 75–77; Cummins' theories 73–77; leveraging language to leverage learning 72–78; overview 66; pedagogical implications 77–78; research, on multilingual pedagogies 78–82; societal benefit from multilingual pedagogy 70–72; UK 66–69
multilingual turn 82–84

294 *Index*

Muñoz, C. 10, 90–91, 97, 99, 100, 101
Munro, M. J. 247, 254
Murphy, J. M. 255
Murphy, V. 281
Murray, D. E. 155
Mutton, T. 132
Myanmar 32, 38
Myles, F. 281–282

Nagengast, B. 116
Nagle, C. 249, 250
Nassaji, H. 165, 168, 177, 212
Nation, I. S. P. 190, 193, 194, 195–196
Nation, K. 223
Nation, P. 183, 184, 195
national identity and national language 36
native language. *see* first language (L1), use of
native-like accent 27
nativelikeness 53–54
nativeness principle 254
native speaker bias 25
native-speaking teachers (NST) 211
Neokleus, G. 210, 217
Netten, J. 91
neural network 188, 189
neurocognitive ageing 56
Newport, E. L. 54
New Zealand 129, 184
Nicholas, R. 236
Nikolov, M. 112, 252
non-Anglophone countries 206
non-interface position 167, 168
non-majority L2 learners and phonics: secondary school students 236–237; university-level learners 237–238; young learners 235–236
non-native speaker teachers (NNST) 202, 211–212
Norris, J. M. 174, 175
Northern Ireland 68
North Macedonia 41, 42
Norway 41, 150
noticing hypothesis 168–169
Novella, M. 175
NTTP 145, 147, 150, 152–153, 155, 158

OETIS programme 150, 153, 155–156
older adults 56
Oller, J. 75
Olsson, E. 96
Oman project 142–143, 145, 150, 153
online games 277, 282

online in-service teacher education 154–157
online learning 131
Online Learning Consortium 154–155
oral communication 232
Orr, D. 154
Ortega, L. 107, 174, 175
orthographic distance effect 228
orthographic rimes 224, 226
Outer Circle countries of Asia 37
output enhancement 171
output hypothesis 169
Oxford, R. 112, 251
Oyman, N. 207

Pakistan 37
PALTAGs 145, 147, 150, 155
pandemic and teaching methods 131
Papi, M. 114, 117
parental support and L2 education 21, 56
Patwa (language) 66
Pawlak, M. 172, 173
Payne, M. 211
pedagogical content knowledge (PCK) 123–124
pedagogical norms, for L2 pronunciation instruction 255
pedagogic purposes, L1 use 211–213
Pérez-Cañado, M. L. 93
Pérez-Vidal, C. 95
performance indicators 134
Perkins, D. N. 267
personality traits 112
Pfenninger, S. E. 57, 58, 280
Philippines 37, 38; knowledge of English in 38; language education in 34–35; living languages in 32
Phillipson, R. 204
phoneme-grapheme correspondences (PGC) 230
phonemes 189, 224, 226, 232, 237
phonemic awareness 226
phonemic coding ability 108
phonetic coding ability 109
phonics, teaching: background 223–224; effects of teaching 233–238; grapheme-phoneme correspondences (GPC) 224, 226; L2 226–238; migrant second language learners 234–235; in non-majority L2 contexts 235–238; factors affecting how to teach 239–240; overview 222–223; phonological decoding 225; phonological decoding, progress in 227; SSC knowledge,

Index 295

importance of 228–233; synthetic and analytic phonics 225–226; 'transfer' and beyond in 228; learners' outcomes without 227–228
Phonics Screening Check 242n4
phonological decoding 242; of beginner learners 232; defined 225; outcomes 226; effects of phonics instruction on 238; progress in 227, 237; role of phonological decoding in L2 learning 229
Pimsleur Language Aptitude Battery (PLAB) 113
Pladevall-Ballester, E. 81, 95
Plonsky, L. 251–252, 268, 270
plurilingualism 42, 43, 46–47
Poland 41, 42
Polio, C. G. 204
Porter, A. 13, 236
Portugal 42
Preevo, M. 76
presentation – practice – production (PPP) procedure 175, 178
Price, D. J. de S. 266
procedural knowledge 167, 169, 170, 175, 177, 266
processability theory 170
processing instruction 170
pronunciation learning: elements of 256; overview 247; setting instructional goals for 254–257; variables influencing 248–254
pseudowords 225, 240, 242n4
Punjabi (language) 66
Purewal, S. 235, 236
pushed output 169
Putonghua (language) 36, 38, 39

quisk 231, 242n4

Ramachandran, S. D. 207
Ramscar, M. 56
randomized controlled trials (RCTs): causal evidence 281; multilingual pedagogy 72; phonics instruction 230, 236
Ranta, L. 109, 173
Raoofi, S. 115
Rapscallion Jones (story) 184, 185, 194
Raschka, C. 209, 211
Rastle, K. 223
reading 117, 229–230
Reading Aloud Tests 225
recasts 169, 171; explicit 175, 177; implicit 172, 175, 177, 178; superiority of prompts over 176

reflective thinking 126
Reljić, G. 74
Renandya, W. A. 13
repetition and frequency 190
RETC 145, 150, 154
retrieval and spacing 189–190
Richards, J. C. 13
rigour 158
Robinson, P. 10, 189
Rogier, D. 98, 99, 100
Rolin-Ianziti, J. 211
Romania 42, 155
Roquet, H. 95
rote-learning ability 108
Rubinstein-Avila, E. 204
Rumlich, D. 93, 94, 96, 100
Russell, V. 175
Russian language 41

Saed, H. A. 208
Sáfár, A. 111
Saito, K. 115, 175, 251–252
Salazar-Noguera, J. 96
Sánchez, L. Z. 80
Sapon 108
Saragi, T. 183, 184
Sardegna, V. G. 251
Savory, C. 236
Sayer, P. 112
Schagen, I. 235, 242n5
Schallert, D. L. 115
Schmidt, R. 169, 187
Schmitt, N. 195
School Direct (school-based models of Initial Teacher Education) 126
Schulman, L. 123
Scotland 68
secondary school students 236–237
second language. *see* L2 (second language)
second language acquisition (SLA): cognitive 204; cognitive-interactionist approach to 169; specialists 165; theories 168, 204
second language teacher education (SLTE) 122–136; assessing student teachers' performance within SLTE programmes 134–135; building research literacy in integrated models 127–128; current debates in 124–125; demand for new forms of SLTE 129; evaluating the effectiveness of SLTE programmes 135–136; knowledge base of language teaching 123–124; knowledge progression when learning to

296   *Index*

teach an L2 129–131; lesson planning templates 132; medium of instruction (MOI) in 133; modelling 133; models of SLTE 126–127; purposes of language teaching and 122–123; relative weighting of practical experience in 128; selection of applicants for SLTE courses 125–126; tools and activities 131–132; video-based observation 133–134; written assignments 132–133

Seedhouse, P. 207, 235, 242n5

self-determination in language teachers 148

self-efficacy in language learning 115–116, 127

self-esteem 112

Seltzer, K. 78

Serbia 42

Sercombe, P. 209, 211

Shanahan, T. E. 226, 235, 236

Shanghainese 36

Shibata, M. 254–255

Shintani, N. 171

Shokrpour, N. 210, 214

Sieh, Y.-C. 81

simple view of reading (SVR) 229

Singapore 37–38

Singleton, D. 55, 57, 58, 90–91, 280

Skehan, P. 108, 109

skill-learning theory 169

skills and content 264–269

Skype 156

Slovakia 42

Slovenia 43

Smit, U. 92

Smith, F. 266

social class 56

social justice 71, 79

social media 154–155, 254

social status of students 71

socio-economic status (SES) 95, 112

Sok, S. 175

Somers, T. 96

sound-to-symbol mappings. *see* symbol-sound correspondences (SSC)

South Korean high school teachers 211

spacing and retrieval 189–190

Spada, N. 106, 175

Spain 42. 205, 224; content and language integrated learning (CLIL) programmes 253; EF EPI index data for 42; English, teaching 91; English education in 41; pronunciation of words in 254; second language teacher education

programmes in 129; teachers of English in 212; young learners in 252

Spanish language 41; language learning apps 282; motivation of adult low-proficiency learners of 249; past tense, knowledge of 176; pronouncing words in 227, 248

Sparks, R. L. 112, 113, 227

spelling, importance of symbol-sound correspondence (SSC) knowledge for 230

SPEX programme 146, 158

split digraph 224

Sri Lanka 37

SSC. *see* symbol-sound correspondences (SSC)

Standard Modern Greek (SMG) 80

Stephens, C. J. 237

Sternberg, R. J. 265

Stoller, F. L. 229

student attitude to L1 use 213–215

student teachers. *see* second language teacher education (SLTE)

Sturm, J. L. 238

subject areas matter 190–191

sub-lexical level 225, 232, 239, 240

Sudan 145, 146

Swahili (language) 66

Swain, M. 73, 169, 204, 266

Swan, M. 265

Sweden 42, 43

Swedish (language) 282

Switzerland 41, 57

symbol-sound correspondences (SSC) 224, 225, 226, 227; affective issues 232–233; coverage 239; French 236; Italian 237–238; knowledge, importance of 228–233; L2, comprehensive programme of instruction in 239; oral communication 232; reading 229–230; sound-to-symbol mappings 230; spelling 230; symbol-to-sound mappings 230; vocabulary acquisition 231–232

symbol-to-sound mappings. *see* symbol-sound correspondences (SSC)

synthetic phonics 225–226

Syria 150

systemic in-service language teacher education 142–158; intensive and distributed in-service work 153–154; introduction 142–143; models of in-service teacher education 143–146; online in-service teacher education 154–157; programme content 150–151;

Index   297

programme evaluation 157–158; programme objectives 148–150; teacher autonomy and motivation 146–148; teacher educators 151–153

Tagalog 35
Taiwan 77, 211
Tan, B. H. 115
target language (TL) 124–125, 133; features, accurate use of 167; forms, use of 177; grammar 165; knowledge 178; sole use of 207; structures, variety of 177–178; *see also* L2 (second language)
task-based language teaching (TBLT) 13
Teacher Activity Group (TAG) approach 145
teacher autonomy and motivation 146–148
teacher education. *see* second language teacher education (SLTE); systemic in-service language teacher education
teacher educators 151–153
teacher leadership and learning programme 151
teacher(s): attitude, to L1 use 213–215; codeswitching 211, 215; experienced 212, 278; of French 211, 227; native-speaking teachers (NST) 211; non-native speaking teachers (NNST) 202, 211–212; position 213–214; in UK 206
Teach for America (school-based models of Initial Teacher Education) 126
teaching: of L2 grammar 166–168; matters of 194–197; methods 23, 110, 150, 155
teaching language *vs.* teaching process: content over skills 264–266; integration 269–271; overview 262; relevance of debate 263–264; skills over content 266–269
technology and L2 learning 25
Tedick, D. J. 102
TEDP 152
TEFL certification 126
Teimouri, Y. 114
Tejas programme 145, 147, **149**, 150, 152–153, 155, 158
Telegram 254, 258n2
tertiary education, foreign languages in 42
text-creation activities 172
Thailand 38
Thompson, T. 234

Tian, L. 215
Tibetan (language) 36
timed analysis 210
TOEFL 38
Tokumoto, M. 254–255
Tomita, Y. 175
Tonzar, C. 81–82
Torgerson, C. J. 230
transfer-appropriate processing (TAP): assumptions 169–170; principles 177
translanguaging 46, 70, 72, 78, 79, 83
Treaty of Maastricht 67
Treaty of the European Community 40
Trofimovich, P. 250
Tucker, G. R. 73
Turkey 42
Twitter 254

Ukraine 154
UNESCO 38, 40
Ungerleider, C. 234
United Kingdom: EAL pupils in 234, 235, 275; government policies in 207; key debates in L2 education in 14–15; languages other than English in 16, 24–25, 212; language teaching in classrooms in 112; linguistic diversity, representation 67–69; L2 learning in 129; 'Modern Foreign Languages' in 207, 280; multilingual pupils in 66–67; systematic programme of phonics instruction in 223; teachers in 206; *see also* English
United States: English Language Learners (ELL) in 16, 20; older immersion learners in 57; school system 16; young secondary school learners in 112
Universal Declaration on Cultural Diversity 40
university-level learners, phonics sessions 237–238
Ur, P. 168
Urdu (language) 66
Üstünel, E. 207
utterance analysis 210

Vallbona, A. 95
Van den Branden, K. 13
Van der Meij, H. 205, 210
Vanhove, J. 54
van IJzendoorn, M. 76
VanPatten, B. 170
variables, influencing L2 pronunciation learning: age 248–249; amount of

298 *Index*

experience 251; autonomy in learning 250–251; cross-language perceptual similarity 249; ethnic identity 250; instruction in contexts of increased L2 exposure 252–253; motivation 249–250; nature of instruction 251–252; quantity and quality of L2 use 253–254

variance, L1/L2 use 211

VEO (online platform) 156

video-based observation 133–134

video-based online teacher education, barriers to **156**

Vietnam 38, 39

vocabulary acquisition 4, 184, 215, 228, 231–232

vocabulary knowledge, developing breadth and depth of 191–194

vocabulary learning 109; frequency, matters of 186–188; input, matters of 188–194; and L1/L2 use 215–216; overview 183–184; teaching, matters of 194–197; through listening to stories 184–186

vocabulary thresholds 187

voluntarism in language teachers 148

Wales 68

Walters, K. 80

Wang, S. 223, 235, 236, 239, 242n5

Webb, S. 195–196

Wedell, M. 152

Wen, Z. 109

Werker, J. F. 54

Wesche, M. B. 110

Weston, D. 146

WhatsApp 153, 155

The White Crane (story) 184, 185, 186, 194

Williams, J. 171, 178

Willis, J. 207

Winch, C. 126

'Windrush generation' 66, 67

Woore, R. 228, 236

word analysis 210

word frequency 185, 186, 193

Wright, T. 152

written assignments 132–133

Wyatt, M. 148

Yang, W. 99, 100

Yiakoumetti, A. 80

Yi (language) 36

Yilmaz, Y. 175

YouGlish 254, 258n1

young learners: L2 instruction for 251; non-native teachers for 252; phonological-based instruction for 235–236; in Spain 252

Zhang, W. 34

Zhao, T. 215

Zhao, X. 205, 210

Zhao, Y. 175

Zhuang (language) 36

Zoom sessions 153, 156